PENGUIN BOOKS

OPENING ARGUMENTS

After leaving the Office of Independent Counsel, Jeffrey Toobin became an Assistant United States Attorney in Brooklyn, New York. He lives with his wife, Amy McIntosh, and their daughter, Ellen, in New York City.

OPENING ARGUMENTS

A Young Lawyer's
First Case:
United States v.
Oliver North

J E F F R E Y   T O O B I N

PENGUIN BOOKS

PENGUIN BOOKS
Published by the Penguin Group
Viking Penguin, a division of Penguin Books USA Inc.,
375 Hudson Street, New York, New York 10014, U.S.A.
Penguin Books Ltd, 27 Wrights Lane,
London W8 5TZ, England
Penguin Books Australia Ltd, Ringwood,
Victoria, Australia
Penguin Books Canada Ltd, 10 Alcorn Avenue, Suite 300,
Toronto, Ontario, Canada M4V 3B2
Penguin Books (N.Z.) Ltd, 182–190 Wairau Road,
Auckland 10, New Zealand

Penguin Books Ltd, Registered Offices:
Harmondsworth, Middlesex, England

First published in the United States of America by
Viking Penguin, a division of Penguin Books USA Inc., 1991
This edition with a new epilogue published in Penguin Books 1992

10 9 8 7 6 5 4 3 2 1

Photo on title page courtesy of The Bettman Archive.

THE LIBRARY OF CONGRESS HAS CATALOGUED THE HARDCOVER AS FOLLOWS:

Toobin, Jeffrey.
Opening arguments : a young lawyer's first case,
U.S. v. Oliver North/Jeffrey Toobin.
p. cm.
Includes index.
ISBN 0-670-83158-1 (hc.)
ISBN 0 14 01.6770 6 (pbk.)
1. North, Oliver—Trials, litigation, etc. 2. Trials
(Conspiracy)—Washington (D.C.) 3. Iran-Contra Affair, 1985–
4. Prosecution—United States—Decision making. 5. United States–
Politics and government—1981–   I. Title.
KF224.N66T66 1991
342.73′0412—dc20 90–50408
[347.302412]

Printed in the United States of America
Set in Sabon and Futura Bold Condensed
Designed by Beth Tondreau Design

TO THE MEMORY OF MY FATHER,
Jerry Toobin

Contents

OPENING
ARGUMENTS

"Who Is Going to Argue for The Government?"

The room was called the "ceremonial" courtroom of the United States Courthouse for the District of Columbia, but the only ceremony it suggested was lunch at a suburban high school. So the courthouse powers recognized that they had to do something to salvage their showpiece, to give it a little of the majesty and solemnity lacking in the room's bare bones.

The answer, they decided, was portraits—oil portraits, portraits by the dozen, portraits selected the way an interior decorator might use yards of books to lend dignity to a den. The pictures were of former judges of the District Court. But most of the portraits loomed up so high on the marble walls that their faces became almost indistinguishable, and their names, placed on simple brass markers, remained a mystery. The looming anonymous faces haunted the vast chamber.

On March 9, 1987, several hundred people packed the courtroom's rows of benches well before the 1:30 P.M. scheduled start of the day's proceedings. To the left of the bench, at the table marked "defendant," a handful of lawyers fidgeted and chatted while awaiting the judge. In the seat nearest the middle of the room was Guy Miller

Struve, partner in the Wall Street firm of Davis, Polk & Wardwell. Over six feet tall, and with a pot belly warning of incipient middle age, Struve had a look of grim importance about him. He also evinced a sense of distance from the hubbub around him, in part because of an uncanny ability to concentrate but also because he was almost completely deaf, and at the moment his two large hearing aids were turned off. Struve arranged and rearranged four perfectly sharpened pencils into precise alignment on the table before him. He was nervous.

At the plaintiff's table, opposite Struve, was Barry Simon, whose intensity crackled where Struve's simmered. Simon got up; he sat down; he played with his collar and with his pencils, which were neither sharpened nor arrayed in a straight line. To Simon's right sat his partner at the Washington law firm of Williams & Connolly, Brendan V. Sullivan, Jr., who exuded an almost ostentatious calm in sharp contrast to the nervous energy being expended beside him. His hair a weathered gray, glasses a scholarly tortoiseshell, Sullivan appeared the picture of an old-fashioned lawyer—an advisor, a counselor at law, as the old title had it, not a combatant.

Next to Sullivan sat his client, Lieutenant Colonel Oliver L. North of the United States Marine Corps. It wasn't the haircut with its ruler-straight part—the haircut that would epitomize his tremendous celebrity four months later—that seemed so noticeable that Monday morning. Nor was it the perfectly pressed uniform, festooned with a fruit salad of decoration. It was, instead, North's smile. There he sat, at the center of the biggest governmental scandal since Watergate, the subject of a major investigation aimed at putting him in jail, a platoon of cameramen camped out at his driveway every morning, and Ollie North was grinning—grinning from ear to ear.

At about a quarter to two, the clerk of the court let out the traditional cry:

"All rise!"

Many judges, affecting humility, prefer to wave their courtroom guests to their seats. No need for that pomp, they say, let's dispense with the ceremony and get to work.

Judge Barrington Parker of the United States District Court for the District of Columbia was not such a judge. His white hair nearly gone, his black skin pasty with age and ill health, Parker appeared at the door to the courtroom and did not even acknowledge the hushed crowd. Parker could scarcely move. He employed the plain metal crutches of the permanently impaired, his legs nearly useless as the result of an automobile accident a decade before. The audience held its collective breath and watched the judge struggle forward. The drama of the moment—a hearing on North's lightning bolt of a lawsuit seeking to have the independent counsel law declared unconstitutional—focused on the figure inching his way across the massive bench. When he finally reached his seat, the audience exhaled and sat down with a thud.

Struve was ready to go. On leave from Davis Polk and now *de facto* second-in-command in the investigation led by his mentor, Independent Counsel (better known as Special Prosecutor) Lawrence E. Walsh, Struve was to argue that the statute under which Walsh was appointed was valid under the Constitution and that his investigation could go forward. As soon as Parker reached his seat, Struve, uninvited, vaulted to the lectern.

Parker had his own plans. "Mr. Struve," he said dryly, "I don't know what you were about to say at this point, but I am about to make a statement as to what this hearing is confined to this afternoon."

A master at the unctuous servility that most lawyers regard as mandatory before judges, Struve slunk back to his seat, saying, "I believe it would be helpful for us all to hear Your Honor's statement."

"Very well." Parker cleared his throat and proceeded. "As far as the Court is concerned, the hearing this afternoon is confined to the several motions to dismiss, one filed by the independent counsel, the other filed on behalf of the attorney general. . . ."

PARKER'S legal jargon sounded so routine. Yet this hearing had emerged from legal and political maneuvering that was not at all ordinary. The future of an investigation that had already reached into the White House was on the line.

The public part of the story began one hundred days earlier, on Tuesday, November 25, 1986, when President Ronald Reagan and

Attorney General Edwin Meese III held a news conference at the White House. The president's voice had an uncharacteristic quaver when he began to read from his prepared text.

"Last Friday," he said, "after becoming concerned whether my national security apparatus had provided me with a complete factual record with respect to the implementation of my policy toward Iran, I directed the attorney general to undertake a review of this matter over the weekend and report to me on Monday." The report, the president said, "led me to conclude that I was not fully informed on the nature of one of the activities undertaken in connection with this initiative. This action raises serious questions of propriety." A stunned press corps looked on in silence.

"Although not directly involved," the president continued, "Vice-admiral John Poindexter has asked to be relieved of his assignment as assistant to the president for national security affairs and to return to another assignment in the Navy. Lieutenant Colonel Oliver North has been relieved of his duties on the National Security Council staff." Then, with a few more words announcing the creation of a special board to review the workings of the National Security Council (NSC), Reagan vanished, leaving Meese to explain the president's tantalizing remarks.

Meese did not disappoint. About three weeks earlier, the press had learned that the Reagan administration had sold arms to the government of Iran in an effort to win the release of American hostages held in Iran. Now, Meese stated, it appeared that some of the proceeds of the arms sales to Iran had been provided to Nicaraguan Democratic Resistance forces who were fighting against the Sandinista government of Nicaragua, that is, to the contras. Meese said this "diversion" had been accomplished by North, with the knowledge of his boss Poindexter.

Privately rejoicing about the blow to the Republican administration, Democrats waxed responsibly about the need to protect the institution of the presidency—and, by the way, did Reagan know? Many Democrats began calling for the appointment of a special prosecutor, known since a 1982 change in the law by the less accusatory title of independent counsel, even though the immediate news reports, prophetically, could not identify the precise crimes that had been committed. The administration at first attempted to fend off the appeals for the appointment of a prosecutor, thus denying that the matter was a full-fledged scandal, but the political heat grew too intense. On December 2 Meese announced that he would seek to have an independent counsel named.

Prosecutions for federal crimes in the United States are generally conducted by the Department of Justice (DOJ), which is run by the attorney general. Congress passed the Ethics in Government Act in 1978 to deal with the situations where wrongdoing is alleged at the highest levels of government, when, in the words of the law, "investigation by the Attorney General may result in a personal, financial, or political conflict of interest." The diversion case, or Iran-Contra affair as it came to be known, represented a classic conflict of interest for the attorney general. Meese had been a top White House advisor before he went to the Justice Department, and his weekend investigation, which prompted the November 25 news conference, would also need to be scrutinized.

Once Meese decided an independent counsel should be appointed, the statute called for a panel of three elderly federal appeals court judges, who were themselves chosen for this duty by the Chief Justice of the United States, to make the selection. On December 19, the panel, which was headed by Judge George MacKinnon, named a former associate of MacKinnon's to the post.

The independent counsel would be Lawrence Edward Walsh, a seventy-four-year-old attorney with a résumé as distinguished as his demeanor. A graduate of Columbia Law School, Walsh had apprenticed with two of New York's greatest prosecutors, J. Edward Lumbard, Jr., later a celebrated appeals court judge in New York, and Thomas Dewey, the New York governor who almost won the presidency in 1948. After Dewey's loss, Walsh rose to prominence in New York Republican circles and was ultimately rewarded by the Eisenhower administration with a lifetime federal judgeship in 1954. Only three years later, however, restless on the bench, Walsh quit and became deputy attorney general—number-two man in the Justice Department—for the remaining three years of Eisenhower's second term. Returning to New York, Walsh, whose brief stint on the bench allowed him a lifetime of being called "Judge," then began twenty years as a senior partner at Davis, Polk & Wardwell, then as now one of the most powerful law firms in the country. In 1981, Walsh left Davis Polk, but, still vigorous at age seventy, he moved to his wife's hometown of Oklahoma City and was practicing law there with the biggest firm in town when he received MacKinnon's call.

As 1987 began, Walsh started to build a staff. He looked first to his protégé at Davis Polk, Guy Struve. A handful of others signed up in January and joined Walsh in an abandoned pair of judge's chambers in the United States Courthouse for the District of Columbia in Washington. Operating in cramped quarters, with about half as many telephones as people, the investigation was soon hit, on February 24, 1987, with a crashing blow.

Shortly after ten that morning, a messenger from the law firm of Williams & Connolly arrived at Walsh's courtroom office. He promptly served Walsh with a lawsuit—turning the tables, with the would-be defendant, Oliver North, accusing the would-be prosecutor. The North suit alleged that the independent counsel provisions of the Ethics in Government Act were unconstitutional, that they violated the "separation of powers" inherent in the Constitution, that only the attorney general or his subordinates could exercise the president's power to "execute the laws." Walsh and his staff waited for their single, tired photocopier to churn out copies of the mammoth document—more than one hundred pages in total. The complaint demanded that the court declare that:

the independent counsel provisions of the act violate the Constitution of the United States. . . .

the appointment of Mr. Walsh as independent counsel under the act violates the Constitution of the United States. . . .

each and every act of the independent counsel and his staff taken in the name of the United States, or otherwise in furtherance of the Court's order of December 19, 1986, is unconstitutional," and

this Court enjoin and restrain defendant Walsh from exercising any and all of the authority and power conferred upon him.

The group read the document in disbelief—and more than a little fear.

JUDGE PARKER began by clearing away some of the procedural underbrush. He noted the various motions that had been filed, made sure all the parties were represented by counsel and then asked a deceptively simple question.

"Mr. Struve, who is going to argue for the government?"

Usually a routine question, the inquiry on this day had no simple answer. There was the independent counsel—he was the special prosecutor. He would be bringing the charges in the Iran-Contra case in the name of the United States. But then there was also the Department of Justice, Walsh's uneasy ally as codefendant in North's lawsuit. Both of them were, in a way, "the government." Yet there was also the plaintiff Oliver North, whose starched uniformed presence spoke more eloquently than any lawyer about his intentions for representing "the government."

After an awkward silence, a Texas drawl emerged from the prosperous-looking gentleman seated next to Struve.

"I am, Your Honor, James Spears, deputy assistant attorney general."

"Are you prepared," the judge asked Spears, "to argue the second motion to dismiss?" The argument in Parker's courtroom was really about two lawsuits. The first was filed against Walsh on February 24. In addition, three days before the hearing, North's attorneys had filed a second lawsuit against Walsh *and* the Justice Department. Struve's team had worked madly over the weekend and prepared a response in the second case for the Judge's consideration on Monday morning. The "government" had not.

"Your Honor," Spears delicately put it, "at this juncture the United States has not completed its second motion to dismiss."

Parker seemed to enjoy watching Spears squirm. "You have not filed a motion to dismiss in connection with the second complaint?" the judge asked, having just heard the answer.

"Not yet, Your Honor. We are under preparation."

"Very well," the judge said with a smile. "You are not only under preparation. You are under pressure."

Judge Parker now gave Struve permission to speak. The lawyer delivered his message in stiff, clipped tones. "As you know, there are two cases pending before Your Honor, both brought by the same plaintiff, Oliver L. North. One was filed almost two weeks ago, the other was filed last Friday.

"As Your Honor knows," Struve decided to stick it to Spears, "*we* have moved to dismiss both of those actions, and we are prepared to address both."

Struve said he would make two arguments. First, he charged that North's two suits were "procedurally infirm"—in short, that North had no right to disrupt the investigation now underway by bringing them at all. Second, Struve said, the independent counsel provisions of the Ethics in Government Act were in fact constitutional.

The crowd displayed a palpable disinterest in Struve's first line of attack. In the days since North filed his suit, the newspapers had speculated avidly about the validity of the law. The press wanted a constitutional showdown, not a niggling contest over judicial niceties. But it was the first argument—the procedural approach—that piqued Judge Parker's interest. Struve said, "It understates the matter to say it is an extraordinary and unusual thing for a court to enjoin an ongoing criminal investigation." Individuals traditionally challenged the actions of a prosecutor after they were indicted, not before. Until charges were filed, Struve noted, courts generally stayed away, believing that the risks of interrupting investigations outweighed any harm that might be done. Before indictment, according to the legal term, such issues were not "ripe for review."

Parker began asking the questions of a careful and cautious trial judge. Advancing elegant new constitutional theories obviously held little appeal for him. It was the biggest case Parker had ever faced, and he did not want to be reversed on appeal. By and large he limited his questions to "Do you have a case to support that?" He wanted precedents—safe legal grounds—on which to make his ruling.

Struve knew that Parker would like the procedural argument. It gave the judge a way out of a sticky situation without having to rule on the constitutionality of the law. So it was with almost a lilt in his voice that Parker asked Struve, "Are you saying in substance that, if the Court rules as far as the defendants are concerned with respect to the procedural matters, that I need not even consider the other?" Struve replied quickly, "That is right, Your Honor."

After Struve's twenty minutes, North's lawyer, Barry Simon, bounded up to the lectern, but Parker moved promptly to show him who was in charge. Before Simon even had a chance to introduce himself, the judge asked, "Mr. Simon, are you prepared to join issue with the procedural challenge to the second complaint, also?" Legal mumbo jumbo like "join issue" left the spectators looking confused but prompted smiles at Struve's table. In other words, the judge was asking whether he could decide both of these cases at once, even though the tardy Spears had not yet submitted his reply in the second matter.

Simon squirmed. Parker asked Simon why the procedural issues were not identical in both cases. Why couldn't both cases be decided together? Simon could not come up with a good reason for distinguishing them, and Parker pressed him: "Did I understand you to say that you are not prepared to join issue on your part with the procedural issue raised in the second complaint?" Simon had nowhere to go and conceded: "Yes, but again, I just want to explain. The point is that independent . . ."

Judge Parker would not let go: "No, no, no. I want to know whether or not you're prepared to address all the arguments on the procedural aspect?" Simon had to surrender. "Your Honor, procedurally, absolutely," he offered weakly, "because it's clear that there's ripeness with respect to the second complaint as well."

North's lawyer had now made the key concession, and the judge had little else to say. He sat, sphinxlike, through the balance of Simon's harangue. As Parker's disinterest grew clearer, Simon's rhetoric flashed hotter. The law, he said, was "absolutely" clear . . . there were "express constitutional" commands. . . . Walsh had "no authority."

Then Simon made the classic error of the zealous advocate—uttering in court what, in the more reflective art of brief-writing, could have been prudently edited away. "We are saying," he said in a voice trembling with outrage, "that a group of what essentially are *vigi-*

lantes, private citizens who have no authority . . . can exercise all the powers." He had, in short, pushed too far.

Parker looked up. At first, just the ferocity of the gaze froze Simon in his tracks. The judge took his eyes off the lectern and muttered with a small grin, "Who are the vigilantes you refer to?"

Seated in a distant corner of Judge Parker's courtroom, I strained to hear what the judge had to say. As he spoke, I smiled broadly and felt, for the first time in at least two weeks, that I could relax.

Because, as Judge Parker asked about real vigilantes in this case, he was looking at Lieutenant Colonel Oliver Laurence North.

CHAPTER ONE

North v. Walsh

Eleven days before the confrontation in Judge Parker's courtroom, I had waited in another tense and silent room. In the vast passenger ship terminal on Pier Eighty-eight at the western edge of Manhattan's Forty-eighth Street, I had joined more than a thousand law school graduates in taking the bar exam.

Unlike law school, the bar exam focuses on the grittiest details of law practice—things like the requirements for a valid will and the difference between assault and battery. In school, it was the Big Picture: Truth, Justice, etc. The bar examiners couldn't have cared less. In a phrase that I would soon be hearing in a very different context, my entire law school education could be dismissed as "NTK," nice to know, but irrelevant to the task at hand.

So I crammed. It had been a long month.

NO ONE had the guts to volunteer in the first moments of my first class at law school, so my contracts professor called out a name at random. "Mr. Sacks," he said, "what seemed to be the problem with the plaintiff's hand in *Hawkins v. McGee?*"

Our professor's words echoed almost verbatim the first classroom scene in *The Paper Chase*, when Professor Kingsfield grilled the luckless Mr. Hart about the case known to generations of law students as "the hairy hand." Eerily, we noted that day, not only had our professor begun with the same case as the movie script, but our Mr. Sacks bore an astonishing resemblance to the actor who played "Mr. Hart" in the movie. The whispered consensus: "weird."

Though our professor treated his first target courteously, I sensed immediately the power of a quick-witted inquisitor to reduce even the smartest student to a stammering fool. The professors' queries followed a recognizable pattern, which I learned well in my own hapless attempts to fend them off.

"If that's true," the professor would reply pleasantly to my initial answer, "then isn't it a fact that . . . ?"

And I would concede the point.

"But doesn't that mean . . . ?" he would continue.

"Well," I would stammer, "I suppose so."

"And then doesn't it follow that . . . ?"

And soon, without a clue that I was heading that way, I was conceding that the law should provide equal punishments for murder and burglary or that parents ought to be able to sell their children or some other equally absurd position. Or just as often, I, or some classmate, would wind up sputtering, "Huh-men-a, huh-men-a," like Ralph Kramden on "The Honeymooners."

It all served to recruit us, unknowing, into the Cult of Complexity. Ideas that once seemed clear grew muddled by the accumulated wisdom of one who has taken torts, property, and civil procedure. Passions moderate; positions soften. Law school leaves a clear, if unspoken, message—not that any one set of values is right or wrong, but that skilled questioning can reduce *any* belief to a contradictory, gooey morass. And since all the old arguments begin to appear threadbare and flawed, it starts to look like less of a compromise to apply your legal skills not on behalf of the migrant workers mentioned in your essay for the admissions committee, but rather for a white-shoe law firm. It's an easy change to make.

I spent one summer at a fancy New York law firm (hell, I wasn't above *that*), and certainly enjoyed the expense-account lunches and the hefty salary. But my most enduring memory of the summer was not the recruiting committee's "booze cruise" around Manhattan or even a day in court, but rather the third-year associate who sat next door and sobbed to me one evening: "Don't work here. Don't. It's so horrible. So horrible. . . ." Big salaries and all, most young lawyers at the firm felt the same way: they hated it.

During law school, I maintained for two years a commuting relationship with Amy McIntosh, whom I would marry the week after graduation. We had met on the college newspaper where, in imitation of genuine newsroom grit, we learned to (and still do) call each other by our last names. McIntosh had taken a job with American Express and moved to New York, my hometown. Our romance had flourished courtesy of the frequent schedules and modest fares of the late (often very late), lamented People Express airline.

With law school ending, I had the luxury of putting off any permanent career choices for a while. In the fall after graduation I was to start a one-year clerkship with the federal court of appeals based in New York. Clerkships allow recent law school graduates to spend a year or two as an assistant to a judge. The duties usually involve reading the briefs in cases, summarizing the arguments in memos, writing first drafts of opinions, and picking up the judge's wife at the train. Working together, in a relationship of unparalleled professional intimacy, judges and clerks frequently establish friendships that long outlast the clerk's tenure in office.

I was fortunate because "my judge"—that's how clerks talk— was J. Edward Lumbard, Jr. Scarcely known outside legal circles, Lumbard is a legend within them. A 1925 graduate of Harvard Law School, he began as a government lawyer and helped Thomas Dewey invent the role of the crusading federal prosecutor in New York. Later Lumbard founded, in league with the World War II spymaster "Wild Bill" Donovan, one of the city's most successful law firms. But public service was Lumbard's first love, and in 1955, he accepted President Dwight D. Eisenhower's call to join the United States Court of Appeals for the Second Circuit. He's been there ever since.

Lumbard thinks like an old trial lawyer—skeptical, practical, cagey. His most famous aphorism hangs, framed, in the offices of judges and lawyers around the country. It says: "Never assume a goddamned thing."

I found that out on my first day on the job, when I gave Judge Lumbard my appointment form to sign. He quickly scanned it and pointed to the last page.

"What's that?" he asked.

"It's my signature, Judge," I replied.

"Who could read it?"

"Uh, I guess nobody."

"Then what the hell good is it?"

"Uh."

And then Lumbard let out the throaty laugh that reverberated so frequently about his chambers. Eighty-five-year-olds, as a rule, don't spend much time in the company of twenty-six-year-olds, but this one seemed to take an almost physical sustenance from the impatient, enthusiastic new charges who arrived each year. There was absolute freedom of speech in the Lumbard chambers and absolutely no majority rule. Still, whatever the subject, whether a knotty copyright problem or the pitching troubles of his (and my) beloved New York Mets, the judge did ultimately give a fair hearing to those of us whom he called, in mock solemnity, his "Assistant Judges."

I had just settled into my clerk's routine when Attorney General Meese held his November 25, 1986, news conference announcing the diversion of funds to the contras. Lumbard took a special pleasure in the appointment of the special prosecutor, his friend Lawrence Walsh. Lumbard had also played an important role in the law governing special prosecutors. From the time the Ethics in Government Act passed in 1978 until 1985, he had served on the three-judge court that selected the independent counsels.

On January 7, 1987, Judge Lumbard's best friend, Judge Walter Mansfield, died suddenly. For more than forty years, the two men had been close colleagues, first in private practice and then on the bench. Lumbard, however, took Mansfield's death with equanimity. At eighty-five, he was well-practiced in the somber art of losing friends. We started fielding calls about funeral services for Mansfield. I took one from Guy Struve, who phoned the day after Mansfield's death. Struve had clerked for Lumbard from 1966 to 1967 and served as the unofficial head of the Lumbard clerks' alumni association. Struve was calling on behalf of Lawrence Walsh, who wanted to attend the Mansfield rites.

"Jeff," Struve said, "There's another matter that I'd appreciate your raising with Judge Lumbard. We at the OIC [Office of Independent Counsel] are starting to build up our staff, and Judge Walsh wanted to know if Judge Lumbard would recommend some particularly outstanding young lawyers to us." Struve made his request as if "particularly outstanding" were a distinct category, like "brown-haired lawyers" or "admiralty lawyers."

Would I ask Judge Lumbard if he had any recommendations? I bit my lip and told Struve, ah, sure.

EXCEPT for those with box scores attached, the first newspaper stories I read to conclusion were those about Watergate. It was two months before my twelfth birthday when five men broke into Democratic party headquarters. The aftermath of this bungled burglary attempt constituted the dominant political event of my childhood. I developed the disdain for Richard Nixon that was all but obligatory on the Upper West Side of Manhattan—I recall my first taste of champagne on the night he resigned, August 8, 1974—but the stories that captured my attention were of the young lawyers working for Special Prosecutor Archibald Cox, who seemed, through the prism of television, like they were changing the world.

Nixon's secretary, Rose Mary Woods, earned an unsought immortality during that period for her improbable tale of how she created the eighteen-and-a-half-minute gap on one of the critical White House tapes, but my chief memory of that story was how it came out. Woods was forced to spill her version of the facts under the barbed interrogation of a prosecutor named Jill Wine Volner. Volner, I remembered reading with astonishment, was just thirty years old.

The Mets (as well as others) had taught me that the good guys didn't always win, but Watergate seemed a happy exception to that rule. Volner and her colleagues appeared on my television lugging big briefcases up the steps to Washington's federal courthouse, and they emerged to take credit for one triumph after another. One by one, their targets were photographed marching alone through the gates of federal prisons: H. R. Haldeman, John Ehrlichman, even John Mitchell, the former attorney general of the United States. The Watergate prosecutors fought the battle for the White House tapes all the way up to the Supreme Court and then won that struggle, too, in a case with the resonant title of *United States v. Nixon*.

To my eyes, it looked less like a job than a crusade—and I wanted to join the next one.

WHEN Lumbard returned to his chambers, I told him of Struve's request, skipping the business about their wanting "particularly outstanding young lawyers." And knowing the judge's preference for bluntness, I charged ahead. "You know, Judge, this is exactly the kind of job I've always wanted to do. Could you put in a word for me with Struve?" Lumbard smiled enigmatically and changed the subject.

The judge must have said something because Struve called me the next day to set up an interview. A day later, I visited Davis Polk's dowdy offices near Wall Street. After bluffing my way through the preliminaries of my interview and trying not to appear too anxious for the chance, I was being ushered out of the conference room when I was seized by panic. There was a vital piece of information that I felt I should, in fairness, tell Struve. The cover-up, I reminded myself, is always worse than the crime.

"I'm sorry to rush back in," I said, "but you should know that I'm not a member of the bar yet." A flicker of discomfort passed over his face. I tried to recover. "But I'm scheduled to take the bar exam next month and, uh, I hope to pass." With a clear conscience, if not high hopes to get the job, I was again politely shown the door.

Bar member or not, I was hired the next day and told to report to a Walsh staff meeting in Washington on January 31. I ran into Lumbard's office and thanked him profusely both for recommending me and for allowing me to leave my clerkship early. "Ah, hell," he growled, "it's a once in a lifetime opportunity. And you don't think you're irreplaceable, do you?"

Astonished by my good fortune, I returned home and cranked up my stereo to play a favorite Elvis Costello song over and over again— a raucous tune about the fall of a decrepit empire. Sure, I thought, we would prosecute some crimes and put some people away. But that would only be the start. The Walsh office would take on Reagan and all the president's men, with their contempt for the Constitution, disdain for the Congress, and hostility to the truth, the qualities epitomized by the diversion scheme. We had nothing less than a blank check to uncover and rectify the misdeeds of a corrupt and dishonorable administration. We wouldn't stop until we reached the top.

And then I played that song—"Oliver's Army"—one more time.

O N the last day of January 1987 I walked for the first time up the same courthouse steps that I had seen dozens of times on television during the Watergate proceedings. On that frigid morning, I joined almost twenty people crowded into the chambers of the late Judge Edward Curran of the federal court for the District of Columbia. Curran had retired in 1971, and his offices remained vacant until the Walsh team disturbed its dusty serenity shortly after the first of the year.

Only a real estate agent would have described the space as having three rooms. There was one spacious office—for the judge—and several appended corridors lined with now-obsolete law books. Three phones rang constantly and were answered occasionally. The only work the staff accomplished took place in a tiny warren of offices that the Federal Bureau of Investigation (FBI) had granted to us in the basement of its headquarters, three blocks up Pennsylvania Avenue.

Walsh had scheduled a staff meeting, his second, and the participants plastered themselves against the walls of his office like freshmen at a high school dance.

Yellow pad on his knee, Guy Struve—rhymes with (and otherwise unrelated to) "groovy"—sat closest to Walsh. Struve started out each day by retrieving a full box of sharpened Mongol brand number-two pencils and placing the box in his jacket breast pocket. As soon as a pencil developed the slightest dullness, he would replace it with another from the box. The process would continue all day. The fate of the pencils returned to the box always remained a mystery. Struve seemed only to use brand new pencils. Was there somewhere a closet full of thousands of perfectly good pencils which Struve had scorned? Not that we ever found.

The most cohesive group of lawyers at the meeting, and those collected around Struve, had come with him from Davis Polk. Chris Mixter, Louise Radin, and Geoff Berman all wore the practiced look of "the associate," attentive and respectful.

Next to them sat Bob Shwartz, scholarly, confident, and, in his late thirties, an elder in this group. He had been a white-collar crime prosecutor in New York and had left a partnership with the New York firm of Debevoise & Plimpton to run Walsh's "flow of funds" investigation. It would be his job to follow the money trail of the arms sales to Iran—who had it and who got it. He, too, had a retinue from his firm: Vicki Been and Bruce Yannett.

Occupying the seat closest to Walsh on his opposite side was Paul Friedman, the president of the District of Columbia Bar Association. He was working part-time for Walsh, helping to ease him into the nuances of Washington criminal practice. He was also temporarily in charge of the second of the three investigating teams, the one looking at the White House and the NSC, focusing on the shredding, lying, and other obstructing of the investigations.

Striding into the meeting late came a figure noticeably different from the lawyerly types who preceded him. John Keker, slick, fortyish, wearing a tie that looked like a postimpressionist lithograph, came from San Francisco and looked it. But he had had a career more like a senatorial candidate than a flower child: Princeton, Vietnam vet (two inches of his left arm lost to an enemy grenade), Yale Law School, clerk to Earl Warren, founder of a respected criminal defense firm. It was Keker's first experience as a prosecutor, and he was charged with investigating the Central American side of Walsh's mandate—how North and others had provided aid to the contras in Nicaragua after Congress banned United States assistance to the rebels.

Like the cool kids who sat in the back of the school bus, one last clique deliberately separated themselves from those whom they suspected of trying to curry favor with Judge Walsh. They were the prosecutors: John Douglass had used his soft Virginia drawl to convict Ronald Pelton of spying; David Zornow, baby-faced but wary, had just helped convict Bronx party boss Stanley Friedman of racketeering; and Michael Bromwich, bearded, balding, and rabbinical, had recently been named the top narcotics prosecutor in the Manhattan United States attorney's office. Surveying their colleagues, they would note (with little prompting) that they, the prosecutors, were the pros—they knew what they were doing.

In this assembly, I was anxious for a familiar face and found one. "Cliff Sloan!" I said, recognizing an acquaintance from law school. Sloan possessed an almost aggressively unassuming manner—he ended most sentences with a mumbled "and stuff"—but he had been a dazzling success in virtually everything he'd done in life. He had run a congressman's office, graduated at the top of his Harvard Law School class, and clerked for Justice John Paul Stevens. I was unsurprised to see him in this setting—and relieved to have someone to sit with.

"With a group this big," Walsh began promptly at half past ten, "we should be done already." The jibe passed unnoticed. But we soon learned it was the way Walsh started every meeting—and most every conversation. We called it "the needle," a seemingly unconscious flick of negative reinforcement to start the day.

Could he really, as the newspapers said, have just had his seventy-fifth birthday? "Judge Walsh," as I learned to address him, retained the sinewy build of an athlete. His three-piece suit, expertly cut from gray wool, hugged the contours of a six-foot, two-inch frame. His hair had gone mostly to silver but it gleamed like the ridges on a new dime.

A Walsh staff meeting unfolded like a decorous revival session; if you had something to say, you said it. The first speaker on this day was the lawyer who was facing the unenviable task of trying to disgorge documents from a reluctant Central Intelligence Agency (CIA). Then our office manager gave a rambling disquisition on office procedures, the gist of which was there weren't any.

John Douglass turned the conversation back to substance by outlining a potential obstruction of justice case against North. It appeared, Douglass said, that during Meese's weekend investigation back in November, North had engaged in massive shredding of key documents. The shredding had first been disclosed only a week after it happened, when the *Los Angeles Times* reported on November 27, 1986, that North was destroying papers even as Meese's Justice Department team was supposed to be investigating the Iran initiative. The press seized on the shredding as the emblem of the corruption of the diversion scheme. And Walsh, ever sensitive to the attentions of the press, wanted immediate follow-up on the story. As he said with some irritation, "I'm still getting seven-eighths of my information from the press, sixty days after I was appointed."

Walsh pressed Douglass for details. He said he was ready to move against North quickly. "You can't play it safe. If you start to let a case like this hang around and let your moment pass," Walsh said, "it may be trouble." Ruminating for a moment on Douglass's story of a desperate North hunched over the shredder, Walsh said, "It has a flavor and a picture to it. It might just remove some of the medals." Walsh had seen North's quivering assertion of the Fifth Amendment at a congressional hearing the previous month. He knew that Oliver North was no ordinary criminal. "I'm not looking for a defensive posture," he said. "We want the public behind us."

Douglass had few additional details. The key, he announced, would be getting a straight story from a key witness, someone named *Vaughn*, who had been less than forthcoming so far.

After we broke for lunch, I asked Sloan, who had preceded me on the staff by two weeks, "Who is this Vaughn who is so important?"

"Who?" he answered.

"You know—the one Douglass kept talking about."

"Oh," he smiled. "Not Vaughn, *Fawn*. Fawn Hall. She was North's secretary."

"Fawn Hall. Is that a real name?"

I WAS assigned to the "legal team," which, under Struve's direction in New York, was supposed to supply research and briefs to the flow of funds, NSC, and Central America investigating teams.

Our first important task was to assemble and secure the key documents in the case. To do so, the usual practice for prosecutors is to go official and issue subpoenas. The intentional violation of a subpoena, whether by destroying or hiding documents, is a crime: obstruction of justice. Prosecutors sometimes agree to negotiate the precise terms of compliance with subpoenas, but their very existence—with their looming threat of obstruction charges—makes a powerful investigating tool. The experienced prosecutors in the office wanted to send them to the administration right away, arguing that subpoenas would give us valuable leverage in a difficult area.

Walsh preferred to issue informal document requests, not subpoenas, to the key government players in our case—the White House, the NSC, and the CIA. President Reagan had offered his full cooperation with the independent counsel and congressional investigations, and given that promise, Walsh thought that subpoenas would look unduly confrontational. In any case, Walsh said, there would be no substantive difference between requests and subpoenas: they both would demand the same set of documents.

The consequences of our cooperative posture soon became apparent. On my first full day on the job, Walsh received word from Peter Wallison, the White House counsel, that Poindexter, the deposed national security advisor, wanted to examine his old files. Poindexter didn't want to take anything, Wallison said, he just wanted to look things over. Did we have any objection?

At that point, we had scarcely examined any of the documents. We didn't want one of our principal targets rummaging in his old files before we had that chance.

The problem was how to tell Wallison. Had we subpoenaed, rather than merely requested, Poindexter's files, the White House probably would not even have considered allowing access to Poindexter. We, as lawyers, had to translate an instinctual reaction into a legal argument. The assignment—a fairly routine bit of legal research—went to me, my first.

The law was clear on the issue. Poindexter had no *right* to see his old papers, but if the White House *wanted* to show them to him, that was not prohibited either. I told Struve of my finding and drafted a letter to Wallison that fudged the issue, stressing that Poindexter could not insist on seeing the documents. Struve approved the text.

As we lacked both a full-time secretary and a word processor, I sat down to retype it. I struggled to give the letter a professional look and presented my best effort to Struve. A demon of a proofreader, he noticed that I had squeezed in an extra letter on one of the lines. He frowned.

"You know," Struve said, "Wallison might not be the only one reading this."

Struve's implication was clear. Our ace in the hole on this issue was public opinion: if reporters knew that the White House was giving special treatment to Poindexter, a known subject of a criminal investigation, it would raise a considerable stink. All that it would take would be for our letter somehow to leak to the press. The letter needed to be presentable. I returned to the keyboard, and the letter ultimately did its job with no leak required: Wallison never let Poindexter return to the scene of the crime.

I SKIPPED the February 24 staff meeting to begin the two-day bar exam in New York. As I walked home after eight mind-numbing hours in the company of inter vivos trusts and collateral estoppel, the afternoon *New York Post* banner headline jolted my stupefied brain: NORTH DROPS BOMB ON PROBE.

The colonel had filed suit to have the independent counsel law declared unconstitutional. The following day, a federal district judge in Washington, Thomas Jackson, had taken the extraordinary step of blocking the perjury indictment of former White House Deputy Chief of Staff Michael K. Deaver because his lawyers had filed essentially the same lawsuit as North's had the day before.

The mere filing of North's suit had no immediate, practical effect on the workings of our office. But Jackson took the accusation against the law seriously enough to stop the Deaver case cold. The curtain might come down on us as well.

Walsh, Struve, and Sloan, who had been meeting around the clock since North filed his case on February 24, struggled to plot a strategy to assure that our investigation would not be thwarted.

In our New York office the next morning, Struve told me the OIC would respond to the suits in two ways, one public and the other very private. The public reply would be to move swiftly to have the lawsuit—designated by North's lawyers as *North v. Walsh*—dismissed. In fact, our preference would have been to try to change the name of the case as well. The instigator of a lawsuit assigns the case its caption, and the initiators of this one, North's law firm of Williams & Connolly, knew that *North v. Walsh*—with its insinuation that a mere criminal suspect was charging an Olympian prosecutor (and not the other way around)—would get under our skin. It did.

Under the rules of the district court, we were permitted several weeks to respond to North's charges. Struve wanted us to take just five days and submit our reply the first thing Monday morning—along with a request that Judge Barrington Parker, who had been assigned the case, give the matter expedited treatment. We would not, Struve vowed, stay on the defensive for long.

The chief basis for North's objection to the independent counsel law was that it allowed a panel of judges to name the prosecutor. North argued that the Constitution permitted only the attorney general—and not members of the judicial branch of government—to name federal law enforcement officials. Indeed, prior to the Ethics in Government Act of 1978, from Teapot Dome to Watergate, the attorney general had always made the choice on the rare occasions when special prosecutors had been named. The private response was based on Walsh's simple idea that history should repeat itself: the attorney general should name a special prosecutor in the Iran-Contra case: Lawrence Walsh. This "new" appointment would, of course, simply ratify the position that Walsh already held. A "parallel appointment," Walsh called it.

The question was how to persuade Attorney General Meese to do it. Struve proposed another well-typed letter to the White House. This one would point out that the attorney general had the power to make the Walsh investigation essentially immune from constitutional challenge. Struve knew that the letter would put Reagan and Meese on the spot. If Meese did *not* give Walsh the parallel appointment, the White House would have to answer some embarrassing questions: Why didn't the administration protect Walsh's probe? What did the administration have to hide?

The very same day that Jackson entered his restraining order in the Deaver case, Walsh sent a polite but insistent letter about a parallel appointment to the White House. We couldn't afford to wait for an answer, because we still had to reply to North's suit. Struve assembled us in New York on Friday, February 27—about thirty-six hours after I finished the bar exam. We had three days to prepare our brief for filing on Monday morning.

As Walsh had benefitted from Struve's loyal service, Struve too had learned the value of loyal apprentices—and no one was more loyal to Struve than Geoff Berman. A gangly six-footer who tried to camouflage his cherub's face with a lawyerly scowl, Berman had become devoted to Struve and Davis Polk during his two years at the firm. And it was he who, on seeing the infant state of Walsh's New York office, with its single, sorry word processor, had the least confidence in our chances for producing a creditable brief by Monday morning. "You know," Berman informed us gravely, "Davis Polk has the best word processors in the city."

Even if we had the best word processors, the task before us looked daunting. North's brief was a paradigm of the Williams & Connolly style—powerful, rhetorical, slashing, and uncompromising—a searing indictment of the notion of an "independent" prosecutor. Only the president, they said, could appoint, supervise, and remove prosecutors. In many ways, this first North brief anticipated struggles that would repeatedly surface in the Iran-Contra affair. Here and throughout the case, North served as the eloquent champion of broad presidential powers—whether the issue was fending off perceived judicial intervention in criminal prosecutions or purported congressional meddling in foreign policy.

We had many possible avenues for reply. In the first place, we would argue that the law was constitutional. Also, we had an argument that comes instinctively to most lawyers—procedural. If North were allowed to bring this case, we would say—trotting out that most lawyerly of argumentative devices, the slippery slope—then anyone who was merely being investigated could tie up his pursuers for years in legal skirmishing.

But Struve had another idea for our brief, one that would, he hoped, work in tandem with the secret letter he had just sent to the White House.

Struve looked to the great Watergate case of *United States v. Nixon* for inspiration. The narrow ruling in that case stated only that the president had to produce the White House tapes in response to a subpoena; that precedent seemed dubiously relevant to the problem that Struve now faced. But Struve noticed one minor argument that Nixon's lawyers had advanced: that the president did not have to comply with any subpoena issued by Leon Jaworski, the special prosecutor whom Nixon himself had hired. In essence, Nixon had argued that he was suing himself—a legal impossibility. The Supreme Court had given this argument the back of its hand, saying that Jaworski was no ordinary law enforcement official but one with "unique authority and tenure," who was allowed to issue subpoenas like any other prosecutor.

The *Nixon* case alone, Struve argued, "established" that the independent counsel statute was valid under the Constitution.

Sloan was dubious. The situation in *Nixon,* Sloan pointed out, was actually very different from the one we now faced, because there the special prosecutor had been appointed by the executive branch and not by a court. The basis of North's constitutional attack was that *only* the attorney general and *not* a court could appoint a special prosecutor.

"That's exactly right, Cliff," Struve said enigmatically, "and that's what I want Williams & Connolly to say."

Before we could question Struve's opaque rationale, our lonely word processor conked out completely, and Struve was left with only one choice. Our team would move to Davis Polk to produce the brief. Hearing the news, Struve's protégé Berman was jubilant, pumping his fist like a pitcher who had just completed a shutout.

The next seventy-two hours passed in a blur, as we worked around the clock and through the weekend to produce a finished product at around 4 A.M. Monday morning. We still had to make copies. Winking at me, Sloan asked Berman, "Geoff, are the Xerox machines here at Davis Polk any good?" Berman didn't hesitate. "Oh, they're great!" And so they were.

N O sooner had we filed our brief on Monday, March 2, than we began to hear that the Justice Department was seriously considering giving us the parallel appointment. Reagan was scheduled to give a major speech on the Iran-Contra situation on Wednesday, and his handlers, we heard, wanted him to seize the initiative by announcing the parallel appointment of Walsh. It would be one way for the president to restore his credibility. But, knowing that they could not offer Walsh the parallel appointment if he wouldn't accept its terms, the Justice officials promised to send us a copy of the appointing regulations before they were announced. Monday and Tuesday passed, however, and we saw no draft regulations.

On the morning of Wednesday, March 4, the day of the president's speech, Justice finally showed us a copy of the regulations for the parallel appointment. A cover letter stated that Meese wanted to announce the issuance of the regulations that afternoon, so that Reagan could say that evening that he had guaranteed that the Walsh investigation would proceed.

The Department of Justice's draft regulations looked like a first-year law student's homework. Filled with typographical and grammatical errors, seemingly produced on an antique typewriter, the document hardly looked like the answer to a president's problems. And the substance was even worse than the style. The regulations carried no guarantees of independence for the Walsh investigation. Meese was, in short, inviting us to work for him.

Struve decided to take Justice's invitation to comment on the regulations literally. He wanted to confront Richard Willard, the assistant attorney general whose office had prepared the regulation. But Struve faced a time bind. He had to accompany Walsh to meet with Meese at the same time he wanted to reply to Willard. So he made his only choice.

"Cliff and Jeff," Struve said, "I hesitate to send anyone as young as you two to negotiate with the Justice Department." Then he paused. "But I suppose it will be all right because I am giving you no negotiating latitude." This was Struve's idea of a vote of confidence. "You are to tell Willard that we will accept the regulation only if we have exactly the same guarantees of independence that we have under the statute. Otherwise, no deal."

Sloan and I raced across Pennsylvania Avenue to the attorney general's enormous domain on Ninth Street. Running down those courthouse steps, I thought of the Watergate special prosecutors and their battles with the Nixon Department of Justice. They had held firm when Justice tried to make them bend. So, I promised myself, would we.

Willard greeted us icily. Sloan quickly made our point: we would accept a parallel appointment only if we would have the same independence as we had under the Ethics in Government Act. At first Willard did not protest and agreed to amend his draft with the statute as a model, but he reserved final judgment until he saw the proposal on paper. He invited us to work out the details with his deputy, James Spears.

"Siddown boys, I hear we got some work to do."

That was our booming greeting as we arrived in the conference room next to Willard's office. "James Spears, deputy assistant A.G., but y'all call me 'Mit,' " he said, thrusting a beefy hand our way. Spears was presiding over a conference table that looked like it had been highjacked from a local kindergarten—with scissors, paste, and tape strewn in random array. Spears and his underlings had taken a photocopy of the statute and simply renumbered the sections to make it into a Justice Department regulation. Since Sloan's and my mandate was not to allow any departure from the text of the statute, we could not have improved upon a photocopy as a place to start.

Shortly after the Meese-Walsh meeting, Struve joined us.

"Mr. Stroo-vay," Spears mispronounced, "good to know you." After recovering from his down home welcome, the born-to-pin-stripes Struve endorsed the "Xerox strategy," although Spears' scrawled edits offended the punctilious New Yorker. Struve volunteered to serve as scribe for all changes on the document, which he accomplished by deploying the six-inch ruler he kept next to his pencils for just this kind of thing.

"No problem, no problem," Spears said as we worked through the document. Finally, near the end of the process, Spears stopped and said, "Well, now, Guy, here we gotta talk."

The section in question concerned removal of independent counsels—the provision guaranteeing our independence. This key section of the law permitted the attorney general to fire an independent counsel only for "good cause." What did good cause mean? The statute didn't say, but it explicitly delegated the authority to review any "good cause" removals to the same three-judge court that appointed the independent counsel. In other words, an independent counsel who was unjustly fired could be reinstated by the three judges. Struve wanted the same promise in the regulations; that is, if Meese ever wanted to dump Walsh, the prosecutor could try and persuade a judge to undo the dismissal.

Here Willard, who had also joined the meeting, balked. He wanted the attorney general's decision to fire an independent counsel to be final and unreviewable.

An unspoken presence suddenly loomed over our debate: the specter of the one special prosecutor who had been dismissed, Archibald Cox, whom Richard Nixon had plucked from office and into legend in the Saturday Night Massacre of 1973. Ed Meese, we vowed, would never do that to us.

Neither Struve nor Willard would budge on the removal power. Willard passed word to the White House that we would not have a deal in time for Reagan's speech.

As a final attempt at breaking the impasse, Willard asked his colleague Charles Cooper, the head of the Justice Department Office of Legal Counsel, to join the meeting. A loyal member of the Meese inner circle, Cooper was also, ironically, a key witness in the Iran-Contra case itself. Meese had chosen him to participate in the famous November 1986 weekend investigation at the White House.

Unlike Spears, Cooper's Southern lilt addressed everyone with elaborate courtesy and curlicue locution. "You see, Guy," he began, "May I call you Guy? We believe that allowing the courts to interfere with the operation of the executive branch is simply unacceptable. It's not that we believe that we would ever have any problem with so fine a man as Judge Walsh. It's our institutional responsibilities to the office of the president."

Willard, however, would still not consent to judicial review. His narrow eyes fixed on Struve—he indulged in none of Spears's or Cooper's regional bonhomie—Willard said flatly: "We cannot do that to the presidency." Struve would not move either. At 8:30 P.M., with the president's speech over and our impasse still unresolved, Struve and Willard agreed to suspend the negotiations and talk again in the morning.

The next morning brought compromise. The heart of the Justice position was that the three-judge court that appointed independent counsels was itself unconstitutional; on that, of course, we disagreed. So both sides decided to gamble that their position would be supported by the courts. Now exchanging drafts by fax machine on Thursday morning, Struve proposed that a fired independent counsel could be reinstated by the three-judge court *"if such court exists at that time. . . ."* Thus, in the event of a firing, the Justice Department could argue that the three-judge court was unconstitutional—that it didn't "exist"—and that there was no judicial review. We were betting that the court's existence would be upheld, that it would still "exist" to review a dismissal.

Willard apparently was willing to live with the uncertainty and accepted Struve's language. Attorney General Meese signed the regulations giving Walsh the parallel appointment early in the afternoon of Thursday, March 5, 1987.

F O R me, the eight days before March 5 passed in a blur, an endless series of researching, drafting, and proofreading sessions, punctuated by negotiations with Justice and fired by Diet Coke. After work on Friday, I saw my wife for the first time in a week. Both of us had grown accustomed to the leisurely hours of my clerkship—not to mention the resulting enhancement of my cooking skills—so we were shellshocked by the separation during my frenzy of work. We turned on the evening news and thought about the prospect of a weekend together. Then Tom Brokaw ruined it.

"Oliver North," the anchorman said, with the bemused smile that laymen use in reporting on complex legal machinations, "today filed a *second* lawsuit, this time charging that yesterday's Justice Department appointment of Lawrence Walsh was unconstitutional."

I knew this meant another weekend stationed at our word processors. Through the many years of our romance, I often marveled at McIntosh's ability to concentrate over long stretches of time.

"McIntosh," I said, tossing a pillow skyward, "*you're* the hard worker in this family. *I* want a weekend off."

No sooner had I begun to speculate about the implications of the second suit than the phone rang. It was Geoff Berman. "Guy would like us to get together at eight tomorrow morning to start drafting our reply in the second case."

Now, the reason Struve wanted to use the *Nixon* case became clear.

In replying to the initial challenge to the independent counsel law, Struve had in the back of his mind that the parallel appointment might be in the works and that North would ultimately challenge it as well. So in responding to the lawsuit against Walsh's appointment under the independent counsel *law,* Struve decided to lay the groundwork for the defense of his appointment under the Justice Department *regulation.* He did so by, in effect, leading with his chin in the first case. He had placed excessive reliance on the *Nixon* case in the hope that North would say that the prosecutor in *Nixon* was indeed different from the one established by the independent counsel law. Wagering that North's lawyers would attempt to look reasonable, Struve thought they would say, "We don't object to special prosecutors appointed by the president, only those appointed by a court"—thereby conceding the legality of the as-yet-nonexistent parallel appointment.

And that is exactly what North's lawyers did. Williams & Connolly had replied to our brief in the first case on Wednesday, March 4, the day before Meese announced the parallel appointment. In their brief, they savaged our reliance on the *Nixon* case. With characteristic ferocity, Williams & Connolly said *Nixon* was "completely off point . . . irrelevant . . . essentially no response at all." As Sloan had pointed out to Struve the week before, they said the special prosecutor in *Nixon* had been appointed by the president through the attorney general, not by some court—and that had made all the difference. Why? As they put it on page twenty of their brief: "Plaintiff North does not assert that the executive branch cannot properly delegate duties to an appropriately appointed special prosecutor and give him 'independence' from the attorney general and the president."

Here was our concession. A principal tenet of the adversary system is to view everything an opponent says with skepticism, if not hostility. But a peculiar corollary to this practice kicks in when a lawyer identifies a concession by an adversary. Dimwits otherwise, opponents become sages when they trip up, even when, as is usually the case, the concession is inadvertent. Little brings lawyers more joy than trapping an unwary foe.

And Struve had a most Struvesque form of fun with this one sentence on page twenty of North's reply brief. "Page twenty." "Page twenty." It became like a mantra in all of our many subsequent briefs on the validity of our investigation. Here, in the course of their brief on the constitutionality of the independent counsel *law*, North's lawyers essentially conceded the constitutionality of the independent counsel *regulation*. As we sat down to reply to North's second suit, we blazoned their concession all over our reply papers.

We wanted to make North look like a nuisance litigator, an instigator of frivolous lawsuits, in short, a lunatic. We pointed out that North had filed two lawsuits in less than two weeks—and we identified them in our papers as "North I" and "North II," as if the procession of cases could be expected to continue indefinitely.

After another Sunday night with the peerless Davis Polk photocopiers, we staggered aboard the Monday morning shuttle to Washington with only one question remaining about the hearing: who should sit where.

To accommodate the press of attention, Judge Parker moved the argument to the ceremonial courtroom in Washington federal court, which features the standard arrangement of two ten-foot-long tables on either side of the lectern. Next to arguing a case, sitting at counsel table is the great prize of the legal profession. But this trophy has a price. An overfull counsel table risks making the other side look like a valiant underdog. We heard through the grapevine that Williams & Connolly, tenacious in pursuit of any edge, specialized in spare seating arrangements. Most judges view this agonized process as an enormous, even comic, waste of time. Still, we worried.

Sloan and I were invited to get to court early and look for an inconspicuous seat near the back. I, for one, was relieved to be sent to Siberia; the strain of the past two weeks left me doubting my ability to stay awake through even the most spirited debate.

By the time we arrived at court—a half-hour before the 1:30 P.M. scheduled start—the vast room had filled to capacity, and we had to talk our way past the guards. Inside, a nervous, almost giddy excitement prevailed, and it took an instant to see why: Oliver North himself was in attendance, his decorated uniform planted securely between his lawyers Barry Simon and Brendan Sullivan at his predictably lean counsel table.

On our side, chaos reigned. In dividing up the table, Struve had not figured on our erstwhile allies, the Department of Justice. The ebullient Mit Spears along with a handful of his colleagues had joined Struve. Then lawyers for the Senate and the House of Representatives—who had asked to be heard as *amicus curiae,* in support of the statute—invited themselves in as well. By the time the full group had assembled, it looked like a popular (if sedate) craps table on a busy night in Las Vegas. Edge to North.

Called by Judge Parker to the podium first, Struve made his points quickly and efficiently. Simon's peripatetic performance bolstered our hopes for victory.

We did not have long to wait. Courtroom rumors—which emerge from the low-level buzz of reporters, law clerks, secretaries, administrative staff, and others less qualified to speculate—had Parker working feverishly on an opinion immediately following the argument. Near the end of the day on March 12, the gossip reached a crescendo, so I walked over to Judge Parker's chambers to see what I could learn. The judge's secretary met me at the door and said, "You're just in time. Here's the first copy."

Reading as I rushed down the hall to Judge Walsh with my prize, I saw that Judge Parker's words left no room for ambiguity: "Colonel North, like any other criminal defendant, can raise his objections by appropriate motions, *if* and *when* an indictment is entered." Parker dismissed both North I and North II on procedural grounds. And even though Parker did not rule on the constitutionality of the Ethics in Government Act, he noted, gratuitously, that "Walsh has offered good reasons to believe that the act will be upheld." We could not have written a better opinion ourselves.

We had done our job. We had guaranteed that the investigation would proceed. But to what end?

CHAPTER TWO

Real Crimes

I spent most of my frantic first weeks trying to pretend I was having less fun than I was. Fencing with Ed Meese's minions? Playing chicken with the White House? Battling Ollie North? I was having the time of my life, but I tried to react to it all with the studied nonchalance I observed among my colleagues.

Just once I couldn't help myself. It was a February morning in the New York office when Struve handed me a three-page memorandum. "We're trying not to make too many copies of this," he said, "so please give it back when you're finished looking it over."

I think my eyes might literally have bulged when I saw the title: "Outline of Potential Charges." This, I thought, was why we were here.

The memo listed the "more likely charges" the OIC was considering bringing, and it began with "Conduct of Covert Hostilities in Nicaragua." This first category was described as the "use of United States government funds and assets . . . to carry on covert hostilities in Nicaragua after the Boland amendment prohibited such expenditures"—the Boland or "one-A" case, as we came to call it, in reference to its position in Struve's memo. The next crime the memo listed was "Use of Tax-Exempt Foundations to Fund Covert Hostilities in Nicaragua," followed by "Diversion of Proceeds of Iranian Arms Transactions." The list was rounded out with "Personal Enrichment" and "Obstruction of Justice."

"This looks great," I told Struve. Violating Boland, I thought—that belonged in the top spot. The Boland amendment banned United States government support for the contras' war in Nicaragua. North and his colleagues, it appeared to me, spent two years systematically violating that congressional restriction.

Sure we should prosecute the more prosaic crimes like "personal enrichment," I thought, but the Boland amendment elevated the Iran-Contra affair beyond ordinary criminality. These people broke that law—brazenly, flagrantly, intentionally. Now our job was to make them pay for it.

In those early days I assumed the OIC was, more or less, just one big happy family, united on the goals and methods for our investigation. I was, however, promptly jolted out of this misconception when I heard Danny Coulson, the chief FBI agent assigned to Walsh's team, muttering after an early staff meeting. "The Boland amendment?" he said, "the *Boland* amendment? What the hell kind of crime is that?

"Sheeet," he added.

Coulson's grumbling was my first clue of a deep split within the OIC. A criminal charge based on the Boland amendment divided us not by political inclination but by professional background. By and large, the professional civil litigators and full-time defense lawyers—Struve, Keker, Mixter—wanted to bring the Boland case. The experienced prosecutors did not.

"C'mon, Danny," Keker said to Coulson (rather indiscreetly) one March lunchtime in the middle of the fast food mall across the street from our offices. "This guy [North] was telling everyone under the sun that he might have to go to jail for violating Boland. This was while he was in the White House. He knew what was coming."

Keker then repeated some of these activities which he had just summarized in a memo to the staff called "The Secret War." North helped Richard Secord, a retired air-force major general, make deliveries of weapons to the contras. . . . He suggested to his boss, then—National Security Advisor Robert McFarlane, that Guatemala be rewarded with increased United States aid for providing phony end-user certificates for arms that reached the contras. . . . He approved a $5.3 million weapons deal that Retired Army Major General John Singlaub had brokered for contra leader Adolfo Calero. . . . He personally paid certain contra leaders. It was a formidable list.

"NTK," sniffed Coulson. Nice to know. "Do you want to win your case or tell a nice story?

"There was too much money floating around this thing," Coulson continued, citing the recently released report on the Iran-Contra affair by the presidentially appointed Tower Commission. "Tower said something like twenty million bucks is out there somewhere. You know we're going to find that that money stuck to somebody. We're here to investigate crimes, John, and that's a nice, simple crime—stealing."

Like Coulson, the experienced prosecutors—Bob Shwartz and Paul Friedman, among others—believed the office should select discreet criminal acts for prosecution rather than charge, in essence, one, big, stinking mess. Charge crimes, they urged—lying, cheating, stealing—not policy disputes.

"Hell," said Coulson, "*I* don't even know if North did violate the Boland amendment." The Boland amendment was actually a series of laws that prohibited only the expenditure of *funds* for military aid to the contras. What government money did North spend? True, Coulson conceded that North used his considerable influence on behalf of the contras, but the law banned expenditures.

"We can say that North spent his own salary to aid the contras," Keker answered. Then he laughed. "I know that's not a hell of a lot of money."

Coulson sniffed, "Don't forget the price of the paper clips he used."

Coulson noted that Boland applied to "the Central Intelligence Agency, the Department of Defense, or any other agency or entity of the United States involved in intelligence activities." North worked at the NSC. Was the NSC "involved in intelligence activities" and thus covered by Boland?

"Berman says yes," Keker answered.

Berman became the resident expert on all matters relating to Boland, and his summary memo on the meaning of the law eventually grew to more than one hundred pages. Given his expertise—he was dubbed "Professor Boland"—we would often come to him with questions about specific activities: Did the Boland amendment apply to NSC employees? Yes, said Berman, *almost* certainly. So did North's activities violate Boland? Yes again, Berman answered, I'm *virtually* certain.

At the lunchtime debate and elsewhere, the Boland opponents within our office sought to make a larger point. Even if we could convince ourselves that Boland applied to North and that he made specific, forbidden expenditures, this was a *criminal* case we were talking about.

We would have to prove every part of our case *beyond a reasonable doubt*—a tough test, and one that juries, with an individual's liberty at stake, take seriously.

After hearing the first round of arguments, I held firm with Struve, Keker, and the other "hawks" on the Boland case. History, I thought, would see the Boland amendment violations by North and the others as their most significant misdeeds. The way they flouted the will of Congress seemed to me more than a mere criminal violation, but a challenge to our constitutional system of checks and balances. They acted like they were above the law.

But was a Boland charge too technical? Did it belong in a criminal court? Were we abusing our power? One office wit summed up the concerns well when he promised us that we would never hear the cry: "Officer, arrest that man—he's violating the Boland amendment!"

Coulson had his own priority for the case. It was a magic-markered sign taped to his desk in the FBI basement: "Follow the money."

Once we tracked down the cash, Coulson promised, we would indeed see that it "stuck to somebody." The key to examining the money trail was to find the records of the shell corporation through which most of the Iran arms money passed.

That shell corporation had no office or employees, and it did not resemble a corporation in the conventional understanding of the word. It was little more than a Swiss bank account, so the question of how to get at its books was not a simple one. One way to do it would have been by giving immunity to Richard Secord or Albert

Hakim, the business partners who ran North's resupply network to the contras and supervised the finances on the arms sales to Iran. But Secord and Hakim were leading suspects in the theft of the money. We had no desire to give them a free ride. In January 1987 we invoked the American-Swiss treaty on criminal investigations and requested that the Swiss government produce the records, but we could not expect answers for close to a year. We needed results *now*.

We decided to try to get the records by subpoenaing the corporation itself, and that created its own problem. The "corporation" had no front door where we could drop off a subpoena. We had to find the person who controlled its books, a central figure in the affair I'll call Mr. Sinbad. We had no idea where he was.

We enlisted the FBI in what turned out to be an updated version of the old vaudeville routine about the process server and the reluctant recipient. The bureau spent several fruitless weeks checking out rumors about Sinbad from South Korea to Dubai until it received a hot tip on April 19, 1987. The report was that Sinbad was registered at the Intercontinental Hotel in Paris. Bill Hassler, the lawyer on our staff coordinating the search for Sinbad, began arranging for the subpoena to be wired to the United States embassy in Paris so that Sinbad could be served.

The first orders arrived in Paris late in the evening of April 19, and Richard Dennis, an FBI agent assigned to the embassy, immediately confirmed that Sinbad was registered at the Intercontinental. The following night, when all the necessary papers finally arrived in Paris, Dennis and a State Department consular officer named Anthony Pinson walked the few blocks from the embassy to the hotel.

At 10:30 that night, they went to Room 3019. They knocked, and a female voice asked who was there. Dennis replied in French that he had a message for Mr. Sinbad that he had to deliver personally. The door opened, and a woman acknowledged the name Sinbad but confessed that she did not speak French. Dennis repeated his message in English. The woman told him to wait and closed the door. A moment later, the woman opened the door and told Dennis to leave whatever he had at the hotel desk. Dennis said that was not possible—the message must be delivered directly to Mr. Sinbad. She said no.

At this point, the door opened sufficiently so that Dennis could see Sinbad's unmistakable figure standing near the bed, the sight rendered especially memorable because the amply fed fellow was wearing only a towel. "Mr. Sinbad," Dennis called out, "I have a subpoena for you."

"Get out of here!" Sinbad replied, and the woman slammed the door.

Dennis did not know if the service would be valid if he left the subpoena at the front desk. He found a pay phone in the hotel and called Hassler in Washington to ask advice. Hassler didn't know the rules either, so he telephoned me in New York for some quick legal research.

I ran to our rudimentary library and quickly found that there was in fact a statute that covered the issuance of United States subpoenas in foreign countries. As fate would have it, the law was known as the Walsh Act and its origins were rooted in another Washington scandal—Teapot Dome.

Led by Senator Thomas J. Walsh of Montana (no relation), Congress passed the law to track down some of President Warren Harding's unsavory friends who, in Walsh's dry phrase on the Senate floor, "found it convenient" to settle in Europe when the investigations began in the 1920s. The law imposed two requirements for the service of a subpoena abroad: first, that service comport with "due process;" second, that delivery comply with the local rules for transmission of legal papers. The first hurdle posed no problem; any method we chose would certainly satisfy the minimal standard of due process. But as for the second—the French rules of service of process—I had no idea.

Knowing of Struve's vast store of legal arcana, I poked my head in his office and asked him what he thought. He admitted that his knowledge more or less stopped at the United States border, and suggested that the only place in New York that might have the information was the Association of the Bar library on Forty-fourth Street. So I bolted for the subway to Times Square, my thoughts on the agent biding his time outside the Sinbads' room.

I had no right to admittance to the Association of the Bar building because I had yet to hear whether I'd passed the bar exam. But I talked my way past the guard and ran up the stairs to the main reading room. There, sounding slightly more crazed than the average New Yorker, I asked what they had in English translation about French civil procedure.

Inside of five minutes, the librarian produced an English version of the French civil code. I not only found the answer to my question, but learned a cultural lesson as well, because article 655 of the code memorializes and sanctifies the great Gallic institution of the concierge. If a guest is not home or refuses to answer his door, under French law, it is always sufficient to leave legal papers with the concierge. As French novelists have always known, these celebrated busybodies, *bien sûr,* will always find their guests.

I found a pay phone at the library and called Hassler with the news. Dennis and Pinson returned to Room 3019, where a DO NOT DISTURB sign now hung forlornly on the door handle. Near the elevator on the fourth floor, they found a house phone down the hall from Sinbad's room.

After giving Dennis a few seconds to return to Sinbad's door, Pinson called Room 3019. Through the door Dennis heard the phone ring and a male voice answer. Pinson got Sinbad to identify himself and then told him that an FBI agent was at that moment sliding a subpoena under his door. Dennis guided the envelope through the crack and walked away. For good measure, they left another copy of the subpoena with the hotel concierge.

We were following the money.

''C O M E on—guess.'' These were the first words David Zornow addressed to me.

On one of my early trips to the Washington office, I heard that it was Zornow's birthday, so I wished him a happy one and asked how many it was. He demanded that I guess.

"I don't know," I said cautiously.

"You have to guess."

"I really have no idea."

When Zornow wanted something, I came to realize, nothing stopped him. "No," he continued, "you gotta guess."

"Okay, okay," I relented. "Thirty-one."

"Right!" he said.

It was always a contest with Zornow. He was always churning, always calculating, always looking for an angle. Notwithstanding our first combative encounter, I thought this was a guy to watch. I could learn something from him.

David (never Dave) Zornow was born and raised in the New York City borough of Queens. After almost three years in Washington his daily routine still included the purchase of the *New York Post* and the *Daily News*. After college Zornow had flirted with New York politics during a brief apprenticeship with then-Assemblyman Andrew Stein. He graduated from Yale Law School in 1980, and then clerked for two years for a federal district judge in New Jersey named Herbert J. Stern.

Zornow's clerkship led to an opportunity to serve as an assistant United States attorney under Rudolph Giuliani in New York City and their triumph over Bronx boss Stanley Friedman—a victory that they won on November 25, 1986.

"You know why I never liked that guy North," Zornow joked to me one day. "When he got fired, he knocked us off the front page." Zornow had an eye for the media as well as an acute radar for office turf battles.

Shortly after joining the OIC, he teamed up with his Southern District of New York colleague Mike Bromwich—the unlikeliest Angeleno. With black hair (what was left of it) and a thick black beard, Bromwich looked the antithesis of the Southern California surfer. And though he swam competitively in high school and ran marathons in his twenties, he had a look of the indoors about him—brown suits and the too-loud laugh of the smartest kid in the class. Mostly, though, he projected an unconscious sincerity. For "the right thing to do," you looked to Bromwich; for career advice, Zornow.

Together, they set off to investigate the private American fund-raisers who had operated with North, chiefly a fellow named Carl "Spitz" Channell.

Like the others on the staff with law enforcement experience, Zornow and Bromwich viewed the Boland case with suspicion. And, like Coulson, they believed in following the money. Working so closely together that they were often called "Zornwich" (much to their mutual annoyance), Zornow and Bromwich cordoned off a small space in our meager offices to pile up the records of Channell's National Endowment for the Preservation of Liberty (NEPL). Slogging through the stack, Zornow and Bromwich discovered that some of the money had seemed to disappear into an account called "toys."

Toys? Toys? What did it mean? Zornow asked, pacing the small office. He did not have to wait long for the answer, because the NEPL crew started spilling their story almost right away.

"Toys" were weapons—weapons for the contras in Nicaragua.

Channell, along with his partner, a former Reagan campaign aide named Richard Miller, specialized in hitting up big-ticket givers to conservative causes, particularly elderly widows. Miller hooked Channell up with North, who told them what weapons the contras needed.

Weapons were an ideal product for Channell to sell. They were dramatic, tangible, useful—and expensive, so he could generate a hefty cash flow for NEPL (invariably pronounced "nepple"). A committed and passionate speaker, the colonel gave a series of speeches to Channell's big givers, and Spitz's blue-haired ladies loved North's gap-toothed sincerity. After a briefing by North and an all-expenses-paid night at the Hay Adams Hotel across from the White House, Channell's appeals for a missile or two from his guests earned generous rewards.

NEPL raised the funds, transferred them to a Cayman Islands account controlled by Miller, and then Miller dispensed those monies at the direction of North, sending much of the proceeds to the Swiss shell corporation controlled by Secord and Hakim. The deal was especially sweet for Channell and Miller, because of the more than $10 million they raised, less than half of that amount found its way to the contras. Their expenses ate up much of the rest.

"Interesting," I said to Zornow when he explained it to me the first time. "But is it illegal? I hear about fundraisers who take a big cut of their proceeds all the time."

"Tax-deductibility, my friend," Zornow said. "That's the key."

Like all fundraisers, Channell knew that people give more if they can deduct the gift from their taxes. A bigger contribution meant a bigger cut for Channell, and the donor's tax deduction didn't cost

Channell a thing. Channell established NEPL under section 501(c)(3) of the Internal Revenue Service (IRS) code, so it could receive tax-deductible contributions. Of course, not any organization qualifies as a 501(c)(3). Only "charities"—churches, schools, hospitals—are granted the precious opportunity to offer tax-deductibility to their donors.

"Channell was telling his donors to take these contributions off their taxes—just like any charitable contribution," Zornow explained. But the tax law says charities may only perform tasks that the government might have to do—run universities, fund medical research, assist the arts, and so on. Providing guns to the contras was not such a purpose, especially when the Congress had forbidden United States government weapons from going to this charity's intended beneficiary.

"If you tell people that they can take deductions for something they can't, like giving arms to the contras," Zornow said, "that's depriving the IRS of money they would otherwise get.

"And that's a crime."

"It is?" I said meekly.

It was.

Or so Bromwich and Zornow informed Channell's and Miller's attorneys in April 1987, and neither Channell nor Miller seemed to have the stomach for a lengthy fight.

But Bromwich and Zornow found that they now faced a curious problem, born of the inbred Washington legal community and the peculiarities of the independent counsel law. Channell was represented by Alexia Morrison, an experienced and respected former federal prosecutor. In fact, Morrison had been appointed a part-time independent counsel herself, to investigate possible obstruction of justice by a former assistant attorney general, Theodore Olson. Rich Miller had retained as his defense counsel Earl Dudley, whom Morrison had named as her deputy in the Olson investigation.

Was this a conflict of interest? Bromwich and Zornow's conversations with Morrison and Dudley came just after Judge Parker dismissed North's suit to invalidate the independent counsel law. Though Parker ruled against North, he did so on procedural grounds, and North was appealing. If the law was unconstitutional, why would anyone plead guilty to an independent counsel? But how could these defense attorneys be expected to give their clients sound advice—advice that might include challenging the independent counsel law—when they themselves were beneficiaries of the law?

The solution reflected the classic lawyer's approach to an ethical dilemma: the hiring of more lawyers. Bromwich and Zornow insisted that before they would accept a plea from either Channell or Miller, they would require each man to hire another lawyer, one unaffiliated with any independent counsel, for the purpose of evaluating the constitutionality of the law and thus the appropriateness of any plea. When these lawyers completed their work (and recommended no challenge to the law), the two fundraisers were ready to fall.

"Look," Zornow explained, "Morrison and Dudley are smart. They know when to make a deal. They know that if they go to trial, we're going to show how these innocent rich folks gave all this money, and Spitz and Rich were living high off the hog. That part isn't illegal, but it creates an atmosphere that no defendant wants to see."

Channell took the first dive. In late April, he agreed to plead guilty to conspiracy to defraud the IRS, punishable (in theory) by up to five years in prison.

Almost more important than the plea itself was Channell's statement in court when he formally pleaded guilty. As is often the case in plea bargains, the plea ceremony had been carefully choreographed by Morrison, Bromwich, and Zornow.

On April 29, 1987, Judge Stanley Harris called the Channell proceedings to order in the federal courthouse. The full complement of the national press corps was there for the first formal court session of Walsh's investigation, and Harris, who had just been appointed to the bench, looked nervous. After stumbling through the first few questions to Channell, Judge Harris reached the highlight of the plea.

"You are charged," Harris read from his script, "with conspiracy in this case, and, of course, it requires two or more persons to have a conspiracy. Are you prepared to state the names of any of those with whom you conspired?"

"Yes, Your Honor," Channell replied.

"Would you please do so?"

"Yes," said Channell quietly. "Colonel North, an official of the National Security Council."

The reporters, gathered more than fifty strong in the back of the courtroom, gasped. Miller later made the same statement during his plea a week later. Our message had been sent: we were closing in.

The day after the Miller plea, I tagged along with Bromwich and Zornow when they scoured the out-of-town newsstands for pictures of themselves in front of the courthouse. It had been a big day for them. They were savoring it.

"*Philadelphia Inquirer*," Zornow said as he began working through the stack, "very nice."

Bromwich reached first for the *Los Angeles Times*. He scanned it. "Good," he said, "my parents will be pleased."

We all were. "But don't kid yourself," Zornow cautioned, "Williams & Connolly won't think much of this deal. Ollie was named as coconspirator, but this crime is not the one they're worried about. Too esoteric. Not enough jury appeal. They can always say that it was Channell and Miller who were the profiteers. Ollie didn't make a dime."

"His motives," Zornow said, lapsing into a parody of a defense lawyer's pleading tone, "were pure. But the shredding—that's a different story. They should be worried about that one. That's a *real* crime."

The hawks and doves at the OIC all agreed on one thing: everyone loved the shredding. But pinning down the shredding story—and doing it fast—pushed us up against a problem that was just beginning to come into focus and one that would dog us throughout the investigation: "national security."

Every aspect of our investigation had been, until recently, among the most tightly guarded national security secrets, and our offices had to comply with the requirements for storing highly classified documents. So our quarters were no mere suite of rooms, but rather a Sensitive Compartmented Information Facility (SCIF).

The precautions began with an armed guard posted twenty-four hours a day at the one unmarked entrance to our suite and extended to the office windows with their shades permanently drawn. We could only type certain documents on special, "tempested" word processors, which had the normal computer innards surrounded by a massive steel box. For some mysterious reason, we were even banned from possessing radios and televisions on the premises. The most disruptive prohibition—especially for lawyers—was that we were even forbidden to discuss most aspects of the investigation over the telephone. To circumvent this prohibition, some lawyers devised a feeble little code to disguise their conversations. For example, when using the phone, they sometimes referred to one principal target of our investigation as "Mr. South."

Even office garbage received special consideration. We were all issued two wastebaskets upon arrival: one for ordinary rubbish, which was collected by the building janitors on their nightly chaperoned rounds, and one for "business trash," which was shredded. Indeed, the piercing whine of the shredders became a regular late-afternoon feature of our lives until we began generating so much classified trash that the task needed to be exported to another site. Charged with the shredding responsibilities, our security staff issued stern, if understandable, reprimands to reprobates who mistakenly tossed their lunch into the wrong container; to shred a document that has been bathed in old coffee is a nasty business.

A veteran FBI agent named George Litzenberg, Jr., orchestrated our security indoctrination, and he promptly earned the nickname "Mad Dog" for the vigilance with which he approached his mission. Cigarette glued to one hand, mug of coffee affixed to the other, he would prowl the halls looking for mislaid documents and errant Styrofoam cups. Though often charmed by Litzenberg's earnestness, the lawyers on the staff soon came to dread his admonitions. Sensing the discontent, he turned briefly to homemade memos, to which he brought the omniscient, passive-voiced style that two decades of FBI directives had instilled in him. "It has been observed," read one, "and become quite evident that particular individuals have been transporting, receiving, duplicating, and distributing highly classified materials." Litzenberg's memos soon degenerated into incomprehensible government-speak, as when he admonished us, "It is the responsibility of the original receiver to ensure the need-to-know and that intended user has the proper access."

Still, in those first days, I silently reveled in my admission to this new covert world. I loved the brightly colored cover sheets on classified documents which told us that their disclosure could cause "extremely serious damage" to the national security. Tempted with that kind of invitation, who could resist diving in? Again, my colleagues affected a bored indifference to their admission to membership in this secret club, but I sensed their satisfaction at being on the inside, or, as North's assistant Robert Earl put it, "in the box." Nothing was off limits! Our blank check extended even to the nation's most priceless secrets.

My naiveté appeared almost painful in retrospect, when I, like the rest of the OIC, recognized that the national security system hung on us like a leech from day one, and it drew blood until we finally fought it off. Even worse, our status as "the government"—at least for purposes of our prosecutions—forced us to accommodate and placate the system rather than, as our instincts came to demand, to fight it as an enemy. Eventually, we came to know that the rush of curiosity we felt on seeing the "Top Secret" label afflicted almost everyone in the government. And we learned that memo writers, capitalizing on this pervasive voyeurism, would label their work accordingly—for no better reason than to reach the top of the in-box. And the secrets, the treasures that provoked those dire warnings ("extremely serious damage") on the cover sheets? We saw that the only way that their disclosure would damage national security would be if our enemies lacked access to *The Washington Post* as well.

All of us had to undergo a full background investigation by the FBI before being allowed access to classified information. These clearances were taking at least a month, so few of us could begin digging into the heart of the case much before March. Walsh sought partial relief through the hiring of John Douglass, the former assistant United States attorney from Virginia. Because Douglass had recently prosecuted the Pelton espionage case, his clearances were fully up to date, and he could start right in talking to witnesses. But there was still a problem. He had also just opened his own law practice in Richmond and could not make a full-time commitment to the OIC. Still, Walsh took what he could get from Douglass and assigned him to the most urgent task in the office—the debriefing of Fawn Hall.

THERE was never any question but that Fawn Hall would receive immunity. An independent counsel had not been appointed to prosecute secretaries, and Hall's savvy lawyer, Plato Cacheris, possessed one of a defense attorney's most useful gifts: knowing how to tantalize a prosecutor with the bombshells his client could provide—if she were immunized. Once Cacheris told us that Hall did know about the shredding, her grant of immunity soon followed. But with her immunity secure, Hall turned into, and remained, a balky and troublesome witness.

In its broad outlines, Hall's story of North's frenzied last week at the NSC had, as Walsh said, "a flavor" that was undeniable. There was a seaminess to it, a sordidness, a *criminality*, that both the Boland and 501(c)(3) tax cases lacked.

During November 1986, Hall reported, North worked around the clock preparing a detailed chronology of the arms sales to Iran. At that time the task of explaining the arms sales consumed the administration. Who approved the sales to Iran and when? How many shipments were there? Were they legal? These questions later paled in public significance after the thunderbolt disclosure of the diversion of the proceeds from these sales to the contras, but they were hot topics for Hall's boss in that final week. Indeed, North's chronology had been an elaborate attempt to fog the record of the arms sales, a task in which he had the support of both his former and current bosses: Robert McFarlane and John Poindexter.

But North, of course, also knew of the contra connection, and he did his best in November 1986 to muddy that trail as well. Hall recalled North obtaining original NSC documents that told of his contra role, editing them with his felt-tip pen and directing her to alter them. Finally, when events seemed to be careening out of control, starting on Friday, November 21, and continuing through the weekend, North and Hall shredded and shredded. Hall said North hovered over his office safe, plucked document after document from the drawers and handed them to her for destruction. They stuffed so much paper into the machine that they had to summon a repairman for an emergency call.

Hall told Douglass her most extraordinary story about the day North was fired, Tuesday, November 25. She said that when NSC security officers came to seal North's office after Meese's press conference announcing the dismissal, she took the altered documents, stuffed them in her boots and skirt and sneaked them past the check-point. What was more, she smuggled these papers in the company of North and the man she understood to be his lawyer, Tom Green. As they arrived at Green's car near the Old Executive Office Building, Hall reported, they all rehearsed what Hall would say if the FBI ever asked (as it was asking now) about any shredding she had done during that last week. "I'll say," she quoted herself telling Green, and coining the words that would become her epitaph, "we shred every day."

As Douglass recounted Hall's revelations at staff meetings, the group percolated with excitement.

"What a story!"

"A jury will eat this up!"

"Some national hero!"

"Let's indict him *now!*"

Douglass, however, tried to dampen the enthusiasm. "Wait a second, folks," he said in his slight twang, "you haven't met Fawn. I promise you that we do not want to pin a case just on her testimony alone."

First and most important, said Douglass, Hall remained intensely loyal to North. They worked together for five years, often around the clock. "She does not want to hurt this guy."

Almost as crucial, Douglass continued, Hall had a poor memory, and details of her stories often changed with each telling. According to Douglass, "She'd start telling one of her stories in a different way and we'd say to her, 'That's not how we heard it the last time,' and she'd start cryin' or complainin' and then we'd try to go over all of it again. This is not an easy witness—she could get eaten up on cross."

Douglass also noted that Hall said that North worked closely with Poindexter and McFarlane in preparing the chronology, raising trou-bling questions about the ultimate assignment of criminal responsi-bility for the colonel's actions. And as for the smuggling of the documents, she said that that was her idea, not North's.

And, finally, said Douglass, "She's still telling us—and with a straight face, too—'We *did* shred every day.'"

Hearing these reports, Walsh believed that someone needed to sit with Hall for at least a solid week and spend hour after hour forcing her to stimulate her memory and her conscience. But Douglass's burgeoning law practice prevented him from devoting a solid chunk of time to Hall. No one else yet had the appropriate clearances to hear her full story. Weeks passed. As February slipped into March and then April, North diverted our office's attention with his civil suit challenging the constitutionality of the independent counsel law.

By the time we extinguished that suit, we began to see Hall's story coming together. But the key moment had passed. We had not moved fast enough. We now knew that the congressional Iran-Contra committees would be giving immunity to Oliver North.

CHAPTER THREE

Taint

"**G**uy," Judge Walsh would ask Struve as almost the first order of business at each week's staff meeting, "what's new on the Hill?"

Walsh's mention of our counterparts, the joint House and Senate committees investigating the Iran-Contra affair, would prompt a symphony of groans from the staff. Smiling sympathetically, Walsh would nevertheless try to quiet the gripes. "They're only doing their jobs up there on the Hill." But we kept thinking "what now?" as we awaited Struve's report. *"What are they doing to us now?"*

We had nothing against the committees; not at the beginning anyway. But differences in style and substance quickly drove a wedge between us. Our mission was simple to define if difficult to achieve: to uncover and prosecute crimes. The stated goal of the congressional committees—to inform the public about the Iran-Contra affair—looked honorable on paper, but their priorities appeared different up close.

My introduction to all of this came when Struve asked me to call one of the senior committee staffers about the order of witnesses in their hearings. I was given the lineup, which included one Bretton Sciaroni, a low-level White House lawyer who had given North some legal advice about the Boland amendment but who had earned enduring fame for his multiple failures on the bar exam.

"Bret Sciaroni?" I said with surprise. He wasn't exactly a central player.

"I know," said the staffer, "but he's such an asshole that everyone wants to beat him up for a while."

The committees often seemed more interested in preening for the television cameras than in investigating the Iran-Contra affair. Indeed, the committees' obsession with their show was a key cause of the major bone of contention between us—immunity.

More than the likes of Sciaroni, the committees needed star witnesses. Few beckoned. CIA Director William Casey underwent surgery for a brain tumor in December 1986 and was not expected to recover. (He died on May 6, 1987.) Former National Security Advisor Robert McFarlane agreed to testify, but he had left the NSC in 1985, before the Iran operation reached full steam. (His suicide attempt, on February 8, 1987, also made him a less-than-promising target for hostile questioning.)

That left only Poindexter and North as candidates. We never quarreled with the committees' decision to give immunity to Poindexter. Alone among the prospective witnesses, he was in a position to know about the president. North, too, held an obvious allure in the committees' attempts to untangle what happened, and we knew that our half-hearted attempts to stop immunity for the colonel were doomed to failure. So immunity was, from day one, largely a fait accompli.

A grant of immunity to North and Poindexter would force them to testify before Congress, but hearing Walsh that first day in January 1987, I didn't know what that meant for the OIC. So, when I returned to my office after that meeting, I looked up the subject of immunity in the manual for United States attorneys. The manual stated that although a witness who testified under a grant of immunity could theoretically still be prosecuted, "successful prosecution would usually be extremely difficult. Consequently, under the circumstances of many cases, use of the [immunity] statute will effectively preclude a future prosecution of the matters to which his/her testimony related."

"Preclude a future prosecution?" I took the book into Struve's office and asked, "Have you seen this?"

He nodded with a grimace. Then he brightened, and I sensed that an assignment was coming.

"Why don't you start seeing what we can do about it?"

I BEGAN by reaching for a book that I always kept handy, the final report of the Watergate special prosecutor. Fourteen Washington winters earlier, I wondered, did the special prosecutor and congressional committee wrestle with these same questions?

Not exactly, I learned, and the difference illustrated, in a small way, a change in the tenor of the times. Special prosecutor Archibald Cox's key targets in the Watergate inquiry were H. R. Haldeman, John Ehrlichman, and John Mitchell, and as they prepared to testify before Senator Sam Ervin's committee, the threat of indictment hung over them just as surely as that prospect confronted Oliver North and John Poindexter in 1987.

In the 1970s, however, all those president's men testified in Congress *without* ever invoking the Fifth Amendment. "Real men" did not do such things in those days; they insisted they had nothing to hide and took the spears in the chest. The Watergate committee and special prosecutor thus never faced an important conflict over immunity, because there was no need for the committees to immunize the big fish.

But North and Poindexter immediately "took five" after November 25, 1986. As was their right, they hid behind the Fifth Amendment until they could extract immunity from Congress. If North was so brave and proud, why did he cower behind the Fifth Amendment? Each time he pleaded the Fifth, his status as a hero only seemed to be enhanced. He and Poindexter could be heroes *and* play the system for all it was worth. To do otherwise, apparently, wasn't courageous; it was just dumb.

The goal of Walsh and Struve was to persuade the committees to put off North's and Poindexter's immunized testimony until the latest possible date. We wanted the time to develop evidence that could not be "tainted" by the immunized statements; it is, after all, impossible to be tainted by what does not yet exist.

Struve actually made a little headway by recognizing the committees' peculiar needs from each of the two principal witnesses. Struve knew that North could provide the committees with a comprehensive narrative of the Iran-Contra affair, but there was no single fact that the committees felt North alone could provide. For North, then, all Struve could do was convince the committees to hold off any examination of him for as long as possible. That turned out to be June 15, 1987.

Poindexter was different. "There's really only one question the committees want to ask Poindexter," Struve told the OIC staff. "Did the president know about the diversion? Once they get an answer to that, they won't be in as big a hurry to hear the rest of his testimony." This gave Struve a little room to maneuver. He sought to find a way to let Congress ask its big question, but then prevent the answer from leaking—and possibly tainting us.

Struve was also betting what the answer would be. At his November 25, 1986, news conference, Attorney General Meese quoted Poindexter as saying the president had not known of the diversion. Like most of the rest of the OIC staff, Struve felt sure that Poindexter would stick to that story in front of Congress. So Struve proposed a deal to the committees: if Poindexter in a private debriefing session said the president did *not* know of the diversion, the committee counsel who interviewed the admiral would keep all aspects of the briefing secret, even from the congressmen and senators on the committees. If, however, Poindexter said that the president did know, the lawyers could tell the members of the committee. If the committee staffers had a bombshell of that magnitude, Struve knew, they could not in good conscience keep it from their bosses.

The committee lawyers bought Struve's proposal and entered into a formal, written "Memorandum of Understanding," signed on March 24 by Struve, Arthur Liman, and John Nields, the chief Senate and House investigators. According to the agreement, Poindexter would be debriefed in private by no more than three committee lawyers on May 2. Liman and Nields agreed not to discuss the results of these private sessions with the members of their committees *except,* according to the agreement, "in the event of certain extraordinary circumstances which have heretofore been discussed and agreed to by counsel for the committees and the IC." (The circumstances themselves were thought to be too sensitive to reduce to writing.)

The "extraordinary circumstances" never came about—Poindexter testified that Reagan did not know of the diversion—and the elaborate precautions in the private briefings served their purpose. There were no leaks to the press of what happened in those private sessions, and we had an extra six weeks to gather evidence without the hazard of taint.

STRUVE'S negotiations succeeded in postponing but not preventing the day of reckoning. While Struve was fencing with the committees, I was trying to figure out how our office could live with the immunity decision, to keep our cases against an immunized North and Poindexter alive.

The major Supreme Court decision about immunity, a case called *Kastigar v. United States,* stated that we could not "use" North's and Poindexter's immunized testimony against them. We would also have the burden of proving that we had not used their testimony. Showing the independent sources of all our evidence would not be enough. We would also have to establish that we had *not* used the defendants' testimony in any way.

So, I realized, our difficulties with prosecuting immunized witnesses, our *Kastigar* problems, as we came to refer to them, could be summarized, if not resolved, neatly: if we wanted to go forward, we could expect two trials, one of the defendants and one of us.

"What I think we've got to do," I told Struve after my research was complete, "is try a belt-and-suspenders approach to saving our cases.

"No one on the staff is going to have any trouble with the 'belt,' " I added, "but the 'suspenders' might create more of a problem."

The belt part of the strategy I suggested was to preserve in one place all the information that the office had collected before the would-be defendants began their immunized testimony. "We've got to be able to show how far our investigation had gotten before they started to testify—what evidence we already had and what leads we were pursuing," I told Struve.

Struve told me to assemble as comprehensive a collection of OIC material as possible and put it "in the can." This process came to be known, inevitably, as "canning."

I thus set out on a brief career as the archivist of a three-month-old office—collecting anything that would memorialize the status of and plans for our investigation, and then literally sealing it all up in boxes.

My problem was I didn't know where to start. I didn't really know how the office kept track of its records. I needed a tutor.

I found one in Roger Diehl, the beefy FBI veteran who supervised the OIC evidence room, which was then still in the FBI building. "Roger," I told him after I tracked him down, "we need to show exactly how much evidence we've collected, so I think what we've got to do is just Xerox everything we've got."

Drumming his fingers on his generous gut, Diehl wasted few words with me.

"You're nuts."

"I am?"

"Ah, *lawyers*," he murmured, articulating the syllables like a slur. A handlettered sign prominently posted in the OIC's FBI office illustrated what many of our bureau colleagues thought of us. It was headed "Investigation Priorities," and read:

1. Hire more lawyers.
2. Please the press.
3. Please the Congress.
4. Hire more lawyers.

But Diehl at least seemed willing to give me a chance so he said, "Come with me," and then he led me through the labyrinthine FBI basement to our evidence room. Opening the door and flipping on the light, he asked, "Do you want to copy all that?"

When my eyes adjusted to the glare, I saw a mountain of cardboard boxes, probably more than a hundred of them. Diehl opened one at random: it contained hundreds of checks and other papers from Spitz Channell's organization.

"How long to copy that one box?" Diehl interrogated me.

"Day, day and a half?" I responded sheepishly.

"Okay, Roger," I added, "you've made your point."

Instead of duplicating all the evidence itself, Diehl suggested we copy the FBI "green sheets"—the inventories of the boxes in the underground warren. Then we added the FBI "302s," the agents' written summaries of all interviews with potential witnesses.

A grand jury dealing exclusively with Iran-Contra matters had been meeting in the courthouse since the end of January. I collected the transcript and exhibits, an excellent record of pre-immunity materials. I tracked down all the subpoenas and document requests that we had sent out, including those for which we had not yet received compliance. That we had asked for the material before the immunized testimony would establish that the statements had not led us to it.

A week into this assignment, I started stacking the canning material in my office, which did not enhance its meager charm. If the battered file cabinets and prison-made desk were not bad enough, the ever-closed blinds gave the room a sickly, fluorescent pallor. My sole attempt to pierce the gloom was a miniature American flag, its pole laced through the shades.

When I finished assembling the existing material, we started writing up new documents to summarize the current state of the investigation. Each of the three teams—White House, Flow of Funds, and Central America—wrote memoranda outlining their investigative progress and plans for the future. In his last act as White House team leader before returning to private practice, Paul Friedman left a memo that, among other things, listed the potential targets and subjects of his investigation. According to Justice Department guidelines, "targets" are likely candidates for indictment; "subjects" are possible targets.

In the middle of a long list of "potential subjects," Friedman recorded the name "President Ronald Reagan." At that time and even after it, we looked for but never found any specific evidence of crimes that the president may have committed, but in the rush to complete the canning project, we erred on the side of inclusiveness. A few weeks after we finished, Friedman realized the significance of listing Reagan as a possible criminal suspect. Though he knew the list had little significance in and of itself, the document could, if leaked, be wildly misinterpreted. So Friedman discreetly tried to collect all the copies of the memo. He found most of them but couldn't get at one; it was, irrevocably, "in the can."

The first of our likely defendants, Albert Hakim, was scheduled to begin giving private testimony under immunity on April 10. He would not testify in public for at least another month, and the results of the private sessions were purportedly not going to be released to the public until Hakim testified in the open. For the Hakim depositions, however, we had not succeeded in arranging for the extraordinary written guarantees of secrecy as we had for the Poindexter sessions. The question was, when to complete our canning—when Hakim began giving his private depositions or when he started his public testimony? Should we wait until the public testimony and use the extra month, or should we trust Congress not to leak the private sessions?

"Jeff," Struve said to me when I presented the choice to him, "I'm surprised even to hear you ask. Given what we know about Congress, this is not even a close question." We would play it safe and seal on April 10. (We also savored the irony that, in obsessing about congressional leaks, we were sharing one of North's own fixations. We weren't wrong either; the highlights of the "private" Hakim depositions promptly leaked to the press.)

By the night of April 9, I had assembled almost the entire canning package, but I still lacked one memo that an OIC lawyer working temporarily at CIA headquarters had sent me by messenger. Pacing the halls, I fumed at no one in particular, "Where the hell is that CIA courier?"

Hearing this, Zornow stuck his head out of his office, lifted an eyebrow and said, "Did you ever think you'd be waiting around for a CIA courier?"

No, I admitted, probably not.

But the courier did eventually show, and I was ready for the finale to the canning project the next morning, when Paul Friedman, another lawyer on our staff, Audrey Strauss, and I appeared in a secret session in Chief Judge Aubrey Robinson's chambers. We were seeking permission to store the canned material in the courthouse safe. There was one precedent for this course of action.

Not all of the Watergate figures played tough guys to the end. John Dean had requested and received immunity for his testimony before Congress. As we were doing with the Iran-Contra figures, the Watergate prosecutors tried to lay down a paper trail for a case against Dean before he gave his immunized testimony. And just as Judge John Sirica permitted those prosecutors to store their material in his safe, Judge Robinson allowed us to do the same.

I promptly returned to our offices to complete the procedure. Litzenberg, the security director, relished the role that I asked him to perform in the canning process. He was to inspect the material, verify the indexes, seal the boxes, and sign the outside—like the wax seal on an eighteenth-century letter. Litzenberg executed his mission with a flourish, scribbling his name all over the cardboard, and then we drove the cargo over to the courthouse.

Sweating in the spring heat, Litzenberg, his assistant Armand Nardi, and I hoisted the seven bulging boxes up the courthouse steps and into the office of Jim Davey, the long-time clerk of the D.C. federal court. Davey led us to the closet with a combination lock that served as the "safe," and, as he undid the combination, he reminisced about the John Dean material that had been stored in the very same place.

"You know," Davey recalled, "Judge Sirica insisted on being the only person to know the combination to this lock. But the guy just could not figure out how to open the thing. He would come down here to open it and then I'd hear him start growling and cussing. So eventually we had to set up a system so that we'd get an assistant United States attorney to open the door each time the judge wanted to get in, and then we'd change the combination until the next time."

Davey also smiled as he saw us struggle to squeeze our big boxes into the narrow closet. As court clerk, he had witnessed firsthand the explosion in the amount of paper the legal system was consuming in recent years.

"Typical lawyers," he muttered. "You know, the Dean material was only two small envelopes."

"Well, Jim," I told Davey, "that might be so, but Dean wound up pleading guilty, so the Watergate prosecutors never had to prove the independence of their case against him.

"And you know who's representing North, don't you?" I asked him. Davey nodded. It was Williams & Connolly, famous as the toughest litigators in the city.

"I think," I said, "we'll need all the space we can get."

T H E canning was the easy part. The "suspenders," as I promised Struve, were going to be a tougher sell around the office. Some courts had suggested that not only could we not *use* the immunized testimony, we could not even *hear* it either.

Audrey Strauss outlined the proposal for the staff. "Our goal should be to have no contact at all with the immunized testimony. That means we can't watch it on television, read it in the newspapers, talk to our families about it—nothing."

An incredulous staff began to cross-examine Strauss on the specifics.

"Are you saying," Strauss was asked, "that when the testimony starts, we can't read newspapers?"

"You can't read any story that might make a reference to the Iran-Contra affair," she answered.

"No television news at all?" "That, too," she replied. Eyes rolled. Cocktail parties? Cover your ears.

"What?" came the nearly universal reply. This was *Washington,* the lawyers said, we had to know what was going on.

"I think it's unworkable," said John Keker, "and I don't know if any court would believe us if we said we did that." Could we—alone among the key players in a national scandal—close our eyes to facts that would be obvious to the most casual newspaper reader? In a city where, according to the cliché, information was power, could we render ourselves uniquely and intentionally disabled?

More importantly, could Walsh himself, who was responsible for the political defense of our office as well as its own legal offensives, bind himself to such an enormous degree?

"I think it's a silly business," Walsh said after he listened quietly to Strauss' recommendations. "I'm not going to put myself in a position to make the judgments I have to make without knowing what is going on on the Hill."

"But, Judge," said Strauss, "it's the only way we can save these cases."

"I don't know if that's true," Walsh answered. Then he turned to Struve. "I want a new memo on *Kastigar,* laying out all the options."

Whenever Walsh received an answer he didn't like, he sent it back. "Look at it again," he said.

So for the junior lawyer on the team, it meant back to the library. I knew that I had looked at all the *Kastigar* cases already, and our recommendations seemed the only way to play it safe.

"Judge," I volunteered, "Audrey's right. We have no choice."

Walsh pursed his lips. "You are talking about doing something that will make me look ridiculous. How can I be the only person in America not reading the newspaper?" His reaction was personal, instinctive, and understandable.

Strauss and I continued to lobby for suspenders, and we gradually began to pick up converts. First Bob Shwartz, then Bromwich and Zornow, even Keker finally came around. Total insulation, they preached to Walsh, was the only way to preserve our cases. Yes, it did seem foolish. Yes, it was a novel attempt. Yes, it might fail. But we had to try.

"Judge," said Bob Shwartz, who never shied away from a fight with Walsh, "North and Poindexter have a Fifth Amendment right to remain silent—a right that Congress is forcibly extracting from them in return for immunity. They have no choice but to testify or be found in contempt. It's our duty as lawyers to do everything we can to avoid learning what they say."

Walsh listened and stewed. It was probably the toughest decision he had to make as independent counsel.

"All right," he said finally, "I'll try." Once again he was demonstrating the flexibility that seemed to be his greatest strength. This office—his office—would not trample anyone's constitutional rights, no matter how badly we wanted convictions.

Stifling an urge toward humor, I prepared a series of no-nonsense memos for Walsh's signature to instruct the staff on how to avoid contact with the immunized testimony. The members of the grand jury also received similar directives. The first of these went out on April 10, the day Hakim's immunity took effect, and it made its points bluntly. Until further notice, it stated, "you should not read any newspaper or magazine articles, watch any television programs or listen to any radio reports that mention Albert Hakim. If you are reading something that makes reference to Mr. Hakim, as soon as you realize that he is being referred to, please stop reading. If you are watching a program or listening to the radio and Mr. Hakim is mentioned, please switch the show off."

Nor was that all. As part of his deal with Congress, Hakim had turned over his Swiss bank records—the same records, which we had chased in the Intercontinental in Paris. The committees, we realized, might use these records to examine other witnesses who appeared before them; if we heard this questioning, we could be accused of using Hakim's immunized "testimony," even though he himself was not testifying. So we instructed the staff to avoid any reference to "Swiss bank records" in connection with the Iran-Contra affair, even if Hakim's name was not mentioned.

The memo landed on every desk at the OIC on April 10, and at first our admonitions proved surprisingly easy to follow. In late April and early May, before the public Iran-Contra hearings began, the media took a brief sabbatical from the story. (It was then preoccupied with the disintegration of Gary Hart's presidential campaign.) There was not, in short, all that much to avoid.

But as the public hearings began with Richard Secord's testimony in May, we realized that the time for half-measures was over. With the advent of the public hearings, when immunized testimony was likely to infect much of the proceedings—in the questions to witnesses, if not in all the answers—Walsh agreed to go all out.

In another memo to the staff, Walsh decreed on May 15 that we were to avoid any media report that "related to the Iran-Contra matter *in any way*." He continued, "If you are watching a television program, or listening to the radio, and any report comes on about the Iran-Contra matter, turn the program off."

We went into total isolation, feeling the lonely unease of a child awaiting his mother's and father's return from an endless parents' night at school. We knew they were talking about us out there, but we couldn't hear what they were saying.

THIS bizarre cutoff from news reports made the whole office edgy. We continued about our business, interviewing witnesses, conducting grand jury proceedings, litigating against those who refused to comply with our subpoenas. But many of us felt, with the advent of the hearings, that the action had shifted to another arena and that we were being left behind.

To combat this malaise and keep everyone abreast of the office's progress, Walsh surprised everyone at our weekly staff meeting with an announcement. "Chris," he said to Chris Todd, a relatively new addition to the staff, "I want a presentation on the obstruction case on June 23." Todd was the full-time replacement for part-timers John Douglass and Paul Friedman, who had returned to their firms as planned. As the head of the NSC team, Todd concentrated on what we generically called the "obstruction case"—North's lies to Congress about NSC support for the contras and his November 1986 cover-up of the Iran arms sales and diversion.

For the past decade, Chris ("just Chris") Todd had been a federal prosecutor in the same New York office that produced Bromwich and Zornow. He had just won a jury conviction against Miami financier Victor Posner and, more importantly in our view, against Posner's lawyers—Williams & Connolly. Todd dressed like an English clubman, an affectation he acquired during a postgraduate year at Oxford. He even looked the part, with a jowly smile and an unruly mop of blondish hair. In an office full of uniform blues and grays, Todd stood out in his wide suspenders and baggy shirts, with their bold stripes and contrasting collars.

But despite the varnish, Todd was pure Texan, the proud product of Lubbock, who preserved his accent like a family heirloom. He had an endless supply of down-home anecdotes, which usually involved pickup trucks, and corn-pone expressions, which, though frequently obscure in meaning, always sounded good. (He would often say, "Wea-ull, that's the difference between the lip and the cup." I would smile and nod, without a clue of what he meant.)

As the group of about twenty lawyers settled into their seats in the windowless conference room on June 23, Todd opened his presentation by saying, "This is our best and dullest case." Everyone knew what he meant by "dull." The public had learned the general facts regarding North's obstruction almost half a year earlier. Over that period, our competitive juices had been stirred by a desire to uncover a more sweeping conspiracy—one involving the Boland amendment or the Iran arms sales. The case Todd outlined had none of those grander elements. It was nothing more and nothing less than an ordinary criminal case. Its simplicity made it the "best" case we had. It was one we could win.

Todd began by summarizing the evidence on what he called the strongest charge: for violation of the statute that prohibited the alteration, destruction, and removal of government documents. He repeated Fawn Hall's story of the chaotic days of late November 1986, when North changed original NSC documents regarding his private efforts to arm the contras in 1985 and then shredded those documents he couldn't alter.

"Doesn't there have to be a 'pending proceeding' for there to be obstruction of justice?" asked Paul Friedman, who still turned up for big OIC events. "Is that what you're calling the Justice Department investigation?" We were leery of describing Meese's weekend foray into the NSC as formal in any legal sense, because the attorney general, no friend of our efforts, had been stressing its loose and extemporaneous quality.

"The PROF notes [North's electronic mail] show that North knew that there was a *congressional* investigation on Iran at this point, and that's enough to satisfy the statute," Todd answered.

"What about the scope of the material we charge was altered?" asked Shwartz, always the most persistent questioner at these events. "How specific can we be?"

Todd then went through some of the altered documents. In one, North cut out a reference to the "current donors" to the contras. In another, North changed a recommendation that the United States increase aid to Guatemala in return for its support for the contras into a bland suggestion for enhanced aid alone—with no hint of a quid pro quo. North's alterations all had the same theme: to obscure the NSC's role in organizing military and financial support for the contras when the Boland amendment was in effect.

Next someone went right to the heart of Fawn Hall's defense of her and North's actions. "The government put a shredder in North's office. What was wrong with his using it?"

Todd smiled. "That's the whole case right there," he said, "this is an intent case. Of course, there's nothing wrong with using the shredder in the normal course of business. But when the shredding is done as part of a pattern of deception, that's a crime. And that's what we have here."

Todd summarized how a series of newspaper stories in the summer of 1985, particularly in *The Miami Herald*, named North as a key figure in the military supply line to the contras. The stories piqued congressional interest, and Democratic Representatives Michael Barnes of Maryland and Lee Hamilton of Indiana wrote North's boss, Robert McFarlane, a series of letters about the accusations. North, Todd continued, drafted the responses to the committees in August and September, and McFarlane signed the final versions.

McFarlane's letters, which Todd distributed to the OIC staff, were riddled with falsehoods. McFarlane told Barnes that "None of us has solicited funds, [or] facilitated contacts for prospective donors." In fact, we had the memos to prove that McFarlane and North repeatedly met with foreigners to goad them to give to the contras. Likewise, McFarlane called the charge that North gave the contras "tactical advice and direction . . . patently untrue." In truth, North provided extensive and detailed advice to the contra military—a fact we could prove through the testimony of those in the Secord resupply network.

As Todd moved to the NSC responses to congressional inquiries in 1986, when Poindexter had replaced McFarlane as national security advisor, Walsh's team grew unusually quiet and attentive. On August 6, 1986, after renewed press reports about North and the contras, the colonel met personally with members of the House intelligence committee in a session in the Situation Room at the White House. At the meeting, North denied that he raised funds for the contras or offered them military advice. He said that he had had no contact with contra fundraiser John Singlaub for twenty months and that his contact with contra activist Robert Owen had been "casual." These were all flat-out lies. And though North had not been put under oath and no transcript had been taken at the meeting with the committee, Todd said the law was clear that unsworn false statements in this kind of proceeding constituted crimes. Besides, two people present took detailed (and substantially identical) notes of North's representations.

Walsh asked for comments and drew rare unanimity. "It'll work," said Todd.

"I like it," added Keker.

Even Audrey Strauss, always a severe skeptic, said it "feels like a real case."

Shwartz, the harshest critic of all, allowed as how he thought at least "certain counts" were strong.

Todd, it appeared, had described the outline of a genuine prosecution. There was more to do, but we had witnesses lined up, documents examined, and defenses analyzed. We were ready to go. *We were ready to go.*

Then, as if a delicious secret had been passed without words around the room, we all began to smile and think the same thing.

Why wait?

I N all of our negotiations with Congress, we had never promised to delay our indictments until after North and Poindexter testified in public. But Congress had other ideas.

On Friday, June 26, the OIC press office received word that a United Press International reporter had called former members of the Watergate special prosecutor's staff to ask them what they would do if they faced Walsh's dilemma: the imminent immunized testimony of North and Poindexter. Those lawyers said they would indict the pair right away, before their testimony. The reporter then called two senators for their reaction and asked whether a deal had been struck. No, said the Senate-House select committee chairman Daniel Inouye, a Democratic senator from Hawaii, there was no agreement with Judge Walsh about the timing of indictments, "but he's an honorable man." Likewise, Republican Orrin Hatch agreed there was no deal, but he added ominously that if North were indicted now, "Walsh is in trouble."

Pretestimony indictments might dissuade North and Poindexter from testifying before the committees at all. Forcing indicted witnesses to testify publicly was literally unprecedented, and it had a suggestion of implicit unfairness—in effect, requiring a criminal defendant to answer an indictment point by point before he stood trial.

Most importantly, we all knew that North would probably refuse to testify under those conditions, choose instead to go into contempt, and fight the matter out in court. Such a confrontation could take years to resolve, and perhaps deprive the committees of their stars forever. This, of course, would help us. If North and Poindexter never gave immunized testimony to Congress, we could indict and try them without any *Kastigar* problems.

But Congress was just then showing how badly it wanted to examine North—even at a cost of its own dignity. According to Struve's deal with the committees, North was to receive immunity on June 15 and testify in public on July 7. The committee planned to use the last two weeks in June to interview North extensively in private in preparation for his testimony. The panel's lawyers were planning on operating by the sound legal principle that one should never ask a question, in a committee or courtroom, to which one does not already know the answer.

But Williams & Connolly had other plans. Once he received the immunity order on June 15, Brendan Sullivan, North's lead lawyer, announced that the colonel would refuse to testify in any private sessions, refuse to speak for more than three days, and refuse to reappear after his first appearances. Sullivan did not want to give the committee lawyers the time to pick North's story apart little by little, so that they could focus on his major weak points in public. He wanted to keep the questioners off balance, struggling to keep up with the colonel as they went along.

It was almost irrelevant that Sullivan's demands were patently absurd; immunized witnesses have no right to insist on conditions for their testimony. Sullivan bet that the committee would lack the guts to fight back, and he was right. The committees caved in on almost all Sullivan's demands. North made only a cursory private appearance before his public testimony, and he never came back after his initial round. North did ultimately testify for more than three days, but, given how he dominated those proceedings, that decision was no concession. In their final report, the committees delicately noted that in responding to North's demands they "struck a balance." Sure, like the one Custer struck with the Sioux at Little Big Horn.

The committees' abject performance at the hands of Williams &

Connolly served to goad our office into contemplating an immediate indictment. *Somebody* had to stand up to this guy.

The obstruction presentation on Tuesday, June 23, took place exactly thirteen days before the scheduled start of North's testimony, so we had no time to waste. Walsh named Todd, Keker, Bromwich, Ken Roth (another former prosecutor from the Southern District of New York who joined the staff part-time) and me to an "indictment committee." We spent Wednesday and Thursday putting the indictment in shape.

Walsh had set a final deadline of Monday, June 29, for a decision on an indictment. For the first time in months, our conference room was vacuumed—a sign that something big was up.

Keker began the Monday meeting by outlining the first count of the indictment. "The conspiracy has two objects," he said, "to violate the Boland amendment and to illegally conceal NSC activities in violation of the Boland amendment. If either one of them is proved," he added, knowing that there was far more enthusiasm for the second prong than the first, "the defendant is guilty."

Chris Todd began wondering out loud how a Boland charge would play to a jury. He was not worried about legal technicalities, but Boland's effect in the courtroom. "What is the theory that we can put in a box?" he asked. "People out there don't know or care about the Boland amendment. How can we make this charge sound *criminal* in laymen's terms?"

To the surprise of Keker, and most everyone else, it was Judge Walsh who jumped in and mounted a vigorous defense of the charge. "My concept is that there was a CIA activity going on in 1984," he said. "Congress wanted to stop it. Notwithstanding that, North said 'we're not going to let that stop us' and moved it over to the NSC."

"Yes," Todd said, "that's a violation of what Congress *intended*, but that's not what Congress *said*. I think what North did was within the letter of the law, and not a violation of criminal law. I see it as morally wrong. But was it criminal? No. What was criminal is that they lied to Congress."

"So you admit that Congress tried to forbid it?" Walsh asked.

"Yes," Todd answered, "they *hoped* to forbid it."

"So," Walsh pressed on, "did North *violate* what Congress said or *avoid* it?"

"It's the distinction between tax avoidance and tax evasion," Todd replied, "and the law has never prevented clever lawyers from finding ways of tax avoidance for their clients."

Todd continued. "If we charge Boland, North's going to call all kinds of people who say that what North did was perfectly legal. And even if they're wrong, when you get into battles of experts about what the law does or does not prohibit, you are creating a monster. Juries are very, very reluctant to find someone guilty of something when that 'something' changes all the time. And that's what we buy with the Boland amendment. Once you play it out at trial, that's trouble."

Still Walsh would not move. "Any time I've gotten in trouble in litigation is when I've not been ready to assert the central core position. We're going to get in trouble if we just pick our 'can't lose' issues. When I know I'm right morally—and have a tough time legally—that's always better."

From there the discussion shifted from the nature of the charges to the timing of the indictment. Earlier that morning, Walsh dictated a list of what he regarded as the pluses and minuses of going forward immediately. He labeled his categories "pro" and "contra."

Shwartz led the contra forces. From his first day on the job, he had loudly opposed the OIC bringing any case that included a Boland charge. "It's not a crime as far as I am concerned," he said. But Shwartz didn't like an obstruction case either. He believed that a case against North would succeed only with a financial angle—if we could "dirty him up" and portray him as a thief.

In the early days, there wasn't much cost to pursuing all avenues of the investigation with equal vigor, tracking down all leads that displayed any promise. But the financial investigation of North had yielded little so far, and it showed few prospects of producing results anytime soon. Our request for the Swiss records was bogged down with the authorities there, and Sinbad had challenged the subpoena we served on him at the Intercontinental Hotel in Paris. We had won in the federal district court, but enforcement was stayed pending his appeal. (Sinbad later won that appeal, though our legal position was vindicated in a separate Supreme Court case in 1988.)

Our search for thieves had not yet yielded results. Struve distilled the argument to its essence: "The 'corruption' here may not be that great. I don't think it's the holy grail. Why should we wait for it?"

Shwartz offered a vague but irrefutable reply. "We keep discovering new evidence all the time," he said. "We should look at it before we commit ourselves."

Keker pressed on for an immediate indictment. "If we wait until North testifies," he predicted, "we are going to be in the ridiculous position of not knowing what North's defenses will be when everyone else in the world does."

I was watching Zornow. He had tried tough white-collar crime cases. He knew what we were going to face. But he also measured his comments carefully in staff meetings so as not to offend potential office allies. Finally, he made an uncharacteristically strong plea for delay. "The most important job this office has is to convict Oliver North," he said, "and our most important constituency is those twelve nonlawyers who will decide whether we win or lose.

"You know," he continued, "every time I've prosecuted a case and heard the judge give the 'proof beyond a reasonable doubt' instruction, I've wanted to crawl under the table. And with a defendant like North, we've got to remember that it is going to be incredibly difficult to get a conviction of any kind.

"I think we need more than just obstruction and 'one-A' [the codeword for the Boland case]. What makes this case is the whole picture—obstruction, diversion, and corruption. And we don't have it yet."

James McCollum, a thoughtful recent Supreme Court clerk, agreed. "No jury will convict North unless they think he's a crook," he said, "and I haven't been convinced he's a crook yet." As for *Kastigar*, McCollum said we may be worrying too much. "*Kastigar* is a rule of law like any other rule of law. The judge will try to do the right thing, and I don't think he's going to throw us out if we wait."

Momentum for delay built steadily as Walsh solicited everyone's views around the room. Danny Coulson of the FBI remarked, "Six or seven months is puberty for an investigation. If you attack the king," he said, referring to North, "you better kill him. And this indictment won't kill him."

"And let's remember," added Mike Bromwich, "that as soon as

we indict, Williams & Connolly is going to create havoc because of their discovery demands. They are going to have us scrambling. We've still got investigating to do, and we'll be so distracted by their demands that we may miss something."

Struve joined Keker in urging action. "I predict," Struve said gravely, "that we will regret this missed opportunity." But the trend seemed to be going the other way. Friedman, Bill Hassler, Cliff Sloan, and Chris Todd all urged delay.

As Walsh continued to canvas his staff, everyone chuckled as he came to a lanky figure the corner—Larry Shtasel, who had been a federal prosecutor in Brooklyn. It was his very first day on the job. Shtasel deferred to those with more than six hours' tenure at the OIC.

I took my turn near the end of the day, when a giddy exhaustion had nearly overcome the group.

"You know," I admitted, "I've found that all afternoon I've been agreeing with the last person I heard." My candor, if not my insight, drew an appreciative laugh, and Keker and Bromwich engaged in a mock duel to make a last impression before I gave my views. With serious misgivings, I joined the majority. I believed that we would have only one shot, and I was not convinced that the "indictment committee's" product was our best.

Walsh professed mixed feelings. "It's always possible to rationalize delay, especially in the law business," he said. "You're never entirely ready." But delay was his decision.

Geoff Stewart, a newer lawyer and one with an eye to proceed, greeted Walsh's ruling with a stage whisper: "Why does North have this mystical effect on authority figures?" The meeting closed with good humor masking nearly universal regret. Even those of us who supported the no-go decision had wistful thoughts about the drama that might have been.

The excitement over, I returned the next day to the New York office, which had assumed a ghostly quality. I had found myself spending nearly all my time in Washington. Having recently learned that I passed the bar exam, I busied myself briefly making arrangements to be sworn in as a lawyer in New York and then left around lunchtime for the July 4 weekend. Disappointed with our failure to act but resigned to the inevitability, I stopped at the video store for an afternoon distraction.

All the President's Men proved irresistible.

Those, I thought, were the days.

J U S T after the holiday weekend, Oliver North began testifying before the congressional Iran-Contra committees.

Each of us on Walsh's staff seemed to have one special problem in our struggle to avoid learning what the colonel said. Mine was sidewalk newspaper dispensers. Until North's testimony began, I never realized how conditioned I was to glance at the headlines behind the glass as I walked along the street. Now, compelled to ignorance, I found myself almost jerking my head in an attempt to avoid the giant letters that heralded the birth of a new folk hero.

North appeared to be everywhere. On the corner outside our office in Washington, they sold buttons with his picture. Mine (of course, I had to have one) featured the proud North gaze and the legend: "I'm a North American!" Walsh's daughter, we later found out, heard a woman ask her hairdresser for a "Betsy North 'do." (Characteristically, we learned this anecdote from a newspaper story about Walsh. He rarely shared his own personal experiences with his staff.)

At no point in the investigation did we feel more helpless than during North's congressional testimony. Aware only of the sizzle that North had produced, we could only speculate about what produced such excitement. Despite my requests to friends and family to forgo any discussion about the hearings with me, my mother could not resist telling me that Brendan Sullivan had announced he was "not a potted plant." Devoid of its context (as it was for me), the comment made little sense. Well, I thought, I never mistook him for a geranium. And though Sullivan's remark did not taint me—North's statements, not Sullivan's, were immunized—it did add to my sense of befuddlement. As Cliff Sloan remarked one day in frustration, "I took this job to learn what went on behind the headlines. Now I can't even read what's *in* the headlines!"

I suffered most in the morning. Up with the alarm (no clock radio), I listened as McIntosh read me the baseball scores. My beloved morning newspaper at a safe distance, I brought a novel to accompany my cereal. It wasn't the same. After navigating around the newsstands on the way to work, the staff could at least retreat to the taint-free sanctuary of our office. This was a far cry from the simple effort of avoiding Hakim's name.

But, by and large, our system for avoiding exposure to the testimony worked. There were minor breaches, which we conscientiously reported to John Douglass in Richmond. After he left the OIC, Douglass agreed to serve as "father confessor" for taint breaches, and we sent him a steady stream of memos and phone calls recounting partially seen newspaper headlines and slips from family members. Guy Struve, always meticulous, reported that an errant front page of the New York *Daily News* had blown in front of him as he was playing with his son in Central Park. Most of our problems were of an equally trivial nature. Journalists, convinced of their own indispensability, reported on our efforts with amused contempt, but we proved that ignorance, if not blissful, was at least possible.

It took some unusual effort. One afternoon during North's testimony, I was reading an old *Sports Illustrated* at lunch in New York's Chinatown. Just after I sat down, I heard the two elderly men at the next table say something about "North." I froze, then, my mind churning, I stuck my fingers in my ears. Recognizing that such eccentricity transcended even the spacious limits of behavior deemed acceptable for lower Manhattan, I decided to step outside the restaurant and collect my thoughts.

I settled on a direct approach. On returning to the restaurant, I marched up to the two men. "Excuse me," I said, "I know this is a strange request, but I work for Lawrence Walsh, the special prosecutor in the Iran-Contra case, and I'm not allowed to hear anything that North said in front of Congress. So I wonder if I could ask you to talk about something else."

With the vacant, wary stare that New Yorkers reserve for subway lunatics, one fellow sized me up. "You work for Walsh?" he asked.

"Yes."

"What are you, a paralegal?" So much for my distinguished lawyer's looks.

"No," I said, "I'm a lawyer."

"Do you work for him here or in St. Louis?" he queried.

St. Louis? Who was this guy?

"Here and in Washington," I explained.

"Okay, we'll change the subject," he replied, now mysteriously satisfied. "And good luck."

Notwithstanding the occasional well-wishes of strangers, we could not help but see that our likely defendant had struck a powerful chord with the American people. Seeing only the ephemera of North's testimony—the buttons, the banners, the pitying looks from our spouses—made the man appear invincible.

Several days after North's testimony ended, Paul Friedman had an experience that seemed to sum up our grim state. Making conversation with the maitre d' at Tiberio, a fashionable Washington restaurant, Friedman asked if anything interesting had happened there lately.

"Well, Vice President Bush was here a few nights ago, and Colonel North was here as well."

"Oh," said Friedman, trying to think of a neutral response, "was the colonel in his full regalia?"

"Oh, *yes*," said the gentleman, beaming at the thought of the man we regarded as a criminal, "and when he left, the whole restaurant gave him a standing ovation."

CHAPTER FOUR

Oh, Elliott

My work on legal issues often led to invitations to attend Judge Walsh's weekly meetings with the investigating teams. A Monday in late April brought me to Keker's Central America team meeting, where I first met Geoffrey Stewart, a new lawyer whom Walsh had hired for a special project.

With his rep bow ties, pastel button-downs, and pinstripe suits bearing just the faintest shine on the elbows, Stewart shifted the sartorial—and political—orientation of the OIC slightly to the right. In his late thirties, he also had acquired the first suggestion of a paunch, giving him a measure of gravity that his cowlicked, sophomore's face had yet to provide. He was, in short, just what the office needed: a Republican who looked it.

Walsh had remembered Stewart from his brief stint at Davis Polk, before the young lawyer emigrated to Washington with President Reagan's election and rose to positions of responsibility in the Justice Department of William French Smith. The demands of a growing family, however, prompted him to flee for the private sector and the D.C. office of the old Boston law firm of Hale & Dorr. He had just won a coveted partnership there when Walsh summoned him, earning from Stewart a commitment to work, part-time, on a single project: Elliott Abrams.

At the April team meeting Stewart was bemoaning the fact that the returns from his fifty-page document request to the State Department had just begun to arrive, and he was swamped.

After the meeting, I decided to volunteer, though this marriage did not seem made in heaven. I was, after all, no southerner, no Republican, and never a willing visitor to Brooks Brothers. But my interest in the subject prompted me to plunge ahead.

"You know," I told Stewart, "Elliott Abrams is kind of a hobby of mine. So if you need some help, let me know."

"Jeff," Stewart said, "you may *already have won* the opportunity to read State Department documents until your eyes bleed and the chance, just possibly, to prosecute the assistant secretary of state for Inter-American Affairs." Thus was born the State Department team, better known around the office as "the two Geoffs"—the spelling a concession to my elder.

I undertook the investigation of Abrams with an enthusiasm that bordered on the unseemly. The prosecution of Abrams would serve as a warning to all those who thought they could dispense truth like charity favored on a chosen few. Getting the bad guys—this was what being a prosecutor was all about.

I N the spring of 1985, President Reagan nominated Elliott Abrams as assistant secretary of state for Central and South America, the top United States policymaker for the region and arguably the second most visible job in the State Department. The position required Senate confirmation. Abrams submitted a résumé for the consideration of the senators.

The résumé, modestly limited to a single page, described nothing less than the foremost diplomat of his generation. Born in January 1948. Graduate of Harvard College and Harvard Law School. Staffer for Henry Jackson, the state of Washington's conservative Democratic senator. As of 1981, assistant secretary of state for International Organization Affairs—at age thirty-two, the youngest assistant secretary in the history of the oldest department in the cabinet. Two years later, assistant secretary for Human Rights and Humanitarian Affairs.

Impressive as these jobs were, they constituted the periphery of power at State. The real power resided at five corners of the maze of corridors that form the sixth floor of the department's headquarters. Those offices belong to the five regional assistant secretaries, the diplomats who supervised our embassies and thus our relations with all the nations of the world. No position was more visible than ARA; the characteristically obscure State Department acronym for Inter-American Affairs.

By 1985, Abrams had already received Senate confirmation for his two previous State posts. A third confirmation seemed little more than a formality in the Republican-controlled body. There was one small problem, a glitch in his otherwise flawless conservative past. From 1977 to 1979, Abrams worked for Senator Daniel Patrick Moynihan. By 1985, the New York Democrat Moynihan had repudiated the neoconservatism in his own past and come to oppose most of the agenda Abrams was selected to implement. Moynihan had even failed on the litmus-test issue for the Republican Right—support for the Nicaraguan contras. Abrams's dilemma, a minor one really, was how to explain his work with Moynihan to conservatives.

But there was a solution. Abrams simply omitted the job and any mention of Moynihan from the résumé submitted to the Senate. He was confirmed without incident.

''I LOVE it,'' said Stewart when I showed him the résumé Abrams submitted to the Senate. "That's our Elliott."

But the résumé, Stewart and I agreed, was an amusing curiosity rather than evidence of a crime. It was *evidence* that we were after. That was the only thing that mattered.

As assistant secretary, we learned, Abrams chaired the Restricted Interagency Group (RIG), which coordinated day-to-day policy in Central America. The most important members of the RIG—the group that Abrams sometimes called the "mini-RIG," "RIG-let," or, if they found themselves on an airplane, "flying RIG"—were Abrams, North as NSC representative, and the chief of the CIA's Central

American Task Force. They represented curious choices to control the nation's most pressing foreign policy problem. None had any experience in the region. None spoke much Spanish. But they were in charge.

By the time Abrams came aboard in mid-1985, North had also blossomed into a full-fledged commander of the contra military. In fact, within two weeks of the day Abrams took office at ARA, North convened an extraordinary all-night meeting in Miami among the contra field commanders and the leaders of Secord's private benefactor enterprise. North informed the would-be revolutionaries that their chaotic procurement practices offended him and that henceforth Secord, and Secord alone, would be supplying them with all their weapons. By that time as well, North had joined with Spitz Channell and Rich Miller to raise money for those purchases. These military and fundraising activities formed the basis of our possible Boland amendment charge against North. Stewart and I set out to learn whether Abrams had joined the conspiracy as well.

My role in the Abrams investigation began with the mountain of State Department documents. Burrowing in the dusty pile, I thought I had quickly found the magic evidence—Abrams' telephone logs, his daily record of all the calls he made and received. Over and over again I saw the same name: *Lieutenant Colonel North . . . Oliver North . . . Ollie . . . North*. Once, twice, even three times a day the two men spoke; sometimes on the secure phone, sometimes on open lines. I showed the caché to Stewart, who seemed impressed, and then, eager to share my discovery, I bustled into Zornow's office.

"Take a look at these," I told Zornow, showing him some representative samples.

"Pretty incredible, huh?" I prompted.

"They talked to each other," Zornow said.

"Abrams," I predicted, still savoring my breakthrough, "will have a hard time saying that he didn't know what North was doing, won't he?"

Zornow shot me a look of pity mixed with contempt. "Not at all," he said. "What do those records show about what was said in their conversations?"

"Well," I sputtered, "nothing, I guess."

"Right—nothing. Abrams will be able to say that they discussed all kinds of things; the scheduling of RIG meetings, legislation on the Hill, anything. And those records can't disprove a word of it."

A prosecutor, Zornow reminded me, could not indulge the easy inferences of a newspaper reader. So North and Abrams spoke a lot. That fact might give a reporter a nice scoop, but it provided little sustenance to a criminal investigator. Even if North and Abrams did nothing *except* scheme to violate the Boland amendment in those phone calls, the records couldn't prove it. Abrams could always say that North never told him about his fundraising and military advising role. Even with the phone records, we didn't have the evidence—*the evidence*—to shoot down that story.

We found copious records of the large RIG meetings, but these turned out to describe innocuous discussions of legislative strategy and the like. We had no way of getting inside the mini-RIG. North and the task force chief were not talking to us, and we wanted, for a time at least, to defer an interview with Abrams.

Besides, here the congressional Iran-Contra committees gave us some help. They scheduled Abrams's testimony for June 2, 1987, near the beginning of their public sessions. As a sitting assistant secretary of state, Abrams could not demand immunity for his testimony and remain in his job. But Abrams's testimony did, however, present sufficient *Kastigar* problems to prevent Stewart and me from seeing him in person. Before we could review the testimony, a "tainted" member of our staff would have to screen it and excise any references Abrams or his questioners made to the immunized statements of other witnesses.

But shortly after Abrams's testimony, Stewart and I obtained an edited videocassette and slipped it into the VCR in our office lunchroom. Televisions were banned by security, but the lunchroom was located outside the boundaries of our SCIF.

"What?" asked Stewart, as we settled in, "no popcorn?"

We heard committee counsel Mark Belnick get right to the heart of the matter. You saw North almost every day, he asked, what did you *think* he was doing?

North, Abrams said, was "the guy who seemed to know the most about the private benefactors" aiding the contras. Abrams said North "once told me . . . that there was a big network out there of people and companies and bank accounts, which nobody else ever said to me," but Abrams asserted he had no idea that North was helping to run that network. Abrams, in short, projected a studied ignorance of North's world.

Belnick pursued Abrams with the obvious follow-up. "Did you ask him for details about that network?"

"No."

"Why not?"

"I was not his supervisor," Abrams replied testily. "He worked for a different agency. I was supervising my people. I did ask him at a couple of occasions . . . whether he was abiding by the law. And on one occasion in particular, I remember he said, 'I have never solicited a nickel.' He may have said a dime. 'I am not breaking a law. I have checked with White House counsel.' "

Abrams cited another reason for his disinterest in North's activities. McFarlane, the national security advisor in 1985, wrote Congress a series of letters in the fall of that year which, according to Abrams, stated "in pretty categorical terms" that North was only monitoring and not aiding the contras.

Hearing that answer, I laughed out loud. "This guy is too much."

By the spring of 1987, when Abrams was testifying, these McFarlane letters had been exposed as full of lies; the OIC had just debated whether to bring criminal charges against both McFarlane and North because of them. But Abrams was now saying *he* relied on them, thereby conveniently adding himself to the list of the NSC's dupes.

With the video rewinding in the machine, Stewart shook his head. "That," he said, "is the smartest 'dumb' man you will ever see." Abrams's professed ignorance of North's actions—as well as his purported reliance on McFarlane's letters—stretched his credibility taut.

"You sound just like [Thomas] Eagleton," I said, quoting the Missouri Senator who had told Abrams, in a celebrated confrontation in the Senate Intelligence Committee, "Oh, Elliott—you're too damn smart not to know."

To refute Abrams's story, however, we needed evidence—specific documents or witnesses showing that Abrams abetted North's secret network. We didn't have the goods.

No, we decided early on, we probably could not make the case to include Abrams in the one-A conspiracy to violate the Boland amendment. But his testimony left another area to pursue, one based on Abrams's own tragicomic foray into the world of covert fundraising.

THE spring of 1986 was a desperate time for the contras, with the administration and Congress still locked in a bitter stalemate over funding for the rebels. But Abrams had an idea.

It was prompted by an obscure provision of the Boland amendment. As a minor concession in the battle over Boland, Congress acceded to an administration request to allow the United States government to solicit foreign governments for funds for the contras. Congress agreed, but said the administration could only solicit funds for "humanitarian" purposes. In addition, the law authorized only the State Department to conduct the solicitations, an attempt to limit the role of the CIA in Nicaragua.

But the legislators—Washington insiders themselves—had another reason for giving this option to State: they regarded the State Department as more trustworthy but less effective than the CIA. They thought that if only State could do the soliciting, it probably wouldn't get done. But Abrams, passionate about the contra cause, wasted no time. By the middle of May in 1986, he had secured Secretary of State George Shultz's approval to solicit money for the contras.

Abrams polled his fellow regional assistant secretaries about which countries to try. He met last with Gaston Sigur, who supervised relations with the Far East. As Abrams recalled it for the Iran-Contra committees, a vision descended on him at the table in Sigur's office, a solution to all their problems, an answer—*the* answer. Brunei.

LONG after Brunei secured its bizarre niche in the Iran-Contra story, the former American ambassador to Brunei, an endearing fuddy duddy with the wonderful State Department name of Barrington King, sat in the OIC and struggled to describe for me the tiny nation where he lived for three years.

In the middle part of this century, he said, Brunei ranked as such an obscure outpost of the British Empire that Her Majesty's government wanted nothing more than to be rid of it. A small sliver of the island of Borneo surrounded on three sides by the nation of Malaysia and on the fourth side by the South China Sea, Brunei could hardly be located in a region Westerners found more obscure. (Even with that description, it took me a while to find it on a map.)

Far from battling for independence after World War II, Brunei's leader, Sultan Omar Ali Saifuddin, rather liked the colonial cocoon. So the sultan, seeking the advantage in this inverted struggle, forced the British hand by abdicating his throne in 1967 and leaving Brunei nominally in the hands of his twenty-one-year-old son. The British Foreign Office declined to turn authority over to the obviously un-qualified junior sultan until 1971, when the Whitehall powers finally threw up their hands and granted Brunei its reluctant autonomy.

The move was characteristic of the British Empire's rotten luck in this century because almost as soon as it severed its colonial ties to Brunei, the oil boom of the 1970s exploded, and Brunei turned out to be a leading beneficiary. Based on the sultan's rights to gigantic reserves under the South China Sea, money poured in to him on an almost unimaginable scale, making him nothing less than the richest man in the world, with a personal fortune estimated in the mid-1980s at $25 billion. The sultan's eighteen-hundred-room palace in the capital city of Bandar Seri Begawan barely put a dent in his budget. What, thought Abrams, was a few million bucks to this guy?

So Brunei it was. Fortuitously, Shultz was scheduled to visit Brunei at the end of June, and Sigur and Abrams knew that a personal appeal from the secretary of state might prompt the young monarch to reach for his checkbook. Sigur advised Ambassador King (who didn't want to dragoon the sultan into Central America), of the project and Abrams told Shultz of the decision to approach Brunei. Shultz tentatively approved.

When Shultz was just about to leave for Brunei, as Abrams re-counted the story for Congress, he realized he had a problem: what if the sultan says yes? In other words, if the Sultan agreed to con-tribute, how would the money actually be passed? Better than anyone, Abrams knew that Congress had carefully scrutinized how "human-itarian" funds were spent. He had endured the scholastic debates with congressmen about wristwatches and night-vision goggles and the like: which were "lethal," and which "humanitarian"? Abrams also knew nothing about covert operations for passing large sums of money. He needed advice.

So he looked to his friend Ollie North. Stewart and I regarded this as curious in the extreme if Abrams really knew nothing of North's secret role in helping the contras. North worked for the NSC, a coordinating entity that ordinarily had *no* operational functions, much less the ability to conduct a covert transaction like this one. In addition, North had no responsibility for administering the humanitarian aid that the United States government was already sending to the contras. How could he be expected to know how to control disbursement of this vast sum? How could he assure that the money would go only to humanitarian aid?

At the time Abrams asked North how the sultan should pass the money to the contras, North was in fact supervising an enormous fundraising network for the contras—an enterprise of which Abrams claimed total ignorance. With funds coming from both Spitz Channel's solicitation of rich Americans and, of course, the Iran arms sales, North had in mid-1986 a vast slush fund at his disposal. Here was Abrams asking, it appeared, if North wanted $10 million more.

Stewart and I scoffed at Abrams's answers to Congress on these questions. He said he asked North where to send the money because North knew the contras and would know where to find their accounts. But didn't the task force chief "know the contras" as well? Yes, but the CIA was not supposed to be involved in the nonhumanitarian funding. Then why not ask the State Department officials who were running the humanitarian aid program? Because they weren't supposed to be involved in this covert program.

So how, Abrams was asked, was the nonlethal restriction going to be applied? Abrams said North was going to set up "a sort of post hoc vouchering system." North would do that? Yes. When? *After* he got the money.

In any event, hearing of Abrams's problem, North cheerfully volunteered to help move the $10 million and told Abrams to stop by his office to pick up the account number to give to the sultan. North, Abrams remembered, was anxious to show off his new office, Room 302 of the Old Executive Office Building, a recently renovated two-story suite with a view of the Washington Monument. Abrams recalled ducking his head into North's fancy digs and saying, "Hey, you owe me an account number."

Fawn Hall later had a characteristically dim recollection of the scene. Both men were rushed, she remembered. North walked out of his office to her adjoining desk and gave her a folder. Pointing to something in the folder, North instructed Hall to type this information on an index card. North gave Hall the account number for Lake Resources, the private Swiss bank account to which he had directed the proceeds of both the Iran arms sales and the Spitz Channel fundraising and from which he had paid for millions in arms for the contras and their secret airstrip in northern Costa Rica. The Lake Resources number was: 386-430-22-1. But Hall typed: 368-430-22-1. Abrams took the card, said thank you and went on his way.

Following Shultz's trip to Brunei, the secretary ordered Ambassador King to put the arm on the sultan for the $10 million. King did. Shortly after the pitch, King heard from the sultan's aide-de-camp—I'll call him Archduke Beluga—that the sultan would provide the cash. Beluga insisted only that a high-level United States official make the final request for the money. A man of the sultan's wealth had attracted his share of fortune hunters, and he wanted a guarantee of the operation's bona fides.

The sultan and his entourage, Abrams learned, would be in London over the weekend of August 8 and would be willing to meet with an American then. Sigur and Abrams discussed it and decided that Abrams would go. Abrams could better answer any questions the Bruneians might have. Informed that Abrams would be the emissary, King said that he should use a pseudonym when telephoning Beluga at London's Connaught Hotel (which, by the way, the sultan owned). Fine, Abrams cabled back, tell Beluga to expect a call on the morning of August 8 from a "Mr. Kenilworth." (Geoff Stewart couldn't resist asking Abrams during one of our later interviews, why "Kenilworth"? "Somebody finally asked me that!" Abrams said with a rare relaxed laugh. The word, he said, was part of his mother's address.)

So Abrams set off to London, carrying Fawn Hall's well-traveled index card, which Abrams had retrieved from the Shultz aide who had taken it to Brunei. Shortly after his arrival, "Mr. Kenilworth" called Beluga at the Connaught and they arranged to meet for a walk in Hyde Park. During the fifteen-minute stroll, Abrams recited a brief history of the contra struggle, asked for Brunei's help, and presented Beluga with the number Fawn Hall had typed for him. Beluga told Abrams that Ambassador King would be informed when the "arrangements had been consummated"—that is, when the money had been deposited.

Abrams did not have long to wait for more good news. Shortly after Abrams's London meeting, King reported that the sultan had transferred the $10 million. Abrams promptly called North and told him to expect the money. Let me know, he told North, when it shows up.

AS summer yielded to fall in 1986, two major events—one long anticipated, the other unexpected, but both equally predictable in retrospect—transformed the administration's contra equation. First, the Democratic-controlled House of Representatives finally approved military aid for the contras. After a close vote on June 25, the official policy of the United States whirled one hundred eighty degrees. The Boland amendment—with flat prohibition on any lethal aid to the contras—was out, and military aid to the contras—$100 million worth—was in.

With the triumph came the second development—hubris. The administration got cocky and sloppy. Even though the Republicans won the House vote in June, House Speaker Thomas "Tip" O'Neill's adroit parliamentary maneuvering prevented the aid from arriving until October. Prudence would have dictated that North use those months to wind down the private supply network which he had built with Secord; they had to fear not just defeat, but its companion, exposure. And because every army suffers some reverses—Secord's ragtag band could hardly expect to be exempt—the enterprise was doomed to public exposure.

The beginning of the end for North came on the night of October 5, when Sandinista antiaircraft fire connected over Nicaragua with a private resupply plane bearing ten thousand pounds of ammunition and three American crewmen. The pilot and copilot—Wallace "Buzz" Sawyer and Bill Cooper—were killed on impact, but one American survived. He had the improbable name of Eugene Hasenfus ("rabbit's foot" in German), but his capture was distinctly bad luck for Elliott Abrams.

Several congressional committees immediately opened an investigation of the Hasenfus downing. Their star witness was Elliott Abrams. Abrams would have to assemble and digest all the facts, prepare the administration line, and testify before the hostile panels all in less than a week. Abrams had two obvious places to begin piecing together the story: the CIA and NSC. At the CIA, Abrams asked the task force chief to put together everything the agency could find about the downed airplane, its occupants, and its sponsors. As far as the CIA was concerned, the task force chief reported to Abrams, they felt that they could deny categorically any involvement with the Hasenfus plane or the entire private benefactor network.

For Abrams, the next place to look was the NSC. After all, the NSC, and particularly North, had been at the center of public and press accusations about American military aid to the contras for more than a year. Secretive though it may be, the CIA was basically a large bureaucracy ill-suited to undertaking a systematic effort to violate the Boland amendment. The NSC, in contrast, with its lean staff and freewheeling style, could move with more stealth in weaving the private benefactors and the contras together. What had the NSC been doing for the contras? What exactly was Ollie North's job? Congress would surely ask those questions. Abrams would need answers.

And faced with all these prospective inquiries about the NSC and his friend North, Abrams did nothing. He didn't ask North what he knew about Hasenfus and company. He didn't ask North where the contras received their money. He ventured before the hostile congressional panels with his ignorance intact.

O N the day that I volunteered to help Stewart in the spring of 1987, my office in Washington contained a single, mostly empty file cabinet. By midsummer, two large cabinets overflowed with the story of Elliott Abrams's life: calendars, memos, messages, cables, notebooks. Stewart and I also interviewed scores of witnesses and traded information with our colleagues who were working on other parts of the case. We were ready to sit down and add it all up.

It was a grumpy time for the Office of Independent Counsel. The congressional hearings were winding toward a close. With North's and Poindexter's testimony recently completed, we had settled into our compelled ignorance with sullen resignation. Discontent about our no-newspapers rule prompted our press officer Jim Wieghart to have his staff start circulating edited stories around the office every day. At least we were able to see some of the Iran-Contra coverage— albeit with many paragraphs crossed out with a black magic marker, like the newspapers read by prisoners in old movies.

Venting our frustrations in private contempt for the committees' investigation, we knew that jealousy intensified our feelings: the committees, at least, were finished and could go home. We recognized that we had just begun. Seven months into our investigation, any indictment we brought could no longer be called "early."

Stewart and I did not, of course, have the last word on whether Elliott Abrams would be indicted, but as those who best knew the evidence against him, our recommendations would carry a certain amount of weight. Like most people, I had bantered around the word "crook" with the same casualness I used with any number of epithets. But Zornow had swatted me out of my infatuation with Abrams's phone records. What I or anyone else thought didn't matter. What we could *prove* did. It was now Stewart's and my job to say what we could prove.

Stewart had traced the ties we had established between Abrams and North. They worked together on the RIG, spoke almost every day, and proclaimed unabashed admiration for one another. Stewart reluctantly concluded, however, that our investigation could proceed no further than our insinuations. Skeptical as we might be about Abrams's explanations, we could not prove specific acts that Abrams knowingly took in support of North's secret war in Nicaragua. The evidence provided no basis for including Abrams with North in a charge for violating the Boland amendment.

"Now of course," Stewart told me with a smile, "this doesn't mean that Abrams isn't guilty of violating the Boland amendment—only that we can't prove that he did."

For my part, I had spent much of the past month assembling and reviewing all of Abrams's previous testimony to congressional committees. I had always thought that if we were going to prosecute Abrams, we would not charge him with violation of the Boland amendment. Even in the egregious example of North, many OIC staff members had reservations about bringing that case; I suspected that a similar charge against Abrams—where the evidence was sure to be less compelling—would never fly. Better, I thought, to keep it simple: get him for lying.

I had gathered into large spiral notebooks every word of Abrams's testimony to Congress in 1985 and 1986. None of his testimony had been under oath, but federal statutes prohibited unsworn false statements just as clearly as they punished perjury.

The key statements came at the congressional hearings after the Hasenfus plane was shot down. Just five days after the Hasenfus crash, Senator John Kerry, a Democrat from Massachusetts and a leading administration critic on the contras, led the questioning in a Senate Foreign Relations Committee hearing:

> SENATOR KERRY: Are you aware . . . of any deal by which, as part of the AWACS transaction [a sale of sophisticated aircraft to Saudi Arabia] or subsequent to the AWACS transaction, [Saudi Arabia] is supplying weapons or assistance to the contras on our behalf?
> MR. ABRAMS: No . . . I think I can say that while I have been assistant secretary, which is about fifteen months, we have not received a dime from a foreign government, not a dime, from any foreign government.
> SENATOR KERRY: "We" being who?
> MR. ABRAMS: The United States.
> SENATOR KERRY: How about the contras?
> MR. ABRAMS: I don't know. But not that I am aware of and not through us.

I did not have to tell Stewart that these answers reeked of falsehood. First, McFarlane disclosed in December 1986 that the Saudis had contributed millions of dollars to the contras. Second, other foreign governments, including two in Asia, had also provided money to the rebels. Third, Abrams himself had chased across the Atlantic in search of money from another foreign government, Brunei.

But I still regarded this statement as inappropriate for a criminal charge. The contributions by the Saudis and the Asian nations were only publicly revealed after the Iran-Contra scandal broke. We had no way to prove that Abrams knew of them when he gave this testimony in October 1986.

In false statement cases, I had learned over the previous month, judges must instruct juries that they may not convict the defendant if his or her statement was literally true, even if it was misleading— just like this one.

As for Brunei, I told Stewart, "Notice that Abrams carefully said that neither the United States nor the contras had *received* any money from foreign governments. At the time Abrams made the statement, that was technically true. The Bruneians had reported that the money had been transferred, but North had not found it. So because the money had not been *received*, Abrams's answer was literally true."

The House intelligence committee on October 14 gave Abrams an even tougher time, I said. Committee Chairman Lee Hamilton pounded away at Abrams and Clair George, head of covert operations at the CIA:

> THE CHAIRMAN: Can anybody assure us that the United States government was not involved, indirectly or directly, in any way in supply of the contras?
>
> MR. ABRAMS: I believe we have already done that, this is, I think, the president has done it, the secretary has done it, and I have done it.
>
> THE CHAIRMAN: So the answer is the United States government was not involved in any way.
>
> MR. ABRAMS: In the supply. Now again, this normal intelligence monitoring is there, but the answer to your question is yes.

Stewart and I smiled at each other as we parsed this one. This, we knew, was close to the line.

"Look," I said, "I agree that Abrams's story is hard to believe. Sure, he *should* have known about North. My own view is that he probably did know. But we don't have the evidence to prove it in court."

Hamilton pursued the point once more. "Just to be clear," he asked Abrams and George, "the United States government has not done anything to facilitate the activities of these private groups, is that a fair statement? We have not furnished any money. We have not furnished any arms. We have not furnished any advice. We have not furnished logistics."

The question neatly tracked what Ollie North had spent the past two years doing.

Clair George, sensing disaster, decided to limit his answer. "Mr. Chairman, I cannot speak for the entire U.S. government." He was not going out on any limb. He would only vouch for the CIA.

"Can you, Mr. Abrams?" Hamilton asked.

"Yes, to the extent of my knowledge that I feel to be complete."

This Abrams statement was a whopper. Even George later expressed astonishment at it. "I found the statements so categorical on the part of Mr. Abrams," George told the Iran-Contra committee, "it was the sort of thought that went through my mind—excuse me, Elliott, but maybe you are the only guy in town that hasn't heard the news. You know, there's a three-inch Nexis pressrun about Ollie North." But Abrams, displaying what Senator Warren Rudman called "an incomprehensible lack of curiosity" about North's activities, apparently never did hear the news. I parsed each word of Hamilton's question: "facilitate" . . . "money" . . . "arms" . . . "advice." We could not *prove* that Abrams knew of it. At least, I told Stewart, we could not *disprove* Abrams's assertion at the Iran-Contra committee hearings that this and other post-Hasenfus statements by him had been "completely honest and completely wrong."

Laughing myself at this point, I savored the irony—that I, of all people, turned out to be Elliott Abrams's great defender. And there was only one more statement to review.

ABRAMS later described November 25, 1986, as "the worst single day I had in six years as assistant secretary." On that point at least, I never heard anyone doubt his word.

At noon on that fateful day, of course, President Reagan and Attorney General Meese disclosed their discovery of the diversion and the departures of Poindexter and North. Like thousands of others throughout the government, Abrams watched the televised news conference in shocked disbelief in his office. Abrams, of course, had special reasons for concern. Not only did the incipient scandal threaten to demolish his Nicaragua policy, he had the more immediate problem of a congressional hearing that very day. In 1986, the New Jersey Democrat, Senator Bill Bradley of the intelligence committee, had insisted on biweekly updates on the situation in Nicaragua, and a session had been slated, coincidentally, for 4:00 that afternoon.

At that session the committee came out growling. The disclosure of the diversion left the senators feeling betrayed and angry—and no one more than Bradley himself. Bradley had jeopardized his future in the Democratic party by voting for the plan to give $100 million in lethal aid to the contras—one of only a handful of Democrats to do so. He had gambled on a Republican policy that was erupting in chaos and scandal.

Testifying with the CIA task force chief, Abrams had few answers. He did not know of the diversion, he said. He did not know how it happened. Moving from the diversion to the more generic question of fundraising for the contras, Bradley asked, "Did either one of you ever discuss the problems of fundraising by the contras with members of the NSC staff?"

"No, I can't remember," was Abrams's ambiguous initial reply.

"Well," Bradley continued, "you would say, gee, they got a lot of problems, they don't have any money. Then you would just sit there and say, what are we going to do? They don't have any money. You never said, you know, maybe he could get the money this way?"

"No," Abrams said. "We're not—you know, we're not in the fundraising business."

Reading these words early in our investigation of Abrams, I sensed immediately the difference between this and his other "wrong" statements, to use the word Abrams preferred to "false." This was a flat-out, bald-faced lie. We might not be able to prove that Abrams knew of North's military operation—or that Abrams knew the contras had "received" funds from foreign countries. But had he discussed fundraising for the contras with North? Yes, in detail and at length. Abrams was very much in the fundraising business.

Peppered with questions about this statement during his Iran-

Contra committee testimony, Abrams responded lamely that he felt he "lacked authority on that day to reveal that solicitation." Rather, he said, he tried to "deflect" any questions about fundraising by giving only "narrowly drawn, technically correct" answers. But Abrams even failed at that—his answer was a lie. Why didn't Abrams just tell Senator Bradley that he was not authorized to discuss the subject? Yes, Abrams conceded, "it would have been relatively easy to do that. It would have been the right thing to do."

Abrams also claimed in his defense that he had corrected the record by calling Senator Bradley shortly after he made the statement. This intrigued and troubled me. I knew that, under the law, recantation did not constitute a defense to the charge of making a false statement. But I still believed that if we charged Abrams with lying to the intelligence committee, a voluntary revision and apology could sway a jury.

Abrams said he realized immediately that his November 25, 1986, testimony had gilded the truth at best, but, as I examined the record, I saw that he did not exactly jump to correct the record. Thanksgiving did shut down official Washington on November 27 and 28, but Abrams had an opportunity at least to mention the problem on the following Saturday. On that evening, we learned, Abrams attended a dinner party at the home of journalist Morton Kondracke, along with John Despres, Senator Bradley's staffer on the intelligence committee. But Abrams did not warn Despres at that time of any pending problems.

Abrams continued to dither all through the following week. Only on Friday, December 5—ten days after his testimony—did Abrams call Bradley to start correcting the record. Why did Abrams wait so long?

So I played a hunch. I decided to see when the Brunei solicitation was disclosed in the press. Searching on the Nexis terminal in our office library, I almost gasped when I saw the answer. Doyle McManus of the *Los Angeles Times* broke the Brunei story on Saturday, December 6. Had McManus called Abrams for comment on the story on December 5, thus tipping him off that the story was about to run? Did Abrams only call Bradley because Abrams knew the story was running in the newspaper the next day?

I ran to examine Abrams's phone logs, which he had turned over to us in response to Stewart's document request. Sure enough, the records showed that McManus called Abrams somewhere around 3:30 P.M. on December 5—the precise time was unclear—and the message was crossed out, indicating that Abrams spoke to McManus on that day.

So did Abrams call Bradley *before* 3:30 P.M., meaning that McManus's scoop came just as a coincidence? Or did Abrams call Bradley *after* 3:30 P.M., indicating that Abrams attempted to cover a lie that he knew was going to be disclosed in the next day's newspaper?

I had three possible sources for learning the timing of the calls: Abrams, McManus, and Bradley. We would save Abrams for last; no investigator relies on the suspect for evidence that others may provide. I moved next to McManus. Questioning reporters raises dicey legal and ethical questions for prosecutors, and I wanted to avoid any false moves. After consulting with my colleagues, we decided that I would call McManus and ask him only about the timing of certain events in which he participated. We would not ask about confidential sources or anything like that—only the time of his call to Abrams on December 5.

McManus greeted me cheerfully on the phone, even after I said I wanted to ask him some questions. Plainly intrigued, McManus said, "Well, maybe we could talk about that, but I think an *exchange* of information might be a better way to do it." Oh, great, I thought. Ever an alert reporter, McManus was trying to recruit me as a source. I said I did not think we could arrange any exchange. In a voice tinged with disappointment, he then admitted that the *Times* policy required him to alert a company lawyer anytime he was contacted by a law enforcement official. I said fine. Not fifteen minutes later, however, an officious attorney from Los Angeles called me to say that the *Times* forbade reporters from giving any informal cooperation to law enforcement. If we wanted to talk to McManus, we would have to subpoena him. Knowing full well that the last thing our office needed was a legal fight with a newspaper, I politely ended the conversation and recognized that Doyle McManus would never be a source.

Next, I wanted to try Bradley, but here again I had to tiptoe around a delicate political situation. Walsh often reminded us that he did not want to pick fights with Congress. He knew that the legislators blanched at revealing much of anything about their internal processes. Still, Walsh agreed to let me contact the Senate legal counsel, and I was able to set up an interview with John Despres, Bradley's aide. When making the appointment, I politely asked Despres if he might bring with him the senator's list of phone messages for December 5, 1986. No problem, he said.

FBI agent Tim Tylicki, my companion through dozens of interviews, joined me in waiting for Despres behind the safelike doors that guard the intelligence committee quarters in the Hart Senate Office Building. Congressional aides often take on qualities of their bosses, and the owlish Despres possessed the same thoughtful demeanor as the former basketball star from New Jersey. Despres was even tall. We chatted for a while, and then I asked to see the phone records. The key message rested on the top of the pile. It read: "To: Senator Bradley. From: Elliott Abrams. Urgent. Please call." The time on the slip, written in the firm hand of Bradley's secretary, read 10:00 A.M., too early to impugn Abrams's motives. I bit my lip and nodded. After making a little more conversation with Despres—I had nothing of substance to ask him—I thanked him and the Senator for their cooperation and went on my way.

STEWART agreed that Abrams's unprompted, if tardy, correction gutted the chances for a case against Abrams for the November 25 statement. I had to concede that, as of the summer of 1987, the evidence against Abrams fell short of that necessary to bring a criminal case on any other statement either.

I didn't enjoy the decision. I knew that some people—not least Elliott Abrams—would construe our failure to indict Abrams as a vindication of him. But I was learning that the power to prosecute should be exercised only when we felt a compelling justification, when we believed that a jury would find proof beyond a reasonable doubt of an individual's guilt. For the rest of my tenure at the OIC, I endured the ribbing of colleagues who would recall my defense of "your friend

Elliott." But they, no less than I, took pride in knowing that exercising restraint in prosecution often takes as much courage as bringing cases.

Some small consolation came from the single page of transcript that I kept in my desk drawer for the remainder of the investigation. It came from December 8, 1986, when Abrams attempted to explain his testimony before the intelligence committee on November 25.

> SENATOR EAGLETON: Were you then in the fundraising business?
>
> MR. ABRAMS: I would say we were in the fundraising business. I take your point.
>
> SENATOR EAGLETON: Take my point? Under oath, my friend, that's perjury. Had you been under oath, that's perjury.
>
> MR. ABRAMS: Well, I don't agree with that.
>
> SENATOR EAGLETON: That's slammer time.
>
> MR. ABRAMS: I don't agree with that, Senator.
>
> SENATOR EAGLETON: Oh, Elliott, you're too damn smart not to know. . . . "We're not in the fundraising business." You *were* in the fundraising business, you and Ollie. You were opening accounts, you had account cards. . . .
>
> MR. ABRAMS: You've heard my testimony.
>
> SENATOR EAGLETON: I've heard it and I want to puke.

CHAPTER FIVE

Democracia sin Ejército

For all that technological innovations like infrared photography and genetic coding have transformed some aspects of law enforcement, the investigation of white-collar crime has changed little in decades. You stare at the documents and you interview the witnesses. And then you do it again.

Computers have helped a little, though the legal profession has, predictably, lagged behind most industries in taking advantage of the new technology. In some ways, Judge Walsh reflected the old order's discomfort with the new. Eyeing me at my usual perch in front of my secretary's word processor—we OIC lawyers did not have our own—he never hid his bafflement that I preferred to compose at the keyboard. But, to his credit, Walsh insisted that our office have access to the latest Justice Department hardware, and, thanks to the efforts of our computer specialist, Patricia Maslinoff, we did.

Maslinoff created a score of different databases to help the investigation. Thanks to a machine that could scan text and place it on the computer—that is, with no typing required—we gained nearly instant access to all of the important material in the case. We could search various transcripts, court hearings, FBI interviews, and even summaries of certain White House and NSC documents for key names, words, or phrases. It was the reluctance of the lawyers, even young ones, to shed their technological inhibitions that most hindered our taking full advantage of Maslinoff's efforts. Fortunately, Geoff Stewart, my partner in the State Department investigation, suffered from no such squeamishness. He loved all gadgets, not just computers. He would, for example, grow almost giddy whipping his pocket photocopier out of his briefcase and making copies of newspapers or phone books, or anything.

Stewart made adept use of the databases in preparing for interviews. Every time he was to meet with someone, he would cull all the references to that person from all the previous FBI "302s," the agents' written summaries of the witnesses' statements. In the late spring of 1987, before his interview of Lewis Tambs, the American ambassador to Costa Rica in 1985 and 1986 and a close friend of North's, Stewart asked the computer to find all previous mentions of Tambs. Among the many entries, Stewart discovered a strange, almost off-hand reference in a document involving a senior administration official—a record Stewart almost certainly would have overlooked if the computer had not flagged it for him. Stewart showed it to me. I, too, had never heard of the project described.

I'll ask Tambs about it, Stewart said.

I N the spring of 1989, during Oliver North's trial, the press discovered the issue of quid pro quos in the Iran-Contra affair. As part of his defense that the entire Reagan administration was arranging aid for the contras in defiance of the Boland amendment, North alleged, in essence, that much of American foreign policy in Central America during the mid-1980s was based on promises of United States support to nations that would, in return, help the anti-Sandinista rebels. The specific arrangements that North identified included a trip by Vice President George Bush to Honduras in 1985 to pressure that country to support the contras. In return for that backing, according to North, Bush promised the Hondurans increased American aid. On the day of North's conviction, *President* Bush's only comment about his own role was that "There was no quid pro quo."

The issue of quid pro quos for the contras percolated around the edges of the Iran-Contra affair since the beginning. The Tower Commission report disclosed that North wrote a memo to McFarlane on March 5, 1985, stating that another Central American country had facilitated several arms shipments to the contras. North recommended to his boss that the United States government increase aid to that country because of this "extraordinary assistance they are providing to the Nicaraguan freedom fighters." Apparently recognizing the impropriety of the quid pro quo he had outlined, North drafted memorandums for McFarlane to send to other top administration officials urging enhanced support for the country. But North studiously avoided mentioning that such aid represented compensation for contra aid. (North also retrieved and rewrote the original of this memo to McFarlane in his frenzy of alterations in November 1986.) In this and other instances, the administration seemed to be attempting to maneuver around the congressional ban on contra aid through a highbrow laundering operation. Instead of assisting the contras directly, Reagan's men simply paid others to provide the assistance.

Walsh's office also recognized the pattern of apparent quid pro quos early in our investigation. The first important question we asked was: "so what?" Was there anything criminal about the conditioning of United States aid on third countries' assistance to the contras? In essence, the Boland amendment prohibited certain government agencies, those "involved in intelligence activities," from spending money on lethal aid to the contras. It did not prohibit the president (or vice president, for that matter) from encouraging third countries to help the contras. Indeed, we had doubts about whether such a restriction on the executive branch would be constitutional. The Supreme Court has traditionally afforded the president wide latitude in conducting foreign policy; personal exhortations by the chief executive or his designees appeared to be at the heart of this power. The Bush approach to Honduras seemed to fall squarely within this constitutionally protected sphere. The specific words of Boland did not forbid this type of behavior. Even if they had, they might have been unenforceable. In addition, the higher the level of the contact, the more difficult we knew it would be to prove a direct quid pro quo. Given the complex web of interests involved in the relationship of the United

States to any other country, we doubted we could prove to a legal certainty that specific aid had been exchanged for specific assistance to the contras.

Still, that analysis did not lead us to end our inquiries—not by a long shot. Quid pro quos had a seaminess irresistible to prosecutors. Unlike some of our more complex theories of Boland amendment violations, we thought a jury might respond well to the tit-for-tat logic of a quid pro quo. The very idea of a quid pro quo suggested a bullying United States administration, one that, unable to persuade the Congress of its views, imposed them on more malleable and vulnerable foreign leaders. If we could prove that an agency that was unequivocally covered by Boland—say, the CIA—made an identifiable expenditure—say, cash—for the specific purpose of encouraging military assistance to the contras—say, the building of an airstrip— that would violate the Boland amendment.

And *that* was what Geoff Stewart appeared to find in the document unearthed by Patty Maslinoff's computer. Following up, we tracked down a series of intelligence cables that seemed to reveal the quid pro quo in stark and revealing terms. Seeing these cables fired my investigative passion more than anything else I had seen in the Iran-Contra investigation so far. The deal smelled. So we set out to ask questions—and perhaps assign responsibility—at the CIA.

A S spring turned to summer of 1987, the players and their roles on Walsh's Central America team were changing. John Keker was spending more time at home in San Francisco. Geoff Stewart was returning to his law firm. Bill Hassler was focusing on Richard Secord.

All of which left Larry Shtasel for investigating the CIA.

Shtasel's passions ranged from international chess competitions to rap music to college basketball (and what he called "the manly art of winning an NCAA basketball pool"). Not spending money was his hobby. Our daily visits to the candy store usually ended with me drumming my fingers while Shtasel compared the cost per ounce of a Milky Way versus a Peppermint Pattie. He was a bachelor with a storm-tossed personal life: a fear-of-commitment poster child. I was a lonely married guy commuting to see my wife. With an adjacent office in a remote corner of the seventh floor—ideal for hiding from unpleasant tasks or people—Shtasel became my closest friend on the Walsh team.

Shtasel was in charge of our liaison with the CIA—making document requests, scheduling interviews, and generally navigating our office through the Langley bureaucracy. He was required to deal with the CIA's Office of General Counsel, an operation that treated our office more or less like a field station of the KGB. Our troubles with the CIA lawyers ranged from the serious—like lost or delayed document production—to the petty. Among the latter was the one lawyer, who, intent on playing spy, refused to use his last name over the telephone, though his identity was no secret to anyone. Taking him at his word, we began referring to him exclusively as "Undercover Bob," even to his face. The ridicule eventually forced him to relent.

Shtasel and I shared the investigation of the quid pro quo project that Stewart had unearthed. In this effort, we were usually accompanied by FBI special agent Tim Tylicki. A rangy Ohio native with only a horseshoe of red hair remaining, Tylicki's characteristic expression was expressionless. His principal joy in his job seemed to be checking the codes on the diplomatic license plates to see what country's officials were double-parking. (He also liked telling the story of how the Soviets' code used to be "DFC"—until the Russians protested when they heard the joke that the letters stood for "Dumb Fucking Commies.") Besides the license plates, Tylicki gave his views on college basketball and nothing else, which at least gave him and Shtasel one subject to discuss. Tylicki's demeanor was so placid, his countenance so impassive, that I was certain if a witness ever told us that a meeting had gone normally except that Oliver North had danced naked with a ukelele, Tylicki's only comment to me afterwards would have been to seek advice on spelling ukelele.

The "smoking gun" cables about the quid pro quo revealed that the project had been suggested in a cable to CIA headquarters by Joe Fernandez, the station chief in San José, Costa Rica. It appeared to be a fairly explicit exchange—the CIA provides the money, and Costa Rica provides the airstrip. The project was described this way in a public stipulation of facts disclosed at North's trial:*

---

* For a discussion of how the stipulation came into being, see Chapter Fifteen.

> In August 1985, Costa Rican President Monge indicated to U.S. officials that he would be willing to provide assistance to the Resistance if the United States government would help fund a certain operation in Costa Rica. The U.S. officials concluded that the operation could be funded if President Monge would take certain specified actions to assist the Resistance.

As the project worked its way through CIA headquarters, a curious transformation occurred. Fernandez was told that the CIA could not endorse or facilitate the airstrip for the contras—but the agency continued to back the "certain operation." Headquarters seemed to be saying one thing and doing another—covering its assets. It was giving the quid pro quo, but not acknowledging it. So Shtasel and I began to interview the CIA personnel involved.

The CIA enjoys a more glamorous reputation than it deserves. If covert operatives strive for a beige sameness of demeanor, the ones I met succeeded—in spades. Only a fellow I'll call "the Smoker" gave a hint of eccentricity. During his interview, the Smoker casually slipped off his loafer and tapped the ashes from his cigarette into his shoe. He then stubbed out the butt inside the heel. When the interview ended, the Smoker slipped the shoe back on and went on his way.

We would usually try to begin our CIA interviews by asking for background information, not because we cared about the answers but in the hope that a little small talk could lighten an atmosphere freighted with contempt and suspicion. But most CIA types failed to observe even these feigned courtesies. I did learn from these background discussions that the days of the Ivy League as a feeding ground for the agency seem to have passed, the change apparently a result of Vietnam, the agency's sullied reputation after the Church Committee disclosures of the 1970s, and, most likely, the diminishing lure of government salaries. Most employees seemed to come from the military. I did come across one Yale man and told him of my surprise at seeing so few Old Blues among his younger comrades. With a small smile he said, "Those were the old days."

Most prosecutors know—as do surprisingly few criminal suspects—that memory loss, real or concocted, can derail virtually any investigation. As Nixon (who knew) said on the White House tapes,

"Just be damned sure you say 'I don't remember; I can't recall.'"

Our friends at the agency knew. With a few courageous exceptions, most of our CIA witnesses suffered stunning memory lapses in our presence. Interviews perking along on stories of life before agency employment ground to absolute halts once substantive questioning began. When these lulls invariably occurred, we deployed an investigator's only hope in such situations: confronting a witness with documents, in the expectation that the paper trail would jog a suppressed recollection.

But paper—like cables between CIA headquarters and its various outposts—produced little more. Indeed, after we presented the cables to the witnesses, the interviews often degenerated into scenes of almost comic passive/aggressive behavior on both sides.

We would show a witness a cable. Eyes narrowed, he would scan it quickly.

"Are you familiar with that document?" we would ask.

"No, I don't think so."

Shtasel's and my reactions would usually vary at this point, as we would fall unconsciously into a Mutt (Larry) and Jeff routine. I would smile, sympathize, and ask whether it was possible to look again and see if any memory at all was triggered. Shtasel, in contrast, would cross and uncross his legs, adjust and readjust his glasses, look skyward and then at the witness and say, "Come on. Just answer the question" or words to that effect.

Neither approach worked, and we would succeed only in prompting what we came to call "The Speech" because we heard it so many times. "You know," it began, "during this period we were working twelve hour days, usually six days a week, and we had to read about two hundred cables a day." At this point, some witnesses would hold their palms about six inches above the table top; others would spread their thumb and forefinger about the same distance and say, "About this many. We can't remember them all."

Nodding at the speech, we would plug on and return to the document before the witness. "Take a look at the bottom of this cable," we would say. "Who does it show wrote it?"

Brief study. "I did."

"And you still have no memory of it?"

Longer pause. Rubbing of eyes. Chin in hand, they would study the document in exaggerated bewilderment, like a desert nomad reading directions for how to build an igloo.

"Nope."

And so it would go until we yielded either to frustration or to boredom.

Though our interviews produced little, our inquiries did establish that the project we were examining typified the real work of the CIA. From Capitol Hill to the movies, attention to the CIA focuses disproportionately on its paramilitary operations, with its poison cigars and private armies well-suited to the needs of screenwriters. But agency jargon characterizes the CIA's paramilitary wing as the "knuckle-dragging world," and the simian analogy reveals a widely held discomfort within the agency with the unsubtle art of secret war. The agency has an ingrained suspicion for the kind of operations that have produced ugly (and public) consequences.

In truth, the CIA relies less on bullets in its covert operations than on a far more effective tool: money. So far as I knew, no one has ever made a sober, public examination of these kinds of CIA expenditures, and my naive mind boggled at the agency's crude calculus in the purchase of influence. Proving the efficacy of capitalism (or perhaps just greed) in achieving results, the recipients of CIA largesse appeared to fall smartly in step with their paymaster's wishes. The more subtle—and ultimately more pernicious—consequences of these payments devolved from how they transformed the benefactor. Those who wrote the checks came to view the recipients as vassals. Preying on the weakness of individuals, our government came to view entire countries as answering to our commands. Foreigners would be damned as "unpredictable," as if they had some obligation to provide us with advance notice of their intentions. I wondered how the American people would react if an ally of ours treated our leaders that way. As I began to understand this quid pro quo project, I felt a keener outrage than I did about any other part of the Iran-Contra affair—more than the lying, the shredding or even the diversion. I recognized in myself a sentiment that I rarely heard another soul in Washington express: I was shocked.

Stymied by the CIA in our effort to learn more about the apparent quid pro quo, we turned to the only other place we could go—Costa Rica.

WHEN we finally received clearance in late July 1987 from our State Department to conduct interviews in Costa Rica, I was subjected to some good-natured ribbing about my impending journey. Good luck, my colleagues said, in venturing into the Central American battlefield. Would I take a helmet? they wondered. I had my own qualms; I had but one life to give for my country but no plans to supply it just then. Fortunately, the worry stemmed more from gringo ignorance than any real danger. Sandwiched between tyrannies of the Left and the Right on the Central American isthmus, south of Nicaragua and north of Panama, Costa Rica was nothing less than a small slice of paradise—a flourishing democracy with an overwhelmingly literate and relatively prosperous population. I was, without question, safer in San José than in the District of Columbia.

In 1948, following an unsuccessful military coup, Costa Rica made a simple but breathtaking decision: they abolished their army. In a region of the world where the military has drained whole societies of their resources and cost hundreds of thousands their lives, Costa Rica escaped. In return for sacrificing its army, Costa Rica achieved the highest standard of living in Central America and forty years of peace. The national slogan announces the secret of the country's success: *democracia sin ejército*. Democracy without an army. That the Costa Rican experiment has worked can be proved in many ways. The raincoated money changers who loiter outside the Banco de Costa Rica brought the message home for me. For all their surreptitious muttering, these fellows give you a paltry few *colones* more for your dollar than does your hotel—eloquent testimony to the stability of this tiny nation.

We had many reasons to take our investigation to Costa Rica. In addition to questions about the quid pro quo project, we wanted to know more about the airstrip that Secord's people had built near the Nicaraguan border. Who had purchased the land and how? We wanted to know about a September 1986 press conference by the minister of public security about the airstrip. According to one of

North's PROF notes to Poindexter, North had scotched this parley with a phone call to President Oscar Arias. What had really happened? Finally, what about this airstrip? What did it look like? Did it represent a serious military asset in the contras' war, or was the attention paid to it much ado about nothing?

Walsh directed that we proceed gingerly in seeking cooperation from any foreign government. Ever sensitive to the charge that the Office of Independent Counsel was meddling in United States foreign policy, we made all our requests for contacts abroad through the State Department. Given our inherently adversarial position with the administration, we did not expect any foreign government to rush to cooperate with us. The State Department, after all, would remain open for business long after Walsh returned to Oklahoma. Thus, somewhat to our surprise, I received a call from a lawyer in the State Department's Office of Legal Counsel in the first week in August to report that Costa Rica's foreign minister would be pleased to meet with us in San José on August 12, 1987. (Minutes after I took that call, a different State Department lawyer called someone else in our office to ask that I not go alone to Costa Rica. Dealing with someone my age, he said, would offend the Costa Ricans. My colleague assured the lawyer that I would be accompanied by an adult.)

JOHN KEKER and I met at the Miami airport on the afternoon of August 11. I showed Keker some notes I brought with me about the people and issues we might confront in Costa Rica. When our conference was over, I followed the instructions of our security staff by tearing the notes into little pieces and distributing the shards among several wastebaskets at the airport. I felt more silly than stealthy.

We were met at San José's Juan Santamaria Airport by an earnest young foreign service officer in the embassy's political section. Given the openness of the Costa Rican government, we had no need to use any subterfuges to conduct our inquiries. That was not the case a few months later when our colleague Bill Lee made a trip to another country in the region. Making arrangements on the telephone with a contra leader, Lee was told to see "the man with the mustache at the Budget Rent-a-Car." Amused at the low-rent cloak-and-dagger,

Lee wondered why the phone seemed to go dead at this point. "Hello? Hello?" Lee said. The fellow came back on and explained, "We were just checking to see if he still has a mustache."

Our young political officer immediately launched into a well-rehearsed spiel—equal parts local color and political briefing. An embassy car—a huge Chevy van that had double-thickness glass and steel-reinforced doors to foil terrorists—whisked us toward downtown. The car seemed almost designed to call attention to itself. Sure enough, our driver told us, "Everybody in San José knows these are embassy cars."

We arrived at the Gran Hotel Costa Rica—at six stories the tallest building in Central America when it was built in 1930—and the streets of downtown still bustled as Keker and I set out to explore just after 11 P.M. Besides the National Theater, a very miniature version of the Paris Opera, San José offers few postcard-pretty locales for the sightseer. It does, however, possess the greatest bar in the world, a wonderfully sinister place called the Key Largo. Just off a busy intersection near our hotel, the bar, located in an old stucco home, sits in an unlikely nest of tropical plants. Auto exhaust has wilted most of the equatorial foliage that should be the city's birthright, but the Key Largo maintains a profusion of these mysterious fronds, all of them, in Raymond Chandler's words, with "nasty meaty leaves and stalks like the newly washed fingers of dead men." Inside, big-game fishing trophies and Bogart memorabilia compete with American music videos for the attention of the curious clientele—quiet Americans, boisterous locals, and, rumor has it, the more-than-occasional prostitute. Up an elaborately carved staircase Japanese tourists lose silently at blackjack to the screeching accompaniment of the pet toucan.

As Keker and I sampled the local beers (wretched, despite my fond hopes), I grew to know him better. Born and raised in suburban Washington, Keker's life had fluctuated between the expected and the unconventional. He had pursued an Ivy League education and married his high school sweetheart. But he had also nurtured and sustained a set of sixties ideals that led him to work first in an environmental public interest law firm and then, for many years, as a public defender in San Francisco. When he decided finally to enter private law practice, he did not exactly join the local establishment. Rather, he started his own firm with a single partner—who promptly took a year off to play professional poker.

Keker neither flaunted the combat experience that cost him part of his left arm, nor refused to discuss it. Yet in his own way, he seemed as powerfully affected by Vietnam as Ollie North was. Keker spoke little about his politics, but the war clearly did not instill in him, as it did in North, a passion for the contra war. Instead, it seemed to have affected Keker more personally than politically. At a minimum Keker shared with North a restless engagement with life, an intensity that I have encountered in few other people. Keker ate, read, listened, and laughed with a ferocious, vital appetite. And when we took occasional runs along the Potomac, he would stop—literally—to smell the flowers.

After a series of meetings at the United States embassy the next morning, Keker and I arrived at the nation's small foreign ministry in the afternoon. Kept waiting the obligatory Central American forty-five minutes, we had time to study the pictures lining the protocol office—which portrayed not only Don Quixoté, King Juan Carlos of Spain, and a hero of the Costa Rican Civil War, but also Abraham Lincoln and John F. Kennedy. Summoned to meet the foreign minister, we entered a modest but ferociously air-conditioned chamber which also featured a Lincoln portrait.

Rodrigo Madrigal Nieto greeted us with a warm handshake and an invitation to his brocaded couch. Madrigal demonstrated how, in a small country, a single individual could cut a swath through virtually all of the nation's public life. A prominent attorney, he had also edited San José's leading newspaper, *La Nacion,* for a time. After serving as a cabinet official in earlier administrations, he had risen to foreign minister under President Arias and helped design the peace initiatives that would earn his patron the Nobel Peace Prize. Around sixty years old, with a full head of white hair and a cultivated, almost aristocratic air, he exuded grace and confidence.

"Mr. Keker," he announced in gently accented English as we sat down. Then he paused and stared. "That is the most extraordinary tie." With its multihued squiggles and dots, it was actually fairly modest by Keker's standards.

"Thank you, sir," Keker said, beaming. I stifled a laugh.

Madrigal resumed. "So how can we assist you?"

Keker then described our interest in seeking interviews with various present and former Costa Rican officials. He said the Office of the Independent Counsel was, of course, only investigating Americans and sought no disruption in relations between the United States and Costa Rica.

Madrigal did not hesitate in his reply. "We are a free country," he said. "You can speak with anyone you like. We have nothing to hide."

Somewhat taken aback by the speed of Madrigal's acquiescence, Keker then identified the specific government individuals with whom we wanted to speak: Benjamin Piza, the former minister of public security; his successor Hernan Garron, who held the news conference about the airstrip; Rodrigo Arias, the brother of the president and his chief aide; and—here Keker took a deep breath—Luis Alberto Monge, the former president whom Arias succeeded in May 1986.

Madrigal again expressed no qualms. "That sounds reasonable," he said. He then walked to his desk and began calling the four men whom we had named. He reached two of them and left elaborate messages for the others—I savored his mellifluous Spanish though I understood little—and returned to ask if he could provide any more assistance.

Keker could think of nothing else. We had expected to receive a polite runaround and return home for the beginning of a lengthy process of diplomatic hand-wringing. All Keker could do was congratulate Madrigal on the peace accord which he and President Arias had sponsored just days before in Guatemala City.

Now it was Madrigal's turn to beam. "Yes," he said, "we are very proud of that." He continued: "We believe it is time for Central Americans to solve their own problems. There has been too much suffering here for too long. We are very small countries, but we have to determine our own destiny—we must." Then he added, lapsing into Spanish: "*Centroamerica por los centroamericanos.*" Central America for Central Americans. "That is what we believe."

With our thanks and admiration, he ushered us to the door.

Recognizing that our stay in Costa Rica would last longer than we had anticipated, Keker and I scrambled to prepare. First, we called Washington and arranged for an OIC paralegal, José Arroyo, to join us as a translator. Then we began reviewing our questions for the people we were going to be interviewing. No sooner did we begin our preparations than Keker received a call saying that Rodrigo Arias would see us right away. At the time I had stepped out for a moment, so Keker visited President Arias's *hermano* alone. His report of the conversation was brief if predictable. In his PROF note to Poindexter on September 6, 1986, North said that he had made "threats/promises" to President Arias based on whether he would cancel the press conference disclosing the airstrip. Rodrigo Arias told Keker not only had the conversation with North never taken place, but no one had made any "threats" to President Arias because of the airstrip.

Keker and I then met at the Ministry of Public Security to speak with its incumbent head, Hernan Garron. As minister, Garron ran Costa Rica's version of a defense establishment—the "civil guard" and "rural guard," the two national civil defense organizations that function similarly to our state police forces. In contrast to the debonair Madrigal, Garron exuded the weary smarts of an old political pro. He had, we were not surprised to learn, spent several years running the San José sewer system. He began our conversation by expressing his amazement at the recently completed Iran-Contra hearings, which, thanks to the Cable News Network, were widely followed in Central America. "The U.S. government," he said, bemused, "is the only one in the world that makes love and war on television."

As for the airstrip, he said that when he took over as minister in May 1986, his predecessor, Piza, told him that the project was being built by a company called Udall Research as a tourism project. Garron knew nothing about any contra involvement. He said that in September of that year he had heard rumors that the strip was being used either by drug traffickers or the contras. At that point he sent the civil guard to place barriers on the strip so that no one could use it. He said that American reporters had heard the rumors about the strip and asked him to answer questions about them. He answered those queries in late September 1986. At that point he said—as he was saying now—he simply wanted the airstrip closed, whatever purposes it may have served in the past. He knew of no pressure on himself or Arias to forestall closing the airstrip or holding the press conference.

Keker asked whether, after all the discussion about the famous airstrip, we could arrange to see it. Garron said there were no roads in the vicinity. Now that the civil guard had blocked the runway with cement barrels, it was only accessible by helicopter. Fine, Keker said, we would arrange to rent one. Garron would have none of it. "We will show it to you," he said, and then rushed off to arrange the details—surprising us once more with Costa Rican openness and generosity.

Garron wore an embarrassed smile when he returned to the room. "I'm sorry," he said, "but we have only three helicopters and they are all being repaired right now." *Democracia sin ejército,* I thought to myself—and they mean *no ejercito.* "But," he added, summoning his pride, "we will fly you around the area to examine it. We will pick you up at your hotel at 7:30 tomorrow morning and take you to the airport."

JOSE ARROYO, our bilingual paralegal, finally arrived in San José late on the night before our journey to the airstrip. His flight to Miami was forced to return to Washington when a flight attendant had a heart attack, and then the aptly named (and now deceased) Challenge Airways canceled his first flight to Costa Rica and lost his luggage on the second. Wearing the same clothes he had put on a day earlier in Washington, he joined Keker and me waiting for our ride to the airport.

At a small side terminal at Juan Santamaria Airport, we were greeted by our young pilot, who directed us toward a four-seat, single-engine propeller plane. Never having ridden in so small an aircraft—and no great partisan of air travel generally—I climbed aboard gingerly.

As we neared the top of the airport's single runway, our pilot began pumping angrily at the foot pedals beneath him. "*Los frenos,*" he muttered. The brakes. In the backseat, I fidgeted while Arroyo stared nervously at the seatback in front of him. Next to the pilot, Keker looked serene. After a little more banging on the pedals, the pilot wrenched open his door, jumped out, and began fiddling with the engine. Still unsatisfied, he radioed to the hangar for a repair van.

During the wait, we wandered around the grass strip by the runway and admired the quiescent volcanos that surround San José on three sides. On this day early in the rainy season, the brilliantly clear sky was beginning to yield to the clouds that, now brushing the top of the mountains, would by afternoon moisten the whole region with a mild shower.

The repair crew finished its work and we all climbed back in for takeoff. Now, however, the motor would not start at all. *"La bateria."* The battery, this time. My knuckles the proverbial white, I decided that this clunker of a plane had trouble written all over it. Summoning the vestiges of my single year of Spanish, I offered, *"Tal vez un otro avion?"* Maybe another plane? Muttering what I took to be profanities, our captain agreed.

Having left our lemon of a Cessna to join the ailing helicopters in the shop, we found a replacement that vaulted into the sky without a hitch. Heading due north toward Nicaragua, we studied the gentle Costa Rican countryside—small farms, rolling hills, and red-roofed houses. We took special note of the occasional dirt landing strips we saw along the way. These bumpy paths, used mostly by crop dusters, looked to be no more than several hundred feet in length. We wanted to compare these inconsequential runways with "the airstrip."

As we reached 12,000 feet, the pilot pointed out the only city of consequence on our route, Liberia, which sat in a small valley on our left. He then began steering the plane both down and west—toward the Pacific coast. Our descent revealed that we were approaching the most remote part of Costa Rica, where a dense, lush forest carpeted the ground as far as we could see. A Costa Rican acquaintance had told us the day before that he had seen jaguars in this region. Off in the distance, about ten miles away, the pilot gestured toward land that looked no different from that beneath us. *"Es Nicaragua,"* he said.

The plane dipped left, and soon the Pacific came into view. When we reached about 1,000 feet, the *capitan* pointed in front of him. He did not have to say anything. There, unmistakably, was the airstrip.

It was both less and more than we expected. The ground had clearly been leveled for use by airplanes, but the runway was unpaved and now largely overgrown with grass. No one would ever mistake it for O'Hare. But the length of the runway stunned us. It was enormous, far longer than any of the other dirt strips we had seen on our journey north. At 6,520 feet, we would later learn, it was the second longest runway in all Costa Rica, second only to that at Juan Santamaria, where the jumbo jets land.

Our overwhelming impression, though, was that Secord's team had selected a terrible place to build an airstrip—of any size. The winds kicked up near the coast, and the strip nestled among rugged mounds on three sides. Takeoffs and landings could thus use the strip in only one direction—over the ocean. Worse than the dangerous hillsides was the still-active riverbed that snaked along the full length of the strip. When the river overflowed, which happened frequently in a region near rain forests, the runway would be rendered unusable. Indeed, North once wrote a panicked PROF note to Poindexter informing him that a plane "got stuck in the mud." Locating the airstrip on such unsuitable ground typified the bumbling incompetence of Secord's operation. (So did his efforts to finance it. When Secord tried to wire the money for constructing the airstrip, he sent it first to the *nation* of Liberia in Africa instead of the Costa Rican *city* of that name.)

The pilot took the plane down to about 500 feet so that I could get a better shot with my camera. Hardly a photo buff, I decided at the last moment to bring my own primitive camera to Costa Rica for just this opportunity. Lacking confidence in my abilities, however, I had planned for the disasters that have dogged my photographic career. I budgeted my pictures so that I could snap my twenty-fourth shot over the airstrip, reload, and then take a few more before we headed for home. My theory was that I was less likely to mangle two rolls of film than one.

When our pilot began our first circumnavigation of the strip, I snapped number twenty-four but did not sense the tug that usually signals the end of a roll of film. I snapped number twenty-five, twenty-six, and twenty-seven. Panic gathered in my chest: there was no film in the camera. I cursed myself and struggled to find my other roll of film. I had half-assumed that any roll that I loaded in a tiny airplane would turn out disastrously. My money had been on that first roll. Now I had to trust the second.

As I diddled with my camera and the plane banked into its second go-around, Arroyo began displaying signs of motion sickness. Our pilot stretched back to open the window near him; in the tumult, I thought it would never have occurred to me to open a window on an airplane. Seeing that the window alone would not address Arroyo's increasingly green condition, the pilot began rummaging in the seats behind him for an air-sickness bag. The effort caused him to take his hand off the steering wheel and the plane—barely 500 feet in the air—lurched toward the ground. Keker found all of this— my bumbling photography, José's rumbling stomach, the plane's . . . tumbling—a laugh riot.

In a brief moment, a modicum of serenity did return. Our *capitan* located a bag, which Arroyo put to productive use several times over the remainder of the trip. I reloaded, or, that is, loaded film into my camera and persuaded our captain to make a few more circles of the strip, so I could have a chance of having something to show for our journey. I did; the pictures turned out fine. Arroyo also survived the journey without any lasting damage, though given his experiences of the past forty-eight hours, he vowed to foreswear air travel for as long as he could. We righted ourselves to enjoy a superlative flight back to San José, skimming the treetops above Costa Rica's incomparable Pacific beaches.

The pilot, tranquil throughout, flipped on the radio for our return flight, and we enjoyed an improbable concert of slightly outdated American pop tunes. We didn't even have to pay extra for headphones.

O U R other interviews in Costa Rica expanded our picture of the birth of the airstrip, but Keker and I failed to nail down the details of the quid pro quo. Our meeting with Ben Piza turned into a frosty encounter. Speaking with Piza, we immediately sensed the tension between Monge's old guard, which had been largely pro-contra, and Arias's new approach, which hewed closer to a line of strict neutrality.

The head of a major liquor distributorship in Costa Rica, Piza met our inquiries about the airstrip warily.

We met with former President Monge in his lavish home in San José, settling in a large office where every inch of the walls was covered by plaques or medallions from his distinguished, but fading, public career. Since late in his term and even in this, his fifteenth month out of office, health and family problems dogged the once-vigorous man. He had supported Arias for president—they belonged to the same party, and Costa Rican presidents may only serve one term—but relations between the two men developed a chill. Monge looked spent.

Monge was of an age when questions prompted stories and speeches rather than answers, and Keker had no intention of treating him with less than the respect due a former head of state. Still, Keker's queries moved delicately into specific actions regarding the contras during Monge's term. At length Monge's voice developed a quaver, and sweat poured from his forehead.

Finally, Keker asked about the quid pro quo. "*Nunca, nunca, nunca*" was Monge's reply. Never, never, never. At that point Keker yielded. He knew that the facts were otherwise, but knew that any more questions would tax our welcome.

And that, in the end, is where our investigation of the Costa Rican quid pro quo concluded. The evidence fell short of that required to convince a jury that a violation of the Boland amendment took place. Because of the curious manner in which the project was handled at Langley, we could not even establish with certainty whom at the CIA we would try to hold responsible. The failure rankled me. For me, this investigation illustrated journalist Michael Kinsley's law of scandal, which holds that the scandal isn't what's illegal; the scandal is what's legal. "There will always be scofflaws," wrote Kinsley in *The New Republic*, "it's the behavior society chooses *not* to punish that tells you about the prevailing ethical standards."

My clearest lesson in the prevailing ethical standards of the CIA came in a chance encounter with an agency officer several months after my trip to Costa Rica. To say that this officer and I were friends would embellish our relationship, but I thought he had been straight with me, and I enjoyed his company.

I decided to ask him what he thought about the project I had been investigating. I made it clear that I wanted his views as a person— just his gut feelings.

His reply took no more than an instant. "Huh," he said, "you ought to see what the Soviets do." That, I recognized, was that. Any follow-up question would be pointless.

My query reminded him of something that he wanted to ask me. "You were in Costa Rica recently, weren't you?"

Keker and I had not hidden our presence from anyone at the embassy in San José, but I was still somewhat surprised that this fellow knew we were there.

"Yes, I was," I said.

"Did anyone there, you know, from the embassy," he continued, "show you around?"

"Yeah," I said, struggling to remember the name of the fellow who had picked us up at the airport and chatted with us in the hallways of the embassy. At last it came to me. I said the name and his job. My companion nodded without comment.

I thought for a moment, then said, "At least he *said* that was his job."

This evoked a smile.

I was learning.

CHAPTER SIX

The Meeting Men

When Bob Shwartz, head of the flow of funds team, went to Paris to interview the Iranian financier and con artist Manucher Ghorbanifar, the prosecutor wasn't supposed to talk about the case on an unsecured telephone line. So his team invented a code and, in an inside joke, gave Shwartz the name "The Meeting Man."

Shwartz hated meetings. He had plenty of opportunities, too, because the OIC staff often spent entire days in rambling, inconclusive conclaves. No toady, Shwartz told Walsh he regarded the meetings as colossal wastes of time. The boss waved off the complaint. Once Shwartz tried to make a morning staff session a little more bearable by bringing doughnuts for everyone. When Walsh walked in and saw the box, he growled, "Get rid of those."

Slow-talking, relentless, Shwartz went his own way. Sometimes it was hard to tell whether his deadpan was merely a strategy or his true face—as when he met with Ghorbanifar, who was about as different from Shwartz as a person can be. (Cliff Sloan, who was there, said he almost laughed out loud because Ghorbanifar so much reminded him of the actor Danny DeVito.) Ghorbanifar irritated Shwartz by showing up late for each day's session and announcing once that he had to leave early. Shwartz asked why. Ghorbanifar said casually that he had a meeting that night "with some Libyan terrorists in Vienna." As only Shwartz would, he blandly asked Ghorbanifar the next morning, "How was your meeting in Vienna?" Ghorbanifar shook his head and muttered through his thick accent, "Oh, dey are berry bad terrorists."

Shwartz believed in one thing: following the money. As he put it in his antiseptic way, "The case against North needs the personal-enrichment angle." Shwartz thought Ollie North was a thief, and we could prove it eventually.

In mid-1985 North began steering Secord and Hakim to the lucrative business of selling arms to the contras. Then North began cutting them in on the even more remunerative trade of American and Israeli weapons to Iran. Secord and Hakim, according to Shwartz, came to see North as their meal ticket, and they were not above priming their pump with a little *baksheesh*—bribery—and North was not above taking it. This theory became known around the OIC as "the golden goose."

To find out whether North had made any extra money, Shwartz looked at whether the colonel's income roughly coincided with his outlays or whether he had been spending unaccounted-for money. Though this probe was an eminently proper law enforcement technique, it also represented a massive invasion of North's privacy.

I was not the only one squirming when I saw us looking into North's private life in such detail. I developed a similar feeling when a witness once told me that the glare of attention so upset one of North's daughters that she had nervously rubbed all the skin off the back of her hand.

But Shwartz's investigation did pay off. Contra leader Adolfo Calero told us that he gave North about $90,000 in traveler's checks. We found that North himself cashed a good number of them—and at places far removed from the contra war, like hosiery emporiums, tire stores, and supermarkets near his Virginia home. The colonel only spent about $4,000 on himself, but it was the first money we could place directly in North's pocket.

Shwartz also pushed hard on a project that had both the promise of a greater payoff and the potential for disaster. In examining the records of Secord's and Hakim's American company, Stanford Technology, Shwartz's team noticed a number of payments to someone named Glenn Robinette. They called him in for an interview. A diminutive, white-haired fellow in his sixties, Robinette had worked in some vague capacity at the CIA for many years before he retired in 1971 to do security consulting. Robinette told Bruce Yannett of Shwartz's team a convoluted story of working occasionally for Secord as a private investigator and building some security features into Oliver North's home. Specifically, a fence.

It later became a ritual of sorts among OIC lawyers to make the almost hour-long drive to Great Falls, Virginia, and take a look at the now-celebrated fence. Our FBI agents, who were the only real Washingtonians among us in our early days, all but licked their chops when they first saw North's address. Great Falls includes some of the choicest real estate in the region, and the agents wondered how a mere colonel could afford to live in horsey splendor. We soon saw how. The modest home squatted on a dusty, treeless plot in Great Falls's only unfashionable neighborhood. As for the fence, it was really an electronic gate with an intercom to the house and a video camera to monitor comings and goings.

We worried about accusing North of any impropriety in connection with the fence because we knew that the colonel had a good reason for wanting some kind of personal protection. North had received a public and very real death threat from a very real terrorist named Abu Nidal in mid-1986. We did not want to trivialize North's concern for the safety of his family. Still, we wanted to know how this fence—or, as we preferred to call it, "the security system"—came into being.

From the beginning Bruce Yannett was suspicious of Robinette's story about the fence, so he decided to subpoena Robinette to testify before the grand jury. Like me, Yannett was a younger member of the staff, and the examination of Robinette would be his first ever in a grand jury. He prepared carefully.

Robinette had given Yannett two bills that he said were for North's security system. One was dated July 2, 1986, for $8,000 and the other, dated September 22, was a dunning notice for the same amount. Robinette also produced two letters from North about the purchase of the security system. In the first, dated May 18, 1986, North suggested that Robinette forgive the bill and instead make the North home "available for commercial endorsement of your firm and the equipment without fee." The second North letter, dated October 1, 1986, seemed to respond to the dunning notice. "Dear Glenn," North wrote:

> Please forgive me for not getting back to you sooner. I've been out of town and we seem to keep missing each other on phone calls. The reason for my first call was to inquire about your note of September 22 [the dunning notice]. We are a bit confused and surely don't want there to be any misunderstanding in that we are very pleased with the security arrangements at the house. I'm also grateful for your looking in on Betsy and the girls now that Stuart is off at school and my hectic pace does not seem to have slowed a bit. Back to the point . . . it was our understanding that we were going to go ahead with the . . . commercial endorsement of your company and the equipment when I retire from the Marine Corps in 1988. If that is not your understanding, we need to get together and talk. . . . We just don't have $8,000 without borrowing it. . . . I don't want you to be caught short, but I don't want to have to resort to holding up gas stations on my way home from work at night either.

"Warm regards," it was signed in North's inimitable left-handed scrawl, "Oliver L. North."

North's second letter had obviously been typed on the same typewriter as the first, except that in the interim, the *e* on the machine had been damaged. That explained North's handwritten postscript. "Please forgive the type," North wrote, "I literally dropped the ball."

Yannett knew from Secord's records that *Secord* had paid Robinette for the security system. What could these letters and bills mean?

When Yannett first took Robinette through the story in front of the grand jury, the former CIA agent stood by his paper trail. He, Robinette, had paid for the system, not Secord. The bills and North's letters were all legitimate, contemporaneous recordings of what really took place.

Moments after Robinette left the grand jury, his lawyer approached Yannett in the hallway.

"How'd it go?" the lawyer said, probably just a way to make conversation. With cheeks set at right angles to his chin and a fastidious near crew cut, Yannett looked like a film noir detective. Now, it turned out, he talked like one, too.

"Fine," he told the lawyer, "except that your client bought himself a perjury rap."

Yannett's tough words had the desired effect. Robinette promptly recanted most of his testimony. In a second appearance before the grand jury, he admitted that Secord had paid for the system. Most importantly for our purposes, Robinette testified that the paperwork about the fence—all of it—was phony. Both Robinette's bills and North's letters were created in December 1986, after North was fired from the NSC.

Shwartz regarded this as devastating evidence against North—worth the risk of raising the issue of the threat on his life. His chatty letters ("we seem to keep missing each other") and everything in them (from the plans for the "commercial endorsement" to the bizarre reference to "holding up gas stations") had been invented by the colonel in order to cover up the fact that the fence had been a gift to him. Even better, the FBI crime lab found that the *e* on the typewriter used in North's second letter had been intentionally defaced. He had not "dropped the ball;" he had tried to make the letters look like they had been typed on two different occasions. At the time I remember forming a vivid picture in my mind of Ollie North intently chiseling away at some poor typing ball in order to embellish a cockamamie story about his fence. Criminal, hell—this guy was a *nut*.

But the story of the fence, evocative as it was, and even the traveler's checks did not leave Shwartz fully confident that we could convince a jury that North was a thief. For that he wanted something more.

"Wait till we get the Swiss records," Shwartz promised. "That will be what we need."

THE letter, dated October 8, 1987, dropped into my in-box like hundreds of others. It came from Abraham Sofaer, the State Department legal advisor, to Judge Walsh. Sofaer wrote Walsh of "a matter of great concern to me as well as to the department"—an incident when "a member of your staff admittedly reviewed certain papers which were extremely sensitive, but which had nothing what-soever to do with the Iran-Contra affair. Distribution of these ma-terials was limited to the president, the secretary [of state] and no more than six other senior officials in the department directly involved in the matter."

"[Y]our staff member," Sofaer went on, "violated applicable se-curity laws and regulations"—and he was "advising the CIA and the Bureau of Diplomatic Security of the compromise of this document." The staff member was me.

The "papers" in question were at ARA—the State Department's Bureau of Inter-American Affairs, run by Elliott Abrams. The State Department had told us that many of the documents covered by Geoff Stewart's original request were still in the "working files" of ARA, so we agreed not to demand that all of them be photocopied. Instead, two retired foreign service officers (FSOs)—honest brokers in the process—would examine the files and mark with yellow Post-its any documents that seemed remotely relevant to the Iran-Contra affair. With the foreign service officers' designations as a starting point, representatives of the OIC would examine the documents in their file cabinets at ARA and mark those we wanted copied and turned over to us.

It fell to me to do it. During my several days in the late summer of 1987 rooting around on the sixth floor of Foggy Bottom, I was not hailed as a distinguished visitor. Everyone at ARA knew who I was and for whom I worked, and the locals tolerated me like a late-paying boarder. To my surprise, my dealings with the political appointees in the department were far more pleasant than my en-counters with the career FSOs. The political types, I realized, rec-ognized the stakes of the Iran-Contra affair ran highest for them; they had the most to lose. Thus, Abrams's special assistant Dan Wattenberg was the soul of cooperation when I needed to know things like the location of the bathroom. In contrast, the foreign service officers, justly confident that they would outlast both Elliott Abrams and me in the bureaucracy, treated me with surly contempt. As one junior FSO said when he met an acquaintance of mine who asked him whether he knew me, "Yeah, I know him." Then he shook his head and said:

"Prick, prick, prick."

In late September, I had received a call from George Taft about the review process. "Wondered whether you had time for a question?" Taft had said. If the official conversational tic of the CIA involved the omission of the definite article when referring to the agency, State Department types tended to eschew the personal pronoun, especially at the beginning of sentences. Taft certainly did. For many years a middle-ranking lawyer with the Office of the Legal Advisor, Taft handled the day-to-day contacts between State and the OIC—namely, me. On one level, Taft embodied much of what the world finds maddening about diplomats. He used politeness as a weapon. He rarely gave a straight answer. He wore the same blue blazer every day. He talked forever. But he was honest and decent, and he tried to do the right thing. I liked him, and he knew it.

Taft's question concerned one of the file drawers I had examined. One of Abrams's deputies—a career official—was concerned that I had seen two especially sensitive documents that were neither "yellow tagged" nor relevant to the Iran-Contra investigation. Taft described these papers in elliptical terms. "Had I seen them?" I had trouble remembering the drawers, much less the specific documents, and I recalled (to myself) with some embarrassment that I had given these files rather cursory attention.

"George," I said, "the subject of one of them does sound somewhat familiar, even though I remember nothing about the substance. And I don't remember anything about the second one." Taft gave me his usual profuse thanks and signed off. I gave the conversation little thought.

The next I heard of it was Sofaer's letter to Walsh. The letter appalled me, though I did have to chuckle at the wacky specificity of "the president, the secretary and no more than six other[s]." I knew that the odds against any secret remaining that tightly held were astronomical. Sofaer's letter made me try to remember what the damned things said; alas, to this day I retain only the dimmest recollection of even the subject of these thunderbolts—and I definitely recall nothing "extremely sensitive."

Sofaer was right about one thing. Our understanding was indeed "clear and unambiguous"—except that his letter had it wrong. We never agreed to look *only* at the yellow-tagged documents. The *purpose* of my review of the files in situ was to make sure that the retired FSOs had marked all the relevant documents. Indeed, in the course of my examination, I had several times added yellow tags to documents that I thought should be produced. I called Geoff Stewart to confirm my understanding of the arrangement with State. He did.

The only thing that worried me—and it concerned me plenty—was Sofaer's line about the CIA and Diplomatic Security. I had visions of my security clearance being withdrawn—or, at least, of struggling in the future to obtain one. I felt determined to guarantee that my file stayed clean. That, in turn, might mean the OIC would have to take on a fight. So I knew immediately what my next task should be: go talk to the boss.

Walsh never exactly discouraged private visits from lawyers on his staff, but neither did he encourage bull sessions. In more than two years on his staff, I only saw Walsh have lunch with someone from the OIC once. It occurred when a fire alarm caused the evacuation of our building around midday, and two lawyers trapped Walsh into an unplanned meal with them. Otherwise, he had a sandwich alone in his room every day. Walsh's office itself bespoke his disdain for quotidian human contact. When I entered it on that October morning, it had not changed in the smallest particular since the day we arrived in March. Walsh put no pictures on the wall. He displayed no family photographs. The government-issue bookcase held no books, and the file cabinets were filled only with material from the case. Still, the door to his corner office was, at least technically, always open. So I walked in.

One never had to worry about making small talk with Judge Walsh. "Judge," I started in, "I wanted to fill you in about that letter from Judge Sofaer." Like Walsh, Sofaer had briefly served as a judge in the Southern District of New York and thus earned a lifetime entitlement to the honorary "Judge." "I wanted to let you know," I continued, "that I think I was playing by the rules we had set down."

"I know, I know," Walsh said quickly, dismissing my worries. "I already spoke to Geoff Stewart about it. He's drafting a letter to them." I was hugely relieved; Walsh would not throw me to the wolves.

"What I want to know," he said almost to himself, "is what was behind it—why did they do this now?" Walsh appeared to believe that virtually all human action—from trivial conversations to major governmental initiatives—emerged from a complex and half-hidden array of motives and inspirations. Nothing is what it seems.

Walsh answered his own question. "The congressional hearings are over, and the story is fading—and we haven't indicted anybody."

"I think people are much less afraid of us than they used to be," I agreed. "They're sick of us, and they think they can push us around."

"We've got to show them that we still mean business," Walsh announced.

So Stewart drafted a curt reply to Sofaer, and Walsh, if anything, made it even tougher. In the letter, dated October 19, Walsh wrote that "we did not consent to accept the department's designations of relevance without question. We have retained the right, as we must, to look at any documents from the department's files that fall within the scope of our investigation." Walsh also addressed my concerns directly. He asked to be "provid[ed] with the names of the officers of the CIA and the Bureau of Diplomatic Security who were contacted by the [State] Department as a result of the incident mentioned in your letter. In addition, I would appreciate learning if members of my staff were identified by name to the CIA or the bureau[.]"

A former prosecutor as well as judge himself, Sofaer promptly recognized that he had been misled about the "understanding" between State and the OIC. In his October 30 response to Walsh, Sofaer ran up the white flag, admitting that the still-unnamed OIC staff member had "act[ed] in good faith and in accordance with the guidance of his superiors." As for the dreaded notification of the CIA and Diplomatic Security, Sofaer wrote that "I have determined not to advise the relevant document security offices of this matter at this time." In other words, the statement in his first letter was only bluster. Sofaer concluded that he was pleased to "have put behind us this temporary misunderstanding. . . . I reiterate the high regard for the professional approach your staff has adopted . . ." And so on.

When I got around to thanking Judge Walsh for standing by me, he made little of the issue. Besides, he saw a new threat on the horizon, one that might make all of our other work irrelevant:

Christmas.

I N the first year of our investigation, the possibility of presidential pardons to some or all of the players in the Iran-Contra affair was the great unmentionable in our offices. To a certain extent our reluctance to discuss the subject came from our powerlessness to do anything about it. The pardon power stands as a great anomaly in the constitutional system of checks and balances. Congress cannot pass its own pardons or reject the president's; nor may the courts review the decision to grant a pardon. In short, if the president wants to issue a pardon, no one can stop him.

Walsh raised the issue at a staff meeting on December 15. "I think we've got to think about the possibility of a pardon before Christmas," he said. Most congressional Democrats would be home for the holidays and thus unable to orchestrate a sustained reaction. "I think there's a substantial chance of it," Walsh continued, "I think we have to be ready."

While I was still thinking what it meant to be "ready" for something over which we had no control, Walsh spelled out his thoughts. "The president may ask us for a report before he does it, and we have to prepare one. We'll talk about the potential charges and the evidence. When the president wants something, I want to be ready," he said. I thought at first that this was Walsh's lawyerly sense of due process at work. He could not imagine that Reagan would act without giving us the opportunity to be heard. Then, as Walsh continued, I had another thought.

Walsh said he had "decided against telling [A.B.] Culvahouse [the White House counsel] that we want to be heard before a pardon is decided on," Walsh said, "That would be too presumptuous. So we'll just prepare as if he had already asked us."

Intensely private where personal matters were concerned—there was even some debate within the office about how many children he had—Walsh was always unusually open with the staff about business-related issues. But this, I sensed, was different. He was so emphatic, so precise in his predictions, that I felt he had some information that he was not disclosing. He seemed to know something was brewing. Walsh added to my impression when he said, "I think there's a forty percent chance of a pardon by Christmas."

I thought Walsh vastly overstated the chances of a pardon. My reasons had less to do with the political calculus of the pardon decision than my sense of Ronald Reagan as a person. My impression of Reagan did not emerge out of any special familiarity with him. Indeed, for all that the president served as a focus of public attention about the Iran-Contra affair ("What did Reagan know?"), he remained a remarkably distant, almost invisible figure for those of us who investigated his White House. His utter passivity in the conduct of the office left us with almost nothing to point to in terms of his involvement in the scandal. As investigators, we could scarcely identify any specific actions he took, much less tie him to actual crimes. Reagan wrote almost no memos; his staff did not send him very many either. His staffers reported that the president often signed documents without reading them, so the mere fact that we saw his signature would not assure that the president had approved—or even noticed—what a document said. Indeed, when staff members did disturb Reagan, they went to peculiar, often astounding, lengths to lighten his load. For example, Reagan apparently did not even bother to read the only memorandum given to him that outlined the plan for direct sales of American weapons to Iran. John Poindexter jotted on the January 17, 1986, memo—a mere two-and-a-half pages long!—that the "president was briefed verbally from this paper."

Yet Reagan's idleness seemed to me to have an emotional as well as a political dimension. He was unburdened by an ethic of sacrifice. For all his surface good nature, he was fundamentally ungenerous to those around him—an impression supported by the stream of memoirs from his most intimate aides. Granting a pardon would expose him to calumny and attack because of an action on behalf of those who served him. Reagan did not go for that sort of thing. Rather, as White House Chief of Staff Donald Regan reported with palpable disgust in his book, this president could not be persuaded, even once, to say thank you to the volunteers who answered his mail.

That kind of man, I thought, would not risk his neck for someone else—even for Ollie North.

On the morning of Friday, December 18, I received an uncharacteristically panicked call from Guy Struve. He wanted me on the pardon patrol. At the time, I was making a rare appearance in the New York office, hoping to take Christmas week off to spend with McIntosh. Struve wanted a draft letter from Walsh to Reagan, urging the president not to grant pardons to McFarlane, North, and Poindexter. He had to have it that very evening. Punctilious as always, Struve instructed me to prepare a three-part presentation. The first would summarize the scope and progress of our investigation. The second would describe the grounds for possible criminal charges against the individuals whom we thought were candidates for pardons. And the third—the third was classic Struve.

Struve said that the president's pardon power appeared to be absolute, but he noticed that in the few cases where the Supreme Court had discussed pardons, it had always been in the context of *following* a criminal conviction. Struve said part three of the memo should suggest that a preindictment pardon would not be legally valid. Anticipating my initial reaction, Struve noted that Gerald Ford's preemptive pardon of Richard Nixon had never been tested by a court. Struve said our presentation should not commit us to fighting the legality of a pardon—just raise the possibility. That, Struve thought, would greatly diminish the political appeal of the pardon. If the White House thought that it might have to fight a messy legal battle after the pardon, the chief political benefit of a pardon—its quick-and-dirty conclusion of the Iran-Contra affair—would evaporate.

So I spent the next eight hours hunched over the word processor writing a seventeen-page letter to the president. The chief crib sheet for my efforts, I noticed with mixed feelings, was the draft indictment we had considered in July; the investigation, alas, had not developed many new facts since that time. I ran the draft up to Struve's home on the Upper East Side of Manhattan and waited for further marching orders.

Struve edited the document on Saturday, and I typed in the changes on Sunday, December 20. With Christmas bearing down on us, we had to get the document to Walsh right away, but we had a problem—

how to send it to him in Washington. Our memorandum for the president was not classified, but given its political sensitivity, we wanted to treat it as if it were. The approved carrier for classified information did not deliver Sunday to Monday, and we were not supposed to use the fax machine for classified material. But we were running out of time.

"I suppose there's nothing in there that the KGB doesn't know already," Struve said, reckoning with his characteristic precision, "or at least what Gorbachev suspects."

Then, he added, speculating on the other possible clandestine recipient of the document: "And if it somehow got to the attention of the White House, that wouldn't be the worst thing in the world either."

I chuckled. "Well, that's the point, isn't it?"

Struve, ever earnest, asked me, "Why are you laughing?"

Rather than explain, I collected the memo and ran it to our fax machine for transmission to Washington.

I heard nothing on Monday or Tuesday, but Judge Walsh woke me at home on Wednesday morning, December 23. He said, "We've got to get this thing ready to go to all the leaders in Congress if there's a pardon." Now, clearly, the purpose of the document had changed. The president could no longer ask us for our views before he issued a Christmas pardon; there was no more time for such a request. Walsh made a few modifications in the text to coincide with its new aim and then signed off.

He called back within five minutes. "We forgot a conclusion," Walsh told me, "saying what we're going to do if there's a pardon."

"Well," I answered, curious myself, "what *are* we going to do if there's a pardon?"

"Do you think we ought to challenge it in court?" Walsh asked me. Struve's legal analysis questioning the validity of preindictment pardons appealed to the indefatigable Walsh. He hated the idea of losing and was willing to consider any strategy, however novel, to keep the possibility of winning alive.

I wasn't sure. Much as I wanted the case to go forward, I thought we might look ridiculous contesting a pardon. Even if we had some legal basis for our position, it might seem that we were out of control, unable to know when to stop.

"Maybe we ought to finesse it," I suggested, really trying to finesse my own answer to Walsh's question. "In any event," I said, "I really think public opinion will be the key factor in seeing whether there's any hope of challenging a pardon."

Sensing that I was dubious of the chances for a pardon, Walsh volunteered that he still thought there was a "one-in-three chance of a pardon by Christmas." Those odds, I noticed, were down seven percent from the previous week.

"I hope you're wrong," I said.

"We'll see," Judge Walsh replied.

So we did. There was no Christmas pardon in 1987, and my memo to the president never circulated outside the OIC. We were left to weigh the odds for a pardon in 1988—when the issue would arise repeatedly in a far more public way.

CHAPTER SEVEN

The Race to the Starting Line

I ran into Bob Shwartz on the elevator on the day late in 1987 when he returned to our offices from the airport carrying a simple cardboard box tied up with twine: the Swiss records of Secord's and Hakim's operation. I studied his face for a clue as to their contents, but the imperturbable Shwartz gave no clue.

Since almost the day Walsh opened shop, lawyers for Willard Zucker had been tantalizing us with stories of how their client, Hakim's financial advisor, could show how the Swiss records revealed financial misdeeds by North. The staff knew Shwartz had talked with Zucker during his trip to Europe, so once the prosecutor entered our SCIF, we accosted him and demanded a quick rundown on what he had learned.

"We met with Willard Zucker for almost five days," he said. According to Zucker, Shwartz said, "Hakim kept pestering him to find a way to help the North family, particularly Betsy North, who was worried about the family's finances." Zucker even made a little joke about it to Hakim. "What do you want me to do," he told Hakim, "rub belly buttons with this lady?"

Zucker did meet with Betsy North at an office Zucker was using in Philadelphia on March 6, 1986. In their brief discussion Betsy

North supplied the names and ages of the four North children and described their educational plans.

"On May 20, 1986," Shwartz continued, "Zucker transferred $200,000 from proceeds of the Iran arms sales into a new account he created. Zucker remembered his joke, so he named the account 'B. Button.' Zucker never saw Betsy again."

"Did Zucker ever tell Betsy or Ollie that he had transferred the money?" Shwartz was asked.

"No."

"Did the Norths sign anything?"

"No. Zucker never even met Ollie."

The room sagged.

"Did anyone ever take money out of the Button account?"

"No."

"Was the Button money supposed to be a gift to North?"

Shwartz spoke with precision: "It seemed clearly *intended* to be a gratuity." He did not have to add that the evidence, as he described it, would not allow us to charge North with *receiving* the gratuity. North could say that he asked his wife to get some general financial advice from the friend of a friend. If Zucker returned to Switzerland and set up an account, that was his business. The Norths could say they never knew anything about any Button account—and we couldn't prove otherwise. As far as North was concerned, Shwartz's trip—and the Swiss records—were a bust.

Walsh's face reddened as Shwartz's presentation continued. For this we had delayed our indictment? For *this*? After a long silence, Walsh snapped at Shwartz, "How can we prosecute Zucker?" Zucker's story was a disappointment, but we had given him immunity in return for it. We *couldn't* prosecute him, the staff gently reminded Walsh. Walsh was merely voicing the frustration that we all shared. At last Walsh said tightly to Shwartz, "I think that was a very full account of your trip. The Button account will be very nice if we ever get it." But he now knew—as did we all—that we never would.

T H E beginning of 1988 brought no improvement in Walsh's mood—not least because North gave the Washington Redskins a rousing (and highly publicized) pep talk before their appearance in the Super

Bowl. After a year of legal research (which included a memo by me considering whether we should prosecute the case under the famed RICO law and name the National Security Council as a "racketeering enterprise"), Walsh assigned David Zornow to settle the issue and draft an indictment in the case.

Ever since he and Bromwich had won guilty pleas from Channell and Miller, Zornow had lacked a niche within the OIC. It was Bromwich whom Walsh called on as Keker's temporary replacement as Central America team leader. Zornow savored the chance to make his mark on the indictment.

In his peculiar habit of assigning any task to a committee rather than an individual, Walsh actually named Zornow "chairman of the indictment committee"—although the committee seemed to include every lawyer on the staff. Needling Zornow about his reborn prominence in the office—as well as his unwillingness to stop Walsh from calling him Dave—we began calling him "Chairman Dave."

Chairman Dave had a prosecutor's instincts. He sought to charge simple crimes. He began with the false statement and obstruction counts—for McFarlane's and North's letters to Congress in the fall of 1985 denying any NSC role in aiding the contras; North's false testimony on the same subject to the House intelligence committee in August 1986; and in the cover-up of November 1986—when North and company were trying to protect the Iran initiative as well as their contra roles. Of course, there was also a count against North for, in the evocative words of the statute, "concealing, removing, mutilating, obliterating, falsifying, and destroying official documents"—the shredding.

The money charges came next: North's misuse of the traveler's checks and his acceptance of the fence—first dubbed "the security system" in the indictment. Also in this category—but, in truth, always a fifth wheel in the case—was North's conspiracy to defraud the IRS for his actions in aiding Channell and Miller in their "tax deductible" fundraising.

When Zornow completed the draft of each count, the lawyers with a special expertise or interest in it would assemble in our conference room. Together with Walsh, they would parse every word, checking both that the legal requirements of the statute were satisfied and that we had the evidence to back up each claim. Walsh even began half-seriously giving letter grades to each of the counts as they passed before him. Demonstrating prescient trial instincts, he awarded the only straight-A to Bruce Yannett when he summarized the evidence concerning North's receipt of the fence.

Late in January, Walsh called the staff together to consider the first count in the case—the charge of conspiracy to violate the Boland amendment. Just what was criminal about North's efforts on behalf of the contras?

Bob Shwartz had a simple answer: nothing. "These people acted in what they thought was a good-faith belief that they were doing what they were supposed to do," he said. "Their endgame lying did not serve to make criminal all that went before it."

But Shwartz was fighting an uphill battle. The failure of the Swiss records to provide a bombshell subtly discredited him in Walsh's mind. Plus, he had a powerful adversary on the Boland question—Guy Struve.

"What we're talking about is running a war off the books," Struve said. "That's criminal."

"We have to balance what the facts and law permit with a sense of fairness," Shwartz answered. "Charging a violation of the Boland amendment is not fair."

The arguments went on for hours, then for days. Walsh polled the staff on the Boland question: five for the count, five against and two on the fence—one of whom was Walsh. We grew achingly familiar with each other's views. Like weathermen in Phoenix, we struggled to come up with new ways to say the same thing. One day, in the middle of yet another meeting about the conspiracy count, the door handle to the conference room broke off, and we were trapped. The metaphor was widely noted at the time.

Walsh would not commit himself to Struve's view—charge a straight violation of Boland—or to Shwartz's—ignore Boland and charge nothing except obstruction of justice. When Bruce Yannett conceded one day that he had been "wavering wildly on Boland for months," Walsh shot back with some embarrassment, "You have a lot of company." Compromises beckoned.

Struve proposed that we charge North with attempting to evade the entire structure of oversight and control for covert operations. "It wasn't so much that North broke a single law, like Boland," Struve said, but that he vaulted over the whole legal system. The proposal drew support more from our exhaustion than our enthusiasm.

At last we agreed that the conspiracy charge would have three parts. The first, and most controversial, would deal with Nicaragua. Part two would charge North, Poindexter, Secord, and Hakim with a scheme of "self-dealing," and part three would charge them with "corrupting a United States government initiative involving the sale of arms" to Iran. As for the first part, the Struve compromise eventually charged North with a conspiracy to defraud the United States:

> By impeding, impairing, defeating and obstructing the lawful governmental functions of the United States, including compliance with legal restrictions governing the conduct of military and covert action activities and congressional control of appropriations and exercise of oversight for such activities, by deceitfully and without legal authorization organizing, directing and concealing a program to continue the funding of and logistical and other support for military and paramilitary operations in Nicaragua by the contras, at a time when the prohibitions of the Boland amendment and other legal restrictions on the execution of covert actions were in effect.

Even for indictments, which have their share of legalese, it was a mouthful. And we all knew it had an academic quality—and little jury appeal. On the day Walsh finally approved it, Bob Shwartz did not attend the staff meeting.

Now all we had to do was decide whom to indict.

IN truth there was only one question mark. North, of course, was at the center. Poindexter, too, moved from more of an observer role in 1985 to be a leading participant in the cover-up in November of the following year. Secord and Hakim helped North transform the arms-for-hostages initiative into a vehicle for North's imperial dreams and their own considerable enrichment. Those four were set.

The question was what to do about Robert McFarlane.

The son of a Democratic congressman from Texas, "Bud" Mc-Farlane had dedicated his life to public service. As Marine officer, he served twice in Vietnam. He was an aide to Henry Kissinger at the National Security Council and to Alexander Haig during Haig's brief tenure as secretary of state in Ronald Reagan's first term. After two years of obscure toil at State, McFarlane emerged as a compromise choice for National Security Advisor in 1983.

Though North preceded McFarlane to the NSC, albeit at a less exalted level, McFarlane grew close to the colonel, a fellow Naval Academy graduate six years his junior. North became devoted to McFarlane as well. He peppered his boss with memos about his activities, keeping McFarlane well informed as North's efforts on behalf of the contras grew more bold. They worked together closely in making possible the Saudi Arabian government's multimillion-dollar gifts to the contras, passing bank account numbers to the Saudi ambassador and arranging for the president to thank King Fahd personally for his largesse. Other than that, McFarlane, perhaps taking a cue from the president's management style, interfered little with North's operations. If he had any reservations about North's work, he left little evidence of it. One scribble beside one of North's ideas in a memo—"I don't think this is legal"—seemed to constitute his only exercise of a restraining hand.

When congressmen began hearing rumors about North's role in assisting the contras in 1985, they wrote to McFarlane for answers. McFarlane asked North to draft the responses. North's drafts—which McFarlane signed and sent on to the representatives almost verbatim—included categorical denials of the congressmen's accusations: the NSC had not solicited third countries for aid for the contras; the NSC had not facilitated private donations to the contras; the NSC did not know where the contras got their money. Finally, no one on the NSC staff had violated the "letter or spirit" of the Boland amendment.

Lies—all of it. And effective, too. McFarlane's ringing defense of North quieted congressional criticism for a full year, long enough for North to integrate the Iran arms sales money into his contra support network. Even after McFarlane quit as National Security

Advisor in December 1985, he kept a hand in some of the covert action programs that began under his watch. His most celebrated mission during this period was his leading the ill-fated trip to Tehran in May 1986, when he unsuccessfully tried to barter two planes full of HAWK missile parts (and one cake) for the American hostages in Beirut.

So, too, did McFarlane join in the cover-up as the Iran initiative began to crumble in November 1986. He contributed large chunks of misleading information to North's chronology of the Iran arms sales. Indeed, even after the diversion became public, McFarlane's lies continued. When he testified before the House Foreign Affairs Committee on December 8, 1986, he was asked whether he was aware of any contributions by the Saudis to the contras—the contributions that he, more than anyone else, had made possible. He replied with his own special brand of gnarled bureaucratese. "The concrete character of that," he said, "is beyond my ken."

All of these facts aside, we always knew that McFarlane would be a troublesome figure to fit into the scheme. Though his false letters made the full flowering of North's enterprise possible, McFarlane left the scene before most of the acts that we regarded as criminal took place. He appeared to have known about the diversion of funds—North made a vague reference to it during their trip to Iran—but he had not actively participated in it. Even the letters were problematic. To prove that McFarlane knew they were false we would have to demonstrate that he knew what North was doing. North's memos to McFarlane strongly suggested what was going on, but without North's testimony—which, of course, we did not have—we might not be able to nail down the proof. Nor did the December 8 statement present a sure thing. As I rather meekly volunteered at one of the many staff meetings where we weighed the case against McFarlane, I didn't know what "beyond my ken" meant. "Oh, God," said Walsh with a laugh, "the schools have gone to hell. Didn't you read Robert Burns?" To my relief, no reply to that question was required. "When you 'ken' something," Walsh explained, "it means you know it." But would a jury know that?

Still, all these reasons for hesitating to prosecute McFarlane paled beside our overriding concern. On February 8, 1987, McFarlane tried to commit suicide by taking an overdose of Valium at his home in suburban Maryland. He had almost performed the consummate act of remorse—one that we could not ignore.

The situation was complicated, too, by the strategy that McFarlane and his lawyer, Leonard Garment, undertook to win his redemption. Almost as soon as McFarlane left the hospital after his suicide attempt, he began giving an astonishing series of interviews to an assortment of journalists. Rather than conduct his rehabilitation with dignity, McFarlane paraded his mental problems—the feelings of inadequacy, the burdens of his father's success—like a rock star peddling a new album. No one forced him to bare his soul in this manner, but, in the end, these degrading spectacles probably did generate an additional measure of sympathy for McFarlane.

Garment also boasted that while McFarlane's colleagues were taking the Fifth Amendment, his client was cooperating with all of the various Iran-Contra investigators. That was true, after a fashion. McFarlane's "cooperation" did, however, include his lies to the House Foreign Affairs Committee—behavior that should not have earned him any bonus points over witnesses who took the Fifth. His interviews with the OIC were often no more satisfactory. For all the remorse that the suicide attempt implied, McFarlane consistently refused to acknowledge that he had done anything wrong. John Keker, who conducted most of the debriefings of McFarlane, seemed alternately amused and stupefied by his subject. "We'd sit there with McFarlane," Keker reported at one staff meeting, "and he'd talk about a subject literally for an hour. And then he'd get into a jam and say, 'You know, I'm trying to be cooperative, but what I've been saying may never have happened at all.'"

A former counsel to President Nixon and an old Washington hand, Garment tried hard to persuade Walsh to drop any plans for prosecuting McFarlane. Unlike Williams & Connolly, Garment did more work at cocktail parties than in courtrooms. We were amused to read, for example, in the January 20, 1988, *Wall Street Journal* that "Mr. Walsh, *according to attorneys familiar with the investigation,* appeared to drop consideration of seeking charges against . . . Robert McFarlane, partly on the ground that jurors wouldn't have much taste for such a case after [his] suicide attempt last year" (emphasis added). False though they were, stories like that one earned Garment the nickname "the Spin Doctor" within our offices.

In contrast to the media buzz, most of us at the OIC always thought the appropriate resolution to our McFarlane problem would be a plea bargain. A plea could help McFarlane by limiting his exposure to jail time. It could assist us by letting us avoid a trial of a near suicide—and giving us a witness who had acknowledged his own wrongdoing to testify against his former colleagues. Plea negotiations actually started in late 1987 and proceeded fitfully for many months. McFarlane and Garment would sometimes seem amenable, then pull back. In a meeting on January 22, 1988, Walsh mentioned that we would want a plea to a felony. Perhaps believing what he had read in the *Journal* two days earlier, McFarlane answered by blowing up in a screaming rage—a memorable sight for those used to his preternatural calm.

A few days later, we even received a remarkable letter from McFarlane that announced flatly that "I will not plead guilty to anything." In the letter McFarlane meditated on his father and the nature of public service and speculated, in his inimitable fashion, about the causes of the Iran-Contra imbroglio. "It is clear," McFarlane wrote, "that serious problems exist in the functioning of our government. Within the executive branch, they derive from a fundamental lack of competence in the broadest sense. Lack of competence as measured in knowledge of history, foreign cultures, basic principles of political discourse, economics, and a host of other essentially academic desiderata." Desiderata?

Days later—notwithstanding McFarlane's vow—the plea talks resumed.

On March 3, Walsh walked into Larry Shtasel's office where Mike Bromwich and I were loitering to tell us that Garment had a new proposal. McFarlane would plead guilty to *misdemeanors* if we would agree not to prosecute him further. Rather than admit to a felony "false statement," McFarlane would confess to the misdemeanor of unlawfully "withholding" information from Congress. This misdemeanor statute actually had a fairly distinguished pedigree in the world of Washington corruption. Both former Attorney General Richard Kleindienst and former CIA Director Richard Helms plea bargained under this law.

As Walsh outlined the deal for the whole staff, McFarlane would plead guilty to four misdemeanors on one condition. He would not sign the form letter that accompanies most guilty pleas. That letter specifically states that if the individual pleading guilty does not continue to give full and truthful cooperation, the plea bargain is off. McFarlane wanted to write his own letter in which he would promise to give truthful testimony. The substantive differences between the two letters were small, but the issue was important to McFarlane. Walsh wanted to know if we should make the deal.

There were audible groans. This, we knew, was a sweet deal for McFarlane. The experienced prosecutors pointed out that virtually all federal judges viewed a "misdemeanor" as a code word for no jail time—even if the statute technically carried a potential prison sentence. In effect, we were agreeing to let Ollie North's boss walk. Worse, we had not nailed down what McFarlane would say at North's and Poindexter's trial. He was still at the stage of wondering whether the stories he told ever "happened at all."

Of the former prosecutors, only Chris Todd pushed hard for the deal. "He only wants to write his own letter because he wants to make it seem like he doesn't have a gun to his head," Todd said. "He doesn't want to be treated like a mob guy."

Bob Shwartz could not contain his contempt. "He's getting misdemeanors," he told Todd. "Mob guys aren't allowed to plea to misdemeanors."

Walsh tried to explain McFarlane's position. "He doesn't want to make it seem like a plea bargain."

"But it *is* a plea bargain," Shwartz shot back.

Bromwich jumped in on Shwartz's side. "He's getting a great deal. We shouldn't be negotiating with him about the letter," said Bromwich.

Others began to question the whole misdemeanor arrangement. Zornow pointed out that Channell had pleaded to a felony. "I'm more offended by a high government official violating the law," he said. "Let's deter the Robert McFarlanes more than the Spitz Channells." Yannett pronounced the deal "a blank check for McFarlane."

I backed Todd and Walsh. "Do you want to try this guy," I asked, "and hear his doctor testify about the suicide attempt?" I also pointed out that in the eleven long months since the Channell and Miller pleas we had shown no signs of progress. This would build our momentum. Why not get rid of a defendant who would present nothing but problems in a trial?

Appearing somewhat shaken by the skepticism to the McFarlane deal, Walsh ultimately decided to agree to it—though he acceded to staff demands not to relent on the letter. McFarlane had to agree to the form letter or it was no deal. True to the predictions of Shwartz, Bromwich, and Zornow, McFarlane stayed with the deal even though he had to sign our letter. He would plead guilty to four misdemeanors—three based on the letters to Congress in 1985 and one based on his lie to the foreign affairs committee in December 1986. McFarlane made it official before Chief Judge Robinson on March 11, 1988.

Although it would take more than a year for most people—and especially me—to realize it, the McFarlane plea bargain turned out to be one of the worst mistakes the OIC made. The deal had poisonous repercussions for our office. First, McFarlane never showed any contrition about his role in the scandal, notwithstanding his suicide attempt. Second, his testimony at the North trial reeked of sanctimony and pride—and severely damaged our case. But third, and most important, McFarlane ultimately revealed himself to be among the most culpable for the Iran-Contra crimes. Our charity toward him turned out to be misplaced indeed.

Regrets about the plea bargain took many forms. One of the most common was an office-wide hostility to Garment for his relentless preening before the press. When the deal-making concerning the plea ended, and McFarlane began to be interviewed by us in detail about his role in the scandal, Garment could not have been less interested in his client's testimony. In fact, he would occasionally fall asleep while McFarlane was talking. And on the first day of the North trial, Garment called one of the more junior lawyers on the staff and demanded tickets to see the opening statements. Told that we had none to give— and that his only option was to stand in line like everyone else—Garment bellowed like a spoiled child. But we could mock Garment all we wanted. The Spin Doctor had taken us to the cleaners.

MARCH 16 brought with it a first taste of the incomparable Washington spring. That balmy day also brought a unanimous vote in the grand jury to bring the indictment we had prepared—all one hundred one pages of it.

The banner headlines that greeted the indictment provided a welcome sign that our work still had an impact outside the seventh floor of our building. But the news that generated the most interest in our office that day was a decision by Chief Judge Aubrey E. Robinson. The district court in Washington remains one of the few federal courts in the nation where the chief judge retains total discretion to assign complex criminal cases to the judge of his choice. It was no coincidence that then–Chief Judge John Sirica handled virtually all of the key Watergate matters. Similarly, we had assumed that Robinson would hoard this decade's case of the century for himself.

But the day of the indictment, Robinson assigned *United States v. John M. Poindexter et al.*, criminal number 88–80, to the Honorable Gerhard A. Gesell.

We got a sense of the Gesell style on the day of the arraignment, March 24, when the four defendants assembled together for the first time. North and Hakim arrived first, about twenty minutes before the 10 A.M. session was to begin. North looked fit and confident in his pinstriped suit and muted blue and red striped tie. Hakim, in contrast, looked like a beat-up old car, his bald olive pate framed by sad eyes and unfashionably long sideburns. Secord, the next to arrive, looked similarly unimpressive—red-faced, fat, and more than a little scared.

John Poindexter arrived last, proceeding at a more regal pace. Still the superior officer, Poindexter could afford to wait. He shook hands with Secord, Hakim, and their lawyers and then marched into a tight bear hug with North. On one level the hug seemed to show the affection between them, but so, too, did they seem to be measuring one another—taking stock of the chances for a united front.

Gesell emerged smartly at 10 A.M. and took immediate control of the proceedings. He walked each defendant through his pleas—Poindexter boomed out his "Not guilty!"—and took care of a few other formalities. We had expected little more than the ceremonial commencement of the case, so Gesell gave us a start when he informed us what was in store.

"As I understand the cases," Gesell said, "having taken judicial notice of the broad immunities that have been granted each of these defendants for their testimony and documents, the court has an independent, *sua sponte* obligation to determine by findings of fact and conclusions of law whether or not this prosecution up to this stage is or is not tainted by the use of immune information.

"My present plan," Gesell continued, "is to schedule as the first order of business the *Kastigar* hearing."

CHAPTER EIGHT

"We're Not in New Jersey"

Three of the four defendants who were indicted on March 16—North, Poindexter, and Hakim—gave widely publicized testimony under congressional grants of immunity during 1987. (Secord testified before Congress voluntarily.) We knew that meant big problems for our case. So we did what people do when they have trouble. We got ourselves a lawyer.

To be precise, we knew that the three defendants would move immediately after their indictment for the cases to be dismissed on the grounds that the OIC had "used" their immunized testimony against them. Gesell's invitation at the arraignment for the defendants to file their *Kastigar* motion showed that the judge intended to take a long and careful look at this issue. That motion would be, we thought, the biggest single obstacle to obtaining convictions. The immunity problem posed more than just a dicey legal issue. The law was fairly simple. Both sides would agree that the OIC was not allowed to "use" the immunized testimony, although the parties would tangle over what exactly constituted "use." Instead, the question in the *Kastigar* hearing would be more fundamental and more troubling. Had we cheated?

Because the *Kastigar* hearing would require Judge Gesell to evaluate the OIC's conduct of the investigation, we believed that our lawyer in the hearing should not have participated in that investigation. We needed an outside counsel to work solely on this motion. With the indictment approaching in early 1988, Walsh cast about for suggestions.

David Zornow, never shy about working the names in his Rolodex, had an idea. Zornow clerked for Judge Herbert Stern on the federal district court in Newark from 1980 to 1982 and remained a protégé of the judge. Before ascending to the bench, Stern was also a successful prosecutor. After thirteen years as a federal judge, Stern had recently entered private practice. Perhaps, Zornow thought, he was our man.

Stern was something of a legend in prosecutorial circles. In 1962, just out of law school, he began working as an assistant district attorney in Manhattan under Frank Hogan. After investigating the murder of Malcolm X, Stern moved to the Justice Department. The Feds dispatched Stern to New Jersey—a state he had scarcely visited at the time.

Stern promptly became the scourge of the New Jersey political netherworld. With his mentor, United States attorney Frederick B. Lacey, Stern prosecuted scores of prominent politicians and organized crime figures (often the same people). In his most celebrated case, he pinned a conviction and long prison term on the sitting mayor of Newark, Hugh Addonizio. He won another victory over Edward Bennett Williams, the great trial lawyer who cofounded Williams & Connolly. When Lacey was named a federal judge in 1970, Senator Clifford Case tapped the thirty-four-year-old Stern as Lacey's successor. Uncomfortable with Stern's independence, however, the Nixon administration refused to nominate Stern for the post. After a public tug-of-war between Case and Attorney General John Mitchell over the Stern appointment—a contest that affixed Stern's halo even more securely—Stern finally got the job. About three years later, and still in his thirties, he became a federal judge.

Knowing Walsh's fondness for former federal judges like himself, Zornow proposed Stern to run our *Kastigar* defense. That both Zornow and Larry Shtasel had clerked for Stern gave him an additional tie to our office. Walsh liked the idea and, after a brief meeting between Judge Walsh and Judge Stern, the deal was sealed on February 9, 1988.

The following day, Walsh asked me to go to see Stern in Newark and brief him on the *Kastigar* issues in the case to date. So, on February 12, I ventured to Stern's office in the middle of Newark's ghostly downtown. Detained on the telephone, Stern invited me to look at what he called his "wall of arrogance"—his collection of political cartoons from his days as a feared prosecutor. When I was ushered into his presence, he appeared to me to be too young to be a federal judge, much less a retired one. He had a full head of thick curly brown hair and mobile, fleshy features on an unlined countenance. It was, I learned, an astonishingly malleable face, with expressions that could shift in an instant from skeptical to satisfied and then to dismayed.

Like Walsh, Stern wasn't much for small talk. "There is going to be a *Kastigar* hearing in this case," he said, "but it must be our job to make it a *posttrial* hearing." He believed, as did everyone else on the staff, that a lengthy hearing before the trial might doom the whole case. Hearings always take longer than expected, generate unexpected new problems, and can never be fully controlled. Also, we might lose. Besides the usual prosecutorial distaste for delay, we had another reason for wanting to get the case to trial soon. President Reagan might pardon the defendants after the November 1988 election.

Trial judges generally have broad discretion on issues such as when to schedule hearings, and a District of Columbia appeals court decision specifically allowed a judge to hold a *Kastigar* hearing either before or after the trial. Stern told me, "We have got to convince Judge Gesell that it is in *his* interest—not ours or the defendants'— to hold the hearing after the trial." Here Stern's perspective as a former judge made a difference. The one thing judges hate most, he said, was wasting their time. We had to prove that a pretrial hearing would not even accomplish what Gesell might hope it would. "The defendants may all be acquitted, some counts may be dismissed, one of the defendants may be acquitted," Stern speculated, "all of those things would make a pretrial hearing a monumental waste of time.

"I see three basic possibilities for how this will work out," Stern continued. "The first is that he puts it all off until posttrial. That of course is the best for us. The second is that he holds some sort of limited hearing, where he satisfies himself as to the systemic integrity of your procedures to protect against the use of immunized testimony. We wouldn't talk about specific incidents in that one, just how your systems worked. That way he can assure himself of your good faith."

Now Stern bunched his eyebrows and turned his large mouth down at the edges. "The third is a full pretrial hearing—where all the prosecutors and all the witnesses have to testify." He paused: "As Louis XIV said, '*après moi, le déluge.*' " Then Stern grew even more grave, infusing his words with more drama than I thought they deserved. "Now, Judge Walsh has promised me total independence in my work. But I tell you I might mandamus Gesell if he decided on *Götterdämmerung.*" Mandamus is an extraordinary midtrial appeal of an order; it almost never works and usually just irritates the judge. "I would *consult* with Judge Walsh before doing that," Stern said precisely, "but I have the authority to do it, and the issue is so important that we might have to take that step."

I grew to marvel at Stern—and his seemingly incompatible character traits. His intense paranoia and total self-confidence. His extravagant self-dramatizations and gritty street smarts. His obsession with secrecy and love of the limelight.

"I don't believe in a lot of memos. I think we should just do what we have to do," he said. If I were to work with him on *Kastigar* issues, Stern said he would probably hire one more lawyer to work exclusively for him. "Too many lawyers is worse than too few," he observed. Where, I thought, have you been for the last year? I was hooked.

FEBRUARY 12 marked a turning point for me in another way as well. On the day I enlisted with Herb Stern, McIntosh agreed to take a new job for American Express that would require her to live almost full-time in Phoenix for at least the next year. I had been spending so little time in New York that it seemed like a good time for her to see a different part of her business. We figured that I would probably be finished at the OIC by the end of 1988, and we might not have this kind of flexibility in our lives again. For the next few months, we thought, we'd try the ungainly New York-Phoenix-Washington commute.

Stern made his debut in front of the full OIC staff on March 31. "This, I believe," he began. Among other rhetorical peculiarities, Stern parted his sentences on the side. His baroque locutions sometimes made him sound like an eighteenth-century Tory who had somehow been born in 1936 New York. "It is my belief," Stern continued, "that we are on the Gerhard Gesell Express, and this train is *moving*. It is my mission—our mission—to stay out of the way."

After that cryptic introduction, Stern showed off his instincts as a lawyer with some savvy speculation on what was going on in Gesell's head at this stage of the case. "If I were Gerhard Gesell," Stern said, "I would want to try this case pretty badly. And if I were Gerhard Gesell, I would want to try this case pretty badly pretty soon"—an allusion to the pardon fears that Stern felt Gesell probably shared. Here Paul Friedman interjected that he had heard through the grapevine that the seventy-seven-year-old Gesell had been acting ten years younger since he was assigned the case.

"It is our job," Stern resumed, "to give the judge the intellectual basis for where he wants to go emotionally anyway." Stern then announced his goal of no pretrial hearing—an objective the staff shared wholeheartedly. "If that nose gets into our tent, it's going to be difficult to draw the curtain," he said. "We cannot win a battle to lose a war. Yet we cannot fight a battle so long so that the war is never finished." If the OIC found itself enmeshed in a lengthy pretrial *Kastigar* hearing, "Well," Stern said, "as Louis XIV said, 'apres moi, le deluge.'" In the three months of our work together, Stern used that expression about a dozen times—always complete with attribution.

For all his legal shrewdness, Stern persisted in announcing opinions instead of just having them. The only highlights of Stern's speech were his repeated references to Walsh as "Ed." At that point, the staff had only heard Walsh called "Judge," even by Struve, who had known the man for decades.

Stern said he wanted to make the following proposal to Judge Gesell: in return for avoiding a pretrial hearing, the government would prosecute its case using only evidence that we had placed "in the can" before the defendants' immunized testimony. Because the prosecution would be using evidence which could not have been "tainted" by the testimony, Stern's theory went, there would be no reason to hold a hearing before the trial.

But could we really agree to give up most of the evidence that we had collected in the past year? Stern was peppered with questions by the skeptical staff, who were annoyed as much by his condescending tone as by the substance of what he had to say. Under his proposal could we, for example, use the Swiss records? We had received them in November 1987—after all of the defendants testified. Stern said we could use them because we had *requested* them before the testimony. It was the same with witnesses whom we first interviewed before the immunized testimony but who only told us their full stories after it. Stern said we could use them as well. "There appears to be some cost to my proposal at the beginning, but by the end," Stern promised, "it will cost you nothing." Stern ultimately agreed only to promise Gesell that the "overwhelming majority"—but not all—of our evidence at trial would come from the can.

Stern's bold proposal, especially given his style of presentation, earned him only suspicion from the OIC staff. The complaint went, sure Stern wants to win *his* motion, even if it hurts *our* trial. Stern sensed the staff's wariness and responded in kind. He would call me almost every day from Newark and ask, "How's the mood down there?"—which I understood to mean whether any new rebellions against him had erupted. I assured him that the situation was stable— for now.

WITH the internal opposition at least temporarily quieted, Stern turned his attention to our first external task: responding to a discovery request that Barry Simon of Williams & Connolly submitted to the OIC on March 30. At the beginning of the case, Williams & Connolly handled virtually all the legal work on behalf of all four defendants. And though Brendan Sullivan was clearly North's lead counsel, Simon alone handled all the legal questions. When a judge once questioned Sullivan's total lack of involvement in the legal arguments, Sullivan pointed to the jury box and said, "I only work when they do."

Discovery requests are the bread-and-butter of modern litigators. They include passages like, "the terms 'documents' and 'documentary materials' include all memorandums, correspondence, reports, studies, transcripts, books, papers, drafts, tangible objects, tape recordings" and on and on, and they provide a good window on the lawyers who write them. Simon's letter was sixteen densely packed pages that not only sought far more "documentary materials" than we would ever provide but more than we even knew existed. And this letter only covered what Simon wanted for one hearing; we could safely assume that it represented only a small fraction of what he would want for the trial. Documents from the OIC—things like Walsh's instructions to the staff for avoiding exposure to the testimony—were just the beginning of what Simon sought in his *Kastigar* discovery demand. He also sought "information reflecting" the OIC staff's personal reading habits; as he helpfully put it, "this includes everything from issues of the *The Washington Post* to *Playboy* to *Veil* [by Bob Woodward]." But that was not all. Simon also wanted any document that "refers, reflects, or relates" to how the staff "dealt with spouses, family members, friends, business and social contacts, members of the press . . . or anyone else to prevent (or report) exposure to any testimony or other information derived from" the immunized testimony. Much as we enjoyed speculating about what might "relate" to how we "dealt with" our "spouses," we knew that Simon's request was comically over inclusive. In a characteristic locution, Stern called the demand "the baying of an insatiable beast."

Stern's position on discovery was simple: the defense should get nothing. If the hearing was going to come after the trial, why should the defense get anything now? Still, the local district court rules said we had to offer to hold a discovery conference with the defendants. I called Simon on April 4 to try and set one up. Judge Gesell had ordered the defendants to submit a brief summary of their legal position—a motion of a "page or two" based on *Kastigar*—on April 7. I wanted to schedule the discovery conference for some time after that date, so we could first see what their motion said. Simon said he wanted the conference before April 7. We hung up without setting a date.

The following day, April 5, Simon sent a blistering letter to Walsh to complain about his conversation with me and to demand that the discovery conference be held before April 7. "Mr. Toobin," Simon wrote, "did not indicate what his role was in this case or whether he was responding on your behalf"—as if I might have found his discovery letter on the street and wandered over to a phone booth to call him about it. The following morning, April 6, I sent Simon a short reply, stating, "Our position remains that we would be glad to meet with you as soon as we have received your motion papers."

Simon's April 7 response to me, coming less than a month after his client was indicted, captured the tone of the relationship between Williams & Connolly and the OIC. The professional courtesies that lawyers routinely extend to one another, even in criminal cases, did not apply in this one. In this case, the lawyers never shook hands. From day one, this was war.

Marked "Personal and Confidential" and delivered by hand, Simon's letter read, in its entirety: "Dear Mr. Toobin: I do not believe that I should have one-on-one conversations with any attorney who is willing to re-create history. To avoid any misunderstandings between us in the future, further communications between us will be in writing or in the presence of witnesses. Very truly yours, Barry S. Simon"

Simon did not send a copy to Judge Gesell. That is what Simon would have done if he had *really* wanted to raise the pitch between us. This missive was just his way of trying to get the last word. When I showed it to Stern, he revealed that he did not always express himself like a member of the House of Lords. He handed it back to me, and said, "Send him a two-word response."

I would meet Simon in person at the discovery conference, which was scheduled for April 8. Shortly before the 2 P.M. start of the meeting, a worried-looking secretary came into my office and said, "I think you better go out to the guard's desk." I hustled that way and about fifteen yards away from the desk—and through the bulletproof door—I heard the raised voices of Barry Simon and Al Stansbury, our new security director, who had replaced George Litzenberg. Like a cop arriving at the scene of a domestic dispute, I asked, "What seems to be the trouble here?" Stansbury said that Simon was refusing to sign the log that we were required to maintain for all visitors to our secured facility, our SCIF. "Is that true, Barry?" I asked.

The top of Simon's bald head turned purple. "I am not signing anything," Simon said. "This office can take lawyers' fingerprints, analyze lawyers' handwriting, and I'm not helping you do your investigation."

Simon usually wrote us several letters a day, hectoring us about what he regarded as the various outrages we had visited upon his client. We already had dozens of examples of his signature from which to choose.

"So you're refusing to attend the discovery conference?" I asked.

Simon knew that I was laying the groundwork for a letter to him. ("Because you refused to attend the discovery conference . . .") These letters between counsel rarely amount to anything, but because they can always be shown to the judge in the case, lawyers take care in writing them.

Simon collected himself and said, "I'm just refusing to sign the book." And Stansbury piped up, "And that means he's not coming in here!"

At this point, Steve Saltzburg arrived. Saltzburg was a University of Virginia law professor who had agreed to work part-time with Stern on *Kastigar* and to run this discovery conference. A calm and thoughtful sort, Saltzburg proposed that we meet in our lunchroom, which was outside the technical boundaries of the SCIF. No one would have to sign in.

We had our meeting. We gave them nothing.

STERN felt that the key to winning the *Kastigar* motion was staying on the offensive—even though the defendants initiated the whole thing. We needed to keep Gesell talking about our proposals, not theirs, listening to our summary of the law, not theirs. The problem was how to go about it.

Stern decided to use Barry Simon's zeal to our advantage. At the arraignment, Gesell had scheduled a public court session for April 12 to discuss the format of the *Kastigar* hearing. Almost as an afterthought, the judge invited the defense to make its first *Kastigar* motion on April 7, "a motion that simply was designed to preserve your legal position, a page or two." Stern focused on those words.

He knew that certain lawyers—like Simon—were incapable of expressing themselves in a page or two. Because he knew that their motion would be much longer than that, Stern decided that we should prepare a response that was even longer—and get the first chance to outline how we thought the *Kastigar* proceedings should unfold. Sure enough, Simon's April 7 motion went well beyond Gesell's page-or-two instruction. The next day we replied in kind: and dropped a bomb.

The idea, Stern said, came from the text of the Fifth Amendment itself. The amendment protects a witness from being "compelled" to give evidence against himself or herself. Of course, when a witness gets immunity, he or she is then "compelled" to answer questions, and those answers may not be used against him or her. But Stern thought an immunized witness was compelled *only* to answer questions, not to give speeches. Nor was he or she compelled to grandstand, or pontificate, or talk about any subject that moved him or her—all the things that made Ollie North's performance in July 1987 so memorable. In short, Stern thought that much of what North said in his "immunized" testimony was not immunized.

The Fifth Amendment privilege against self-incrimination, Stern wrote in our April 8 brief, "protects only *compelled* disclosures. . . . The privilege does not protect voluntary answers or the 'spontaneous outpouring of testimony,'" as the Supreme Court once said. Stern rejoiced when Bob Longstreth, who had joined our team, found that quote because Stern felt it captured North's behavior so well.

Nor was that all, according to Stern. Any time a witness waived the privilege once, "subsequent related testimony" could be used against him. What was more, Stern said the prosecution could use volunteered answers "even where they do no more than repeat previously compelled information." And Stern could not resist a shot at the celebrated Brendan Sullivan. Because the cases we cited involved witnesses who had testified alone in front of grand juries, Stern reasoned, the principle "clearly applies when the witness testifies and volunteers information with able and experienced counsel by his side." To drive home his point, Stern added a massive appendix to our brief. Longstreth created the appendix by parsing every word North said to Congress and labeling those portions of North's testimony that he felt were volunteered and thus unimmunized. I was spared helping Longstreth with this tedious task because I was still "untainted" by exposure to North's testimony.

The press ate this brief up. On the day we filed it, I later learned, the networks mined their archives and showed some of the portions of the North testimony that we claimed were volunteered.

Stern never seriously expected that Gesell would ultimately rule that any part of North's testimony was not immunized. His legal argument was rather novel, and it relied more on common sense than precedent. Indeed, shortly after the reports on our brief hit the press, I received a call from Laurence Tribe, the Harvard professor who had helped us defend the independent counsel law. Tribe, who I knew from law school as a man who takes the Constitution seriously, said he had "serious reservations" about our argument. How could a judge, Tribe asked, sit down and differentiate between the compelled and the volunteered? Tribe asserted that the task would be a practical impossibility.

Stern's point was not that different from Tribe's. Stern included the massive appendix to show Gesell that untangling the "volunteered" from the "compelled" testimony would be a huge, time-consuming task. If Gesell wanted to do it at all, he certainly would not want to try it before the trial. So Stern never wanted Judge Gesell to decide which part of North's testimony was compelled and which was volunteered. Rather, his argument represented another tactic in the effort to persuade Gesell to defer all consideration of immunity issues until after the trial.

We would receive our first sense of how Judge Gesell felt about these issues at the April 12 status conference. A packed gallery greeted both sides when they arrived for the 10 A.M. start. The counsel tables also filled up quickly. We had eight lawyers at our table, and there were four defendants and five lawyers at the other—with an assortment of seconds sitting just behind them in the well. "I'm a little troubled," Judge Gesell said upon taking the bench, "there don't seem to be enough lawyers here."

Gesell savored the deep chuckle that greeted his opening remark. One perk judges enjoy is that lawyers always laugh at their jokes. But Gerhard Gesell did not look like he needed anyone's approval.

Perhaps the confidence came from a model upbringing by his father (the distinguished child psychologist Arnold Gesell), or the two decades of practice with Washington's eminent firm of Covington & Burling, or two more decades as a star of the federal trial bench—or maybe, as we thought in moments of frustration with him, he was just a nasty old cuss. At the beginning of this day, however, Gesell looked as jolly as a Frans Hals peasant—red-faced, white-haired, and ready for action.

We never had to wait long to know how Gesell felt about the issue before him. He read the briefs and made up his mind. Afterward he let the lawyers talk for just about as long as they wanted—usually to no effect. April 12 was typical.

"As you know," he said, "this is a pretrial which I set up at the time of the arraignment." Then he essentially decided the question that he had convened the group to discuss. He said it was "obviously going to be necessary to review *Kastigar* problems at a later stage as well as at a preliminary stage. . . . The reason I want to approach the problem in two bites is because it did not appear to the Court that it would be wise for the Court to embark on what looks as though it is going to be a fairly lengthy trial unless the Court was satisfied that the prosecutor has developed sufficient proof independently of the immunities granted to the defendant." The judge would hold a limited hearing to examine our systems for avoiding the immunized testimony—but not launch a full-scale investigation into whether those procedures worked. Stern's middle course.

Gesell added in a rather irritated tone that he had "no intention of following the suggestion of Mr. Stern in his papers . . . that the first step involved in this process is to determine" whether the defendants volunteered testimony and thus waived their immunity. "Those are matters down the line," the judge said. Irritated or not, Gesell did just what Stern wanted on this issue. "Down the line" was precisely where Stern wanted it. After a few more words, Gesell invited Stern to the podium and asked a specific question about discovery.

Instead of answering the question, Stern said, "I wonder if you would allow me to just address, Your Honor, for a moment and then return to Your Honor's questions although I'll be glad to—"

Gesell's round head began sinking into his robe. "Oh, yes, you can," the judge said, adding after a pause, "if you wish."

"Thank you, Your Honor," said Stern. "Your Honor has of course the right to conduct a hearing in any form that you want at any time that you want."

This was the first of several occasions when Stern chose to enlighten Gesell on the limits of his authority—reminders Gesell did not enjoy hearing. "That's why I'm telling you how I'm intending to do it," Gesell responded.

"Your Honor also indicated that you would give counsel, in your words, ample time to brief these issues. . . ."

"Well," Gesell said, "this is the time. We're going to decide it today."

It later became an OIC parlor game to speculate on the origins of Judge Gesell's immediate and intense antipathy to Stern. One theory traced the enmity to Stern's reputation during his days as a judge. Stern had spent a good deal of his time giving lectures and conducting trial advocacy seminars—all for handsome fees. He always ranked near the top of the list when federal judges declared their outside income each year. Even worse, the very week that Stern appeared before Judge Gesell, a movie based on Stern's book, *Judgment in Berlin,* opened in Washington. The story concerned how Stern conducted a trial in Berlin of a young German accused of highjacking an airplane and, as every reviewer noted, the film included an extremely flattering portrayal of one Herbert J. Stern. Stern's activities didn't violate any ethical rules—they just did not endear him to his colleagues on the bench.

An equally popular theory tied Stern's problems to his performance. Stern had superb insight into Gesell as a judge—and none at all into Gesell as a human being. The chemistry between the two men was, to put it mildly, poor. Gesell liked straight answers. Stern did not give them. Stern's oracular style, permissible when he was running his own show as a judge, immediately got under Gesell's skin.

The irony was, the judge was going our way. Still, Stern could not take yes for an answer and undertook several filibusters that seemed only to irritate Gesell more. Almost every time Gesell asked him a question, Stern requested permission to answer it—a verbal tic that nettled the judge. It was almost a relief to see Simon stand up.

Simon did not irk Gesell the way Stern did, but he had less success on the merits: he could not persuade the judge to hold a full-blown, multiwitness hearing. Gesell did seem interested in Simon's claim that the testimony of certain prosecution witnesses had been "shaped and modified" by their exposure to the defendants' immunized testimony. Simon was pressing on one of our greatest fears. Much as we prosecutors protected against using the immunized testimony ourselves, we could do relatively little to prevent our witnesses from using it. Simon vowed that if he were allowed to call a witness, he could "draw blood fairly quickly" in proving that the witness had used the immunized testimony. Based on this promise, Gesell said he would let the defendants call a witness at the *Kastigar* hearing. But except on that point, the judge stuck by his vision of a very brief and limited hearing.

Stern had only to escape with his life at this stage. He had won. But when Gesell said he wanted to schedule the *Kastigar* hearing for Monday and Tuesday, April 25 and 26, Stern returned his head to the chopping block. He told Gesell he had a schedule conflict, saying, "I mean, I hate not to fulfill an obligation to a client that I did not know would conflict with Your Honor's schedule."

With that Gesell snapped, "Well, it isn't a question of my schedule. Let me see if counsel understands. I have a trial set in another matter every day with only what was to have been my vacation between now and the end of the year. . . . And those cases are set. . . . You may not be aware of how this Court operates, but I'm receiving new cases to try every day. . . . It isn't a question of my convenience. I don't have any convenience. I have a duty, not a convenience. So it isn't a question of my schedule. It's just a question of what's fair and appropriate for the interest of counsel here."

Stern did not give up. "If Your Honor cannot accommodate me on Wednesday instead of Monday—"

Still impatient, Gesell asked, "Is that a federal case you've got?"

Stern paused and thought. Then he spoke very deliberately. "There was a little girl killed by a truck whose family expects me to be in court, in state court. It is my duty to be there, but if I cannot accommodate both, either someone will substitute for me either here or there."

The pathos moved Gesell not at all. The date did not change.

O N April 18, I received a call at the office from *The Washington Post* reporter George Lardner. We were acquaintances because Lardner had interviewed Judge Lumbard for a profile of Walsh while I was still clerking in New York. Lardner had seen my name on our *Kastigar* briefs and wanted my comments for a piece on Stern. I told Lardner I had to get permission to speak with him. After hanging up with Lardner, I called our press officer, Jim Wieghart.

Wieghart went back to the old days of print journalism, when reporters worried more about bumming their next cigarette than lowering their cholesterol. Doritos and chocolate milk was Wieghart's idea of an afternoon snack. First a reporter for the *Milwaukee Sentinel* and later a columnist and editor of the New York *Daily News,* Wieghart had dragged his nicotine-filled lungs around the country in a dozen political campaigns and covered half-a-dozen scandals. He had seen it all. He also thought public officials in Washington—especially lawyers—displayed an unnecessary paranoia about talking to reporters. Could I talk to Lardner? Sure, Wieghart said. Just use common sense.

I called Lardner back, and he began asking a few innocuous questions about Stern. I answered the same way. "Stern clearly has his eye on the ball as to what's important: getting this case to trial promptly and fairly." But then Lardner began pressing me about Stern's effectiveness the previous week. What did I think of Stern's rapport with Gesell? Would it improve? I did not want to see Stern the victim of a hatchet job in the *Post.* I asked Lardner if we could speak "on background," and he agreed.

Look, I said, Gesell gave Stern virtually everything he wanted. A story that said Stern "lost" the argument would miss the boat. Sure, I told Lardner, Stern did not win any points on style. But it was a well-established oral argument technique to resist the judge at first and then appear to be "giving in"—when the compromise position was your goal all along. Look at the bottom line, I urged Lardner.

Lardner signed off cheerfully, and I thought little about the interview until the profile of Stern appeared in the April 20 *Post*. The piece, written by Lardner and Joe Pichirallo, basically adopted the line I had pressed on Lardner. It noted that "Stern held forth at length, pontificating as though he were still on the bench." But it added that, "In the end, however, Gesell gave Stern, and Walsh's office, almost everything they wanted." Then came the following sentence:

> Lawyers who know Stern suspect he planned it that way from the outset, deliberately resisting Gesell at the beginning so that he could seem to be 'giving in' at the end.

Other nearby quotes in the article were attributed to "a colleague" and a "Walsh staff member." Reading the paper in the morning, I knew this was trouble. When Gesell saw this story, he might feel like Stern had dealt dishonestly with him, had "gamed" him. I thought the *Post* story might aggravate their already abysmal relationship. When I arrived at the office, I heard through the grapevine that Walsh was apoplectic about the "giving in" paragraph.

I had not wanted Lardner to quote my account of Stern's strategy. I just wanted to give Lardner the background that would allow him to write a more accurate piece. How could he have done this to me? Much later, I reconstructed the scenario. I told Lardner that my comments were to be "on background." That journalistic term meant that Lardner could use my words, just not attribute them to me. That's what he did. I *should* have said my comments were "off the record." That would have meant that Lardner could not have quoted my observations at all. Lardner had played by the rules; I had screwed up.

To my relief, Walsh never confronted me about the incident. Rather, he issued a curt memo on April 20 to the full OIC staff stating that Walsh personally would have to approve all further contacts with the press. Henceforth, I talked to Lardner about the weather. My single, amateurish attempt at spin control was my last. I was lucky not to get fired.

I N an order dated April 13, Gesell officially confined the *Kastigar* hearing to an examination of Walsh himself and one other "draw blood" witness of Simon's choosing. Or so we thought.

On Wednesday, April 20, Barry Simon filed both a "Motion to Reconsider" Gesell's order and a request to delay the planned April 25 hearing. Ever anxious to stay off the defensive, Stern ordered Longstreth and me to respond by Thursday at noon.

Gesell beat us to the punch. The judge saw that not only was Simon trying to get him to change his order, the defense lawyer was laying the groundwork for an appeal of that order. But Gesell knew that appeals courts are reluctant to consider any issue that has not been "finally" decided by the district court—especially in a midtrial appeal. So even before the judge had received our response, Gesell on the morning of Thursday, April 21, denied the request for a delay in the hearing but did nothing about Simon's Motion to Reconsider. A denial of the Motion to Reconsider, Gesell knew, might be an appealable order, so he ignored it. Gesell's gamesmanship—denying one motion and disregarding the other—foreclosed Simon's effort to run to the court of appeals.

That alone, however, did not deter Simon. On the morning of Friday, April 22, he called our office and asked if we would accept service (that is, the physical delivery) of subpoenas for individual lawyers in our office. Simon was persisting in trying to have our lawyers testify on April 25. We said we would accept the service. This move was another attempt to ignore Gesell's order, which had specifically stated that only Walsh and one other witness would testify at the April 25 hearing. Stern directed Longstreth and me to start immediately at work on a motion to quash the subpoenas to our lawyers—even before we received them.

Stern ordered us to mince no words in our motion to quash, and we didn't. "The defendants," we wrote, "have done everything possible to subvert the Court's order and to undermine the decisions that the Court made." We threw caution—and subtlety—to the wind. "No momentary tactical advantage is worth abandoning the rule of law in this Court," we wrote. "Deliberate violations of judicial orders threaten the rule of law."

At 4 P.M. on Friday, we received the actual subpoenas to our lawyers. Williams & Connolly chose an eclectic group: Struve, Friedman, Hassler, Zornow, Keker, Todd, Douglass, and Sloan. Ever meticulous, Williams & Connolly supplied each one of them with a check for the standard $30 witness fee—and, incidentally, a prized souvenir of the case.

Longstreth and I plugged the eight names into the motion to quash that we had already prepared. We ran it over to Gesell's chambers at 4:30 P.M. Fifteen minutes later, Gesell's clerk called to say the judge had issued an order. "Counsel for defendants," Gesell wrote, "shall advise any person subpoenaed . . . that they are excused from appearing at the courthouse pending further order of the Court." It might have been a new legal speed record: subpoenas rejected within an hour of their being served. Better yet, Gesell was excusing *all* witnesses except Walsh from testifying. As punishment for violating his order, Gesell was forbidding the defense from calling its "draw blood" witness. And once more Gesell demonstrated his special savvy. He did not exactly say the subpoenas were "quashed." Had he done so, the defense might have appealed. Instead, Gesell just excused the recipients from attending, "pending further order of the Court." He made sure his order was not "final." Again, Gesell used a quirky word formulation to deny the defendants the right to an appeal. This judge was rolling.

N O W all we had to do was survive Walsh's testimony. Stern wanted Walsh to say as little as possible. His approach seemed based on the old political adage, "no one ever lost an election because of something he did not say in the campaign." Stern would limit his direct examination of Walsh to a bare minimum, and hope that Sullivan would not bring out anything too damaging on cross.

Judge Walsh knew—as do most lawyers—that lawyers make awful witnesses. Lawyers hedge, equivocate, and niggle on the stand. These problems are exacerbated in a criminal case. The most standard criminal defense technique is to "put the prosecution on trial." Any fact-finders—judges or jury—are less likely to find fault with the defendant if they believe that the accusers in the case have themselves bent the rules. Usually, defense lawyers must satisfy themselves by implying their critique of the prosecutor; here, Brendan Sullivan was handed a defense lawyer's dream. For him, putting the prosecution on trial would not be a metaphor. It would be a reality.

So Walsh did what he tended to do in difficult situations, which was surround himself with layers of assistants. He called Struve in—that was always the first step—and then he re-enlisted Audrey Strauss and Paul Friedman to reacquaint him with the procedures we had used to screen ourselves from the immunized testimony. He had Cliff Sloan and me assemble all the documentation for the steps the office had taken. Finally, on the afternoon of Sunday, April 24, when Stern departed after a hasty run-through of Walsh's testimony, Walsh buried himself in old documents, summaries of the documents and outlines of the summaries. I had never seen him so nervous.

It was hard to blame him. Walsh was going to have to acknowledge that our procedures had not been foolproof. We had made mistakes. And he was going to be examined by someone whose sole objective would be to make him look like a fool at best and a liar at worst. And, finally, there was another thing, one that many of us thought, but few would admit. Walsh was going to be dueling Brendan Sullivan—the man we understood to be the hero of the Iran-Contra hearings, loudly proclaimed as the best lawyer in the country. This would be no ordinary cross-examination.

GESELL began the Monday session with a bitter denunciation of the defense attorneys for violating his orders over the past week. He took the rare step of telling the defendants that he was addressing them and not their lawyers. Gesell said, "Now, it's not unusual for defendants in a criminal case to make a decision that they're not going to cooperate with the Court and so instruct their lawyers, and they have an absolute right to do that. . . . Whether you three men of experience and wisdom in affairs instruct your lawyers [to do that] is your business alone. You can do it either way you want. . . . I will undertake in every way I know how to provide you with a fair trial. But the court's orders are going to be complied with."

That stinging rebuke made it look like Stern would not be the judge's only target. Gesell directed the hearing to begin and summoned Walsh to the stand.

Standing at his chair by the counsel table, Stern first had a question for Gesell. "Your Honor," he said, "I'm unfamiliar with your procedure. Where should I inquire from?"

Gesell's head began to recede once more. He gestured toward a small sign at counsel table. "The sign says you're to do it from the podium, and I suggest that's what you should do . . . *sir*." Gesell made the word sound like an epithet.

Stern decided to pursue the issue. "By the way, Judge," Stern explained as he made his way toward the lectern, "the sign doesn't say anything. It just says state your name. That's all."

"Well," said Gesell, obviously uninterested in the topic. "There is a sign somewhere. . . ."

Stern could not leave it alone, saying, "I just wanted you to know I can read."

"All right, Mr. Stern," said Gesell, his impatience mounting, "you may proceed." We were approximately one minute into the hearing.

Walsh began testifying by explaining our "canning" procedures—the placing of our evidence and leads under seal before the defendants gave their immunized testimony. Then he spoke of our efforts to avoid learning the contents of the testimony. "It was clear that we were not going to read it, and we weren't going to listen to it," Walsh said, "and then there were procedures that I put in place to try to minimize the dangers of inadvertent exposure to it."

Hands poised somewhat nervously on his knees, Walsh spoke haltingly, but he radiated integrity. Certainly, his success did not come from calling forth perfectly constructed sentences. Rather, Walsh lapsed almost immediately into what we at the OIC sometimes called his "Jimmy Stewart thing"—when, like the actor, Walsh would sputter a series of related clauses rather than completed thoughts. But the effect was much like when the upstanding Stewart spoke. It seemed that Walsh hesitated because he was trying so hard to tell the truth, to repeat the facts just precisely the way they happened. This was "Mr. Walsh Goes to Washington." Gesell was entranced.

With Walsh, that is. As for Stern, there was no détente. About ten minutes into Stern's examination, Poindexter's lawyer, Richard Beckler, made an objection on a fairly minor point. Stern responded and then Beckler spoke again. Irritated, Stern raised his voice and said to Beckler, "I don't need any help with that. . . . I heard very well."

This, for some reason, enraged Gesell. "Now, Mr. Stern," Gesell lectured, "that kind of comment is not permitted in Courtroom Six. We do not engage in personal comments back and forth between the two tables. You'll address the Court, but you will not act in that fashion again."

Taken aback by this tirade, Stern could only say, "I apologize."

But Gesell was not finished. He fixed his eyes on Stern and muttered in a voice soaked with contempt, "We're not in New Jersey."

Having drawn blood on both Stern and the Garden State, Gesell disdained further attacks on the luckless attorney. Stern, too, decided that he had had enough. For one thing, he had planned on a short examination of Walsh; for another, he wanted to get the hell out of there.

Less than half-an-hour into the hearing, it was Brendan Sullivan's turn. He trudged to the podium bearing an enormous black binder and shot Walsh a look as cold as a February rain. Sullivan had stringy white hair that looked like it had been that color for years, and his skin bore the pallor of the sedentary. One day in court, Sullivan mentioned that he was forty-five years old. He looked sixty.

Sullivan did not say good morning. Instead, he began by asking Walsh about "breaches" in our system for avoiding exposure to the testimony. It was a sensible place for him to start. Stern had focused on when the system worked; Sullivan on when it failed.

"Now," Sullivan said, "did you yourself have exposure to tainted information?"

"Yes," said Walsh.

"And did you make a record of it?"

"Yes."

Sullivan was warming up. What had Walsh heard?

But Sullivan changed his tack—saving for later the exposure of Walsh's personal sins—and moved instead to the origins of our system for avoiding taint. He directed Walsh's attention to one of the documents we had turned over to the defense, a memorandum from Audrey Strauss and me to Walsh outlining our procedures. Sullivan asked, "These were recommendations by fairly young attorneys in your office, weren't they?" Strauss had practiced law exclusively in New York, and was, I assumed, unknown to Williams & Connolly. Why, Sullivan was asking, did you listen to this kid Toobin?

I did not want to be a subject of this examination. But Walsh either misunderstood the question or decided to be generous. "Very seasoned attorneys," Walsh said of the authors of the memo. Sort of, I thought.

"Well," Sullivan pursued, "younger than I and younger than you?"

This gave the seventy-six-year-old Walsh a perfect opening. "Well," he said, "from my vantage point everybody looks young." This got a small giggle.

Then Gesell, aged seventy-seven, chimed in, "I understand that, Mr. Walsh." He, of course, got a bigger laugh. Recognizing that he was forging an alliance between the two golden agers before him, Sullivan fled from the topic of my experience. No one was happier than I to see him go.

But Sullivan stepped into trouble when he united Gesell and Walsh in common cause. As Walsh's testimony continued, the bond between the septuagenarians grew stronger. Gesell began protecting Walsh, sometimes amplifying the prosecutor's comments, other times interrupting Sullivan.

Sullivan's worst moments came when he tried to ridicule the effectiveness of our procedures, and, by implication, Walsh. Sullivan focused in on the period of time when, according to our rules, we could watch some televised news, but no stories about the immunized defendants. Sullivan tried to make it sound like you had to be a gymnast to comply with the rules.

Following the regulations, Sullivan suggested, "might even depend on how rigorously they adhered to your instructions by virtue of how far they were away from the TV?"

Walsh replied calmly, "If they couldn't be close to the TV, they better leave it shut off."

"Well," Sullivan continued, "did you specifically tell them to stay close to the TV?"

"I told them what I did."

"Which was what?"

"If you have your hand on the button or on the remote control, you can do that." It was a rather bizarre moment—Walsh recounting how he used his television clicker.

"Is that what you did?"

"That's what I did."

"Watching every minute and the minute a name came up, you would flick it off?" Sullivan did not hide his disbelief. Sullivan gave his glasses a small tug—as if they had been blown askew by the falsehood that had just come their way. He did this a lot here.

"That's right," Walsh replied. Walsh's deadly earnestness made his story entirely believable.

Still, Sullivan pressed on. "You would agree with me, sir," he asked Walsh, "that it is a very subjective standard, isn't it?"

Finally, Walsh grew annoyed with Sullivan—with his tone as much as his questions. Walsh was a man used to being treated with some deference, and the spectacle of being treated like a criminal defendant no doubt affected him. But Walsh did not explode. Instead he reached the heart of our whole efforts to screen ourselves off from the immunized testimony. Sullivan tried to make it seem like we were playing a game with the defendant's rights. Walsh made clear he did not see his responsibilities as any game.

"It is as objective as I thought reasonably workable," Walsh said, "and then in addition to that, there is the added care that has to be subjective, that every person on this staff who was spending fifteen months of his life on this investigation knows he is jeopardizing the investigation if he is careless. Now that is subjective, but it is based upon a very high objective standard."

In its style as much as its substance, Walsh's answer buried Sullivan. When Sullivan got around to asking about Walsh's three incidents of exposure, the defense lawyer evoked a thud rather than a climax. Walsh had glimpsed one newspaper headline during the Poindexter testimony, and the other two "breaches" were similarly inconsequential. None of them related to the charges against the defendants. The incidents were just specific enough to be credible and just minor enough to be irrelevant to Gesell's resolution of the *Kastigar* motion.

After a break on Tuesday, the hearing concluded on Wednesday, April 27. When Sullivan finished, Beckler and Dick Janis, Hakim's lawyer, had the opportunity to cross-examine Walsh, but succeeded only in joining Stern in Gesell's doghouse. Late on Wednesday afternoon, Walsh was excused. Gesell announced a briefing schedule, took care of a few housekeeping matters, and then stopped for a final order of business.

"Mr. Walsh," Gesell said, "I want to say something to you personally." Those of us at the prosecution table looked up in concern. "I've been around as long as you, I guess, a little older, at the trial bar and around courts. And I want to say that I'd never before experienced the prosecutor having to spend two solid days on the stand explaining his case, and I want to thank you for the guidance you've given the Court in your frank testimony about your problems."

Stern allowed himself a small, satisfied smile. He leaned over and whispered to me. "Huh," he said, "do you think he's gonna dismiss this case?" No, I conceded, probably not. Our witness had been a winner.

SHORTLY after the hearing, the defense filed its formal *Kastigar* motion, we responded to it in writing, and then Gesell heard oral arguments on the issue on May 26. Stern managed to survive an entire day in Courtroom Six without a serious blow-up with Gesell, and we seemed well on the way to an easy victory. Just before the end of the day, however, Barry Simon persuaded Gesell to allow him to call a few more witnesses to the stand on June 13.

But Williams & Connolly's overzealousness rescued us once more. On June 8, North's lawyers issued a blizzard of subpoenas for people and documents in preparation for the hearing. In the true Stern style, we moved to quash them that very day. And in a repeat of his earlier remedy, Gesell not only voided North's subpoenas, but he canceled the whole hearing—based on W & C's violation of court orders.

Less than a week later, on June 16, Gesell administered the coup de grace to the defendants' *Kastigar* motion. In a detailed, thirty-six-page opinion, Gesell gave a ringing endorsement to the way Walsh conducted the investigation. Gesell found "a scrupulous awareness of the strictures against exposure [to the immunized testimony] and a conscientious attempt to avoid even the most remote possibility of taint." The judge also quoted liberally from our instructions to the staff to avoid any contact with the immunized testimony—the documents that Audrey Strauss and I had slaved over more than a year earlier. For me, it was a tremendously satisfying victory.

But no one enjoyed it more than Herb Stern. When the decision came in, I faxed it to him in New Jersey, and he called back immediately to savor some of the fine points. Who could blame him? He had suffered for this triumph, and notwithstanding his very public humiliations, his strategy had been vindicated in every respect.

Of his skeptics, and there were several, he asked, "What are they saying now? Huh? Huh?" I assured Stern that he was universally regarded as our savior.

To Stern's inevitable query about the mood in the office, I answered dutifully that, thanks to him, the mood was good. Very good.

My answer, alas, was only partly true.

CHAPTER NINE

Cuckoo Clock

Judge Gesell did indeed elevate our spirits with his order of June 16 dismissing the defendants' *Kastigar* motion. But good as the news on *Kastigar* was—and it was very good—we were still stunned by a decision Gesell had made days earlier. On June 8, Gesell had ordered the four defendants tried separately.

From the moment he took charge, Gesell recognized that the defendants would bury him (and the case) in motions and other legal challenges if he did not keep the proceedings under firm control. So even though the judge concentrated on the *Kastigar* motion during the first three months after the indictment, he kept moving forward on other fronts as well, resolving most of these routine preliminary matters with dispatch. For example, when the defendants tried to have the case moved out of Washington because of excessive pretrial publicity, the judge waved the objection aside with an opinion of only a couple of paragraphs. We gave the Watergate defendants a fair trial, he ruled, so this one would stay put as well. Judge Gesell even refused to decamp from his beloved Courtroom Six for a more spacious chamber in the same building. Throngs of spectators had to be turned away every day during the North trial.

We expected a similarly curt rejection of the defendants' demands for a severance, that is, their requests for Gesell to grant them four separate trials. We didn't even originally pay much heed to this particular defense motion, though it reminded us that our problems based on the defendants' immunity did not disappear with the demise of the *Kastigar* motion. The defendants' claim was based on an assertion that each defendant might seek to introduce the immunized congressional testimony of his codefendants in order to exculpate himself. For example, North might want to introduce Poindexter's immunized testimony during the trial. Poindexter's immunized testimony could not be introduced in Poindexter's own trial, the defendants' reasoning went, so Gesell should grant a severance. If, in a severed trial, North wanted to introduce Poindexter's testimony, North could do so without harm to Poindexter's rights.

We regarded this reasoning as screwy. In the first place, the defendants never pointed to any specific testimony that they wanted to introduce or said how that testimony was relevant, much less exculpatory. In addition, we argued, this congressional testimony would be hearsay evidence in a criminal trial and thus not admissible in any event. In short, we regarded the defendants' severance arguments as a pile of hypothetical concerns—*if* the testimony is relevant, *if* it's exculpatory, *if* it's admissible—designed to carve up our case.

We lost. When Walsh returned to Thirteenth Street from the court session where Gesell announced his severance decision, the lawyers gathered in our conference room like the traumatized survivors of a natural disaster. The severance would make all of the individual cases harder to win. Prosecutors always prefer group trials to individual proceedings because they let a jury see a full picture of a conspiracy—a partnership in crime—and because they sometimes allow the government to bootstrap weaker cases along with stronger ones.

The severance also shattered our unstated but widely shared goal of finishing the trial—and thus our jobs—by the end of 1988. For those on the staff who had made personal sacrifices to work with the OIC as well as for others who simply preferred not to devote three or four years to this single investigation, the severance felt like a punch in the gut.

With the severance Gesell also dumped a crucial dilemma in our laps: who to try first. The judge directed us to choose between North and Poindexter (that is, not Secord or Hakim) because the Ethics in Government Act made our first priority the prosecution of government officials. We tried to persuade the judge to allow a joint trial of North and Poindexter before two different juries. We theorized that one group of jurors could be excused whenever the immunized testimony of "their" defendant was being introduced. But, as we knew he would, Gesell quickly rejected this cumbersome idea—not least because Courtroom Six lacked sufficient floor space for the plan to work.

Walsh cast about for suggestions for our first trial. At the outset the staff displayed an unusual reticence. It wasn't that we were indifferent to the selection confronting us. It was, in fact, just the opposite. We couldn't wait for the combat of trial, and for one person to be tried first.

Finally, Mike Bromwich gave voice to the unspoken consensus: Oliver North.

Bromwich said that after we convicted North, we could give him immunity and force him to testify in the later trials. Because North worked at the center of the conspiracy and had the most contact with each of the others, he could offer the most damaging evidence. Bromwich's suggestion met with immediate and universal approval.

We wanted a conviction, and we wanted North. We knew that we would have to lead with our strongest case. In order to have any chance of prosecuting the rest of the group, we had to win the first one. One crucial fact made the North case stand out: we could put money in North's pocket—make him look like a thief—something that we could not do with Poindexter. We might not be able to prove that North took the Belly Button money, but we thought we could prove he stole the traveler's checks and illegally accepted the security system. The shredding, too, had the feel of a real crime, not a lawyers' technicality. For a jury of laymen, we knew that would make an enormous difference.

The strength of our case was not the only reason to name North first. After a year and a half on the job, many of us had come to believe that Oliver North was at the red-hot center of the illegalities in the Iran-Contra affair. In some respects, that realization constituted a disappointment; every prosecutor hopes some day to thunder that the corruption stretches "all the way to the top!" But it hadn't—at least not that we could prove to a jury. North, we knew, would be plenty for us to handle—a man whom the president regarded as a "national hero," and one who, according to the speeches he was giving around the nation, repented not a single action he took at the White House. We wanted his lawyers, too. We wanted the celebrity Sullivan and his sidekick Simon, the legal tic.

In candid moments in that brief intense period after the severance, several of us admitted to sharing the same passion. We had seen enough of Ollie and his lawyers. We were human beings—and we wanted to beat their asses.

On June 9, 1988, the Office of Independent Counsel designated Oliver North as the first defendant to be tried.

ANOTHER foreboding sign also arrived on our doorstep just days before our *Kastigar* victory. Immediately after the indictment, we began giving the defendants discovery material: that is, the documents they could use to prepare their defenses. Our initial approach had been simple: we turned over everything we had. If we had seen it, so could the defendants.

On May 23, the defendants informed us that our policy would not satisfy them—not by a long shot. On that date, they sought classified information above and beyond the 100,000 Secret and Top Secret documents that we had already produced to them. Like their *Kastigar* document demand, this was no ordinary request. The defendants' May 23 submission sought documents for about one hundred forty-seven of the nation's most tightly guarded intelligence and covert action operations. The request itself, not to mention the documents it sought, was so highly classified that our security director Al Stansbury had to invent a whole separate category beyond Top Secret for it. Though most of our staff was by then inured to the thrill of the words "Top Secret," many of us still gaped at what seemed like all of the nation's most confidential information arrayed in one folder. Even David Zornow, whose political tastes generally ran toward the race for Queens district attorney, pronounced North's discovery demand "the first interesting document I've read in this case."

The May 23 document request represented the opening salvo in a war over classified information that would, in the coming months, repeatedly bring the North case to the brink of dismissal. We planned for months to defeat the defendants' *Kastigar* motion and reaped enormous dividends for it. By contrast, we had failed to anticipate our classified information problems. We simply conducted our investigation and brought our indictment based solely on our judgments as prosecutors. We never sought permission from the intelligence agencies for where we could pursue our mandate; to do so would have represented a shocking abdication of our independence. Since these agencies included several people whom we were investigating, we could scarcely rely on their word for where to stop.

To the extent that we considered the issue of classified information at all, we waved it off as largely having been dealt with by the congressional Iran-Contra committees. After all, we reasoned, they were holding public hearings, so everything important must have been declassified. "So much of it," Walsh said to Gesell at the arraignment, "has been on the Hill already."

In a funny way, Walsh was right. Virtually all of the information relevant to the trial of Oliver North had been disclosed during the time of the Iran-Contra hearings—either in the hearings themselves or in press reports about them. But that, as we came to learn, did not necessarily help us as we began our lengthy struggle over classified information. We were still discovering one true secret of the charmed circle of national security insiders: that what is labeled secret often is not.

My own enlightenment on this topic began during one of my early days on the State Department investigation, when a State lawyer took me into her office, closed the door, and informed me that she had something important to tell me. Unscrewing the combination to her office safe, she said that the State Department had decided to show the OIC some documents that were arguably within the purview of our investigation, but contained information of such sensitivity that she was personally imploring me to limit the distribution as closely as possible. I braced myself and accepted the papers in the same grave spirit in which they were offered. Then I read them.

Several days later, I walked into the office of Cliff Sloan, who I knew had seen these documents as well. Following the State lawyer's example, I closed Sloan's door and guardedly asked a question. Did you get the same speech about how sensitive this material was? Sloan had. But hadn't this super-classified stuff been reported in *The Washington Post?* Yup, Sloan said. In fact, hadn't there been extensive reporting about it? True enough, Sloan said. And then we just started to laugh—which seemed the only appropriate response to the charade to which we had been treated.

But why had the State lawyer done that? Why did she and her colleagues bother to classify information that was already well known to the public? Why did they go to such absurd lengths to protect what we came to call "fictional secrets?" They did have an answer of sorts. Whenever we complained, we were informed of the supposed difference between "disclosures" and "acknowledgments." When a fact had merely been disclosed in the media, according to our sources, the administration could say to its allies that the United States government had not *officially* confirmed that fact—even if the newspaper stories cited, as they invariably did, unnamed government officials. So the classified information regulations did not apply to administration officials leaking classified information to their favorite reporters; but they did, apparently, apply to us—when we were only trying to play by the rules. In truth, then, the four-cornered debate among the judge, the defense, the prosecution, and the administration that consumed the next three months had almost nothing to do with "secrets," as that word is conventionally used in the English language. Rather, it was fictional secrets—unsecret secrets, *non*secrets.

Judge Gesell realized sooner than did the OIC the importance—and difficulty—of managing the classified information process. On the day of the arraignment, he flagged not only *Kastigar* but also classified information as the chief pretrial obstacles to be negotiated. In dealing with classified information, Gesell would be guided by a peculiar law called the Classified Information Procedures Act of 1980—CIPA, for short. Congress passed CIPA in an effort to deal with the problem of "graymail," the claims by criminal defendants that, in order to defend themselves, they needed to disclose national security secrets. CIPA establishes a convoluted series of procedures that has the effect of giving the government the opportunity to preview any classified information the defendant seeks to disclose. This advance peek by the government gives it several options: the government may argue to the judge that the material is irrelevant to the case and thus should not be allowed into evidence; the government may declassify the evidence and allow it to be introduced; or the government may forbid its disclosure. If the government decides that the classified information sought by the defendant may not be revealed, the judge must then decide whether the defendant can still receive a fair trial—whether, in other words, to dismiss the case.

For all the complexities, Gesell cut to the heart of the issue when he vowed early on that he would not conduct a "cuckoo clock" trial—one where the jury would have to enter and leave the courtroom at regular intervals while the government's security experts tried to censor testimony or exhibits. There would be a fair, straight trial, said Gesell, or there wouldn't be one at all.

The defendants, of course, wanted no trial. They sought to clot the case so full of classified information that the administration would never let it take place.

During their years at the NSC, North and Poindexter were perfectly situated to know all the most delicate national security secrets in every part of the government. Now, faced with trial, they pressed all the hot buttons. To some extent, we played into their hands. By charging an extremely broad conspiracy, we opened the door to their use of a very broad defense. They would attempt to prove other, classified "collateral acts." In other words, because our conspiracy charge was phrased in such an open and convoluted manner, the defendants could point to other activities they had undertaken at the NSC and say, in effect, "We did this all the time. How can you charge us with breaking the law?" Their analogies to these other, highly classified activities were not close, to say the least, but they were clearly going to try to make them—if only to graymail the administration into forcing a dismissal of the case. Sensing the cynicism at the heart of their May 23 submission, Judge Gesell denied it—in total.

This action—Gesell's denial of their classified discovery request—prompted a characteristic reaction from Williams & Connolly: a savage denunciation of the decision as "arbitrary, baseless, and in our view totally irrational." Angry as most lawyers get at judges, some litigators worry about offending the figure who, for better or worse, will be deciding many more issues affecting their client. Not W & C. We would occasionally feel a perverse kind of admiration for the recklessness with which they denounced Gesell and urged him to change his prior rulings. In one brief, Barry Simon informed the judge that another pair of his decisions in the case were "most notable for their arbitrariness, their superficiality, and their unprecedented denial of due process." At one point Williams & Connolly, presumably with straight faces, wrote that "Counsel do not easily question the fundamental fairness of a proceeding." But, they hastened to add, in this case, "silence is not possible." Apparently, it never was.

Sometimes the clanking of the Williams & Connolly outrage machine did its job. On July 8, Gesell modified his position banning discovery about all one hundred forty-seven programs and instead ordered the administration to produce documents for about twenty of the programs before August 1. The judge also threw something our way that day. He set a trial date of September 20, 1988, making clear his determination to see the case through to completion and giving all our pretrial preparations a focus and goal. But we knew that the grant of the classified discovery would jeopardize the trial date—and ignite the OIC's first direct clash with the Reagan administration over classified information.

To this point the administration had remained in the background during our trial preparation. A small group of lawyers from various agencies—ultimately known as the Inter-Agency Group or IAG—was declassifying the documents that we planned to use in our case against North, but our office had not yet tested the administration's resolve to allow us to go forward. Gesell's July 8 order forced the first such test. It required the various national security agencies to go back in their files and dredge up material relating to some of their most secret activities of the past ten years—and do it within three weeks. The responses of the agencies tipped us off to their willingness to cooperate with the OIC and in the process revealed something of their institutional personalities.

The Department of Defense (DOD) had no objection to complying but, given the efficiency of its record-keeping, DOD doubted it could find the documents at all, much less within three weeks. This gargantuan department, we were informed, had no central filing system, and each of the services would have to conduct separate document searches. Also, DOD employees sometimes worked in different locations from where their documents were stored. It was a mess.

The State Department, too, gave profuse vows of cooperation, but it also wasn't sure where to look. Besides, it said, anyone who might know anything was posted overseas at the moment.

The CIA answered that it would produce some, but not all, of what was sought. As it had from the beginning, the CIA refused to come through with anything that it regarded, under its elastic definition, as involving intelligence "sources and methods."

The passive-aggressive CIA seemed the soul of cooperation compared to the National Security Agency (NSA), which is usually (and justifiably) referred to as the "super-secret NSA." It first responded to Gesell's order by informing us that it did not think that any NSA employees had high enough clearances even to look through the relevant files. These were, apparently, metasecrets: documents too sensitive to be seen by *anyone*.

As for the National Security Council, well, it said, it could probably do it—and make the deadline. The NSC lived up to its reputation as lean, flexible, and responsive, qualities which, ironically, led the government into the Iran-Contra mess in the first place.

Eventually, Walsh summoned all his genteel doggedness and pushed and pulled the agencies into trying to comply with Gesell's order. For the most part, they did, although Walsh had to inform the judge that the administration would not be able to make the August 1 deadline for all of the documents. For some of them, Walsh had to agree to a peculiar condition: the defense team would have to examine some of the most highly sensitive documents at the OIC offices on Thirteenth Street, because the agencies did not want any more photocopies made. This led to several unusual scenes. One took place on a midsummer afternoon in our seventh floor men's room, when Al Stansbury, Bob Longstreth, and I were enjoying an animated discussion of our softball triumph the previous day over the Justice Department Torts Division. As we were talking, the door to the room jerked open and a pleasantly disheveled fellow bounded in, his unbuttoned shirtsleeves flapping in the breeze. He rushed by and asked with a smile, "Is this where you hold your meetings?" I answered, "Only about softball"—which remain the only three words I have ever said to Oliver North.

With the granting of access to even twenty of the one hundred forty-seven categories, the camel's nose, as Herb Stern would say, was in the tent. Having found the passageway to at least some of the crown jewels, the North team went into a stall—designed to avoid at all costs a trial on September 20. Beginning in June, Williams & Connolly began what amounted to another prolonged tantrum, meant to delay the trial. "Having demanded that the floodgates be opened and that he receive torrents of irrelevant material requiring cursory review at best," Cliff Sloan wrote in one of our response briefs, "the defendant cannot now be heard to complain that he is drowning."

But complain he did. Forcing the case to go to trial on September 20, Williams & Connolly wrote, "would cause a proceeding without even a semblance of fairness and run afoul of the most basic principles of due process required by the Constitution."

North's team also asserted that the case should not be tried during the 1988 presidential campaign. They gave Gesell videotapes of speeches by keynote speaker Ann Richards and Senator Edward Kennedy at the Democratic Convention, which, they said, "included biting references to the 'Iran-Contra' issue." The defense added that "[i]n its frantic rush to trial before the election, the Court seems to have abandoned all sense of what is possible and what is fair," and even attacked the September 20 trial date because they wanted a vacation. Referring to Gesell's statement in court that his family and pets would be going on their holiday without him this year, the North team, perhaps surrendering to giddiness, wrote: "We learned in open court . . . that even the Court's dog will be vacationing in Maine. Defense counsel deserve no less."

The final blow to the September 20 trial date came when North was required, on August 2, to submit the list of classified documents he wanted to use at trial. North "complied" with this deadline by submitting a list of documents that was two hundred sixty-five single-spaced pages long. He had simply regurgitated all the classified documents that we had given to him in discovery. Because the defense "*cannot possibly* review (much less analyze and organize)" these documents, North's team claimed, it was designating virtually all of them as potential trial exhibits.

Though I was not a regular member of our CIPA team, Walsh recruited me to help draft our reply to this North blizzard. He wanted not my legal expertise, he said, but what he called my ability to put legal arguments in colloquial terms. So we struck back the next day, with a brief denouncing North's "telephone-book-sized submission [as] merely the latest move in defendant's struggle to have this trial postponed and to subvert the procedures of this Court." In the brief, we recommended that as a sanction for North's failure to submit a reasonable list of classified documents, he be precluded from disclosing "any classified information whatsoever" at the trial. This would have been a draconian remedy, but North had invited it by not even attempting to comply with the Court's orders. The question was, had North's brinkmanship angered Gesell enough for the judge to impose this "death penalty" and go ahead with the trial?

North came back on the morning of August 4 with his by-now-familiar litany about the impossibilities of meeting Gesell's deadlines, and Walsh directed me to have a reply in by that same afternoon. I assumed my familiar position at my secretary's word processor and, working with John Barrett, a new lawyer who had been hired as a CIPA specialist, began to bang out a response. We produced what I thought was a fairly hard-hitting reply and showed it to Walsh at about 2 P.M. A half-hour later, Walsh returned with a lengthy typed insert, which he had dictated to his secretary. Walsh rarely wrote any briefs himself, so I was surprised to see him adding substantially to Barrett's and my effort. When we looked at what Walsh had written, Barrett and I stared at each other in shock. It looked like our adversaries' rage turned inside out. Walsh denounced the defense for their "megalomaniacal" strategy, which constituted, he said, "monstrous foolishness."

The two of us sat and wondered what to do. I often said that my greatest contribution to the OIC was my recruitment of John Barrett to the staff. We were classmates in law school, and when Walsh said he wanted to hire a young lawyer to work on CIPA, I immediately sought him out. (Most of our staff was hired this way; old boys networks being what they are, the office's predominantly white and male cast should be no surprise.) Walsh said the CIPA lawyer would not be involved in the investigation or trial of the case, so he could be "tainted" by exposure to North's immunized testimony; Barrett admitted he was tainted, "thoroughly."

Barrett agreed that Walsh's insert pushed too far. We consulted with some of our more senior colleagues, who agreed with us, though they did not volunteer to tell Walsh as much. I tried to tone down Walsh's rhetoric and handed him our new draft. He noticed my substantial changes and studied them carefully. "Well," he finally told me, "if I can't get my biggest hatchet man to agree with me, I guess we ought to change it."

The brief didn't work. On August 5, the day after we submitted it, Judge Gesell abruptly canceled the September 20 trial date. Even worse, Gesell completely revised the schedule for the North case, pushing the next stage in the CIPA process back from the second week in August to the second week in November. The order set no new date for the trial, but the earliest possible time now looked to be January of 1989. The judge would be joining his dog in Maine after all.

This was, after the severance, the second enormous blow of the summer. It might have been inevitable; six months between the indictment and a trial of this complexity would have been exceptionally fast. Once Walsh was forced to concede that the administration would not produce all of the classified discovery by Gesell's August 1 deadline, the forces for delay began to look irresistible. Williams & Connolly could stall and diddle and whine—and avoid any sanction for it.

T H E melancholy staff took the loss of the September trial hard. Most people focused immediately on what they regarded as the greatly increased chances for a presidential pardon of North. That, we had assumed, was the true subtext of W & C's frantic effort to have the trial postponed. Surely, no one on either side thought that President Reagan would issue a pardon to North before the November election;

and even during the lame-duck period a pardon in the midst of a trial also seemed unlikely. But now North's lawyers had arranged it so that, at Christmastime 1988, the president would be faced only with a case seemingly bogged down in the pretrial ooze. Why *wouldn't* he pardon North?

The day after Gesell's order, Walsh headed home to Oklahoma for a three-week vacation. A couple of days after Walsh left town, David Zornow invited the legal staff to his in-laws' home in the Maryland suburbs. We mostly sat by the pool and pondered our fate, but there was also one item on the agenda for the afternoon. Several months earlier, Zornow had suggested to Walsh that the office arrange for a group photograph to provide us with a memento of our service on the case—and offer a rare stroke to staff morale. A photographer was retained and a date selected—and then doubts crept in. Our office had been repeatedly criticized in the press (particularly on *The Wall Street Journal* editorial page) and in our defendants' briefs for our "unlimited" staff and budget. A staff picture would surely have to include all of our growing group of alumni lawyers and our sizable corps of part-timers. Adding them to our core group of about twenty lawyers would mean a very large group photo. What if, Walsh wondered, the photograph fell into "the wrong hands?" He decided it was not worth the risk. The staff photo was canceled.

The *official* photo, that is. In the dimming twilight of a beer-soaked summer afternoon in Chevy Chase, Bruce Yannett's camera snapped a bedraggled group portrait. Perhaps, we thought at that grim juncture, this might be all we had to show for our efforts.

OCCASIONAL skirmishes between the two sides punctuated the following ten weeks, but the period up to the presidential election passed for most of us in gloomy uncertainty. Spirits at the OIC sunk to a new low. We faced what looked like an even worse prospect than losing the case: not knowing whether a Reagan pardon or our CIPA woes were going to allow us to try it at all. At least a trial— even an unsuccessful one—has a beginning and an end. Much as it offended their consciences, several lawyers on the staff voiced not- so-secret hopes for a pardon, which would deliver us from our uncertainties and make us instant martyrs in the bargain. During one of our many lunchtime straw polls about a pardon, I predicted no pardon and lost eleven to one.

We hit bottom in October when both Cliff Sloan and Bruce Yannett announced that they would soon be leaving the OIC. Two of the original younger lawyers on the staff, they embodied the optimistic spirit with which so many of us started the investigation. Sloan in particular held a central position in the office because he was so obviously Judge Walsh's favorite—a status he kept while remaining popular with his peers. Among those who remained, "sinking ship" analogies popped frequently into conversations.

I thought about quitting as well. McIntosh and my commute had worked out somewhat better than we had expected; we had managed to meet, in one city or another, about three weekends a month. But we tolerated the arrangement only because we knew it would soon end, and the current round of delays threatened the finality on which we had been counting. Even worse, McIntosh suffered a medical emergency in Phoenix in the last week in October. I rushed out to see her, and we returned together to New York where she underwent surgery. She recovered quickly, and Judge Walsh generously allowed me several weeks off to be with her during her recuperation. But we suffered long over the question of whether this crazy commute was any way to live.

Ultimately, McIntosh and I decided that I would not leave Washington right away, but we did the next best thing. We set a deadline of April 1989. That would mark one year since our three-city commute had begun and more than two since I began at the OIC. Win or lose, trial completed or not, I would depart the OIC and join McIntosh in Phoenix no later than the end of April.

When the November 1988 round of CIPA proceedings began, it looked like a virtual replay of what went on in August. Shortly before November 14, the date when North was to disclose the classified documents he sought to introduce at the trial, W & C submitted a brief stating that "[i]t is *physically impossible* for the defense to complete its review of the classified documents and prepare" its CIPA notice by that date. "Tens of thousands of documents remain," they continued, "as to which the defense has not even had time to conduct a *preliminary review*[.]" The stall had commenced again. As in August, the defense submitted another telephone-book-sized list of the documents it wanted to use, this one four hundred ninety-one pages long and including about thirty thousand pages worth of documents. Again we asked Gesell to preclude North from using *any* of them.

Judges usually make their views known in written orders, but Gesell knew that a courtroom full of reporters would make a more efficient medium for the particular message he wanted to deliver on November 21. Following a morning of harangues from both sides on a variety of minor issues, Gesell began reading from a text—addressing not the parties present, but the president of the United States.

"As far as the court is aware," Gesell began, "the president has made no effort whatsoever to prevent this case from going forward. Quite the contrary." Indeed, Gesell said, the president's administration had appointed the independent counsel in the case and even made some progress declassifying some of the documents for the trial. Gesell, too, promised to do his part to protect real secrets—regarding things like the names of our intelligence operatives and their continuing efforts to free the hostages. "But a far more difficult situation for those who may have foreign policy or national security concerns is presented by the trial *testimony*," he said.

A savvy trial judge, Gesell knew that while the administration could censor documents in advance, witnesses posed a separate problem. Gesell said that during the trial witnesses "will be subject to intense cross-examination. The Constitution does not permit the Court to take this testimony in secret, as did the Congress. It must be public." Gesell then disavowed any intention—or even ability—to censor the freewheeling give-and-take of a trial. "The Court," he said, "can define the broad limits of what is relevant, but it cannot even attempt to define the precise scope of each question and answer within the relevant area."

Then Gesell issued his challenge. "Accordingly," he said, "if on analysis this imminent prospect gives ground for presidential action to protect any perceived threat to the foreign policy obligations which the president has, or the intelligence needs of the country, the Constitution, and the statutes provide various courses which he may take." Then, as if the point needed to be made any clearer, Gesell concluded: "The Court has a very limited role. It will continue to strive for a fair trial. But under the Constitution it is for the president, not North or any witness, to protect the prerogatives of the president's office if he deems them unduly threatened."

Gesell knew he could not affix a hermetic barrier to separate the classified from the unclassified in his courtroom. He could see that North was being overinclusive, but so, too, did he recognize that some of what the defendant listed *was* necessary to his defense. The judge lacked both the time and the temperament to quibble, one fictional secret after another, over what precisely could be disclosed. Instead, he tried to break the logjam, saying to the president that if he really believed these "secrets" needed to be protected, he should just pardon North right now. It was a classic Gesell maneuver.

Our team in court that day returned to our Thirteenth Street base announcing that the case was as good as over—and some were smiling. Now, they said, Reagan had his opening. He could claim that, confronted with a judge who was unwilling to protect vital national secrets, he had no choice except to end the trial. That afternoon Walsh asked Mike Bromwich to survey each lawyer on the staff for suggestions about what we should do in the event of a pardon. Do we challenge the pardon in court? Should we prosecute the others beside North? Should we allow Channell, Miller, and McFarlane to withdraw their guilty pleas? Bromwich drew mostly inconclusive groans in reply.

We weren't the only people to interpret the events of the day as paving the way for the end of the case. Late on that last Monday before Thanksgiving, Walsh received a hand-delivered envelope from Williams & Connolly. It was a commercial greeting card with a turkey on the front saying "Gobble, Gobble, Gobble." The message inside said, "Happy Thanksgiving," and the signature—apparently genuine—read "Brendan V. Sullivan, Jr."

Thanksgiving passed without a pardon, but the case still looked headed for demise. The administration seemed to be reaching out for ways to push us around. Shortly after Gesell's challenge to Reagan, we received curt letters from Assistant Attorney General Ed Dennis, head of the criminal division, and A.B. Culvahouse, the White House counsel, informing us that the administration was finished making compromises in the effort to bring the case to trial. We were looking over the abyss.

On December 21, we were told, the administration planned to hold a cabinet-level session at the White House, where all remaining national security issues concerning the North trial would be resolved. Walsh was not invited to attend the meeting, so he decided to make our case in writing. If the North case blew up altogether, we could show the congressional intelligence committees just how our position had been laid out before the administration. Thus, a couple of days before the cabinet-level meeting, Walsh submitted a thick package to all of the top Reagan aides—Attorney General Richard Thornburgh, Secretary of State George Shultz, and CIA Director William Webster—who held the fate of our case in their hands.

It had been prepared in two parts by Evan Wolfson, a "tainted" lawyer who had recently joined the staff from the Brooklyn district attorney's office. The first section, a thirty-page brief, explained how Gesell had already ruled that any of the genuine secrets about which the administration was worried would not be allowed into the case.

Wolfson devoted the second part of the package—the key part—to attacking the administration position on fictional secrets. Here Wolfson showed how most of these subjects had already received "pervasive publicity," attaching a forty-five-page list of press clippings to drive the point home. But we knew that because of the disclosure/acknowledgment distinction, even the torrent of press clippings would not alone do the job. So Wolfson did his best to preempt that argument as well. He collected a separate, almost-as-thick group of public references to the fictional secrets that were drawn exclusively from "official" sources. He gathered them from a variety of locations within the government—the declassified testimony, depositions, and report of the congressional Iran-Contra committee, the Tower Commission, and on-the-record statements made by various administration spokesmen. (Because this task required examining the congressional committee's material, including the immunized testimony, a "tainted" lawyer had to do it.) With these references, we told the administration, *you yourselves* have allowed these "secrets" to be disclosed. Why hold our case hostage to protect them?

On the afternoon of December 21, Walsh gathered the staff to report the results of the cabinet meeting, which had just been telephoned to him.

"Well," said Walsh, "we didn't lose everything, but we lost *almost* everything." The administration would allow us to disclose that Saudi Arabia had donated money to the contras—a fact that had been common knowledge for approximately a year. Certain other country names would be allowed as well. We were shut out completely as far as the National Security Agency was concerned. In fact, the NSA had insisted—and the cabinet had apparently agreed—that no one at the trial could even make a generic reference to that agency's work.

The NSA had played a minor but real role in supporting the sale of American arms to Iran—a fact that, by December 1988, was known to anyone who cared. Indeed, in Attorney General Meese's nationally televised news conference (November 25, 1986), he specifically said that the NSA was involved. But the administration was acquiescing to more than just the NSA's demand that its own role in the Iran arms sales be covered up; it was agreeing to censor the NSA's very existence. This agency of the United States government had a budget far larger than that of the CIA and had been the subject of books, which described its monitoring of phone calls and other communications in mind-numbing detail. In fact, around the time of the cabinet-level meeting, the Public Broadcasting System showed a documentary that included interviews with the jailed spy John Walker, who calmly recited how he turned over code books and plans for some of the NSA's most sophisticated equipment to the Soviets. Our adversaries, in short, had the ability to build our machines themselves. And the NSA was forbidding us from mentioning its work at the trial.

The meeting rumbled to an inconclusive close. Chris Mixter, who had been handling our relations with the administration on CIPA, raised the possibility of our asking Judge Gesell to reconsider his prior CIPA rulings. Or, Mixter said, we should consider appealing Gesell's orders in the hope that the circuit court might provide the precise guarantees of nondisclosure that the administration regarded as mandatory. This was what the administration lawyers wanted us to do. They wanted Gesell to follow their exact script in ruling certain subjects forever off-limits to North—subjects that included both genuine and fictional secrets.

The thought of an appeal turned my stomach—not least because the accompanying delay would probably eat up most of the time left until my self-imposed April deadline for leaving. John Keker said the prospect of an appeal in a case that had already gone on this long began to look like a "*Bleak House* situation." And more importantly, Keker added, Gesell had protected all of the genuine secrets. The judge, in short, was right. So why should we appeal?

Just before five o'clock, Chris Mixter's secretary stuck her head in the conference room door to say he had a call from the Justice Department.

As Mixter left to take the call, our press spokesman Jim Wieghart cracked, "Tell him we all resigned in protest."

Walsh smiled and added, "Don't tell him that—they'll all go out and have a drink to celebrate."

But Wieghart was serious. When the staff meeting broke up, Wieghart began going from office to office soliciting support for a public protest of the administration's intransigence on classified information. Wieghart said we had played along with the administration for long enough. If we appealed or asked Gesell to reconsider his prior orders, that would mean we bought into the administration's approach to the problem. It was time to take a stand. If the OIC didn't start fighting back, Wieghart said, he would resign and denounce the administration—and the OIC for its cowardice.

Evan Wolfson joined Wieghart in the nascent protest movement. A fiery New Yorker with little patience for the deliberative pace of the OIC, Wolfson was spoiling for a confrontation. He drafted a short, punchy public release stating that the administration was making a fair trial of North impossible. About six of us hovered around Wolfson at the word processor as he banged out his position. Almost the entire office felt energized by finally confronting the administration rather than placating it, as we had tried to do so far. Then, in an almost melodramatic flourish to illustrate our unity on the issue, Wolfson attached the name of every lawyer on the staff to the document—just as the Supreme Court used to do with its most important desegregation decisions. The obvious (and intended) implication of

Wolfson's draft was that we would all resign in protest if the administration continued its current course.

Wolfson sent his draft to Walsh at his suite at the Watergate Hotel—he stayed there not for symbolic reasons but because he had lived there once before—and many of us remained at the office to speculate about how he would react to our proposal to get tough with the administration. To the surprise of many, Walsh did not reject it out of hand, but he did decide to wait out Christmas and New Year's before taking this final stand. Walsh knew that, with the Reagan administration winding down, Washington was closing tighter than usual this year for the holidays. If we hoped to ignite public outrage, the last week in December was not the time to do it. Better to wait a week.

President Reagan departed for his California vacation without leaving behind so much as a rumor that a pardon was imminent. It wasn't that Reagan seemed any less favorably disposed toward the colonel, but rather that a pardon no longer seemed necessary. Our final indignity, it appeared, would be that the end to our case would come not with the constitutional grandeur of a pardon but because of an obscure statute called the Classified Information Procedures Act. They didn't even need a presidential act of grace to beat us. Instead, the case against Oliver North was, in John Keker's words, "being pecked to death by ducks."

So we thought until Friday, December 30, 1988, the last working day of the year—and the first day of the rest of the case. For on that day Oliver North's lawyers came to our rescue.

CHAPTER TEN

May It Please the Court

Throughout all the maneuvering about CIPA, Judge Gesell kept moving forward on all the small tasks necessary to bring the case to trial. Late in 1988 he made sure that the federal courthouse sent out jury notices to assemble an adequate pool of potential jurors. He arranged for the defense team to have access to an office where they could assemble before and after court sessions. He ordered the United States marshals to set up adequate security for the courtroom, and directed the clerk to distribute press passes. As long as the possibility still existed that the trial might take place, Gesell was going to be prepared.

As ever, Barry Simon had some further demands for Gesell. At the end of a typically rancorous pretrial session about CIPA in late December, Simon said, "We would strongly suggest that the Court actually set a trial date. We're in a position where we can't serve trial subpoenas for the appearance of witnesses—"

Gesell, incredulous, cut him off.

"Do you want me to do it now?" Gesell asked Simon. "I will."

Simon did. "There's a change of administration," he said. "People going to the four corners of the earth and we would like to get subpoenas out on individuals. . . ."

"All right," Gesell barked. "The trial will start January 31 at nine-thirty in the morning."

Simon, of course, wanted a later trial date, so he began to pester Gesell once more, saying, "And we do object to the date, Your Honor, but—"

But Gesell had had enough of him. "That's the date," he said, leaving the subject emphatically closed.

Amid our general CIPA panic of that time, most of us paid little attention to the reason why Simon demanded a trial date, but his hidden agenda became clear as I watched the news with McIntosh on the Friday night before New Year's weekend. The lead story on that broadcast—as it would be front-page news across the country on New Year's Eve—announced that Oliver North had subpoenaed Ronald Reagan and George Bush to testify as defense witnesses in his trial. Simon asked for a trial date so he could issue his subpoenas and give his witnesses a specific day when the trial would begin.

This last bomb in North's arsenal transformed the complexion of the CIPA debate. North's subpoena swept the great unanswered question of the Iran-Contra affair—what did Reagan know?—back into the forefront.

Most importantly for us, North's subpoenas had the unintended effect of softening the administration's positions on a broad range of classified information issues. North's presidential subpoenas demonstrated, more clearly than any other episode so far, that political rather than national security considerations governed the administration's decisions on classified information. If the administration shut down the case now, with subpoenas outstanding to Reagan and Bush, the odor of cover-up would be too strong. Any CIPA-related dismissal would look like the administration used classified information as a pretext to keep the two Republican presidents off the stand. North had improved our hand dramatically.

Flexibility and accommodation became the administration watchwords. Gesell, too, cooperated by issuing two orders in January that reassured the administration that he would not let North open the floodgates to any classified information he felt might help him win his case.

The OIC had to make one more concession as well, but the sacrifice was one that many on the staff felt only too happy to offer. Virtually all of the difficult issues regarding classified information arose because of counts one and two against North, the charge of conspiracy to defraud the United States and the charge of theft of government property. Because we had phrased those counts so broadly, North in defending himself would have a sublime opportunity to introduce evidence of other, highly classified programs in order to prove that his activities were legal. With these two counts, we had lobbed CIPA timebombs into our own camp. Our "concession" was to rid ourselves of them.

There was considerable sentiment to do it. Several of the lawyers—especially the experienced prosecutors—had almost immediate doubts about how these highly complex crimes would play to a jury. We would sometimes read aloud the tortured results of our compromise wording and wonder how any collection of twelve nonlawyers would understand them, much less find the accusations proved beyond a reasonable doubt. Of course, a case including only the twelve remaining counts, which dealt chiefly with North's various deceptions, left us open to the classic defense lawyer's response to any false statement case: "The prosecutors charge my client with lying but they don't say that his underlying activity was illegal—so why would he have lied about it?" That could be a powerful defense, but many of us believed that the cardinal virtue of these remaining crimes—their simplicity—more than made up for the risks.

A trial without counts one and two would allow us to shear dozens of names from our witness list, an important advantage in a case where many of our witnesses liked the defendant far more than they cared for us. For all of these reasons, many on the staff had been willing, even anxious, to solve our classified information problems by dropping these counts. It would also, some of us felt, boost the chances for a conviction in the bargain.

Judge Walsh met with Attorney General Dick Thornburgh on January 4, 1989, to make the deal. We would drop the counts one and two, and, in return, the administration would guarantee that the remaining counts proceed unimpeded to trial. The deal was announced the following day. As Thornburgh said definitively on the television news program "Nightline" that evening, Walsh's decision to dismiss counts one and two meant that the case "will go to trial on the remaining dozen counts."

THE motives of the North team for their subpoena of Reagan and Bush always mystified me. The move seemed symptomatic of their schizoid approach to classified information throughout the case. In most respects, they displayed the utmost cynicism in attempting to use national security to get their client off the hook. Their massive submissions of documents that they supposedly wanted to use during the trial were clearly nothing more than attempts to blow up the prosecution case—pure graymail. But the subpoenas to Reagan and Bush were apparently sincere, if ill-timed, attempts to obtain testimony that they thought would aid North's defense. Here, North's team passed up a tremendous opportunity to use our classified information problems to their advantage.

Their cynical use of classified information and their sincere effort to subpoena Reagan and Bush had in common the fanatical urge to push forward on all fronts all the time. They were undone by the same energy and aggressiveness that so often brought them success. Had they held off on their subpoenas for as little as a week, they might have seen the whole case against North disappear. But they couldn't restrain themselves—and lost their chance.

Notwithstanding a spate of news stories about North's "winning maneuver" leading to the demise of the first and second counts, he had lost more than he won. Instead of no trial, or a tangled, difficult-to-prove case, Williams & Connolly faced a trial on the toughest, simplest counts against Oliver North. Provided, of course, that the OIC had someone to try it.

THE opportunity to serve as chief prosecutor in this decade's "trial of the century" was, of course, the greatest plum Walsh had to bestow. The struggle over who would receive it—a battle at once bitter and poignant—absorbed as much psychic energy as any internal issue the OIC confronted, and it was left unresolved until a desperately late hour.

Walsh's choice came down to Bob Shwartz or John Keker. Certainly any selection based on commitment to the OIC would have favored Bob Shwartz. Unlike Struve, Friedman, and Keker, Shwartz had cut all his ties with his law firm and worked full-time on the case in Washington. The methodical, almost plodding Shwartz once admitted that at first he did not even know it was possible to work part-time as a prosecutor. The thought, he said, had never occurred to him.

Shwartz also demonstrated his single-mindedness in his approach to the case. From Shwartz's first day at the office, he viewed the Iran-Contra affair as, at its core, a simple case of larceny. In his view, North favored Secord and Hakim with the chance to jack up their arms prices to the contras and Iranians, and the arms dealers paid off North in return. To Shwartz, the key was the Belly Button account, the Swiss bank account that Hakim allegedly established to help the North family. For him, the Button account was the hinge on which the rest of the case turned.

Though it was difficult to imagine two more different men, Walsh always had a soft spot for John Keker. Keker's breezy informality posed a vivid contrast to Walsh's starched civility; it was, for example, a safe bet that Minister Madrigal would have found nothing extraordinary in any of Walsh's ties. But Keker projected an electric self-confidence that seemed almost to intimidate the older man. So, too, the ever-present knowledge that this carefree spirit, this mellow Californian, had fought with valor in Vietnam surely aided his cause as well. Keker faced life with a relaxed smile because he knew—he had learned—what mattered.

Still, Keker on paper would represent an odd choice to lead the prosecution of Oliver North. Keker had tried dozens of criminal cases as a defense attorney but not a single one as a prosecutor. But Walsh came to believe, as did many others, that the North case would come down to the testimony of the defendant on the stand. Who better to cross-examine the colonel than his fellow ex-Marine? Keker would not be intimidated by the legend of Ollie.

The debate over the indictment highlighted the tensions between Shwartz and Keker. Shwartz voiced outright contempt for the Boland amendment charge. "This," he would say, shaking his head, "is a criminal case, and the Boland amendment is not a criminal law." But Shwartz's credibility was subtly undermined by our disappointment with the Swiss records. They had dashed our hope of pinning the Button account on North. And with that loss, Shwartz lost his charter. In the last of our marathon sessions drafting the indictment, Bob Shwartz did not attend. He left the OIC, dignity intact, shortly after the indictment in March of 1988.

But even with Shwartz gone, Walsh would not make a commitment to allow Keker to try the case. To the surprise of virtually everyone on the staff, it became apparent that Judge Walsh had another candidate in mind for lead counsel: Lawrence Walsh. In Watergate, the only obvious parallel to Walsh's Iran-Contra investigation, special prosecutor Leon Jaworski had not personally tried any of the cases, and we all had assumed that Walsh, too, would delegate this job. For one thing, Walsh turned seventy-seven in January 1989. The trial of any lawsuit requires tremendous stamina, and as hotly contested and highly publicized as the North case would be, all the lawyers would be pushed to their limits. Court sessions would last all day, and then the lawyers would return to their offices to prepare their next witnesses, check the admissibility of their evidence, anticipate defense moves, and plot strategy—in all, play an exhausting young man's game. Walsh ran the OIC with vigor, and he managed to tolerate his weekly shuttle home to Oklahoma City, an ability that I, with my own exhausting commute, particularly admired. But could he stand the daily pounding of a trial?

Walsh never said that he could, but he never said that he couldn't either. Walsh's failure to make up his mind opened the door for two new candidates to emerge in the trial sweepstakes: Mike Bromwich and David Zornow. When the office opened in early 1987, the staff was arrayed in three distinct layers. At the top sat the team leaders, all in their forties. The second group featured those a decade younger and less than ten years out of law school: Bromwich, Zornow, and Mixter. Those of us in the last category, "the younger lawyers," figured in the race for slots on the trial team only as sounding boards for the contestants.

Bromwich and Zornow advanced in the hierarchy in part because of their achievements for the OIC: their skillful negotiations of the

Channell and Miller pleas, Zornow's drafting of the indictment, Bromwich's supervision of the grand jury. Just as importantly, the two former Southern District of New York prosecutors had hung in when others had bailed out. Bromwich was promoted to CIA team leader when Keker scaled back his commitment to the OIC in late 1987, and Zornow replaced Shwartz in flow of funds in early 1988. Unlike Mixter who as a long-time associate at Davis Polk had never tried anything, Bromwich and Zornow had prosecuted many cases between them. With Keker, who had no prior experience as a government lawyer, the trio made a logical team.

Still, Walsh would not make up his mind. First the severance and then the loss of the September trial date let Walsh put off the decision. But as the CIPA process moved forward, witnesses began arriving in our offices in order to go through final preparations for their testimony. A floating cast of characters would walk them through their lines because it remained unclear which lawyer would examine them at the trial. Robert Owen, North's courier to Central America, claimed during Brendan Sullivan's cross-examination of him that he had met with thirteen different lawyers during his interviews with the OIC. Owen's experience was not unique.

In late fall, Walsh began talking to Keker about their doing the trial together, a scenario that Keker agreed to consider—as long as Walsh would settle the issue one way or the other. Finally, Keker grew fed up with what amounted to a continuing audition for the job. He came from a tradition where a lawyer got the feel of his witnesses, what they were like as people, learned their idiosyncracies before he put them on the stand. This took time. In contrast, senior partners at Davis Polk worked with witnesses based on scripts prepared by younger lawyers, so Walsh did not fully appreciate Keker's urgency.

In the first week of December, Keker told Walsh that he wanted to be placed in sole charge of the trial or he would leave the OIC. When Walsh equivocated, Keker told the rest of the staff he was quitting. But Walsh, as Keker well knew, did not want to try the case with Zornow and Bromwich, whose combined ages fell more than a decade short of Walsh's own. Minute by minute, the lawyers on the staff followed the tangle of negotiations, as Keker paced the long corridor between his office and Walsh's corner. When Keker left for San Francisco on December 10, he told us he would not be coming back.

The breakthrough occurred when the media-savvy Zornow proposed that Keker insist to Walsh that the OIC issue a press release announcing the Keker-Bromwich-Zornow trial team. Walsh, Zornow contended, would only regard a public commitment as irrevocable, and on December 16, Walsh gave in and approved the press release. At last the decision was made.

Walsh had fought to keep the North case, I felt certain, not out of ego or vanity, but out of an overwhelming sense of responsibility. It was his office, his investigation, his trial, and his duty to accept the consequences. Walsh may even have felt that the staff regarded his delegation of this difficult mission as the abdication of an obligation. But we, and I, certainly would never know.

Days after his reluctant surrender of the North case to Keker, I spotted Walsh in the tense solitude of his office, peering at the light that penetrated the closed blinds. He remained, as ever, alone.

N O W firmly in charge, Keker wanted action. Why not, Keker suggested, try to get North's notebooks?

In interviews with our office, witnesses would often recall Oliver North's penchant for taking notes on all of his meetings. His left elbow splayed out parallel to his torso, North would fill one government-issued stenographic pad after another and then stack the used ones in the credenza lining the wall of his office. On the day he was fired, however, all the notebooks were gone—presumably bundled off by the colonel in the panic of his last days at the NSC.

From almost day one, we wanted them. They would constitute a priceless trove of information on all of North's activities. In a case involving just North's false statements (that is, without the conspiracy counts), the value of the notebooks would be enhanced even more. To prove a conspiracy, we would have to establish that North knew he was breaking the law. But to prove the charged lies, which basically constituted North's denial of actions he took on behalf of the contras, we would only need to confirm that North's activities had taken place. The notebooks, it seemed safe to say, would do just that.

Since my first days at the OIC, one of my assignments had been to figure out how to get them. By December 1988, I had assembled a mountain of legal research on the question. By that time, I had agonized for so long and written so many memos about the notebooks I came to refer to the subject as "my Vietnam." I got in, but I couldn't get out.

Rule 17(c) of the Federal Rules of Criminal Procedure allows both sides in a criminal trial to obtain certain documents from each other just before the first witness takes the stand. Keker asked me to prepare a 17(c) subpoena for the notebooks.

I did so, filing it on December 22, and North, as we expected, objected to turning over the notebooks, citing his Fifth Amendment right against self-incrimination. In a recent series of cases, the Supreme Court had said, in essence, that as long as the government had not "compelled" a defendant to write down what was subpoenaed—as surely no one had compelled North to keep his detailed notes—the paper records were not protected by the Fifth Amendment. But the lower courts had resisted this trend, apparently offended by the thought of defendants turning over the personal records that might lead to their convictions. Exceptions to the Supreme Court's rule sprouted up, as did exceptions to the exceptions. Working with Dan Meltzer, a Harvard law professor who served as a consultant to our office, I drafted a brief urging Gesell to see the muddled law our way.

When the judge issued an order on Tuesday, January 17, scheduling an oral argument on the notebooks subpoena for eight days later, Keker confronted a dicey question: who should argue the motion. Needing to prepare his opening statement as well as almost a dozen witnesses, Keker lacked the time or the inclination to master the squirrelly legal issues raised by the subpoena. Bromwich and Zornow also were swamped with pretrial preparations. Dan Meltzer knew the law but had not immersed himself in the facts behind the subpoena. Besides, he said, he taught class on Wednesdays.

I knew Keker well enough to be straight with him. Soon after Gesell's scheduling order, I approached him in his office.

"Look," I said, "I'll try not to sound too eager." I wanted to argue the motion. I knew the facts and the law. I had no other commitments. I could do it. The downside required no elaboration, for Keker knew it as well as I did. I had never before so much as opened my mouth in a courtroom, and *United States v. North* seemed a somewhat high-profile place to make my debut. After a quick conference with Bromwich and Zornow—whom I had primed (well, begged, really) to back me—Keker told me to go ahead. He said he would tell Walsh later.

The next several days passed in a blur of frantic preparations, though the time included a weekend in Phoenix, which I spent worrying whether an East Coast snowstorm would prevent my return. So relieved was Keker to have the subpoena out of his hands that he would not even schedule a moot court—a practice session—until the afternoon of Tuesday, January 24, the day before my argument. Shortly after noon on that day, almost a dozen of my colleagues trooped into our familiar posts around the conference table. But instead of taking my usual place, I moved to the head, set my papers on an overturned trash can and, suppressing a nervous giggle, began my spiel.

"May it please the Court."

Larry Shtasel, my best friend, looked like he'd just chewed on a lemon. It broke my concentration.

"What was wrong with that?" I asked, stunned that I made a faux pas so quickly.

" 'May it please the Court'?" Shtasel repeated. "This isn't the Supreme Court. Why don't you just say 'good morning'?"

At that Mike Bromwich cut in. "That's not what Walsh told me. The first time I argued in this case, I said 'good morning,' and Walsh told me afterwards I was 'pretty informal.' " Shtasel was incredulous. This set off a round of debate on the proper way to begin an argument, a subject of about as much concern to judges as the lawyers' seating arrangements—none. Eventually I interrupted this scholarly debate. "Hello?" I reclaimed their attention.

The rehearsal went well. Since I had spent the last week gorging myself on legal precedents that I had been gathering for more than a year, I figured I knew more about the law than my colleagues. None of their questions threw me, and I handled myself okay.

As the session closed, Keker instructed me to avoid lengthy speeches or fancy rhetoric. "He'll have read the briefs," Keker said. "Don't get cute. When he asks you something, be sure to give him a straight answer."

As we were walking out, David Zornow offered some aesthetic

advice. Gesturing at my chest, he said, "Just don't wear that pimp tie." Zornow did not share my fondness for Italian fashion.

Nervous puttering absorbed the rest of my afternoon until an uncomfortable-looking Keker padded into my office at around 5 P.M.

"I've got some bad news for you," he said. "Judge Walsh doesn't want you to do this argument. He thinks Gesell will be offended seeing someone your age."

"I'm not surprised," I said, and I wasn't. Walsh spent, I thought, an inordinate amount of time speculating about the emotions of Judge Gesell—not what the judge would *do,* but how he would *feel.* This was all right, but I believed Gesell could not have cared less who stood before him. The judge often said he needed "help" from lawyers in oral arguments, and I could not believe he worried about who gave it to him.

With the trial less than a week away, I knew Keker had greater concerns than me, but I decided to press him.

"John, I really want you to go to bat for me on this one. I'm ready. I know the issues. It's just not fair," I said. Was I groveling? You bet.

"I know," he said. "I know." Then he began rubbing his face with the weariness of one unused to decision-making by committee. He paced my tiny office and pointed to a beautiful bouquet of flowers perched on my file cabinet.

"What's that?" he asked distractedly.

I started to laugh. "I don't know if you want to know.

"Amy sent them to me for good luck for tomorrow."

"All right, all right," Keker said, and trooped back for an appeal to Walsh.

The next fifteen minutes passed like an eternity. Should I continue to prepare? Should I storm off? Mostly I did nothing.

Finally Keker reappeared in my doorway. He held his arm aloft like a Roman emperor weighing the fate of a gladiator and, after a pause, gave me a thumbs up. Then he pointed at me.

"Now don't fuck up."

KEKER'S damaged left elbow gave a small, almost jaunty flap as I followed him into Courtroom Six the next morning. Keker, I noticed, wore a gray suit with erratic red pinstripes and one of his most exotic blue ties, which bore a design looking like it had been stenciled by a freethinking child. In contrast, I had heeded Zornow's counsel: navy suit, white shirt, and painfully restrained red tie. Outside the courtroom Zornow had grabbed it, inspected it for a moment, and nodded sagely.

Every trial establishes its own rhythms, and in the ten months since indictment the North case had set its own cadence as well. The government always arrived first, usually about fifteen minutes before the opening, and its lawyers walked slowly down the center aisle past the seven rows of wooden benches and then through the yard-high swinging wood gate that marked "the well." Walsh invariably took the seat at the left front of the rectangular table set at a right angle to Judge Gesell's thronelike bench. Others followed in his wake, Bromwich behind Walsh, Zornow at the rear head of the table, and Keker opposite Walsh on the right side. On January 25, I took my place in back of Keker.

The Williams & Connolly swagger extended to the dangerous precision with which they timed their arrival in court. Two minutes before the appointed hour, Barry Simon, invariably bearing two litigation bags the size of fire hydrants, would patter into the well and take the lead seat at the far right of the defense table. Though clearly the chief defense counsel, Brendan Sullivan ceded the place of honor to his colleague, as he did virtually all of the talking at the pretrial sessions. In the only major change in the defense team since I first laid eyes on them in the hearing before Judge Parker in March of 1987, they had abandoned their pretense of lean staffing on the case. Three more lawyers followed the leading pair: two associates, Nicole Seligman and John Cline, and one fairly senior partner, Terrence O'Donnell. The latter attorney attended every court session, but he appeared uniquely functionless in the operation of the defense camp. Mystified by his role, we at the OIC privately began calling O'Donnell "Hankie"—for the dapper triangle of silk that always peeked out of his jacket's breast pocket.

North followed his squad of lawyers into the room and moved at a more leisurely pace. In the almost two years since the session before Judge Parker, he had assumed the easy grace of a celebrity. Even accompanied by two bodyguards, he found ways to display his legendary courtesy, contriving to hold open the courtroom door for any woman within ten paces and flashing his gap-toothed smile to the world at large. His suits fit him with the precision of a department store mannequin, and his ties always featured an excruciatingly symmetrical dimple in the center of the knot. If the case was taking its toll, I didn't see it.

Gesell was prompt. On this Wednesday morning, he bounded to his seat at the apogee of the oak bench and announced that he had issued an order in one of the several minor pretrial matters that still needed to be resolved. Walsh had meetings scheduled with administration officials that morning, but, ever respectful of Gesell, he had planned to seek permission to be excused from the hearing rather than simply not show up. But Gesell was talking so fast that Walsh never had the chance to ask to leave.

"All right," Gesell said to Keker. "I'll hear you on the motion."

Keker arose and spoke from his place. "Your Honor," he said, "Mr. Jeffrey Toobin will argue for the government on the 17(c) subpoena motion."

"Very well," the judge said, shuffling papers.

Two final thoughts flashed through my consciousness as I gathered the thick black binder that would serve as my crutch at the lectern. My mind first went back to a videotape I remembered from law school featuring the late Irving Younger, a legendary judge, law professor, and trial lawyer (for a time at Williams & Connolly). Younger was describing attorneys' first appearances in court and the various fates he had seen on these maiden voyages. But one thought, Younger said gravely, united all of these counsel as they took that first step to the podium, one wish gave them a small plot of common ground. " 'Please, God,' " Younger quoted this lawyers' prayer, " 'don't let me throw up.' "

The nearly invisible smile that this thought evoked allowed me to camouflage the second emotion, one that grabbed at me even as it clashed with the prosecutor's cynical savoir faire I had tried so hard to cultivate. My second thought was that this was the proudest moment of my life.

"Good morning, Your Honor, and may it please the Court." So

had I chosen to resolve the scholarly debate that attended my rehearsal.

"In the course of his duties at the National Security Council," I continued, "Oliver North used and kept spiral notebooks. He used them to take notes on meetings and conversations. He used them to assist in reconstructing events, and he used them to dictate memoranda of presidential and other meetings. The government has sought a trial subpoena for production of these notebooks, and the defendant has objected, principally on Fifth Amendment grounds."

It was as close as I came to a speech because Gesell jumped in with his first question.

"Well," Gesell said, "the first question I have for you with respect to that is what makes you think these are presidential records covered by the Presidential Records Act?"

We had asserted in our brief that because North used the notebooks in the course of his duties at the NSC, they actually belonged to the federal government. Congress passed the Presidential Records Act of 1978 in its anger at President Nixon's attempt to control his papers after he left office. Starting with the president inaugurated in 1981, the law said, the federal government would own any "documentary materials . . . created" in the executive office of the president. Under a body of law called the "collective entity doctrine," individuals may not assert their Fifth Amendment rights in refusing to produce papers that belong to a "collective entity"—like a corporation, a labor union, or a government. Thus, under our reasoning, the Fifth Amendment offered North no shelter from our demand for the return of this government property.

I answered Gesell, "Because the Presidential Records Act defines what's covered by the Presidential Records Act"—inartful phrasing, to be sure.

But Gesell had a more specific question in mind. The judge observed that these records were created at the National Security Council. Wasn't the NSC a separate agency from the executive office of the president—and thus not covered by the Presidential Records Act?

Hearing Gesell's words, I thought to myself that I would have kissed Dan Meltzer if he had been handy. In the final stages of drafting our brief, the professor had raised that very question. Was the NSC part of the executive office of the president? Of course, I said to him, where else would it be? But Meltzer had pushed me to find a citation to that effect, a task that I completed grudgingly. Now, thanks to Meltzer's prodding, I had the statute on the tip of my tongue.

"At 3 United States Code, section 101, there's a note that explicitly includes the National Security Council within the executive office of the president," I told the judge.

"Where is that found? I'm unaware of that," Gesell said, fishing for a pencil. "Give me the citation." I repeated the number of the statute.

Then the white-haired, red-faced judge flashed me the smile that every reporter covering the trial compared, at one point or another, to Santa Claus. "All right, thank you," he said. "I didn't mean to interrupt you but I've got a few questions like that that I want to get clear as we go along." I exhaled.

Yet as my argument proceeded, Gesell gradually underlined his skepticism for our position. He noted the tangled precedents on the legal question and pressed me on why we wanted to bother with the issue at this late date. He appeared to be searching for a way to dispose of it.

"What evidence have you got," he asked, "that there's anything in these spiral notebooks, if they exist, which is relevant and material?" He knew, of course, that I could not tell him what was in the notebooks. That was why we wanted to see them. "Well," Gesell said, "in other words, you hope to find something."

"Well—," I started.

"Is that a fair statement?" he demanded, still a fierce cross-examiner twenty-five years after he tried his last case.

"It's a fair statement," I replied, "to say that we don't know the details of what's in these notebooks."

"All right," Gesell concluded, "and there's nothing specific you can tell me that you have evidence of what's in there."

"We do not know the contents of these notebooks," I confessed.

Barry Simon sprung to the lectern and offered the four words with which he began almost every argument.

"Very briefly, Your Honor," he began, and it rarely was. Here, however, Gesell let him go pretty much uninterrupted. Simon began by stating that "we don't concede the existence or possession of any documents." This evoked snickers from the press gallery, and I could imagine the reason. Fawn Hall had told our office that she had seen North's notebooks stacked in Brendan Sullivan's office. Although I did not know for sure, I assumed that, as part of his immunity deal with Congress, North had turned over the notebooks to the House and Senate investigators and some portions, in turn, had been publicly released. (That was, in fact, the case.) Now Simon, as was his right, refused to concede the "existence" of documents that all the reporters had seen—though we at the government's table had not.

I offered a brief rebuttal, but the tide seemed headed North's way. My ability to come up with a prompt answer to Gesell's first question did earn me respectful treatment for the rest of the argument. I grew comfortable replying to the judge, but I could tell I was in a squeeze. Gesell had already decided several difficult legal issues in the case—most of them in our favor—and any one of them might give North grounds for appeal if he were convicted. Here, we were asking for another close ruling to go our way. It did not look like it would.

As the team walked through the winter chill back to Thirteenth Street, I listened to my peers tell me I had done well under difficult circumstances.

"Good job," said Zornow, who retained his New Yorker's bluntness. "You're gonna lose."

I did. Just two days after the argument, Cathy Clay, our gravelly voiced, five-foot-tall document specialist, ran into my office and jabbed a freshly photocopied six-page Gesell opinion at me. As the official conduit for all papers arriving at the OIC, Clay exercised a diplomatic touch in deciding which lawyer deserved the first look at them. These I saw first. "Sorry, kid," she growled.

The opinion displayed Gesell at his most shrewd. He noted the confused legal precedents on the Fifth Amendment issues, so he focused his ruling on what he called our inadequate factual showing—our failure to identify just what the notebooks said. This shift in emphasis protected him against any realistic hope for an appeal by our side, because Gesell knew that appeals courts, while quick to disagree with district courts' legal theories, rarely quibbled with what they call "findings of fact." Thus, as with the judge's rebuffs to

North's *Kastigar* strategy, he was again angling to keep the case out of the hands of the court of appeals.

Gesell also made clear in his opinion that if North took the stand in his own defense he would have to fork over the notebooks to us, because a defendant who testifies at his own trial waives all Fifth Amendment rights. Gesell probably suspected, as did we, that Sullivan could not resist unveiling to the jury the voice that held the whole nation in thrall. Thus, Gesell thought, the prosecution would in any event see the notebooks in due course; why should he stretch the law to give us a head start?

Of course, all of those explanations made eminent sense, but they did not quell my disappointment at losing my first argument. I took some small pleasure in a sentence Gesell buried in a footnote: "The NSC is part of the executive office of the president. 3 U.S.C. Sec. 101 . . ." At least the judge had listened to *something* I had to say. And, as Keker told me, the notebooks subpoena had forced W & C to defend their ground for a change—instead of the endless rounds of our own retreats, whether on CIPA, severance, or simply more delay. Now, he said, the coast was clear. All that remained was the trial.

CHAPTER ELEVEN

The Drop Dead List

The last round of pretrial CIPA battles with the administration took the greatest psychological toll because it began when we thought we had left these problems behind us. Hadn't we done all this already? Did we have to live with even more uncertainty? After all this time, couldn't we just *get on with it*?

The administration's new spirit of accommodation in light of the Reagan and Bush subpoenas seemed initially to have resolved most of the classified information problems in the case. Recognizing that a trial would happen, the administration instead turned its attention to establishing a list of certain subjects that it regarded as absolutely "nondisclosable." In late January the "drop dead list," as it came to be called, included about ten categories of information.

But in the last days of January the intelligence agencies' lawyers began urging us to obtain one final ruling from Gesell stating that these "drop dead" subjects could never be disclosed during the trial. We believed that the judge's many prior orders on CIPA had already done just that. Why, we asked the administration, should we make Gesell—who was, at this point, as sick of CIPA as anyone—revisit these settled issues? But we have to be *sure*, said the agencies, and they ultimately prevailed on our day-to-day liaison with them, the former Davis Polk associate Chris Mixter, to do their bidding. So, at the behest of the agencies, Mixter began submitting requests for Gesell to "modify" his previous orders to make absolutely certain that these subjects would not be disclosed.

Gesell would have none of it. He had issued half-a-dozen orders relating to CIPA already, and he was not going to start repeating himself to accommodate the paranoid fantasies of what he called the "security gurus." As Zornow squeezed next to me in Al Stansbury's car outside the courthouse one day in early February, he said, "I feel sick—I really do."

Zornow, as he readily admitted, was something of a hypochondriac, but in this case the knot in my own stomach was more than just a sympathetic pain. On that day Zornow, Bromwich, Keker, and I sat in morose silence for the short ride back to Thirteenth Street.

When we returned to Thirteenth Street, Keker told Walsh it was "nut-cutting time." It had been Keker's duty to stand at the podium each day and absorb Gesell's wrath after the judge read Mixter's splenetic calls for changes in the CIPA orders. Keker said Gesell had ruled as fairly as we could expect. If the OIC appealed any of Gesell's CIPA rulings at this point, Keker said, "I'm going home to California."

He pleaded with Walsh, "Don't you understand? These people [in the intelligence agencies] are insatiable. They'll never be satisfied. If we take this appeal, and win it, even then they'll still have problems."

As Jim Wieghart bluntly put it, "If the Justice Department wants to pull the plug on this case, let them do it.

"But don't *you* do it, Judge," he told Walsh.

"Look," Wieghart continued, "Gesell remembers the Pentagon Papers case. He heard all these same agencies say that the sky was falling and all these terrible things would happen if he let them publish it. So Gesell stopped publication, but the Supreme Court reversed him and let it all come out—and not a goddamned thing happened. He's still pissed about that.

"Hell," Wieghart added, his newspaperman's voice filled with disgust, "I've yet to see a real secret in this case."

Keker offered a compromise solution. We would make one last try to persuade Gesell to rule out the drop dead list, except this time the OIC would prepare the motion without involving the intelligence agencies. We would phrase the motion in our own words, and, most importantly, abandon the shrill tone that our latest pleadings had adopted. Mixter, whom I half-jokingly accused of developing Stockholm syndrome for identifying with his captors in the intelligence agencies, said Gesell had become a hopeless case and an appeal was our only hope. Walsh agreed to try Keker's approach.

As we left Walsh's office, Keker told me to draft the new motion. "Remember," he said, "the tone will mean everything here. Be nice."

As I sat down to work on the project with John Barrett, I made my first alteration in the atmospherics by changing the title that Mixter had been using. His motions demanded "modifications" of Gesell's orders; mine asked for "clarification." We then turned to the drop dead list itself. The list, as previously submitted to Gesell, included lots of vague, open-ended phrases like "operational methodology" and "related topics." I struck all those words and honed the categories down to what I understood to be the nub of the agencies' concerns.

Then, later that night, Walsh rushed into Keker's office to say that he had learned that just as we had become fed up with the administration, so they now felt the same way about us. Walsh said that on the following day, February 8, the Justice Department would be filing its own motion asking Gesell to reopen the entire CIPA procedure and start from scratch in evaluating which documents would be admissible and which would not. If Gesell agreed, of course, this would delay the trial for weeks, if not months. Though the prospects for an explosion that would destroy the case never looked higher, we all viewed this coming clash with a certain amount of relief. At least now we would end the pretense of an alliance with the administration—and join the battle against it.

The court session the next day, February 8, began auspiciously. Gesell said that the brief we had submitted that morning—the toned-down version of the drop dead list prepared by Keker, Barrett, and me—looked promising. The judge said he thought he could live with it. Saltzburg, the Virginia professor who worked with Stern at the OIC, was now a deputy assistant attorney general representing the administration in the North case. Gesell asked Saltzburg what was wrong with our list. Were there even more topics, additional areas, that had to be kept off-limits?

"Yes," said Saltzburg.

"Why don't you mention them now?" Gesell asked. "What are they?"

"The reason I don't, Your Honor," Saltzburg said, "is these are—"

Gesell was almost too disgusted to speak. He knew why Saltzburg couldn't say what the new topics were. "You don't *know* what they are," said the judge.

Saltzburg conceded that he did not. "The specific items, I do not know what they are." The administration was objecting to our version of the drop dead list on the grounds that it was underinclusive— but declining to say what subjects should be added to it. Keker was right. They *were* insatiable.

Gesell gave Saltzburg his most patronizing grin. "Yes. Well, you see it's very difficult for me to rule on them."

Saltzburg tried. No one on our staff really blamed him for the unreasonable positions he was compelled to take. Saltzburg stood, we knew, at the end of a long line of administration officials who could make their outrageous demands outside of Judge Gesell's penetrating gaze. "If I knew," Saltzburg said, "I would state them for you right now. I don't." It was a pathetic display.

When Saltzburg finished, it was the defense's turn to speak. For once it was Brendan Sullivan and not Barry Simon who arose when the time came for the defense to give its view.

Sullivan urged Gesell to think about his client. Oliver North, Sullivan said, "worked in a secret world. Sixteen hours a day for four years. Everything he did was secret. Everything he thought was secret. Maybe five percent of his work was not secret."

Then, pausing for effect, Sullivan wheeled at the podium and addressed the "gurus" who were assembled in the back of the courtroom. "It's coming out," Sullivan almost yelled, referring to the secrets that they held so dear. "I'm warning you, it's coming out. Listen to me. Read my lips."

Then he returned his attention to Gesell. "It's coming out," Sullivan said, "because I believe you're dedicated to fairness and you're not going to let this man hang as a scapegoat in this case."

Gesell was moved. "I've said so," the judge muttered.

So the conflict between the OIC and the administration was now officially joined. Gesell said he would sign our latest motion, but he would do no more. If the Justice Department tried to appeal any of his rulings, the judge said that was its business. As far as he was concerned, on tomorrow morning, Thursday, February 9, jury selection would continue, with both sides exercising their peremptory challenges. Gesell would then swear in the jury and allow opening statements to begin in the afternoon.

All this would happen, Gesell said dryly, as long as the court of appeals did not tell him to do otherwise.

THE ability to pick a jury ranks as one of the most prized—and most claimed—skills in lawyers' repertoires. The talent is prized because the right jury can more than compensate for other failings; lawyers never care why they win as long as they do win. Shibboleths predominate in the received wisdom of jury selection. The ideal prosecution juror is said to be a little old Lutheran lady in pearls—quick to judge and slow to forgive. Defense lawyers seek out men with mustaches or beards—indicating a taste for independence, iconoclasm, and perhaps rebellion.

In all cases, lawyers subject these truisms to exceptions, and in the trial of Oliver North, their value bordered on negligible. Prosecutors generally look for jurors who unquestioningly obey authority. But in this case, such a world view might lead to sympathy for the defendant, who would be asserting that he was just following orders. So, too, defense lawyers incline toward those on the political Left. But here the defendant was a hero of the Right, and liberals would not share North's belief in the contra cause. In the end, in this case, as ultimately in most others, the lawyers went with their gut instincts and hoped for the best.

Jury selection in the North case veered close to the norm in that it offered a panel of citizens their first chance to fall in love with a judge. Jurors almost always look to the judge as a voice of sanity and fairness. A judge's voice will never impart that urgent sense of need, of pleading, that fills every lawyer's word to the jury. Jurors sense that, unlike the lawyers, the judge wants nothing from them. A judge will usually treat them with respect, even affection, and welcome them into a benign conspiracy of the only unbiased people in the courtroom.

Few did this better than Gerhard Gesell, who charmed the nervous people who found themselves under such unusual scrutiny.

"Now," said Gesell to one Ms. Marks in a typical exchange, "you say that you get your news from conversation with friends and *The Washington Post*."

"Well," the potential juror answered, "the only thing I read in *The Washington Post* is the funnies."

Gesell, fascinated, asked, "Which one do you like?"

" 'Peanuts.' "

The judge confided, "I kind of like 'Li'l Abner.' Do you read 'Li'l Abner'?"

"No," said the now-smiling Ms. Marks, "mostly just 'Dagwood' and 'Peanuts.' "

"Yes," the judge answered, seemingly lost in thought, "Mark Trail is in great trouble now," referring to a fairly obscure figure in the *Post* funnies and earning a rich laugh from the press gallery. Returning to the subject, Gesell said, "I gather from what you're saying here that you . . . never heard of Colonel North?"

"I heard my girlfriend mention him once."

And so it went—for almost two weeks. The biggest surprise of the jury selection process came in the hard line that North's lawyers took in excusing anyone who had any real knowledge of the Iran-Contra scandal or North's testimony at the congressional hearings. Under our reading of *Kastigar* and the rules relating to immunity, jurors did not have to be completely ignorant of North's testimony, only possess an open mind about him. But Gesell sustained Sullivan's objections to all jurors who had more than the most rudimentary knowledge of the Iran-Contra affair. Keker did not object to this strategy. He, of course, knew nothing of what North said at the hearings, but no one could avoid seeing how popular North became with many of those who did hear him. We at the OIC thought that

Sullivan would seek out those potential jurors who had listened to North. But if Sullivan wanted to excise this group, we would not quarrel with him.

For all that lawyers claim that they spend jury selection sizing up the jurors, they also use the time to ingratiate themselves with them. Brendan Sullivan, the snarling scourge of Congress, was now purring questions like, "Do you like to go to the movies?" Keker played it straighter, though he, too, was working the angles. When one young man described himself as a big Washington Redskins fan, Keker asked how much he would be influenced if the team's quarterback, Doug Williams, testified at the trial. (Ever since North's pep speech to the Skins before the Super Bowl, we had nervously anticipated several character witnesses drawn from the team.) The young juror, as Keker knew he would, responded that the evidence would make no special impact; Williams was "just a man," after all. Keker thus inoculated this juror for any potential Williams appearance and even raised the suspicion that such an appearance would look like pandering.

Mind games like that one occupied the lawyers through the first week in February until Gesell assembled a corps of forty-five "qualified" potential jurors on the afternoon of February 8. The following morning, all of them reassembled in the jurors' lounge, so that they could be called back into the courtroom and both sides allowed to exercise their preemptory challenges—that is, their right to disqualify jurors not "for cause," but for any reason they chose.

The tense ritual began when the bailiff led the first twelve jurors into the box at about 10 A.M. on the morning of the ninth. Barry Simon named two of the jurors, who were excused and then replaced with two more. Simon rejected the one white person among the forty-five, a woman in a peasant dress who we (and probably W & C) guessed had a "U.S. Out of Central America" poster in her apartment. Keker removed one juror, then dropped another who retained, we thought, an excessive fondness for his years in the military. The process continued until, as the federal rule allowed, the defense exercised ten preemptories and the government six.

At the end, twelve jurors and six alternates were arrayed to Gesell's right, all with the hesitant smiles of students on the first day of school.

GESELL now faced a bizarre dilemma. The time was 10:45 on Thursday morning, February 9. The jury was selected, and Keker and Sullivan had their opening statements ready. Earlier in the morning, however, the Justice Department had made its motion demanding that Gesell delay the trial and start the CIPA process all over again. Gesell denied the motion as soon as he took the bench at 9:30, but he knew that Justice planned to appeal. At this moment the judge had not yet heard of any stay entered by the court of appeals, so he was, technically, free to begin. But the appeals court had had only about an hour to read the papers and make up its mind; a stay might still be issued at any moment. Should Gesell start the trial or not?

The faces of both Keker and Sullivan bore the strain of the legal maelstrom in which they were living. Keker did not even know which way he wanted Gesell to go. Of course, Keker longed for the opportunity to start the case. But if Gesell swore in the jury and *then* the court of appeals granted a stay, North might be able to argue that a second trial constituted "double jeopardy" under the Fifth Amendment.

Gesell remained calm and called a brief recess. When the judge returned to the bench at 11:30 A.M., he announced that the court of appeals had entered an "administrative stay" on the North trial. That meant the appeals court simply wanted time to gather the papers and think about what to do. Administrative stays sometimes lasted as little as an hour, so Gesell might still be able to start the trial after lunch. The judge thus dismissed everyone until 2 P.M.

When we reconvened, it appeared that Judge Gesell had not digested his sandwich any better than the jittery lawyers. With the administrative stay still in place, even Gesell couldn't stand the tension. He decided he would not swear in the jury and would, instead, send everyone home. "I see no reason," he said, "to keep counsel on sort of a tenterhooks as to whether or not they're going to be making an opening. . . . I think we ought to shut down until Monday and come together Monday and see if on Monday there's any news.

"So I think," he concluded with a weary smile, "the best thing to do is just take a vacation. I really believe that all of us perhaps would benefit with a good night's sleep."

The next few days featured some of the most frenzied legal maneuvering and political posturing of the case, with events moving so fast that we sometimes had trouble distinguishing the good news from the bad. Some of us did not even know what outcome we wanted. Our frustration with the uncertainties surrounding the trial left many of us hoping as much for finality as victory—for this final conflict over classified information to settle the issue of whether this case would go to trial, one way or the other.

The first news awaited us on our return to Thirteenth Street after Gesell dismissed us on Thursday afternoon. At 4 P.M., the court of appeals denied the stay sought by Justice, a victory made all the sweeter by the presence on the appeals panel of Laurence Silberman, the conservative judge who had struck down the Independent Counsel law as unconstitutional. If we could coax Silberman to our side, we thought, we must be right. Justice would, apparently, play out the string with a plea for the Supreme Court to stay the trial, but no one regarded that possibility as very likely. We had won.

We all felt we should have. Our argument had an enviable simplicity. The Independent Counsel statute, which the Supreme Court had since upheld by reversing Silberman's earlier opinion, gave Walsh's office the absolute right to conduct the North trial as well as any appeals in it; that is what, the Supreme Court held, an "independent" prosecutor does. As for classified information, the OIC fully conceded that domain to the administration. But here we had an ace in the hole. CIPA included a specific provision—section 6(e)—that said if the attorney general wanted to prevent any classified material from being disclosed at a trial, he need only say so by identifying the off-limits information in a "6(e) affidavit." We did not question the attorney general's right to file a 6(e) affidavit. He could do it at any time and bind us with his judgments. But, we argued, the attorney general could protect classified information *only* by submitting a 6(e) affidavit and not by appealing our case.

The obvious question was, why didn't the Justice Department just put the drop dead list in an affidavit and calm the administration worries once and for all? Why, indeed, hadn't the gurus filed the affidavit at the *start* of the CIPA process and spared everyone the agony that followed? The answer lies in the politics that dominated the CIPA process in the North case from beginning to end. The administration never wanted to file a 6(e) affidavit because doing so would have forced it to commit to paper the final, specific list of secrets that would cause the North case to drop dead. Had the gurus submitted their list and the case collapsed, they knew the congressional intelligence committees would take a hard look at that list. Though by February the list had been shorn of its most outrageous fictional secrets, it still contained material that would evoke only yawns for any reasonably astute observer of the world scene. Congressmen and senators would ask, "You killed the North case for *that?*"—and smell cover-up.

So the administration tried to hedge. Instead of just ruling out the drop dead list, the Justice Department sought to force us to appeal Gesell's CIPA orders and, when we wouldn't, tried to appeal those rulings itself. This way, the administration got to complain about Gesell's "procedures" and "lack of adequate safeguards," but it never had to bite the bullet and identify just what secrets were at risk and why they mattered. The court of appeals, not to mention Judge Gesell, didn't buy it.

The Justice Department did appeal to the Supreme Court, and a certain gallows humor took over as we commenced writing our brief. If we lost and the Supreme Court allowed the Justice Department to appeal, the North case would descend into an endless swamp of appellate proceedings. But if we *won* and the Supreme Court let the case proceed, that might be even worse. The Justice Department's 6(e) affidavit might forbid the disclosure of so much material that Gesell, concerned about North's ability to defend himself, would dismiss the case. Either way, the prognosis looked grim.

Friday, a team of Geoff Berman, Evan Wolfson, Bill Treanor (another long-time member of Struve's legal group), and I started writing. As the most skilled typist in the bunch, I assumed the position behind the word processor and pecked out our joint effort with my three colleagues huddled around me. We knew that the Supreme Court—and particularly the William Rehnquist court—demonstrated an almost Pavlovian reaction to administration claims of dangers to national security, so our brief hit repeatedly on the attorney general's authority to file the affidavit and stanch any flow of secrets. "The attorney general," we said, "at all times retains unquestioned authority to prevent any harm simply by prohibiting the disclosure of appropriately classified information."

The solicitor general's office, which represented the Justice Department in the Supreme Court, told us it would be filing its request for a stay on Saturday morning, February 11, so we prepared to receive its brief, answer a few of its arguments in our papers, and file our completed response at about noon. The solicitor general had given the case, number A-643, the cumbersome title of "*United States v. Oliver North; Dick Thornburgh, attorney general of the United States, Applicant.*" I changed the cover of our brief to reflect what I regarded as the true nature of the conflict before the Supreme Court: "*A-643, Dick Thornburgh, Attorney General v. Lawrence E. Walsh, Independent Counsel.*" Might as well, I thought, go out with a bang.

Saturday, February 11, was the day I gave up. The case against Oliver North, I decided that night, was never going to trial. I had kept the faith through the pardon watch, the severance, the loss of the September 1988 trial date, and the untold CIPA crises, but this, I believed, was the end. In the glow of the first weeks of the Bush presidency, the sacrifice of North's trial seemed almost appropriate to the mood of the country, a final cutting of ties to one unfortunate legacy of the Reagan years.

McIntosh suggested that I might be hoarse from crying wolf for the past two years. No, I said, this was different. This was *it.*

EXCEPT that it wasn't. Unknown at the time to the OIC, the key event had taken place the previous day, Friday, February 10, when Senators David Boren and William Cohen, chairman and vice chairman, respectively, of the Senate intelligence committee, wrote Attorney General Thornburgh a letter informing him that they had scheduled an appearance for him before them on February 21. The letter asked Thornburgh to "tell the committee precisely what concerns for the protection of intelligence prompted" the dismissal of the first two charges in *United States v. Oliver L. North*. "In light of recent events," the letter went on, "the committee wishes to expedite its inquiry." (In the best congressional style, the letter to Thornburgh was soon leaked to the press.)

Thus the administration knew on Friday that it was going to have to start defending its conduct in the North trial—and soon. Late Saturday night, while I was whining to McIntosh, Steve Saltzburg and one of his Justice Department peers, acting with the urgency of those who have received instructions from on high, summoned Keker and Barrett to discuss a "compromise." The Justice team suddenly wanted only a face-saving escape from its fix. Now, once again, the administration wanted to escape blame for ending the North trial. The result of this hasty collaboration was a nine-page joint motion of the Independent Counsel and Department of Justice for, as the title of the submission styled it, "Final Pretrial Clarification Concerning Classified Information." All Justice demanded, it turned out, was for Gesell to state for no less than the third time that the drop dead list was off-limits. In return, we agreed to state that the "attorney general will have an opportunity during the trial to file a CIPA section 6(e) affidavit that will finally and conclusively bar disclosure of specific classified information"—something that we ourselves had already said half-a-dozen times.

Shortly after noon on Sunday, Barrett rushed the filing over to the courthouse where Judge Gesell's clerk read it to him at his farm outside Washington. With the Justice Department and the OIC now allied, the administration could end its bid in the Supreme Court and the case could finally get started.

As part of the deal for the joint motion, Saltzburg had agreed to call the clerk's office at the Supreme Court to withdraw the Justice Department's request for a stay on Sunday morning, just after we filed the DOJ-OIC brief. With no motion for a stay pending, the North case could then proceed on Monday morning. But, as Saltzburg later admitted, he forgot to make the call to the Supreme Court. And at 3 P.M. on Sunday, Frank Lorson of the Supreme Court clerk's office telephoned me to say that "Chief Justice Rehnquist has entered a stay in the North case."

"You're kidding," I said.

He wasn't. As Rehnquist's order slid out of the fax machine, I could scarcely believe it. Here we were on the brink of a deal with Justice. Better than that, we *had* a deal, and now the Supreme Court was gumming up the works. The news of the day would now headline the Supreme Court stay, and that would open the door to further haggling with Justice. Rehnquist's order offered one silver lining, in that he only stayed "trial proceedings" in the case and not *all* proceedings. This way, Gesell still had the authority to issue the final CIPA order we sought in the joint motion and *then* Justice could withdraw its request for a stay.

And that, in effect, is what happened. It took a few days longer than if Saltzburg had remembered to make his phone call to the Supreme Court, and Gesell made some cranky noises during court sessions at the beginning of the following week, but he ultimately did agree to issue an order along the lines of the one we requested on Sunday afternoon.

On Wednesday, February 15, the Justice Department finally asked the Supreme Court to lift its stay and the High Court did so within an hour of receiving the request. "I am pleased," said Attorney General Thornburgh's prepared statement, "that a mechanism has been developed that will permit the trial to go forward while ensuring that I can fulfill the responsibility imposed on me by the Congress to protect the national security interests of the United States." Thornburgh thus played one of the oldest political tricks in the book: he declared victory and walked away.

It was ludicrous. On the brink of a trial the previous Wednesday, we had been subjected to a week of frantic legal and emotional gyrations, and, thanks to the not-so-discreet application of some political heat, we had returned to exactly where we had started. Nothing had changed. *Nothing had changed.*

Except now we had a case to try.

CHAPTER TWELVE

Judges of the Facts

"**B**ring in the jurors." I savored the words. Not only had I doubted whether Judge Gesell would ever say them, but I almost didn't hear them when he did.

The intimate scale of the Gesell courtroom left even OIC staffers scrounging for seats. Only John Barrett avoided this fate. Throughout the trial he was deputized to sit in the back row of the courtroom with the members of the Inter-Agency Group, who were monitoring the proceedings for security breaches. "My spies," Barrett called this dour clique. For the rest of the staff, Larry Shtasel devised a system for apportioning our limited number of trial passes, an arrangement only slightly less complicated than the financing of the arms sales to Iran.

I had no assigned pass for opening day and had to stand with the regular folks or miss the pageant altogether. I arrived at the court-house at 6:55 A.M. on Tuesday, February 21, and still stood no better than ninth place on the line outside Courtroom Six. (As the trial progressed, I was able to finagle regular access to the courtroom.)

The size of the courtroom also limited the number of reporters, a fact that certain media eminences learned, to their chagrin, only after they showed up. One columnist from *The Washington Post* threw a tantrum when told he could not pass the threshold. A far more dignified figure was cut by the reedy white-haired gentleman who followed only five minutes behind me. Though probably the most distinguished trial journalist in the nation, Murray Kempton ceded the single *Newsday* pass to the paper's beat reporter. Kempton, dapper in a three-piece suit and a heavily starched cotton shirt, stood on line like any other citizen—except that he was reading a battered volume of Proust.

Even on this first day, Gesell had to settle a few final disputes before he could allow the trial to begin.

"Good morning," the judge said to the citizens before him, and they answered "Good morning," in the sweet sing-song of eighteen voices speaking at once.

Gesell offered a few gentle words of instructions—"You're now judges. You're judges of the facts. . . . You must not as judges hear one witness or hear another and say, 'Well, that's it,' You must wait until you see all the evidence. . . . I urge you to be prompt . . . each morning at nine-thirty"—and then he turned the stage over to John Keker.

"Thank you, Your Honor," Keker said, "and good morning ladies and gentlemen."

"Good morning," came the smiling response.

The lectern and microphone, usually directly in front of the judge, had been moved this one day to the government's counsel table. Keker could thus face the twelve jurors and six alternates squarely, his body not five feet away from the closest of them.

"Since a picture is worth a thousand words," he began in a serious tone, "I want to start with a word picture. November 21, 1986. It was a Friday about a week before Thanksgiving that year. On November 21, 1986, this gentleman right here, Lieutenant Colonel Oliver North, walked into his office at the Old Executive Office Building—that's the huge building that looks like a wedding cake over there at Seventeenth and Pennsylvania, right next to the White House."

Keker called him Colonel North on that day and throughout the trial. Keker had debated at some length with Bromwich and Zornow about how the prosecution should refer to the defendant. Did "colonel" dignify him too much? Should they try to stick to "Mr."? The trial team ultimately decided that the members of the jury, always sensitive to pretense and false notes, would frown on our making a big deal out of it. Everyone called him Colonel North. So would we.

Colonel North, Keker told the jury, "knew when he walked into his office that the Congress of the United States wanted to know what he had been doing for the last two years. And he knew when he walked into his office that the attorney general of the United States was sending his people to look at records and documents in Colonel North's office that showed what he had been doing for the last two years.

"And Colonel North went into his office," Keker said, his voice picking up speed, "and the first thing he did was take some of those records and change them and make them look like he hadn't been doing what he had been doing for the last two years. And the next thing he did was go over to his file cabinet, and open up the drawer and begin to go through his file cabinet and take out a record and hand it to his secretary. And his secretary fed it into a machine called a shredder, that grinds the record up into little dots that you can't read. . . . And after he had done that for a while, going all through these file cabinets, this drawer, that drawer, he went over to his computer, a computer that was used to send messages to other people—to his bosses, to other people where he worked—and he began to erase the messages that he had in his computer. And then sometime that weekend he smuggled some documents, records, out of his office, and then a couple of days later, he went to see the attorney general of the United States."

Now Keker slowed down, emphasizing each word. North "met with the attorney general and some of his top assistants, and when they asked him questions about something very important for them to know, he lied."

Here Keker took a breath, for both he and the jury needed a respite from the vivid description he had provided. Still speaking slowly, Keker said, "The evidence in this case is going to show that these were crimes and that the reason for these crimes was that Colonel North was covering up crimes he had already committed."

That was his punch line, and now he circled back to begin again. In his first opening statement as a prosecutor, Keker adopted a classic strategy. Pick one image to plant immediately in the jurors' minds, and then let them relax for a little while.

"Let me go back and introduce myself again," Keker continued, "because I haven't seen some of you for a long time." Not only had the examination of the jurors begun three full weeks earlier, but they had all been excused for our last week-long CIPA crisis. "I'm John Keker. With Mr. Michael Bromwich and Mr. David Zornow, we have the honor to present this case on behalf of the United States.

"I want to start by thanking you for your willingness to serve on this important case. I know that at this stage sometimes jurors are a little nervous and apprehensive." Here Keker paused and smiled. "I'm a little nervous," he admitted, and the disarming candor won him understanding nods. "You sit there," he told the jury, "and you worry 'How am I going to remember it all, I don't know what the rules are going to be?' and things like that, but I think you'll find . . . you'll have plenty of time to find out what the evidence is."

Keker then slowly returned to the facts, and began, in his earnest, conversational manner, going through the whole story. Jurors invariably tell lawyers that they try to stuff too much information into their opening statements, but most advocates heed this counsel more in theory than in practice. According to Irving Younger, the two most valuable words of advice a litigator ever hears are "sit down." Keker displayed an admirable restraint in summarizing the case, though, at almost ninety minutes, his opening did begin to drag at the end.

Following his introduction, he gave a very brief account of the struggle in Nicaragua, explaining how the United States government came to support the contra rebels and then how Congress cut off that assistance. "But Oliver North and his bosses," said Keker, "didn't stop supporting the contras in this war." When Congress got suspicious and asked about North's activities, they were "lied to"— first by North and McFarlane, "North's boss," in the fall of 1985 and then by North alone in August of 1986. These people "decided they would place themselves above the law and not tell Congress about Colonel North's activities."

Then Keker moved to the personal enrichment side of the story, the $4,000 in traveler's checks that North received from contra leader Adolfo Calero and then used "like it was his personal piggy bank." North "would go to the Giant [supermarket]. . . . He took his family on a trip and paid for it with Calero's traveler's checks. He wanted new tires for his car. . . ." Keker spoke of the fence, "the gift of [a] $14,000 . . . security system, for Colonel North's home out in Great Falls, Virginia," and North's "very elaborate cover-up of this security system." Keker brought his narrative to a close talking about the disintegration of the Iranian initiative to free the hostages in November 1986. When Congress and the attorney general started asking questions about Iran, Keker said, North first tried to destroy the evidence of his deeds and then he lied again.

At last Keker turned to North as a person—and where he fit into the schemes Keker had outlined. "The person on trial here is Oliver North," Keker said. "It's his guilt or innocence that you'll be asked to decide by your verdict." He added, a touch defensively, "The fact that other people are or may be guilty of some of these same crimes is not a defense in this case." Keker said the jury would hear of North's heroic deeds in the Marines. For those claims, the ex-Marine prosecutor summoned the one rhetorical flourish of his opening: "As a Marine you swear to uphold the Constitution. Being a Marine is an honor, not an excuse. Being a Marine is a responsibility, not a defense.

"Ladies and gentlemen," he concluded, "there is, as it says in the Bible, a time and a place for everything. This is the time for you to be judges, judges of the facts. To do that you have to be fair, but you're also going to have to be firm. . . . For Oliver North, it's a time for judgment. It's a time to decide whether or not he did place himself above the law, whether or not the normal rules at some point stopped applying to him.

"The evidence in this case is going to show that when the time came for Oliver North to tell the truth, he lied. When the time came for Oliver North to come clean, he shredded, he erased, he altered. When the time came for Oliver North to let the light shine in, he covered up.

"When the time comes for you, ladies and gentlemen, to deliberate and reach your verdict, the government will ask you to return a verdict of guilty as to all of those twelve charges. I thank you very much for your attention this morning."

Judge Gesell did not let the silence linger for more than a moment. "Mr. Sullivan?" he said.

"Your Honor," Sullivan answered, "I'll be glad to use the time rather than break for lunch." The time was 11:30, an hour when Gesell ordinarly would begin his lunch recess, which in no event began later than noon. But Sullivan did not want Keker's words echoing in the jurors' ears as they left for the ninety-minute intermission. Yes, Sullivan said, he would use the time.

"I've found over the years," Brendan Sullivan began, that "jurors sometimes spend the first two weeks figuring out who is who." So, he said, since the courtroom "is our workplace, I would like you to know who people are generally." Sullivan identified his four colleagues at the defense table, the court reporters, the deputy clerk, Judge Gesell's law clerk, and the bailiff. He also begged the jury's indulgence for the delays they might have to endure during the trial.

" 'L.A. Law' boggles my mind," Sullivan confided. "I watch that show, and here I am a lawyer. I don't know why I'm interested. And in that one-hour show, they've got three trials going. . . . There are four fist fights, one shooting, and two romantic scenes in forty-five minutes. No wonder we are thrilled in watching shows like that. But TV is not life, as we all know. Life is hard work. There is a lot of boredom in it."

And then, at long last, he turned to his client and Sullivan's smile, which never came easily to his pale, pained face, vanished, rarely to be seen again over the next two months. He summarized North's defense in a single paragraph, announcing each sentence as if it were a point on a list. "You should know early on that the defense says to you: absolutely not guilty to all charges. That's why Colonel North is here.

"He never broke the law. He acted within the law at all times. He followed the instructions of the highest ranking officials of the United States of America. He protected the secrets that he was ordered to protect, to save the lives of many people, many sources, many relationships. That's what he was ordered to do, and he followed his orders as any Marine Corps officer and any officer that worked at the National Security Council.

"He never," Sullivan said, holding his thumb and forefinger about an inch apart, "had this much criminal intent—none, never, never."

Just before the lunch break, he turned to one of a defense attorney's most standard and most effective lines of attack. "This is a criminal courtroom," he said. "The government has an enormous burden, like climbing Mount Everest. They have to prove all of the case beyond a reasonable doubt. Those are the magic words—'beyond a reasonable doubt.' " If the point needed any more emphasis, "I'm going to write that word on there [an easel which he had set up] and ask that you remember it."

In this trial, Sullivan promised that the jurors would be confronted with "a million initials . . . the FBI, the CIA, the NSC . . . and they are going to drive you nuts like they drive me nuts. I'm going to ask you to remember only one, and I made up this one. I made this up, BARD—beyond a reasonable doubt, beyond a reasonable doubt."

After the lunch break, Sullivan worked his way methodically through the indictment. The first four counts relate to "letters that were sent to congressmen," said Sullivan, "not Oliver North's letters. He did not sign the letters. They're charging him with a crime for letters really that his boss sent, McFarlane."

"Now," Sullivan continued, "remember something about McFarlane. He's a cabinet officer—one of the top fifteen most powerful people in the country." Gesturing to North, Sullivan said, "This man is a lieutenant colonel. Think how far the gap is between a lieutenant colonel and a cabinet officer." McFarlane's office, Sullivan said, as he would repeat throughout the trial, was "less than a hundred steps from the president of the United States. That's the man who wrote the letters that the government wants you to convict Oliver North for in this courtroom."

As for the "lies" in August and November 1986, those were "informal" meetings, where there was no transcript taken and no oath sworn. Sullivan answered the shredding charge by saying that North "was told by a cabinet-level officer to clean up the operations. . . . That's a term which means that you take action to protect the secrets at all costs." As for the traveler's checks, North "was entitled to the traveler's checks that he had. He was entitled to spend them the way he did. He kept meticulous records at that time of an accounting."

Having plucked off the counts one by one, Sullivan now described the defendant as a human being, "what makes Oliver North tick." Here Sullivan went through the North biography—altar boy, Naval midshipman, boxing champion, war hero in Vietnam, who, in the words of the citation on his Silver Star medal, acted "with total disregard of the machine gun fire directed at him by the enemy. "The Vietnam experience," Sullivan said, "shaped him, molded him. It does something to you." As a result of his success in the Marine Corps, Sullivan continued, North was rewarded with an assignment to the NSC in 1981.

Lawyers sometimes judge their adversary's effectiveness by how uncomfortable they feel in listening, and, at that point, I, for one, was squirming. Sullivan had fingered all our weak points—the holes in our case—and his portrait of North stirred me, as it must have moved the jury. By God, I hated to admit, this lawyer lived up to his billing.

But then something happened. Brendan Sullivan revealed that he had fallen prey to one of the most common pitfalls of the criminal defense business: spending too much time with the client. Because instead of continuing to hammer away at the flaws in our case, Sullivan shifted gears and gave the jury a seminar on anticommunism, circa 1953. "Communism is easy to remember," he said, "because all the things that we enjoy, communism is just the opposite. No freedom of press. No freedom to worship. Communism calls religion the opiate of the people. No freedom of speech. No freedom to own property. No freedom to do what you want."

Sullivan showed the jury a huge world map and pointed out how the Soviet Union was "taking this country and taking that country, and taking a country here, like a cancer." He dwelled for a while on "communist Cuba," with its "communist runways" for communist airplanes, and then he moved on to "communist Nicaragua," which had its own communist runways. This harangue went on for close to an hour—all John Foster Dulles and no Oliver North. Through this speech the lawyer ostensibly sought to show the motives for North's actions, but Sullivan found himself so wrapped up in ideological rhetoric, that this portion of the opening lost almost all meaning for the issues at hand. One did not have to be a communist sympathizer to find a political address out of place and irrelevant in the courtroom. By the time the defendant returned to Sullivan's story, into the third hour of his opening statement, the lawyer seemed to have lost the jurors.

He did retrieve them in the final moments, when he returned to the facts of the case. As Sullivan surveyed North's last days at the NSC, he claimed that North was told "that if things went bad, if things went real bad, he might have to be a scapegoat. He might have to be the one that's blamed for things, be a fall guy for the president." The president himself, Sullivan claimed, felt that way, because just a few hours after North was fired on November 25, 1986, "something very unusual happened.

"The phone rang, and North answered it," Sullivan said quietly. "It was the president of the United States. The president of the United States said to North, 'You are a true American hero. Thank you,' and hung up.

"Six hours after he was fired," Sullivan mused, letting the words hang in the air. Would the president, came the unspoken questions, do that for a *criminal?* If North had *not* been doing the president's bidding, why did Reagan make that call?

At the end Sullivan contemplated the Marine Corps motto: *semper fidelis,* always faithful. North, Sullivan said, "lives with that Marine Corps motto today. He was always faithful, *semper fidelis,* always faithful to his country, to his commander in chief, to his family, to those whose lives depended on him. And finally you'll see from the evidence that Lieutenant Colonel Oliver North has in the end been abandoned by his government."

Sullivan's powerful peroration told us he would not be playing it safe. He would, it appeared, concede that North committed the acts charged in the indictment but gamble that the jury would absolve him all the same. Sullivan would point the finger up the chain of command—at McFarlane, at Poindexter, even at President Reagan—in the hope that the jury would not permit the buck to stop on North's desk.

Our response was simple—as Keker put it, "The fact that other people are or may be guilty of some of these same crimes is not a defense in this case." But hearing Sullivan's powerful plea for the little guy reminded us that our answer for this jury may have sounded more of tinny legalism than American justice.

''CHAIRMAN HAMILTON,'' said John Keker in his fifth question to our first witness, "In addition to work and education, have you been honored by the Indiana Hall of Fame for basketball playing?"

"Yes," came the humble response from crew-cut Congressman Lee Hamilton, "I'm a member of the Indiana Basketball Hall of Fame."

Keker had, to put it mildly, an unusual style of direct examination. As a career defense attorney, he specialized in cross-examination, where leading questions—that is, questions that suggest their own answer—are permitted. In cross, a lawyer is supposed to draw attention to himself and force the witness to say as little as possible, ideally limiting the target to "yes" and "no," In direct questioning, however, a lawyer attempts to fade into invisibility, allowing the witness, as much as possible, to tell an uninterrupted version of his or her own story. The conventional legal wisdom holds, for example, that the ideal question on direct examination is, "And what happened next?"

Keker possessed many skills, but fading into invisibility was never one of them. He injected himself into direct examination far more than most prosecutors, and tried to keep the proceedings lively, which in this trial was rarely a challenge. Sometimes, if Keker could get away with it, that style meant asking one leading question after another, if only to plow through a boring stretch of testimony. Sometimes it meant asking about a little something that might liven up the jury's day—like learning that this gangly Hoosier could play ball.

But that was not our chief purpose in leading off our witnesses with Lee Hamilton. Prosecutors generally adopt a "horseshoe" strategy in making their cases: concentrate the strong material in the beginning and end of the case, where it might stick more permanently in the jurors' minds, and put the boring or less helpful testimony in the middle. Through Hamilton—a dignified figure of erect carriage and conspicuous integrity—we hoped to humanize the crime of "lying to Congress." North, we wanted to suggest, did not just lie to some marble building, but to this nice man.

From 1984 to 1986, Hamilton served as chairman of the House Permanent Select Committee on Intelligence (HPSCI) and sent some of the letters to which North drafted false responses for McFarlane in the fall of 1985. After exploring with Hamilton the importance of HPSCI's role—overseeing covert action, passing on the intelligence agencies' budgets—Keker asked whether the committee needed "accurate information from executive branch officials?"

"Absolutely," came Hamilton's reply. "We cannot fulfill our responsibility unless we have accurate information from the executive branch."

Hamilton marched through the chronology well enough, the letters to McFarlane in the fall of 1985 and the face-to-face session with North in August 1986. But we needed something more than the straight facts from Hamilton. Sullivan's opening had stressed how North lived in a "secret world," where people trusted their lives to North's confidence. We wanted to establish that the acknowledged sensitivity of North's work did not translate into a license to lie. As Keker previewed in his opening, "Chairman Hamilton will also tell you something . . . that all of you I'm sure learned at your mother's knee. There's a difference between keeping secrets and telling lies. And you don't have to tell lies to keep secrets. And the intelligence committees are set up that way. . . . The need for secrecy is no excuse for lying to Congress. Lying to Congress is a crime."

Hamilton detailed how his committee met in a super-secure "special room on the fourth floor of the United States Capitol building, right under the Capitol dome," how its staff obtained top-level security clearances, how the law placed no information off-limits to their inquiries.

After this recitation, Keker bluntly reached for the heart of the matter. "Chairman Hamilton," he asked, "in our system of government, is there any situation where it's all right just to go ahead and lie to the House intelligence committee?"

"No," said Hamilton, just as Sullivan was rising to object. Keker knew his question called for Hamilton both to speculate and to give a legal conclusion, neither of which he could permissibly do. The judge sustained the objection, but he couldn't, as Keker also knew, unring the bell.

Sullivan's cross-examination of Hamilton began predictably enough, as he established that his letters were to McFarlane, not North, and the answers came not in formal, sworn testimony, but through informal means, like letters. Sullivan, however, soon started moving far afield from the charges against North. He began showing Hamilton some of the classified documents the defense had collected during discovery, specifically requests for information that Hamilton had sent to the CIA from 1984 through 1986 and the answers Hamilton received. Keker repeatedly objected, questioning the relevance of this line of inquiry.

This was the first salvo in a battle that Sullivan and Keker would wage throughout the case. Sullivan had a theory. As he said at a bench conference, "We have a situation with respect to a willful blindness. [Hamilton's committee] knew full well significant amounts of information regarding the very matter that they're inquiring of Colonel North." Hamilton, according to Sullivan, knew what North was doing and was "willing to look the other way," because he didn't want to cross a popular president. Sullivan said CIA officials, too, knew of North's role in Central America, and they were willing to deny any knowledge to Hamilton's committee. It was, in short, all one grand conspiracy: Hamilton, the CIA, and North—except now everyone was pretending only North was involved.

The grand conspiracy theory had one important supporter: Gerhard Gesell. As he made his position known at bench conferences, Gesell said candidly he thought the CIA and the State Department, as well as the NSC, had lied to Congress about Nicaragua throughout the period in question, and, what was more, he thought that Hamilton knew these agencies were not telling the truth. But, according to Gesell, the congressman lacked the political will to protest, so he just accepted the false information.

All of this placed Keker in an extraordinarily difficult bind. He did not want to appear to be defending State and CIA and saying that North was the only malefactor in the whole government; for one thing, Keker himself did not believe it, though he knew Sullivan could point fingers a lot more easily than we could bring charges. Still, as Keker said of the defense, "If they want to call" one of these high-ranking government officials, "and get him to say he knew all this and lied to Congress, I'd love to hear it."

Keker felt his most important mission—indeed his only objective—was to keep the judge and jury focused on Oliver North. Throughout the trial, Keker argued that Sullivan should not be allowed to pursue this line of argument because the grand conspiracy argument was irrelevant to this criminal trial. "I'm ready to believe the CIA doesn't tell the truth about anything," Keker told Gesell early in the case. "I don't want to defend Elliott Abrams, Clair George [the head of covert operations at the CIA] and everybody else in this case. I don't want to prosecute them either," he added. "I would like to deal with Lieutenant Colonel Oliver North, and that's the basis of [my relevance] objection."

Gesell fudged to get through Hamilton's testimony, and allowed Sullivan to probe somewhat outside the precise contours of the case. But the judge did not resolve the larger conflict that would flare throughout the trial: whether the defendant would be permitted to put the whole Reagan administration on trial along with him.

KEKER had one last question for Lee Hamilton. "We've heard that many of the contras were poor people or small farmers." In his opening, Sullivan had sung a lengthy hymn to the heroic labors of the contras. "Were there some contras who caused some of the congressmen concern who were not poor people or small farmers? Such as National Guardsmen?"

Sullivan bounded out of his seat. "Objection."

"Sustained."

Keker tried another tack. "Were there charges of human rights abuses by the contras that caused some congressmen to think that a military solution to the problem in Nicaragua was not the way to go?"

Gesell permitted this question, and Hamilton noted that not all the contras fit the noble profile that Sullivan had given them. Keker wanted the jury to have this thought in mind when the next witness lumbered to the stand, the barrel-chested contra leader Adolfo Calero. Keker did not want the jury to love this contra, because this contra surely did not love Keker.

Calero embodied many of the problems that we faced in our direct case against North. Like many of our witnesses, Calero adored North and loathed us. No prosecutor wants to rely on such a witness, but we had no choice. The indictment charged that North had lied to Meese on November 23, 1986, by stating, among other things, that he, North, had advised Adolfo Calero to open bank accounts in Switzerland to receive the diverted Iranian arms sales proceeds. Further, we needed Calero to establish that he had given North $90,000 in traveler's checks because we charged North with using about $4,000 worth of these for his own purposes.

Keker's objective, then, was to get the facts we needed from Calero and usher him off the stand as quickly as possible. But Calero could not relinquish a stage before a room full of reporters without giving them a speech or two. Keker made the mistake of asking him to "tell the jury . . . something of your background." This prompted a lengthy address about his "American education" that left him "imbued in the ideals of democracy, freedom, and justice" and his struggle against the Sandinistas, who had "intimate ties to the Soviet Union whom I always considered an enemy and to Cuba, Fidel Castro."

Calero tried so hard to take control of the examination that Keker essentially began crossexamining him, in a largely futile attempt to limit his orations. Sullivan did not object to this bizarre format, but Gesell finally butted in, saying (as he had admonished Keker before), "I think you ought to frame your questions in the normal mode of direct examination." This painful sparring went on for about an hour, when Keker, satisfied that he had drawn out the necessary facts, turned the witness over to Sullivan.

This "cross-examination" more resembled a love fest, so much so, in fact, that it took on an antic quality. Sullivan asked, "Would you try to tell the ladies and gentlemen of the jury, as best you can, who is this guy, Colonel North? What did he do for you?"

"Well," said Calero, "for us he became sort of a savior. . . . We felt abandoned, we felt that we couldn't feed our people, and that we had no way of getting support any place. And then all of a sudden, we were introduced to this man with whom we became more and more familiar as time went on, and . . . our men, even though they were Nicaraguans and were not Americans, seemed to be as important for him as Americans. . . . We developed a very—a tremendously human relationship. . . . I would say we are tremendously grateful to him. . . . The Nicaraguan people have a tremendous appreciation for this man. So much so . . . that they're going to erect a monument for him once we free Nicaragua."

So spoke Adolfo Calero, prosecution witness.

ROB OWEN had served as North's courier to Central America, carrying North's plans of battle in the contra war with the Sandinistas and transferring money—traveler's checks—to contra commanders. Owen's testimony was crucial to proving the false statements counts. Several of those charges were based on North's denials of any involvement with contra military operations. North had also said he had "not advised or guided" Owen with respect to the contras and had only "casual contact" with him. Owen could put the lie to these assertions.

A graduate of Stanford, Owen had gone to work for then Senator Dan Quayle of Indiana in the early 1980s and then for a Washington public relations firm that proposed doing some image repair for the contras. There Owen came under North's charismatic spell, and the young conservative drifted into running errands for North in the battlefields of Central America, often at great personal risk. Owen was both utterly sincere and entirely unsuited for this dangerous line of work. One intelligence officer once said, "You know, when the Soviets want to fight a guerrilla war, they send in guys who've spent ten years fighting in the bush in some place like Angola." Then, equally bemused and contemptuous, he added, "And who do we send? Rob Owen." Andover '74.

The principal documentary evidence that Mike Bromwich would introduce through Owen's testimony was his reports from the field to North—detailed memos recounting how he had passed along North's instructions to the contra fighters. An experienced prosecutor, Bromwich posed a distinct stylistic contrast to Keker. This veteran of a dozen narcotics trials moved crisply through Owen's story in about a day. Bromwich even finished with a flourish. The OIC had used North's calendar book and schedule cards to construct a chart with a densely packed list recounting dozens of meetings between Owen and North from 1984 to 1986. Bromwich got Owen to verify the accuracy of the chart and even to say that several of their meetings were not listed.

"What is your best estimate," Bromwich asked Owen, "as to how many meetings you had with [North] from 1984 through early August 1986?"—the date of North's HPSCI testimony.

"Somewhere around one hundred," Owen said. This, the jury could see, was not just "casual contact." That these last words of Owen's direct testimony came at the end of a Friday afternoon—for the jury to savor over the weekend—made them all the sweeter.

CHAPTER THIRTEEN

One Fleeting Second

In most federal courtrooms, the examining attorney stands at a podium at the far end of the jury box, so the witness can look directly into the jurors' eyes when testifying. Not so in Courtroom Six. Judge Gesell decreed that, when lawyers were questioning witnesses, the lectern would remain anchored directly in front of the bench. So, as the witnesses spoke, they were compelled to look over the shoulder of the attorney making the inquiries to the defense table. In a case where most of the witnesses retained a deep affection for the defendant, W & C mined the potential in this arrangement. Thus, as each of his friends took the stand, Oliver North positioned his chair so that he could gaze directly into the witness's eyes.

This unnerved Rob Owen. By the time of his testimony, Owen had been largely cured of his fascination with North; after all, though Owen was never prosecuted, the association with the colonel had caused the young man more than a year of grief. But the sight of North over Brendan Sullivan's shoulder on Monday morning, February 27, 1989, revived all the hero worship that led Owen to risk his life for North during their two years of work together. In cross-examination, Sullivan milked Owen's infatuation, urging him to describe how he and North had forged their friendship in their shared passion for the people of Nicaragua.

Sullivan, for instance, prompted Owen to say how many people from various parts of the United States government he had met with in Central America during the course of his duties for North. This theme was meant to develop the "grand conspiracy" theory; Sullivan wanted to show that North's activities were not secret to anyone who cared to know.

About midway through the morning, Sullivan called Owen's attention to one of his memos to North, one dated August 25, 1985, which Bromwich had already introduced during the witness's direct testimony. In the form that Bromwich introduced it, however, one of the names Owen mentioned in the memo had been blacked out by the Inter-Agency Group, which had censored all of our exhibits prior to their use in open court. Sullivan wanted to use the memo, but he also sought to have the name disclosed.

The name was Ben Piza, the minister of public security under President Monge in Costa Rica and a key figure in assisting North and Owen to build the secret airstrip on the contras' southern front. Piza later visited Washington and made a five-minute courtesy call on President Reagan. (When Keker and I visited Piza in San José, we saw the photo of him in the Oval Office with Reagan.) Sullivan wanted to use Piza's name because he wanted to link up Piza's involvement with the southern front and the picture-taking session with Reagan. The lawyer thought that the juxtaposition of these events would show that the president authorized North's actions.

Approaching the bench to argue about the use of Piza's name, Keker and Bromwich knew that they had to fight hard on this one. The administration regarded certain dealings with foreign officials as pure drop dead material. It could not come out. At first Gesell went along with the administration view, telling Sullivan, "You can bring out that information, but you have to protect the name." That is, Sullivan could say what Piza did, but he had to refer to him as a "high Costa Rican government official." But Sullivan kept battling, saying that the generic reference alone could not make his point.

With the lawyers gathered at a conference around Gesell's bench, the spectators could hear little and see only the intense bobbing of the lawyers' heads. Bromwich held firm: "We have no objection to the disclosure of these underlying facts," he said. "The only fact we object to is the disclosure of the man's name." Gesell, however, was warming to Sullivan's view, telling Keker, "He has a witness on the stand who cannot tell him the names of the people that were in the room that planned the airport, and he is intending to show down the line that the president embraced this man, had pictures taken with him, and knew that he was helping with logistical matters in the area." Keker replied, "All that can come out without naming the man. . . . We can make up a name for him. We can call him Costa Rican official 'Mr. Big.' "

But Sullivan won Gesell over. Sullivan had, in the judge's words, brought the case "home to Poppa"—to Reagan. "The name is coming in," said Gesell. Keker had to ask for a recess to consult with the intelligence agencies about whether they would allow the trial to go forward if Piza was named.

With the day's testimony abruptly halted, the press buzzed with news of this first CIPA explosion of the trial. Nina Totenberg, the National Public Radio legal affairs correspondent, sang out, "Cuckoo, cuckoo"—an off-key reminder that Gesell's fears of a "cuckoo clock trial" were coming true. As they gathered in the hallway after Gesell sent the jury home, the reporters knew that the dispute arose over an Owen memo to North dated August 25, 1985. So they set out to find the mysterious name in the memo.

They did not have to look very far. The National Security Archive, a Washington think tank devoted to obtaining and assembling declassified government documents, had been monitoring the North trial from the start. Over the past two years, the Archive had obtained Iran-Contra documents from a variety of sources, including the Christic Institute, which had filed a flaky lawsuit against Owen and others in the private benefactor network. Before the suit was dismissed, the institute had obtained a trove of material from discovery in the case. In fact, Owen had turned over to the Christics all of his memos to North—in completely uncensored form—and the Christics, in turn, had passed the papers to the National Security Archive. So, just after the North trial recessed on Monday, the Archive triumphantly sent the complete set of Owen's memos to every newspaper in town—

and proclaimed that Ben Piza was the name that caused all the fuss.

Reporters must have had a good laugh in printing Piza's name in Tuesday's paper—the "secret" name that halted the trial—but the danger to the OIC was only just becoming apparent. When North's lawyers learned that the Owen memos had been disclosed in the Christic suit, they called Thomas Hyland, Owen's lawyer, to ask about it. You mean, they asked Hyland, these memos, which the OIC that very afternoon fought to keep secret, have been public for months? Right, said Hyland. What was more, Hyland said he told the OIC about it just a couple of weeks ago.

O N February 10, two weeks before the trial started, Owen arrived for one of his many preparation sessions at the OIC. He was accompanied by his lawyer, Hyland, and was met by Mike Bromwich and Larry Shtasel. As the prosecutors were putting Owen through his paces, Hyland asked why the copies of the Owen memos that Bromwich and Shtasel were using had portions blacked out. Bromwich told him that the Inter-Agency Group regarded these sections as "classified" and would not allow them to be released to the public.

"That's bizarre," said Hyland. He said he had complete copies of all the memos, and no one ever told him anything about their being classified. In fact, he said, he had turned over uncensored copies to the Christic Institute in June 1987 as part of its civil suit against Owen.

Bromwich told Hyland that this was "a problem," and summoned Al Stansbury, the OIC security director, but the matter lay dormant until the brouhaha in court on February 28. After court that day, Williams & Connolly called Hyland and learned that Bromwich knew—three weeks before the confrontation in Gesell's courtroom about disclosing Piza's name—that the Christic Institute already had full text of the memo. Barry Simon, as was his wont, was outraged: W & C had spent the day fighting to use a memo that the OIC knew was already public.

The situation was rich with irony. The "government secrets" at issue had never been classified like normal national security documents because North was running a freelance government on the sly with friends like Owen. Because of North's largesse, Rob Owen was privy to some of the most sensitive information in the executive branch. Indeed, count one of our indictment, which we had by then dropped, stated that North's operation of this off-the-books public/private partnership was at the heart of his crime. But now North's lawyer was shocked that the government could not properly manage the secrets to which North's initiative had given birth.

But Simon did not stop to savor the ironies and instead worked through Monday night writing a motion to dismiss all the charges against North based on Mike Bromwich's "prosecutorial misconduct." North's lawyers charged that by not revealing to the defense and the Court that the Owen memos had been turned over to the Christic Institute—and, even worse, arguing that Piza's name should not be disclosed—Bromwich had committed "a fraud on the defense."

Gesell came out on Tuesday morning, March 1, snarling at Keker and the prosecution. The judge dismissed the jury for the day and demanded an immediate hearing on the charge of prosecutorial misconduct, muttering darkly that if the defense accusations were true, "The implications are foregone." He gave both sides the morning to prepare and called a hearing for 1:30, where Bromwich, Shtasel, and Stansbury would testify. The stakes: whether the case against Oliver North should be thrown out because of the "misconduct" of one Michael Bromwich.

A S the news of the crisis rocketed back to Thirteenth Street, the reaction of those of us who were not in court that day found a rare internal consensus for the OIC. Prosecutorial misconduct by Mike Bromwich? Impossible.

I decided I couldn't miss this spectacle and cadged a pass for the afternoon hearing. Shortly before lunch, I ran to the courthouse and the empty judge's chamber that was serving as our courtroom headquarters. Walking in, I saw Shtasel alone in the foyer, his six-foot three-inch frame bouncing around the furniture like a slinky toy.

"Look at this," Shtasel snapped, jabbing his finger at his chest.

I looked. Saw nothing. "At what?" I said.

"Pink shirt," said Shtasel. I agreed. Pink.

"So?"

"Stern always said you always wear a *white* shirt to court," Shtasel replied, "and I'm going to have to testify in a pink shirt." Shtasel, like Zornow, had clerked for Herb Stern and still relied on the former judge's courtroom bromides.

"Oh, boy," I told him, "I'm glad not too much panic has set in around here.

"Look," I continued, "I think I can get you immunity if you agree to give up Brommy."

Shtasel, unamused, resumed his pacing until, shortly before 1:30 P.M., Keker, Zornow, and Bromwich emerged from the back room where they had been preparing Bromwich's testimony. The five of us walked grimly down to Courtroom Six, where the three North prosecutors took their seats at counsel table and Shtasel joined me in the front row.

"All right, Mr. Sullivan," said Judge Gesell, "it's your motion."

Sullivan first called Tom Hyland, Owen's lawyer, who recounted the February 10 meeting with Bromwich and Shtasel. "Did you tell them at that meeting specifically that you provided these same documents [including the August 25, 1985 memo] to the Christic Institute?"

"Absolutely," Hyland replied.

Hyland's direct testimony added little to the motion papers W & C had filed the night before, but Keker decided to regain the initiative with a brutal cross-examination. He brought out that Hyland knew long before February 10 that the Owen memos were classified but did nothing to protect them. Even better, Keker insinuated a smarmy little conspiracy among Owen and North's lawyers to embarrass the prosecution. Keker asked if there were "social" contacts among North and his defense team and Hyland and Owen. Hyland said there were.

"And these would be lunches in the Williams & Connolly dining room?"

Hyland admitted that was so.

Keker finished with a zinger. Hyland volunteered that North himself had been subpoenaed in the Christic Institute suit against Owen, and that the subpoena had been quashed. Keker asked who represented North in the effort to have his subpoena quashed? Hyland professed ignorance.

"You don't know," Keker asked, incredulous, "who represented Colonel North in an effort to get that subpoena quashed?"

"No," said Hyland, but everyone knew: W & C. Maybe, Keker implied, those lawyers weren't as ignorant as they said they were about what documents had been turned over in the Christic case. Maybe it was the prosecution and not the defense who had been sandbagged here.

Moments later, the main event: the testimony of Mike Bromwich, in an effort to save both the case and his reputation. Keker first elicited Bromwich's princely résumé—Harvard College, Harvard Law School, Kennedy School of Government, four years at the United States Attorney's Office, where he was chief of the narcotics unit. Keker then went to the heart of Bromwich's defense.

"In your work at the Office of Independent Counsel," Keker asked, "have you become familiar with an issue that in some ways plagued our office about information that has appeared someplace in the public domain, a newspaper or a magazine or maybe in the hands of a private individual, that is nevertheless classified by the government of the United States?"

"Yes, sir," said Bromwich, "on many occasions."

The fact that something has appeared in public, said Bromwich, "does not mean that it's not classified. On a variety of occasions with respect to various facts, even though the facts may have been in the newspaper or known to people outside our office or other places . . . I have nevertheless been told that that does not mean the material is unclassified. . . ."

"In fact," Keker interjected, "before counts one and two of this indictment against Mr. North were dismissed, did our office prepare a rather fat list of items that we understood were classified, with references to public disclosures of those items in various newspapers, magazines, and so on and submit that to the intelligence community?" Keker was referring to Evan Wolfson's package distributed to the administration before the December 21, 1988, cabinet meeting.

"Yes," Bromwich answered, explaining that the situation with

Owen was especially "anomalous" because "Colonel North was working with a private citizen to do things that normally the government does and as a result, information was gathered and documents were prepared that, had they been done through normal government channels, would have been properly classified. Here we had that same kind of information which was sitting in private hands and for that reason had not been classified."

Gesell immediately understood Bromwich's point. He asked Bromwich if information "has fallen into the hands of the public, even from a private citizen, the classification people take the view that they can step in and put a stamp on it and give it a new status, right?"

"That's my understanding, Your Honor."

And that, in essence, was Bromwich's defense. We *also* think the rules are stupid, but we've had to live with them.

Keker threw Bromwich one more softball, but an important one. Had he, as W & C charged, manipulated the situation with classified information for tactical advantage? No, Bromwich said, he found the whole classified information problem "quite a handicap"—which was the understatement of the year.

"As a prosecutor in this case, which would be easier," Keker asked in his final question, "dealing with these redacted documents or having all of this underlying information that is still classified come out?"

That, too, was easy. "Have all the classified information come out."

As Brendan Sullivan marched to the podium for the cross-examination, one had to marvel at how he had managed, for a second time, to make real the metaphor of putting the prosecution on trial.

"Mr. Bromwich," said Sullivan without a smile, "you acknowledge, I take it, that on February 10, 1989, you were fully informed that the Owen to North memoranda were in the hands of the Christic Institute?"

"I wouldn't say fully informed, sir," Bromwich replied icily, "no." He said that fact had been mentioned briefly. So the cross-examination went, with Bromwich refusing each Sullivan sally at putting words in his mouth.

Sullivan, at last, reached the heart of his accusation against Bromwich. "So when you came to court last Friday," Sullivan asked, "and began presenting the evidence from Mr. Owen, you still had not heard back anything about the fact that the documents you were using in court were out in the hands of at least the Christic Institute?"

"That suggests, Mr. Sullivan," Bromwich replied, "that I had thought about it since February 10, 1989, which I had not. I was focusing on a lot of other things. . . ."

"Now, on Friday," Sullivan continued, his voice drenched with contempt, "at the time you were dealing with these very documents, one document after another, . . . it didn't occur to you for one fleeting second that the very documents you were using in a redacted classified form were out in the hands of the Christic Institute?"

Bromwich stared hard at the gray-haired man before him. "Not for one fleeting second, Mr. Sullivan."

Gesell believed Bromwich. The hearing petered out soon thereafter, though Al Stansbury did have to testify and admit that he had not followed up at all after learning of the breach on February 10.

Before the end of the day, Gesell made clear that he would not dismiss the case against North and, in an opinion on the prosecutorial misconduct motion issued later that week, completely exonerated Bromwich and Shtasel of any wrongdoing, though he labeled Stansbury "incompetent." Gesell directed his fury where it belonged—at the classifying authorities who operated by such mysterious rules and then changed their flimsy dictates when the spirit moved them.

The OIC had won, but just barely.

Near the end of the hearing, Gesell spoke words that provided no comfort on Thirteenth Street. "I have a case now," he said, "where we're through two-and-a-half witnesses and so far the jury has been held out of the courtroom two-and-a-half weeks. And I've got fifty witnesses at least ahead of me.

"And I think somebody had better begin to start thinking about that."

CHAPTER FOURTEEN

Not the Truth, Per Se

During his cross-examination of Owen, Brendan Sullivan made a special effort to emphasize that, in Owen's view, "Colonel North was extremely meticulous" about tracking the traveler's checks he had given to Owen for distribution in Central America. Agreeing with Sullivan's characterization, Owen elaborated that "every time [North] gave me money, he would take out a ledger which he kept in his safe and write down the serial numbers." Sullivan suggested on several occasions that by maintaining this "meticulous" ledger book, North demonstrated that he was using the checks only for official business and not as a personal piggy bank.

Bromwich knew of an important exception to North's supposed business-only fastidiousness about the traveler's checks. When Owen was married on October 19, 1985, North had arrived at the wedding with an unusual gift: $1,000 worth of the traveler's checks. Bromwich wanted to call special attention to this most personal expenditure by North.

But Bromwich hardly had the chance—because, when he turned to the subject, Judge Gesell took over the questioning. "Where were you," Gesell asked Owen, "when you got the traveler's checks?"

"I was at my wedding reception in southern Virginia, down on the Tidewater."

"Who gave it to you?"

"Colonel North."

Gesell then smirked and asked in a voice thick with sarcasm, "Did he have his book with him?" and the question alone brought down the house. "No, Judge," Owen said, laughing himself, "I didn't see it anyway."

The move was arguably improper. Gesell was clearly showing that he believed North was less than painstaking in dispensing the checks, but we loved it. "You know," Keker said after court, "this almost felt like a real trial today." At the rate we were going, that alone seemed like cause for celebration.

But more was to come. After Owen was finished late on Wednesday morning, March 1, David Zornow, in his first appearance of the trial, briskly marched retired Major General John Singlaub through his direct testimony, completing it by the end of the day. The former army general described how he and North had worked together to solicit contributions to the contras from two Asian nations and how they had met together frequently on a variety of contra-related matters from 1983 to 1986. (One of North's charged false statements to the House intelligence committee on August 6, 1986, was that he had not had any contact with Singlaub in twenty months.)

With his brush-top hairdo and hubcap ears, "Black Jack" Singlaub was a favorite around the Office of Independent Counsel, one of a special category of witnesses who combined passionate politics with complete honesty. Singlaub had devoted a good chunk of his life to fighting for the contras, but he had always done so in an open and forthright way. The extreme version of this character type was Felix Rodriguez, otherwise known as Max Gomez, the former CIA agent who served as the contact for North's "private benefactor" network in El Salvador. When Rodriguez first appeared in our offices, he insisted, in return for his cooperation, on two of the more unusual "conditions" in law-enforcement history. Rodriguez would speak to us, he said, only if he did *not* hire a lawyer and did *not* receive immunity. We acquiesced.

That kind of fearlessness, which Rodriguez shared with Singlaub, made them difficult figures to dislike, and they both appeared to return the good feelings. At one point, Singlaub even bestowed his highest praise upon Bromwich and Zornow in a conversation just before his testimony. Though he had never exchanged so much as a single word about politics with the two prosecutors, he beamed and called them "good anticommunists."

Still, Singlaub caused us a good deal of worry as a trial witness because some areas of his testimony looked like a CIPA mine field; he was another private individual who, according to the administration, knew many "nondisclosable" government secrets. Even worse, Gesell had agreed to proceed with the trial following Owen's disastrous testimony only on a provisional basis. Gesell said he "thought that there was some advantage in going with another witness to see whether what happened with respect to Owen was an exception or a rule." Another blowup, in other words, might prompt him to scuttle the whole case. Thus, we awaited Sullivan's cross-examination of Singlaub, which promised to aim for all of the hot buttons, with more than the usual degree of concern.

Late Wednesday evening, however, Keker was summoned to an unusual conference call with Sullivan and Judge Gesell. Sullivan wanted to inform us of his plans for the cross-examination of Singlaub: there wouldn't be any. Keker feigned nonchalance on the telephone but he and everyone else at the OIC were stunned. The Singlaub cross presented Sullivan with a golden opportunity to create the CIPA crisis that would shove Gesell over the edge—and the case with it. And, independent of CIPA, Singlaub had even offered some fairly damaging testimony against North regarding the false-statement counts, the kind most attorneys would have wanted to address in cross-examination. But as in their December 30 subpoenas to Reagan and Bush, Williams & Connolly came, inexplicably, to our rescue.

Why did it happen? Why wasn't Singlaub cross-examined? No one could say for sure. We heard rumors of a personal rift between North and Singlaub, but that alone would not have justified Sullivan's squandering a chance to end the case. Could Sullivan have been trying to send a subliminal message to the jury that he regarded Singlaub's testimony as inconsequential? Perhaps so, but Sullivan still could

have tried—as he had done so often before—to exploit our
CIPA woes.

Whatever Sullivan's reasons, when he waived his chance to cross-
examine Singlaub, we took full advantage. Bromwich started Thursday morning with Rafael Quintero, a leading member of North's
private resupply effort for the contras, and he completed his testimony
just after lunch. Richard Gadd, another private benefactor, followed,
and he finished up without incident as well. By Friday, March 3,
when Gesell had said he was going to reevaluate how the CIPA
process was working, we had churned through three witnesses since
the Owen fiasco. The threat of the CIPA disaster receded. All of a
sudden, we were rolling.

Even Spitz Channell did his part. A nervous, delicate fellow, Channell fretted endlessly about his testimony, and many in our camp
wondered just what would come out of his mouth when he finally
took the stand—almost two years to the day after his guilty plea to
conspiracy to defraud the IRS. But Channell managed to keep himself
together for almost a full day of direct testimony under Bromwich's
questioning. He told of his background in fundraising—"I worked
very closely with what is called the high dollar or maximum dollar
contribution process, where I would meet with individuals alone,"
he said, in Washington-speak for hitting up rich people—and the
creation of the National Endowment for the Preservation of Liberty.
He then moved to how, under North's direction, he had come to use
that tax-exempt foundation to raise money for weapons for the contras. The testimony helped both the rather esoteric conspiracy to
defraud the IRS count and the false-statement charges where North
denied soliciting money.

But Channell also told a story that had the potential to help us on
all the counts—and, indeed, on the most important issue in the case.
Sullivan had stressed in his opening that North never had a smidgen
of criminal intent, that is, that his client never believed he was doing
anything wrong. As Sullivan's cross-examination of the first witnesses
evolved, we saw that he was not going to challenge in any great detail
our version of the facts. Sullivan was conceding that North did all
these things—helped the contras raise money and assisted them in
their battle plans—but never in the colonel's wildest dreams did it

occur to him that any of these activities were improper, much less criminal.

But, then, Bromwich had Channell tell of an incident that took place on September 11, 1985. Channell had chartered a private plane to take North to a dinner meeting in Dallas with Bunker Hunt, of the famous Texas Hunts, so they could ask the oil heir to ante up for the Freedom Fighters.

"He is a rich man, right?" Bromwich asked.

"Used to be," said Channell, knowing of the magnate's recent woes in the silver market.

Channell and North dined with Hunt at the Petroleum Club, on top of a Dallas skyscraper, and toward the end of the evening Channell made a direct pitch for cash. After Channell's plea, the three men waited in the restaurant foyer for a taxi to bring North back to the airport. While Channell strained to see whether his assistant, Dan Conrad, had flagged a cab for North, the colonel and the oilman talked nearby at a banquette.

"Mr. Channell," Bromwich asked, "were you able to hear any parts of their conversation?"

"A little."

"And would you please describe what it is that you overheard?"

"Well," Channell said, "Bunker and Colonel North talked about this fellow named [Roberto] d'Aubuisson. I think he's in El Salvador. They discussed a little bit about the Somoza history in Nicaragua . . . and one thing that stuck in my mind—it just stuck in my mind. . . . Bunker said to him, 'What are you going to do? Do you mind getting in trouble for this?' And Ollie said, 'No, I don't care if I have to go to jail for this, and I don't care if I have to lie to Congress about this.' . . . It just stuck."

To this point in the trial, North had mostly kept his head down taking notes almost continuously, no matter how insignificant the testimony. But as Channell said these words, North for once put down his pen and stared vacantly ahead of him. Several jurors pointed scowls North's way. They knew it, North knew it, and we knew it: we had drawn blood.

And so, of course, did Brendan Sullivan. The lawyer promptly rose to examine what he called, in a sarcastic tone, that "conversation that you overheard while you were looking down forty stories to see if Mr. Conrad hailed a cab."

Sullivan was fearless. He walked Channell through the conversation once more, at the risk of implanting the story even more securely in the jurors' memories—but then he lowered the boom.

"Now," Sullivan asked, "you've described it very differently in the past, haven't you?"

"I don't think so," Channell offered meekly.

"You don't?" Sullivan sneered, and then took off on a tour de force of cross-examination. He put several of Channell's prior statements to government investigators in front of him, and each version of the "lobby conversation" contained differences. His composure slipping, Channell tried with little success to explain the inconsistencies. As if this were not bad enough, Judge Gesell soon jumped into the act.

"And how do you explain," the judge said to the now-cowering witness, "that you told the jury that this 'stuck' in your mind and you had no doubt about it?"

"Because it has . . ." Channell bleated, "and it was very interesting how long—"

"You've got three versions already," Gesell shot at him.

"It has—"

"What 'stuck' in your mind," Gesell continued, "when you told the jury it 'stuck' in your mind?"

"That Colonel North said what he did . . ."

Gesell turned away in disgust, and Sullivan resumed his offensive. "Sometimes when you have such an urge to cooperate with the prosecution," he whispered to Channell, "there is a little danger that you might put words in somebody's mouth that really don't belong in the mouth, is that fair to say?"

"Well," Channell answered, "I'm sure there is that temptation, of course," and Sullivan let the words linger in the air.

Gesell decided that Sullivan's flogging of the witness had been insufficient, so as Sullivan finally yielded the floor, the judge turned to the jury and made a little speech. "My instructions are the same to you, ladies and gentlemen of the jury, as to each and every statement that has been pointed out, you may consider them in connection with your appraisal of the credibility of this witness." A more subtle tack would have been for Gesell to force Channell to wear a sandwich board saying "LIAR."

Sullivan's cross of Channell illustrated one of the hidden costs the congressional investigation imposed on the OIC. The Hill probe of the NEPL side of the Iran-Contra story had been a particularly inept affair, featuring repeated examinations of Channell under oath. A law called the Jencks Act requires prosecutors to turn over to the defense in a criminal case all prior statements of government witnesses. Because human beings inevitably tell stories with slight differences each time—changes which can be exploited in cross-examination—prosecutors generally try to keep Jencks material to a minimum. But Congress lacked any such inhibitions, and, with Channell, the OIC had to supply Sullivan with the ammunition to torpedo our own witness.

On redirect Bromwich made a game effort to rehabilitate Channell and the "lobby conversation." The prosecutor tried to show that Channell's versions did not vary as much as Sullivan suggested they did. Still, what looked at first like a knockout wound up as a draw at best.

When Channell and a few other minor NEPL witnesses finished their testimony later that week, we felt that we could take our first deep breath. Through Congressman Hamilton we offered the text of the charged false statements, and through the witnesses who followed we established that the assertions in the 1985 letters and the 1986 testimony were false. At this point in the trial, the jury could scarcely have doubted that North *did* solicit money for the contras and that he *did* give them tactical advice—contrary to the representations to Congress.

But we extracted these facts from our witnesses at a price. With the exception of Hamilton, the witnesses lavished North with the most extraordinary praise. Dick Gadd called him a "national hero." Rafael Quintero, in his fractured English, called North's "devotion to duty . . . a work of art." Bob Dutton, who worked with Gadd and Secord in Central America, said North worked so hard that "he almost killed himself." One day, according to Dutton, when he was complaining about his own high blood pressure, North said, " 'That's not too bad. Mine is 205 over 180.' And at that time he pulled his eyelid down and the blood vessels in his eyes were breaking under the tremendous pressure." The adulation occasionally took on an almost comic tone, as when Joseph Coors, the beer baron and NEPL contributor, volunteered out of the blue when answering the very first question put to him that he considered North "a tremendously wonderful patriotic American." When Coors finished his testimony, he walked over to the defendant and clasped his hand. Prosecution witnesses all.

In our private counsels we discounted the effect of all this adulation. After all, we noted bravely, everyone had friends. But in the end criminal trials come down to personal judgments—one man, good or bad—and the jury must have started wondering how anyone could find fault with this protagonist. Was this Colonel North a *criminal?* Should the buck stop here?

What about his boss, anyway?

AT one point we had thought about beginning the trial with the testimony of Robert McFarlane. A central figure in the story, McFarlane could frame the entire case for the jury and give it some context. We vacillated on the subject until the last minute but ultimately decided to push him into the middle, the bottom of our trial horseshoe, where the prosecution generally puts its weakest proof. Our indecision on where to place McFarlane—as well as our resolution of that quandary—symbolized our discomfort with this crucial witness.

Not for nothing do prosecutors (in private) call cooperating witnesses, or informers, "scumbag witnesses." Their very presence broadcasts their betrayal and disloyalty, qualities that, like powerful pesticides, offend mightily even in support of the best causes. Scumbags' motives are as clear as they are repellent: to save their own skins. Prosecutors try to fend off the inevitable (and ferocious) attacks on cooperators in defense attorneys' summations. The witness, says the government lawyer, "is not the *government*'s friend. He is the *defendant*'s friend." But the joust is hollow. The jurors may believe a scumbag, but they'll never like him.

We weren't even sure what we wanted McFarlane to say on the stand. The former national security advisor had pleaded guilty to four misdemeanors, three of them based on the very same letters for which North was charged with felonies. Just before North's trial, he had been sentenced to probation. We wanted McFarlane to say that he had known the letters were false and that he personally had done something wrong in signing them. We did not want McFarlane to absorb all of the blame; we had to let the jury know that North, too, had been in on the deception from the start and had prepared the false drafts. At the same time, we did not want McFarlane to fob *all* of the responsibility on North.

On Friday morning, March 10, dour as always, Robert McFarlane strutted to the witness stand. His suit was too tight and his fingernails bore a shiny new coat of clear polish. In spite of everything, he still preened.

For the first time in the trial, Keker appeared uncomfortable at the podium. He could spar with a buffoon like Calero without any hesitation, but the combination of our need for—and contempt for—McFarlane threw Keker off stride. So, too, the personal chemistry between the two men during their many preparation sessions had been abysmal. Near the end, in fact, Keker more or less gave up trying to prepare McFarlane's direct testimony. Even off the stand, McFarlane's vagueness, memory lapses, and evasions grew so infuriating that Keker figured he would simply approach him as he would a witness to cross-examine—and hope for the best.

Keker tried never to hide anything from the jury. He quickly established that McFarlane had pleaded guilty in March 1988 to "four separate charges" of withholding information from the Congress of the United States. From there he bored on.

"After pleading guilty to these charges, Mr. McFarlane," Keker said unsteadily, "did you try to commit—or excuse me. After committing these crimes, before pleading guilty, did you try to commit suicide?" Keker's bumbling registered his discomfort with asking such a raw question, but McFarlane dutifully answered in the affirmative.

Keker moved to one of the most difficult areas he had to navigate. At a meeting of top-level officials in 1984 to consider soliciting third-country support to the contras, President Reagan had said, according to the minutes, "If such a story gets out, we'll all be hanging by our thumbs in front of the White House until we find out who did it." North and Sullivan had seized on this remark as justifying his lies to Congress. No less than the president, North claimed, gave the command to withhold information.

"Do you remember," Keker asked, "attending a meeting where President Reagan said something like that?"

"Well," said McFarlane, "I remember hearing him say words to that effect, yes. . . ."

"And what was he referring to? Was he referring to leaks to the— if you know?" This question was typical of the leading, cross-examination-style interrogation that Keker lapsed into with McFarlane on the stand.

"No doubt that," said McFarlane in typically garbled syntax, "that were public and would lead Congress to react."

This was a tepid version of what Keker wanted McFarlane to say. Reagan had forbidden any leaks to the press; he had *not* ordered lies to Congress. "Did you understand when he said words to that effect that that was an order to people in his administration to lie to the Congress of the United States?"

"No, I think to just not let the information become public."

Keker then broadened the point. "Do you ever recall hearing the president of the United States, Ronald Reagan, instruct you or anyone else in your presence to lie to the Congress of the United States?"

"No."

"About anything?"

"No."

In order to establish that both McFarlane and North knew the 1985 letters to Congress were false, Keker had to show McFarlane all of the various memos North had sent him about his activities on behalf of the contras. One after another, these documents demonstrated North's direct role in providing money and military direction to the rebels.

And here the trouble began. Though McFarlane pleaded guilty to his misdemeanors, he consistently refused to acknowledge that he did anything wrong. He would accept global responsibility for his own actions and those of his subordinates. "It was, again, my responsibility," McFarlane said. "Whatever he had done, I was responsible for, and also I was the one who should properly be accountable for what the staff did."

But when it came down to what he himself had done, McFarlane waffled. He didn't even admit that he had solicited money from Saudi Arabia for the contras. When McFarlane said that the money was "given," not "solicited," an incredulous Gesell asked the witness to repeat himself.

"You didn't solicit it, you say?" said the judge.

"Right, sir," said McFarlane. "It was volunteered by other countries."

The problems became worse when Keker came to the drafting of the responses to Congressman Hamilton's letters in the fall of 1985. When he received these inquiries, McFarlane said that he had asked his staff to collect all of the memos North had written about his own contra role. Looking through them, McFarlane recalled for the court, he found that some were "problem documents."

"Meaning what?" Keker asked.

"It seemed to me from an examination" of these documents, McFarlane said, "that there were many that, were I in the place of a congressman, I might find expressing activities that the Congress didn't want done, something against the law, perhaps, or something at least that they would ask a question about. And since I was responsible and anything that occurred was my fault, I wanted to know everything that I could so as to be able to respond in a proper way." So he called in North and the two of them went over the problem documents.

And what did they decide to do about them? North, according to McFarlane, "said he would rewrite" the memos "to make sure" that they were "clear." The two of them decided to doctor the record to make it appear (falsely) that North was not actively helping the contras. Yet McFarlane persisted in saying that the changes in the memos were meant solely to "clarify" them, not to change their substance.

Gesell had been fidgeting slightly throughout the McFarlane examination, but now he could not control himself. He began jumping in frequently, sneering questions and instructions to the witness as if he were a slow-witted child. As McFarlane's mind wandered off on some tangent, Gesell snapped, "We're not interested in what you had in your mind. We're interested in what was said to you and what you said to him. . . . We're not at all interested in you at all in terms of your mind."

This was more than a judge's pique at a witness. McFarlane seemed unwilling and perhaps even incapable of distinguishing truth from fiction, and his sanctimonious demeanor suggested that he did not find the effort worth making. At one point McFarlane mentioned almost perfunctorily that during one of the fall 1985 drafting sessions for responding to the Hamilton letters, North had handed him a rewritten memo dated from May of that year. Gesell stared at McFarlane and said, "This was in August, right?"

"August or September, yes, sir."

"And the memorandum comes for you dated May, right?"

"That's correct," said the witness, and the judge gathered his robes around him and sunk deeply into his chair. He was appalled.

As Keker turned to the letters to Congress themselves, the prosecutor also had trouble keeping his composure. He asked, "Was there any discussion on providing less than fully truthful answers to Congress between you and Colonel North?"

"Not per se, no," he said, perhaps the ultimate McFarlane obfuscation.

"You say, 'not per se,'" Keker quoted back to him, trying to untangle the thoughts for the jury. "'Per se' means not for itself?"

"As such," said McFarlane. "The—I'm trying to provide a truthful answer without going to the obvious precedent that goes back years about correspondence with the Congress. . . ."

"What do you mean by that?" Gesell barked.

McFarlane foundered around a little more. "You don't lie," he said, "you put your own interpretation on what the truth is."

Now it was Keker's turn to be disgusted. "When you say you 'put your own interpretation on what the truth is,' do you turn night into day?"

"No, certainly not," said McFarlane, suddenly offended. Then he paused. "You present the truth as it best expresses your behavior"—whatever that meant.

Keker decided to make a simple point. "Did you ever order or ask Colonel North in drafting replies to these letters to put lies in them?"

"No."

"Did you have any authority to tell somebody that worked for you to lie to Congress?"

"No."

Keker had no trouble with McFarlane about broad statements of policy. The only problem was he couldn't get a straight answer on any facts of the case. Judge Gesell summed it up in a bench conference: "I can take full responsibility for the sinking of the *Lusitania,* but everybody would know I didn't know anything about it. But the fact of the matter is this man was right at the center of what was going on and he says he doesn't know."

Even a simple question—was McFarlane's letter to Hamilton true?—yielded the following gibberish:

"As written, no. In context, I think so, but it's wrong to write it, I agree. I'm wrong."

Or when Keker asked whether North had been candid with him before they wrote the letters:

"No," said McFarlane, "but he was probably trying to protect me. I mean, it's my fault."

"I don't understand," Gesell interjected in an icy tone, "will you explain that?"

"Well, I'm not sure I can, Your Honor"—one of the few unambiguously true statements McFarlane made. But Gesell pressed on.

"You say he was trying to protect you," the judge said.

"Yes."

"That suggests he thought that you knew what he knew."

"No, sir," said McFarlane, "it suggests that if he had told me what he knew that I would have gotten into trouble and perhaps him as well, but that in my behalf he didn't want me to get gratuitously into trouble, if he could avoid it."

"All right," sighed Gesell, which it wasn't.

McFarlane delivered his speeches with a lack of inflection that made the meaning of his words even more impenetrable. As Keker wound up the second day of McFarlane's direct testimony, having forsaken the hope of scoring points and seeking only to plow through the remainder of the story, there was one last piece of business to settle. On February 8, 1987, the day before McFarlane tried to take his own life, he wrote several suicide notes, including one to Lee Hamilton. (Only in Washington do people write suicide notes to congressional committee chairmen.) When asked by Hamilton's committee in December 1986 about third-country contributions to the contras, McFarlane had testified that the "concrete character of that is beyond my ken"—a statement for which he later pleaded guilty to withholding information from Congress.

The suicide letter, said McFarlane, was intended to provide "a full accounting for my actions with the Congress." In it, as Keker read the letter out loud in court, McFarlane told Hamilton that " 'in 1984 a foreign national [the Saudi ambassador] offered to contribute to the support of the contras.' " McFarlane told him where he should send his money. " 'I have no knowledge,' " Keker quoted the letter, " 'as to the precise amount the individual donated. I would estimate it may have come to as much as $5 million.' "

His recitation of the letter completed, Keker paused and asked: "Okay. Now, this is just complete nonsense, isn't it?"

The transformation in McFarlane was immediate and intense. He reddened, tensed and appeared ready to vault out of his chair. Then, for the first time, he lost control. McFarlane screamed, "It is not!"

McFarlane's letter *was* nonsense, of course. He knew the Saudis first gave the contras $1 million per month and then $2 million per month, with a grand total of $32 million. Keker followed up McFarlane's outburst by asking whether the $5 million figure in the letter was way off.

"Well, Mr. Keker," McFarlane said, his voice still many decibels above its usual murmur, "if I had sat down the day before I tried to take my life and tried to parse every last dime I know about that went to the contras, it probably would have come out different. If that's your point, I'm dead wrong."

That bizarre confrontation at last brought McFarlane's direct testimony to a close. In a bench conference with the lawyers afterwards, Judge Gesell said, "This man"—he could scarcely bring himself to utter the name—"has told so many stories since he has been on direct that there isn't any way to know what he believes or what he knows. He is an intensely unreliable witness in almost every respect of his testimony." Pity mingled with contempt as Gesell continued: "I'm not at all sure that it's intentional on his part. I'm not at all sure he isn't a victim, a physical victim, of what he has been going through. But the fact of the matter is, he is not a reliable witness."

CHAPTER FIFTEEN

A Poor
Lieutenant Colonel

Was Oliver North, Brendan Sullivan asked Robert McFarlane, "the kind of man that you knew that, if you were in a desperate life or death struggle in the military in the jungle somewhere, he'd be the kind of man you'd select to be at your right hand . . . ?"

"Yes."

"He's the kind of man," Sullivan resumed, "that if the boat was going down you'd want him in your life raft because he'd find a way to save the lives of the people in the boat, wouldn't he?"

"Yes."

"He's that kind of man," said Sullivan, enjoying himself now. "He has a special quality about him that people look to him. In fact, he has a passionate sense of wanting to save human life, doesn't he?"

"Yes."

Following his spoon-fed encomiums, Sullivan skillfully guided McFarlane through the various drafts of the three letters he sent to Congress in the fall of 1985. The attorney established that McFarlane contributed as much as North to them, and, as for one of them, North had relatively little to do with its creation. Then Sullivan pulled out an enormous black binder and dumped it in front of the witness.

"Mr. McFarlane," Sullivan said, "let me direct your attention to the time period of February 1985. I take it that that was a time period in which the members of the National Security Council were interested in doing what they could to assist the Freedom Fighters who were then very limited in the amount of help they could receive from the United States government, correct?"

"Yes."

Sullivan then asked McFarlane to look at the first of eighteen tabs in the binder, a copy of a memo from North and another NSC staffer to McFarlane on February 11, 1985.

"Now," Sullivan said, "the memo written by Colonel North and Mr. [Raymond] Burghardt essentially says that the letter you are about to send [from President Reagan to President Suazo of Honduras] sets up a strategy for enticing the Hondurans to greater support for the Nicaraguan Resistance, correct?"

"Yes."

"And the word 'enticing' means give them something so that they will cooperate with the goals of the United States in assisting these Freedom Fighters?"

"Yes."

Sullivan continued, "And you are saying further that a letter from President Reagan to President Suazo should be sent indicating the United States commitment to continued support for the Nicaraguan Resistance and to the defense of Honduran sovereignty, correct?"

"Yes."

"And in this letter," Sullivan plodded on, "you indicate . . . that the expedited military deliveries, economic funding, and other benefits should be offered privately as an incentive to the Hondurans for their continued support for the contras?"

"That's right," said McFarlane.

Sullivan was beginning to demonstrate that everyone in the administration, from President Reagan on down, was involved in the offer and delivery of quid pro quos to third countries that agreed to help the contras. This first document was only the beginning. Sullivan believed that these efforts, packaged together, represented an American effort every bit as significant as what North did for the contras. And he wanted to say that to the jury.

When Sullivan made that intention known before the trial, the administration security gurus had a collective conniption. They regarded these sorts of bilateral "liaison" relationships as exquisitely secret. In the last struggle about classified information before the trial, an awkward (and temporary) compromise was reached. The prosecution agreed to "admit" as true for the purposes of this case that many of the quid pro quo initiatives took place. A list of the initiatives was placed in a forty-four-page document that, according to the pretrial agreement, the defense could use any way it wanted at the trial. The document was prepared by Williams & Connolly and edited by both the OIC and the security gurus, and it occupied a peculiar place in the trial.

The disclosures of these quid pro quos became, for the media, the principal "news" of the trial, and we watched in some perplexity the administration—and President Bush specifically—deny that they had taken place. We had concluded long before the North trial that these arrangements, though unseemly, violated no criminal statute. The practice of foreign relations is, after all, the trading of chits among nations. The real surprise would have been if the Reagan Administration did *not* bring its influence to bear about its consuming obsession in the region. Bush's denial was absurd—an automatic reaction in the cycle of accusation-and-denial that characterizes the Washington journalism. Were there quid pro quos for the contras? Of course.

Most of the documents Sullivan used had been released to the public in one form or another over the past two years, but his arrangement of them all together gave them a new significance. They added up to a powerful picture of an administration with extreme contempt for Congress's legislated desire to end United States support for the war in Nicaragua. Clearly, Sullivan was right when he said that North was not the only administration official who helped the contras on the sly during the period of the Boland amendment.

But what did any of this have to do with the case? As Keker stated in his increasingly forlorn objections to Sullivan's cross-examination of McFarlane, North was charged with lying to Congress. This quid quo pro material, said Keker, had no relevance to North's guilt or innocence. Now that we had dropped count one, he argued, Judge

Gesell should exclude testimony about the legality of North's operation in Central America. What the president or the CIA or anyone else in the government may have done to help the contras did not bear on whether North should be convicted of the twelve charges against him. But Gesell gave Sullivan free rein.

As for the effect of all this on the jury, it was difficult to say. For starters, the presentation was stupefyingly dull, as Sullivan read from the documents and McFarlane, with utter passivity, contributed an occasional "yes" and "that's right." (Careful observers would have noticed that Mike Bromwich slipped a copy of *Street & Smith's* baseball preview magazine inside his black binder and was assessing the Dodgers' lineup to McFarlane's droning accompaniment.) But even if they did not understand the relevance of each document presented, the jurors must have been affected by the sight of McFarlane's inert acceptance of everything Sullivan said. One message was both clear and true: Ollie North's boss was in on everything right up to his fancy haircut.

Keker couldn't resist a wisecrack to open his redirect questioning. "Good afternoon, Mr. McFarlane," Keker said. "As I understand your testimony on cross . . . when you were asked questions about various events having to do with assisting the contras, your testimony, if I can summarize it, was pretty much, 'yes,' 'that's right,' and 'correct'?" The spectators giggled. McFarlane did not respond.

Keker's redirect succeeded no better than did his direct, again because of the absence of clear objectives about McFarlane's testimony. Keker had no desire to "rehabilitate" this witness; there was no truthful core of McFarlane's testimony to protect. Still, the government had called McFarlane to the stand, and thus regarded some of his testimony as truthful and incriminating to North. But we never succeeded in getting it across.

McFarlane's performance cast a pall over our team. Our frustration was compounded because we knew that we had shot ourselves in the foot by allowing McFarlane to plea to misdemeanors. Whatever else the jurors took away from McFarlane's testimony, they saw the case bog down in an abstruse debate about foreign policy. And when it came to assessing responsibility, North's boss consigned it all to himself. We had lost the thread of moral passion, of right and wrong, that prosecutors must weave through every moment in a trial. The flavor of criminality disappeared. Roger Diehl, the dumpster-sized FBI supervisor who was my old partner from our days "canning" two years earlier, put it best when he visited Thirteenth Street on the day McFarlane stepped down.

"Hey, Toobin," Diehl said, deadpan, "when is the prosecution going to start calling *its* witnesses in this case?" That, I had to admit, was a good question.

O N the morning of March 21, Glenn Robinette trod meekly into the courtroom with his white hair and half-moon glasses. Keker asked him to state his name. "Mr. Robinette," Keker said, "you have a gentle voice. We've got some water there. It's important that everyone in the jury box hear you, so [please] speak as though you're talking to the two gentlemen at the end of the box. It's particularly important because one of them knows something about security systems, so I want them all to hear." Keker was referring to one of the alternates, who also worked in the security business. As a trial lawyer, Keker tried always to make a point of remembering that the jurors were human beings, with lives and interests of their own, and, not incidentally, Keker liked to remind them that he remembered.

Cued to the water glass, Robinette promptly spilled it all over himself. Just as they beat their Santa Claus comparisons into the ground with Gesell, reporters wore out the Inspector Clouseau analogies with Robinette. He was so inept, so incompetent, that it somehow added to the credibility of his story. *No one* could make this stuff up.

After a brief mention of his twenty-year CIA career, Robinette described how his friend Dick Secord had hired him to do some private security consulting in 1986. In April of that year, Robinette said Secord "told me of his friend or his associate named Colonel North who was experiencing rather frightening episodes" because of threats on his life from a terrorist named Abu Nidal. In his own brand of government-speak, Robinette said Secord asked him if "that's the kind of thing I could handle and/or would I be interested in attempting to give some support." Shortly thereafter, Robinette said, he began talking with Colonel North, visiting the North home and making plans to install a security system. Robinette launched into a rambling discourse about the difficulties of making the system work: "I just simply thought we could put it up in a tree or in a box away from the weather, that at any time if anyone opened [the] mailbox, the camera would be automatically activated, but I ran into more technical difficulty with several suppliers. . . ." The system was completed by early summer 1986.

Did Robinette ever discuss the price of the system with North?

"I recall his response," Robinette testified, "as simply saying, 'Well, remember, I'm a poor Lieutenant Colonel. . . .'"

But, as Robinette continued, he said General Secord sent him checks to cover the full cost of the system—about $14,000.

"Why didn't you go to Colonel North for the money?" Keker asked. "It was his security system."

"I had no reason to go to Colonel North," Robinette answered blandly, "I was working with General Secord."

Keker then moved ahead to December of 1986, when North had been fired and the Iran-Contra affair had exploded. Robinette said he received a telephone call from North shortly after he was dismissed from the NSC. "What did he say?" asked Keker.

"We exchanged—I was quite pleased to hear from him, surprised, thinking that he was quite busy. . . ."

Like everyone else in the courtroom, Keker could see Robinette was stalling, reluctant to describe the substance of this conversation. So Keker cut him off sternly: "I want to hear what he said and what you said, Mr. Robinette."

"Well, 'How are you? How are things going?' Or vice versa. I said the same thing to him. . . . We exchanged a few comments about his family and his children. I know he likes children, and he knows I like children so we talked about that for a few moments. . . ." This filibuster only made the facts of the conversation that much more enticing for the audience.

Finally, according to Robinette, North "said something to the effect of, 'Hey buddy, you never sent me a bill for that . . . security work you did for me.' And I probably said, 'That's right.' "

Keker feigned surprise. "You didn't say anything about General Secord having already paid for the system?"

"No, sir."

Was Robinette's testimony truthful? Probably not. Both he and North knew that Secord had paid Robinette for the work, and they probably discussed frankly the need for a cover story. But maybe their conversation did unfold just as Robinette described it. In that case, the two men would have *pretended* that the price of the fence had not been covered and then *pretended* to create a paper trail regarding the payments.

Whatever exactly was said in this conversation with North in December, Robinette followed up on it by typing up a new pair of bills for the security system. He prepared the first one for $8,000 and dated it July 2, 1986. "When you prepared this," Keker asked, "was this a real bill or was it a phony bill?"

"It should be considered as a phony bill," Robinette admitted.

Keker then introduced the second fake bill Robinette created in December, this one styled a dunning notice and dated September 22, 1986, for the same $8,000.

Regarding this second bill, Keker suggested that "everything on here is phony?"

"Well," Robinette offered, "the bill is 'real.' I typed it, but—"

Keker and the whole courtroom broke out in laughter. "Okay," said Keker. "In a philosophical sense, it's real. But what it talks about is not real. The dates aren't real and so on."

"Yes," Robinette allowed.

"Phony paperwork?"

"Yes, it's a false document."

Robinette then admitted that he "received two documents, two letters" from North shortly after he submitted the phony bills, sometime later in December 1986, and Keker introduced these letters as government exhibits 132 and 133.

Judge Gesell had given the lawyers a good deal of freedom in using visual aids in the courtroom, and Keker had placed an overhead projector and screen directly in front of the jury. He placed a transparency of exhibit 132 on the glass, let the jury study it for a moment, and then read through the letter with the witness.

The exhibit was a letter—delivered to Robinette in December 1986—dated "18 May 1986," addressed "Dear Mr. Robinette" and signed "Oliver L. North."

"My wife and I," North wrote, "have considered your kind offer to expedite the installation of a security system at our home in Great Falls. . . ." The letter continued by purporting to agree to proceed in the "terms we discussed in our last meeting," which allowed the Norths to choose between a loan of the equipment for use as a "commercial endorsement . . . without fee" or payment in twenty-four installments. Keker got Robinette to agree that he and North had never discussed these or any other payment options. Keker walked Robinette through the letter, sentence by sentence. Each one contained an abundance of lies.

Then Keker placed exhibit 133 on the projector, the second North-to-Robinette letter, this one dated October 1, 1986. The date of the letter, as Keker pointed out, fit with the phony dunning notice Robinette had sent on September 22. Again Keker worked slowly through each sentence. " 'I've been out of town and we seem to keep missing each other's phone calls,' " North wrote. In the letter North gently protested to Robinette that he thought the system would be paid for through "the first option for reimbursement [through] commercial endorsement"—an "option" that the jury had just learned was a figment of North's imagination.

Keker read more slowly as he reached the end of the letter. " 'I don't want you to be caught short, but I don't want to resort to holding up gas stations on my way home from work at night either.' " North's vivid little joke left a sinister residue in the courtroom.

A stream of witnesses calling North a "tremendously wonderful American patriot" could not alter the fact that he had concocted an elaborate cover-up. Nor could Sullivan's cross-examination of Robinette, which sputtered ineffectually for less than an hour, change the day's impression. Even the best lawyer could not help North refute this kind of evidence.

On the day of Robinette's testimony I happened to be sitting in the rear of the courtroom, next to a group from American Christian Tours (ACT). By late March, the North trial had become a regular stop on the Washington tourist circuit for those willing to arise early and brave the long lines. Most of the visitors, like those from ACT, adored the handsome colonel, and they glowed when they saw him walk through the doorway. When North stopped to sign autographs on his way out, his two beefy bodyguards invariably had to extricate him from the crush of attention.

The young fellow from ACT who sat next to me listened intently to Robinette's testimony. When the ordeal ended, I saw his innocent face darken. "He's not my hero anymore," he whispered to a friend next to him.

N O other witness had as dramatic an impact as Robinette. Relatively few factual issues were in dispute between the two sides, so most of our remaining witnesses proceeded pretty much unchallenged. The case would come down to a question of North's intent. The defense did not dispute that North had committed the acts charged in the indictment. The question was, would the jury accept Sullivan's claim of a pure heart on the part of his client and let him off the hook?

Still, we had to work our way through a troubling array of witnesses. Fawn Hall came shortly after Robinette. Including her flowing blonde mane, Hall pushed six feet, and when she swept into the courtroom, several jurors readjusted their glasses for a better look. They saw her do her best for her former boss. Hall's memory, never too strong to start with, had deteriorated further in the two-and-a-half years since North was fired. But Keker did a skillful job of refreshing her memory with her grand jury testimony, and Hall did admit several damaging facts against North. Yes, she conceded, on Friday, November 21, 1986, she had shredded documents with North. Keker asked if the amount of shredding was unusual on that day.

"We shred every day," she advised, "but I had never shredded phone logs and PROF notes and paper in that volume, no."

So, too, she admitted altering original NSC documents during that last week in November, changing the same memos that McFarlane had described as "problems" when he and North were composing the letters to Congress more than a year before.

Finally—and this was the most damaging—she described smuggling documents out of the Old Executive Office Building on the day North was fired, November 25. For all her faltering memory, the story still had a burlesque feel to it. Hall said she had stuffed "the

Tehran minutes into one of [my] boots and the copies of the altered documents in the other." As for the PROF notes, she "folded them, I think, into quarters, [and] placed them inside the back of my skirt so they were just secured there." With the documents secreted in her clothes, she asked North if he could "see anything," and he hurried her out the door.

Judge Gesell did not treat Hall with the deference to which she apparently believed her celebrity status entitled her. When the judge instructed her at one point, "Please shut your mouth when I'm talking," Hall burst into tears on the stand.

For his part, Sullivan miscalculated with excessive solicitude for Hall's histrionics. He called her "Fawn," the only witness he addressed by first name, and prompted more whimpering from Hall with the simple question, "Did you get to know [North's] family?" Trying to comfort her, Sullivan said, "Try to relax now. Don't— because if you cry, I might cry, and the whole courtroom would be embarrassed if lawyers cry, okay?" It seemed contrived. The jurors— no fools in judging human nature—regarded these episodes with long, cold stares.

North's deputy at the NSC, Robert Earl, followed shortly after Hall, and he told of shredding documents with Hall and North and then lying to the FBI when agents began asking about it. As with Hall, the testimony had a seamy quality, an effect enhanced, not diminished, by the witness's obvious affection for Ollie.

Even an unexpected source gave us a valuable boost. Kelly Williams, the kind of bland, competent, middle-aged bureaucrat who fills the capital's car pools, ran the maintenance section for the White House computers. Under Zornow's questioning, Williams described the PROF electronic mail system, using layman's terms to show how the office terminals worked. After a little more background, Zornow moved to a discussion of the backup system for the PROF notes, and it was possible to sense a certain restlessness among the jurors as they wondered why Zornow felt the subject merited such detailed treatment.

But Zornow pressed on, and Williams described how the computers made duplicate copies of all the messages in a White House employee's file every week. How many messages, Zornow asked, were in Colonel North's file on November 15, 1986? Six hundred and ninety-eight, said Williams. How about November 22, 1986? "There were seven hundred thirty-seven notes."

How many notes were there one week later, by the time North was fired?

Williams took a deep breath: "As of the time that that backup tape was taken, there was one note in the note log."

How could this change have happened? Zornow asked. North, said Williams, "would have to have deleted seven hundred thirty-six notes." So while North had been shredding paper documents, he had been performing the electronic equivalent as well.

And what was the one remaining document? North, according to Williams, had left a memo that allowed him to send electronic messages directly to John Poindexter, without any other NSC officials seeing a copy. And how did North use this direct channel? Williams said he needed only to use the right code words. And what were those code words?

"PRIVATE BLANK CHECK"—a fitting epitaph for the National Security Council of the Reagan era.

FOR each witness in the government's case, the OIC assigned two attorneys—the trial lawyer who would examine the individual, and a younger lawyer who would assemble the exhibits, schedule the preparation sessions, and know the witness's story so completely that any deviations could be spotted and corrected. I was the junior lawyer designated for the last three witnesses in the government's case: Edwin Meese, Charles Cooper, and John Richardson.

We had proceeded in roughly chronological order, and now it was time for November 1986. As the administration scrambled to cope with the Iran arms sales disclosure in that month, it became obsessed with the first of the four shipments to Iran. This first sale—of eighteen HAWK antiaircraft missiles—had taken place in November 1985 with the weapons shipped from Israel to Iran on a CIA-owned airline. At the time of the shipment, however, President Reagan had not yet signed a "finding" authorizing the CIA to assist in the shipment of arms. So a year later, in November 1986, the administration—and

North, specifically—began putting out the phony story that everyone had thought the shipments contained "oil drilling equipment," not missiles.

Who knew what was on the November 1985 delivery to Iran? That was the key issue. North's lies on that subject formed the basis for count six of the indictment, which charged him with "preparing a false chronology" of the arms sales. To prove it, we had to start with Ed Meese. I basically stumbled into the Meese assignment, after Cliff Sloan left the OIC, but I came to spend many hours in Meese's memorable presence.

His face was always red, a dense latticework of tiny burst vessels. He walked with a stiff-legged lumbering gait that was almost a limp. Every day I laid eyes on him, he wore a tie with lots of tiny portraits of Adam Smith, patron saint of the free market. Meese was so insistently, disarmingly friendly that it was occasionally possible to forget for a moment that he made every effort to destroy the case against Oliver North.

John Keker learned all this rather late. He hadn't worked with Meese as extensively as he had with other major witnesses in the case, and we squeezed our sessions with Meese into the early evening hours after the first few days of the trial. But we both began to see that Meese suffered the most convenient memory lapses and offered the strangest judgments for an attorney general of the United States. Still, especially since count eight of the indictment charged North with lying to Meese in a face-to-face interview on November 23, 1986, Keker hoped that he could extract from Meese some measure of indignation, if not outrage, at the colonel. For example, in our last preparation session before Meese's testimony, Keker thought he would test the former attorney general with a real softball. "Now, Mr. Meese," Keker said in this dress rehearsal, "if I were to ask you tomorrow, is it ever all right to lie to the attorney general, what would you say?"

As Meese paused, and paused, Keker and I looked at each other in horror. "Well," Meese said at long last, "I'm not sure." You're not sure! I thought in silence. "Now," Meese continued, "if I worked at the White House and the attorney general was that traitor . . ." Meese was obviously searching his memory for the name, and Keker and I, almost involuntarily, piped up together, "Ramsey Clark?" "Yes, right," Meese said amiably. "If he were the attorney general, I'm not sure what I would do."

Meese was sworn in as a witness early in the afternoon of Tuesday, March 28, and Keker began moving him gingerly through the facts. Given the chance, we thought, Meese would screw us, so Keker pared down his testimony to the bare essentials. Meese had heard President Reagan's disastrous news conference on November 19, 1986, and complained that evening to John Poindexter about the president's lack of preparation for the questions about the Iran arms sales. Poindexter then invited Meese to a meeting in the White House the next day where the relevant players would be assembling a chronology of the arms sales to be used in various rounds of upcoming congressional testimony.

Meese attended the November 20 meeting—though he had almost no memory of what went on there—but was informed later that day that there were still differing recollections about how the arms sales had transpired. So, on Friday, November 21, Meese met with President Reagan, who instructed him to do "a general review of the situation, to talk with the people involved" and report back to him on Monday morning. Meese assembled a group of his closest advisors and they spent the weekend interviewing the relevant players and gathering the facts. The last thing the group did was interview Colonel North on Sunday, November 23—another event of which the former attorney general had precious little memory.

Keker raced through the material in an hour, and he did not pause to question what was, in many respects, a very odd story. In the first place, Meese remembered almost nothing except those facts for which a paper record existed. A cynic would have suggested that he had planned it that way. Moreover, his weekend "investigation" seemed as much designed to avoid learning the facts as it did to seek them out. As soon as he received the go-ahead from President Reagan on Friday, Meese called Poindexter to tell him that his men would be coming over on Saturday; Poindexter promptly told North, who, in turn, spent most of the afternoon shredding documents with Hall and Earl. Meese also deputized for the weekend three assistants who lacked so much as a single day of law enforcement experience among them. And they did not even bother to interview three of the key figures in the affair—John Poindexter, William Casey, and Ronald Reagan. Finally, in the interview with North, Meese chose to excuse himself at a crucial moment—to pick up his wife from the airport. As the prosecution was vouching for the seriousness of Meese's inquiry, Keker had no reason to dwell on these problems. Brendan Sullivan did.

It was that casualness of Meese's efforts—the errand at the airport, the lack of interview transcripts, the general air of nonchalance— that Sullivan exploited on cross-examination. Sullivan started by establishing the close personal and political ties between Meese and President Reagan, and went on to show that Meese himself had had some awareness of the Iran arms sales as they unfolded in 1986. Sullivan's gist was that Meese and the president saw the Iran issue as a political problem, not a criminal issue, and Meese seemed only too happy to assist the defense in making this point.

"It was absolutely clear in your mind," Sullivan suggested to Meese, "that you were not conducting a criminal investigation or a formal investigation of any kind, is that correct?"

"Yes, sir," Meese said.

"Indeed," Sullivan continued, "you were acting basically as a counselor or a friend of the president to try to gather together information that was . . . in the heads of many of the people that were closest to him?"

"Yes, sir."

Sullivan was effectively debunking the idea of our filing criminal charges based on Meese's haphazard, informal inquiry. Nothing in the weekend, Sullivan prompted, was more casual than the interview of North on Sunday. "Is it fair to say," the lawyer asked Meese, that "this [was] almost like coworkers in the administration . . . trying to figure out what the facts were?"

"That's correct."

It was an outrageous answer. Meese had testified earlier in the day that the Iran crisis looked so serious at the time that he feared the president might be impeached. And on that weekend, North was the only person who could tell him what had happened. Meese gathered his team, called in North on a Sunday afternoon, and confronted him on the issue that might bring down the president of the United States—and, according to his testimony, he did not even care whether North told him the truth. All it was, Meese told Sullivan, was a chat among coworkers. Sullivan could not have scripted it any better himself.

CHARLES COOPER, while no more favorably disposed toward our office, cut a far more dignified figure from that of his former boss. Cooper, at least, *did* mind being lied to.

We called Cooper principally to testify about the November 20, 1986, meeting at the White House, where assorted administration figures had planned future congressional testimony about the Iran arms sales. A CIA lawyer had brought a piece of draft testimony to the meeting that stated "We in CIA did not find out" that missiles had been shipped to Iran in November 1985 until January of the following year. At the meeting, North had insisted that the statement in the proposed testimony be broadened to "No one in the United States government found" out that HAWKs had been shipped until January. North, of course, knew at the time that HAWKs were being shipped, but he wanted to peddle the false story to Congress.

Under questioning by Zornow, Cooper described North at the meeting saying that the original phrasing of the congressional testimony "could and would leave the inference that people in the United States government outside of the CIA may have known that the HAWK missiles were on the plane before January. His point was that no one in the United States government knew there were HAWKs on the plane until January, and so we ought to make that point quite clear in the testimony." At North's urging, Cooper had scratched in his own handwriting on the draft testimony, "No one in the USG"— a document we introduced into evidence. But as soon as Zornow showed the jury that document, he placed on the overhead projector two PROF notes that North had written in November 1985 and which described the HAWK shipment in detail. The PROFs convincingly put the lie to North's statements at the November 20 meeting.

At age thirty-one, our youngest witness, John Richardson, came last. He had gone to work for Ed Meese at the White House as little more than a volunteer fresh out of a judicial clerkship in 1983. His intelligence and good nature propelled him up the ladder until Meese named him his chief of staff at the Justice Department in 1986. Despite the grandeur of his title, Richardson's position really amounted to that of senior personal assistant. Still, Meese trusted him completely and tapped him along with Chuck Cooper and Brad Reynolds to conduct the famous weekend investigation in November of 1986.

Richardson and I with our youth in common flirted with being friends. To be sure, vast gulfs separated us; the differences only started with our politics. But I sensed in "J. R." a decency that I never found in most of his administration colleagues. Words that might seem artificial coming from the mouth of another seemed genuine coming from Richardson—as on the day, shortly before his testimony, when we were reviewing for the umpteenth time how he and Reynolds had discovered the "diversion memo" in North's office on November 22, 1986.

"You know," Richardson told Mike Bromwich and me, "that new book, *Landslide* [by Jane Mayer and Doyle McManus], says that when Brad first showed me the memo, I said, 'Oh, Jesus.' But I know that's not true," Richardson continued in his guileless way, "because I only say that when I pray."

We needed just one thing from Richardson as a witness. He had been the note taker at Meese's November 23 interview with North, and we had to establish what exactly North said. Of course, if Meese had conducted his weekend investigation professionally and used a stenographer or even an FBI agent—people who recorded statements for a living—this part of our trial would have entailed much less risk for us. But all we had was J. R.

During the last few months before the trial, I became numbingly familiar with Richardson's twenty-nine pages of notes from the North interview. Even though Richardson had excellent handwriting—so did Ed Meese—they were a long way from a verbatim record. But Richardson supplied us with a secret weapon, a fabulous memory for the events of that Sunday afternoon. As Bromwich moved Richardson carefully through the interview with notes, J. R. recited

North's statements just as they were phrased in the indictment. It was a classy way to finish.

RICHARDSON left the stand in the early afternoon of Thursday, March 30, and Gesell dismissed the jury for the weekend, telling them that "a good deal of lawyering . . . has to be done" before they returned for the beginning of the defense case on Monday.

Several days earlier, after we informed the defense that we would soon complete our case, Williams & Connolly announced, with typical bravado, that Ronald Reagan would be their first witness. The defense had subpoenaed the then-president on December 30, but Gesell had let the issue lie until the lawyers gave a specific date for his testimony. So, just after Richardson stepped down, Gesell held a hearing to determine whether Reagan would be called to testify.

The OIC was definitely of two minds on the subject. On the one hand, we were as curious as anyone about establishing, under oath, what Reagan knew. Keker, in particular, could scarcely resist the thought of crossexamining a president of the United States. But we sought always to keep the trial focused on Oliver North. Reagan would present a tremendous distraction for the jury, and, most importantly, there had been no evidence that the president instructed North to do any of the acts for which he was charged. So, once we sorted out our real priorities, we argued that because Reagan could provide no relevant evidence, Gesell should quash the subpoena to him.

Ronald Reagan's personal lawyer, Theodore Olson, and the Justice Department both argued that, as a constitutional matter of presidential power, Reagan could not be called to the stand. Most of us at the OIC regarded this position as politically odious and legally incorrect, but we bit our collective tongues in the interest of the case as a whole. (When Reagan was called as a witness by John Poindexter in his trial in 1990, the former president dropped his legal challenge and gave a voluntary, videotaped deposition.) I know I offered a silent cheer to (of all people) Barry Simon as he said in the hearing, "Two hundred years ago, Chief Justice John Marshall said the president is different from a sovereign. He is elected by the masses and when he leaves office he goes back to the masses."

Judge Gesell clearly did not regard the presidency as imperial or untouchable, and he appeared offended by the broad constitutional claims made on Reagan's behalf. Yet as the hearing on the Reagan subpoena unfolded, we could see that the OIC's relevance argument, which was weakly refuted by W & C, gave Gesell the perfect escape. Reagan's legendary inattention to his duties also played in our favor; Gesell had to know, as did we, that the former president would not in any event remember anything of importance for the trial. By deciding the issue on relevance grounds, the judge could skirt the legal issue of whether a former president could ever be called to testify and hold only that the defendant in this case had made an inadequate showing to require Reagan to appear.

Which is, in essence, what Gesell did. In a five-page decision handed down the day after the hearing, on Friday, March 31, Gesell wrote, "The trial record presently contains no proof that defendant North ever received any authorization from President Reagan to engage in the illegal conduct alleged, either directly or indirectly, orally or in writing." Furthermore, we noted with interest about a battle still to come, Gesell stated, "Whether or not authorization is a defense, authorization is not established by atmosphere, surmise, or inference." While certainly welcome, our victory on the Reagan subpoena left us with a somewhat hollow feeling, the knowledge that the trial would be forever regarded with a sense of what might have been. We believed that Reagan's testimony would have made no difference, but we and everyone else could never know for sure.

Gesell's other ruling on the last Friday in March left us with no mixed emotions. At the conclusion of the government's case in every criminal trial, the defense asks the judge to dismiss some or all of the counts, on the ground that the jury could not possibly find the defendant guilty beyond a reasonable doubt. Judges often reject these motions as a matter of course, but they also sometimes take the opportunity to drop a count or two or otherwise signal that the prosecution has not done its job.

Gerhard Gesell apparently entertained no such thoughts about *United States v. Oliver North.* As soon as arguments finished on the motion on Friday afternoon, Gesell boomed out in a strong and even voice, "Giving full play to the right of the jury to determine credibility, weigh the evidence, and draw justifiable inferences of fact, a reasonable mind might fairly conclude quite beyond a reasonable doubt that the defendant is guilty of each and all of these counts." All twelve charges would go to the jury.

"*Quite* beyond a reasonable doubt." Keker couldn't suppress a smile as he listened to Gesell's small embellishment on our behalf. North, listening just as intently, looked slightly stricken at Gesell's words, which was also a most sensible reaction.

The prosecution team assembled back at Thirteenth Street in a state of exuberant exhaustion. We had not won this case, not by a long shot, but there were many moments over the past two months—and two years—when we thought even this day would never come. The perils of congressional committees, presidential pardons, classified information, and, we had to admit, skilled defense counsel, had not stopped us from placing before the jury enough evidence to find Oliver North guilty of twelve felonies. We paused to savor the moment.

One person did not join in the celebration because he had left earlier that day for a weekend in Oklahoma City. As the North trial took place, Lawrence Walsh still prowled the corridors above Thirteenth Street but he gave Keker a completely free hand to run the trial. Many on the staff had predicted that Walsh would find it impossible to resist meddling, but he exercised what must have seemed like superhuman restraint to stay out of Keker's way. Alone among the OIC staff—including lawyers, FBI agents, secretaries, and clerks—Walsh did not see a single moment of the North trial. He did not want to interfere.

Keker was met at the celebration not only by his smiling colleagues but by one more letter from Barry Simon demanding that we produce another meaningless document. Even the trial did not slow Simon's torrent of nudging correspondence. So Keker took a little liberty just this once. He prepared a cover letter stating that the document Simon sought was enclosed, grabbed one of our cardboard cover sheets that blared "Top Secret," and stapled the cover sheet to a blank piece of paper.

Then he scrawled on the piece of paper: "April Fools!"

Keker showed the package to me and told me he would send the real document about fifteen minutes after the phony. I weighed the consequences, considered the options, and offered my advice:

"Do it! Do it!"

As I left the office that evening, I thought my counsel had been heeded and the joke played. But John Barrett, the prototypical cooler head, had prevailed and talked Keker out of it. I told Keker of my disappointment that night at our small office party to cheer the end of the government's case.

"Ah, hell," Keker said, "if you want to have fun, don't be a lawyer."

CHAPTER SIXTEEN

Pawn in a Chess Game

For the first six weeks of the trial, one document occupied a prominent place on my desk and served as the blueprint for my work days. The transcript of Brendan Sullivan's opening statement became so familiar to me that I could, by the end of the trial, recite parts of it by heart.

Every prosecutor looks to the opposing counsel's opening statement for clues about the defendant's strategy. But we at the OIC had special reason to scrutinize Sullivan's words. We had gone to paralyzing extremes to avoid contact with North's immunized testimony. We had covered ourselves with such a shroud of ignorance that we knew less about what the defense was up to than the prosecutor of any other case.

Because Sullivan's statement was voluntary, it could not "taint" us with North's immunized testimony—even if the lawyer chose to repeat word for word what North told Congress. The opening statement was thus a gold mine of leads to North's defense.

My job was to follow the leads. In the spirit of title inflation that infected the OIC, along with the rest of the government, Keker named me "head of the defense team" before the trial, responsible for anticipating North's moves at the trial and tracking down the evidence to thwart them. The designation implied that the team contained other members, which it did not. My mission was essentially a personal one: to get inside Brendan Sullivan's head.

Like any skilled defense attorney, Sullivan knew that someone would be parsing his words carefully, with an eye to highlighting any evidence promised in his opening but never produced for the jury. Most of his opening statement stayed safely within the usual rhetoric of defense jury addresses: a hymn to the defendant's character, an explication of his honorable motives, and an attack on the weaknesses of the indictment. But Sullivan did cite some specifics, too.

The most important of these had to do with one of the central counts against North—for shredding and destroying documents. Sullivan had stated that North shredded "to protect the operations and the people in [the documents] because he was told by a cabinet-level officer to clean up the operations. To clean up the operations. That's a term which means that you take action to protect the secrets at all costs." This was a new one for us. Who was this "cabinet-level officer"? Sullivan did not keep us in suspense for long, because as he went through the facts for a final time and reached his crescendo, he said, "At that time, the CIA director, a close friend of the president of the United States, a cabinet officer, a member of the National Security Council, told North to clean up the operation—clean it up." So that, we realized, would be the defense theme: blame it all on good old Bill Casey.

William Casey was in many ways the odd man out in the OIC's investigation for the simple reason that you can only prosecute the living. As prosecutors rather than historians, we did not spend much time weighing the moot question of whether Casey committed any crime. And for all that the former CIA director figured in the mythology of the Iran-Contra affair, the little time we did spend on Casey produced only a trickle of incriminating evidence. No papers remained that showed that Casey was informed about North's private resupply network to the contras, and we never identified any congressional testimony where Casey told a flat-out provable falsehood. His telephone records established that he spoke regularly with North, but that alone proved nothing. For his part, former CIA Deputy Director John McMahon, a close Casey aide and one of the most decent men I encountered in the administration, swore that Casey was not part of North's team.

We did have one clue that said otherwise. In his book *Veil*, Bob Woodward asserted that Casey had, while recuperating from brain surgery in his hospital bed, acknowledged complicity in the diversion of funds to the contras. Our taint rules permitted us to read that portion of Woodward's book because it did not refer to or "use" North's immunized testimony. Like the rest of the world, we had some doubts about whether Woodward's bedside conversation with Casey actually took place, but the writer's record of credibility surpassed that of most of our own witnesses. The question thus arose of whether, or how, to learn more about Casey's "confession."

Some lawyers on the staff believed we should follow up on the disclosure in *Veil* by interviewing Woodward about it. However, even if Woodward agreed to talk, others pointed out, anything he told us about Casey's statements would be hearsay evidence and thus inadmissible in any trial. Not so, said the first group, because of an archaic and seldom-used exception to the hearsay rule concerning the "dying declarations" of witnesses. This exception is based on the dubious premise that, according to an old saying, "a man will not meet his maker with a lie upon his lips." According to this theory, we could argue that as Casey prepared to face his own judgment day, he decided to come clean with Bob Woodward.

As the most recent veteran of the bar exam, which is the only place most lawyers ever see the issue of dying declarations, I did some legal research on the question. I found that under current law, Casey's alleged statement about the diversion did not qualify as an admissible dying declaration. In federal courts, the rule now only applies in homicide cases and only then regarding the "cause or circumstances" of the victim's death—as when a gunshot victim points and says, "He did it!" and then dies in someone's arms. (It is *very* rare.) We figured we might be able to shoehorn Woodward's quotes into another exception to the hearsay rule, but after the initial excitement about *Veil* slackened, so did our interest in tracking down the star reporter from *The Washington Post*. Casey's purported statements about the diversion were too vague to be useful in court, and, anyway, most of us figured Woodward would probably wind up squeezing us for more information than we could ever get out of him.

William Casey remained a mystery.

THE defense case began with two relatively inconsequential witnesses who testified about a few tangential matters and then (like most government witnesses) to North's high character. General P. X. Kelly had recently retired as commandant of the Marine Corps and he brought a compelling aura of rectitude and authority with him to the stand. Kelly testified that both Jeanne Kirkpatrick and William Casey urged him to extend North's tenure at the NSC because the young colonel was doing such an excellent job. He didn't have much to say as a witness but Keker, the old Marine, practically fell all over himself making nice to the commandant.

Ellen Garwood, the next witness, posed a distinct contrast. The most generous of Spitz Channell's blue-haired ladies—she gave $2 million to the contras—Garwood rambled semicoherently about communism in Greece and Turkey and eventually got around to refuting a rather peripheral matter in Channell's testimony.

It did not add up to much of anything, and, with two witnesses completed in less than an hour, we felt we had yet to be wounded. A brief appearance by Stanley Sporkin, CIA general counsel in 1985 and 1986 and a colleague of Gesell's on the federal bench at the time of his testimony, probably hurt North more than it helped him. Sullivan tried to extract some muddled story from Sporkin about his knowledge of the November 1985 HAWK shipment, but Zornow, in cross-examination, decided to take advantage of the judge's appearance to make a simpler point. Did CIA Director Casey, Zornow asked, ever ask you to lie?

"No, sir," said Sporkin, indignant at the suggestion.

To your knowledge, did Casey authorize "anybody in the government to shred and destroy documents?"

"No, sir."

Zornow turned to Sporkin's own earlier congressional testimony and asked whether he "believed that in any way it would have been appropriate for you to lie to Congress in December of 1986 in answer to their questions?"

"I've been around a long time," Sporkin said, "and I'm not going to start now and I wasn't going to start then. You tell it straight." A strange trial this was: the government witnesses helped the defendant, and—so far at least—the defense witnesses assisted the prosecution.

Vince Cannistraro opened his testimony by noting mysteriously that he had "lived abroad in a number of countries over the years" and worked for the CIA from 1982 to 1984.

Cannistraro testified primarily about two meetings in William Casey's office in 1984, just before the most restrictive version of the Boland amendment took effect. At the first of these meetings, which, according to Cannistraro, included various agency officials and contra leaders, "Bill Casey, speaking on behalf of the president of the United States, wanted to assure the Freedom Fighters that the United States government would find a way to continue its support to the Freedom Fighters" even after Boland. Cannistraro stated that Casey "explained that Colonel North, as a member of the National Security Council, would not be subject to [the Boland] restrictions and that Colonel North would be a principal point of reference" between the United States and the contras. Casey, according to Cannistraro, then "said that he had discussed this with the president of the United States and that it was agreed with the president that this was how it should be handled."

This testimony made a difference. It showed not only that CIA Director William Casey authorized North to assist the contras, but that President Reagan blessed the arrangement as well. True, Cannistraro's testimony did not suggest that Casey or Reagan instructed North to lie about the operation—and that was what he was charged with—but it made North's function look so central to the administration that he of all people should not be called to account for its failings. John Barrett, whom I often accused of overstating the importance of any individual piece of testimony, returned to Thirteenth Street after the day and said, "We are in *bad* trouble."

KEKER brought a new demeanor with him to the podium on April 4 to begin the cross of Cannistraro. Gone was the ingratiating smile and casual banter; in its place a grim resolve. "I'm John Keker, representing the government in this case," he told the witness.

First question: "When did director of the CIA Casey die?"

"I believe he died in 1987," said Cannistraro, who could tell what was soon to come.

"You know," said Keker, with almost a sneer, "that it's easy to blame things on a dead man, don't you?"

"Yes, sir."

Fearlessly, Keker let Cannistraro repeat the whole damaging story but then the lawyer began to close the vise: "Do you remember being asked about that same meeting when you testified before the grand jury in this case?"

Cannistraro did remember, and he began to backpedal. "I do not believe," he said, "I addressed that specific point in the answers to the grand jury." Keker then read the grand jury testimony, which Chris Mixter of our staff had skillfully elicited almost two years earlier. In the grand jury Cannistraro said nothing about any Casey instructions to North to take over the liaison relationship with the contras, much less anything about authorization from the president. Mixter gave him plenty of chances to tell the story, but Cannistraro never did. Now on the stand, he admitted, "I did not address those questions at the grand jury meeting."

Keker shot at him: "And that was because you forgot them or because you were deliberately withholding information?"

"No," said Cannistraro, who was now floundering, "because that was the nature of the preparation that I had been led to by the Office of Independent Counsel." Gesell jumped in and began badgering Cannistraro about why his testimony in the grand jury differed so dramatically from his statements in open court. For his part, Keker was merciless. "You didn't tell [the grand jury about this meeting] because they didn't ask, or you didn't tell them because you wanted to lie to them?"

"Please," Cannistraro sputtered.

"Please what?" Keker spit back. Freed of the discipline of direct examination, Keker was flourishing.

Cannistraro's grand jury testimony was a gold mine that Keker had only begun to quarry. Keker was exploiting a quirk in the Jencks Act, the law that requires the prosecution to show the defense all prior statements of government witnesses. When the defense calls a witness—as North called Cannistraro—the Jencks Act does *not* require the government to turn over his earlier statements, like grand jury testimony. Because prosecutors take grand jury testimony unencumbered by defense attorneys and unburdened by any legal obligation to elicit information helpful to the defense, the transcripts tend to be chock-full of damaging assertions about the defendant. So, lacking access to these previous statements, criminal defendants tend to call few witnesses at trials and instead concentrate their efforts on crossexamining those called by the government. But Williams & Connolly, ever cocky, decided to gamble that Cannistraro's grand jury testimony would not come back to haunt them.

They lost.

North had shared with Cannistraro some of the letters the colonel had drafted for McFarlane to send to Capitol Hill. "He showed you some of his answers, right?" Keker asked. "He did," said Cannistraro.

"And what was your response?" asked Keker. "What *physically* did you do when he showed you the answers that he was giving to these questions?" The jury and audience looked quizzical at this odd question. "Physically"? At first Cannistraro told Keker only what he *said* to North, so Keker pushed him.

"Did you do anything with your hands?"

Cannistraro now literally began squirming in his seat. "Are you going back to the grand jury testimony?" he asked.

"I am trying to get the truth, Mr. Cannistraro." Keker was raising his voice in irritation, but he couldn't suppress a smile. Keker was going to enjoy it as much as the witness was going to suffer. "Did you do anything with your hands. . . ."

"Well, truth requires objectivity, not advocacy," Cannistraro said meaninglessly. He was stalling. "I am not sure this falls into the category of objectivity if you ask me to make that gesture." He looked around hopelessly. "But I will if you want me to."

"What did you do?" Keker just repeated.

"Your Honor," Cannistraro looked with basset hound eyes to Gesell, "do I have to answer that?"

"Yes," said Gesell, "you do."

"Okay," said the moping witness, "I suggested that . . ." and Cannistraro placed his hand on his nose and then extended his arm about two feet.

There had been laughs before in Courtroom Six but with Cannistraro's long-awaited gesture, the room collapsed. Guffaws came from Judge Gesell, the jury, the press—everyone—except, of course, for the witness and those at the defense table.

"You went like this," Keker said, and he repeated the gesture, dramatically flinging his arm straight out from his nose. "Like a long nose?"

Cannistraro managed a small smile and, reacting to Keker's flourish, said, "Not *that* long."

"Okay," Keker said, when order was restored. "And that comes from what story? I mean, whose nose grew in our childhood books?"

"I guess I read different childhood books than you did," Cannistraro said.

"Just tell us."

"I think you are trying to get at the Pinocchio story."

"I am," said Keker, "trying to get at the Pinocchio story."

Keker had still another twist for the barbecue skewer. "Was Colonel North considered to be a trustworthy person in terms of what he told you?"

Cannistraro paused slightly before answering, as if struggling to remember what other statement Keker would taunt him with now. He offered some bland words about North being generally trustworthy. Then Keker began his litany once more: "Do you recall testifying on that subject before the grand jury?"

"Yes, I do."

"And do you remember saying anything about four grains of salt?"

The opaque reference prompted Cannistraro to sigh in surrender. "It was either four or three. I don't remember."

Keker enlightened everyone by reading from the grand jury transcript. "Do you recall testifying, 'With Colonel North you could never be certain that what he was telling you was true or was fantasy or was being told you deliberately to mislead you. So my normal modus operandi when receiving information from Colonel North, as I'm sure it was for most people who knew him for some time, was to take everything with about four grains of salt and try to sort it out from there.' " The laughter almost drowned out the last words of Keker's recitation.

CHASTENED by the Cannistraro fiasco, North and his team decided to wrap up the peripheral matters in their case fairly quickly. The most dramatic of the defense witnesses was David Jacobsen, who was held for seventeen months as a hostage in Lebanon. He transfixed a still and respectful courtroom with his description of life in captivity. "I was chained, blindfolded in my underwear, in a basement dungeon." With the precision of one who felt compelled to keep track, Jacobsen said, "I saw the sun twice and the moon once in seventeen months." Jacobsen met North on November 3, 1986, at the American embassy in Beirut, where North had risked his life to see that Jacobsen's release took place.

North hoped other hostages would be freed with Jacobsen in early November, but Jacobsen turned out to be the only one. As the two men were flying back toward the West, Jacobsen testified, "I looked at Colonel North and I saw that he had tears in his eyes. And I said, 'Colonel, what is wrong?' He said, 'David, it is nothing to do with you. . . . I am discouraged that today other men are still remaining there in a dangerous situation in Lebanon, and I am happy you are free, but I just wish everybody else could be.' So that they could enjoy the same joy of freedom that I was experiencing that moment. He was sincerely concerned about the freedom of those men."

The truth was that through his sponsorship of the sleazy profiteers Secord and Hakim—whom the government of Iran eventually recognized were overcharging for the weapons—North had done as much to endanger the hostages as to bring them home. But now, Keker knew, was not the time to make that point. When his turn for cross-examination of this witness came, he rose and said, "We have no questions for Mr. Jacobsen." Turning to the witness and acknowledging, in a small way, the man's ordeal, Keker said, "Thank you, sir."

OLIVER NORTH did not *have* to testify at his trial. Like any criminal defendant, he could have sat through the proceedings and heard Judge Gesell go to great lengths to instruct the jurors to "draw no inference" from the defendant's silence.

We knew North would testify. Defendants in white-collar cases take the stand more often than those accused of violent crime, but, more importantly, Oliver North was a man whose soldierly defiance and schoolboy charm once held the entire nation spellbound. A savvy player like Sullivan knew that the skills that make a good congressional witness do not necessarily translate equally well to the courtroom. Still, Sullivan could not afford to conserve North's skills as a communicator.

Sullivan's opening statement flashed the signal that he would more than likely put North on. By emphasizing CIA Director Casey's supposed command that North "clean up the operation," Sullivan was making that authorization of North's actions a linchpin of the defense. He had to provide the evidence to back it up. Casey couldn't repeat his instruction for the jury, and this evidence would be inadmissible hearsay if anyone else tried to testify about it. It could only come from North's own mouth.

Final confirmation arrived in a phone call from a Williams & Connolly functionary at shortly after 7 P.M. on Wednesday, April 5: North would take the stand the next day. Though we expected the news, the confirmation struck our office like a lightning bolt. It was time for the main event.

THE line outside Courtroom Six engulfed the entire second floor of the federal courthouse on Thursday morning. A crowd of almost three hundred people materialized in response to the news of North's appearance. Disappointment awaited virtually all of them. After the fifty reporters, nine courtroom artists, half-dozen security gurus, and various peripheral members of the prosecution and defense teams (like me), the public was allowed about a dozen seats.

Gesell possessed a keen ear for distractions—"No newspapers in this courtroom!" he would snap at the slightest rustle—but this morning only the click of Oliver North's heels against the marble floor disturbed the silence as he marched to the stand directly after lunch. He placed one hand on the courtroom Bible and lifted his other at the precise right angle that had been immortalized in thousands of photographs some six hundred days earlier.

North had officially retired from the Marines, so he had traded the crisp Marine greens with their sparkling array of decorations for a somberly elegant blue suit. The erect, martial bearing remained. He even sat at attention, his back never touching the rear of his chair. Confident, nearly smug, he did not smile.

Sullivan walked slowly to the podium and said with an unexpected lilt, "So you're Colonel North." It was the grim attorney's single attempt at public wit in the year since the indictment, but it did break the tension.

"Yes, sir, I am," North responded and flashed his famous, gap-toothed grin.

The voice. That *voice*. It scratched just a little, and North converted this technical flaw into an astonishing sense of sincerity, even intimacy. The tiny catch could make it seem that he was on the verge of tears, hesitating as he proceeded, keeping his emotions just barely under control. I was transfixed, not only by the timbre but by my recognition that, famous as this man was, I had almost never before heard that sound before. I never fully realized until that moment the success of our insulation efforts.

North had been trained exceptionally well. "Don't look at me," Sullivan must have told him, "look at the jury." He made lots of eye contact with the jurors, who, accustomed to witnesses gazing away from them and toward the podium, stared intently back at him.

Sullivan gave his client a little time to get settled. He asked about North's family. "I am married to my wife Betsy," he said, gesturing toward the front row, "who is out there. We have four lovely children." The jury could scarcely have missed them. Almost every day, about half an hour into the day's session, Betsy would promenade down the aisle, usually with some assortment of the kids or a clergyman in full regalia. Williams & Connolly did not miss a trick.

"One does a lot of paper." That was North's general (and generally accurate) summary of his duties at the NSC. Sullivan gradually moved him toward his two principal areas of responsibility—counterterrorism and Nicaragua—and the people he dealt with on those issues. Asked to describe William Casey, North gave a little nod and told the jury, "Director Casey was, in my humble estimation, a remarkable man. At age seventy plus, he had more energy than I have or even these lawyers of mine." But were they friends? No. "He was a man that I respected and admired, obviously very close to the president. [Our relationship] was one of a subordinate to a superior."

At the time the Boland amendment kicked in, North said that Casey essentially turned over responsibility for supporting the contras from the CIA to him at the NSC. "I understood it very clearly to be that I would be the one to replace the CIA. . . ." There was, said North, "basically what we would call a hand-off, just like in basketball, I suppose. You got the ball—go on with it." The "basketball" reference struck me as a little contrived and perhaps patronizing for a Washington jury; you see a lot more hand-offs in *football* than you do in "the city game."

Part of his new responsibilities, North said, came in the area of public relations and fundraising. He said he would give briefings to various visitors to the White House, some of whom came from groups like Spitz Channell's NEPL. "Colonel," Sullivan said casually, "I would like for you at this time to come down and demonstrate what it was that you said at that time in those briefings. . . ."

The W & C team moved a large screen into the courtroom after lunch, so Keker knew what was coming. Quietly but insistently—he did not want the jury to think him rude to North—Keker asked to be heard at a bench conference before North could agree to Sullivan's request. Sullivan was asking permission for his client to give a speech to the jury—with slides, no less. This kind of thing just doesn't happen in criminal trials. Along with the rest of us, Keker thought Gesell would never allow it.

"You vowed," Keker reminded the judge at the bench, that this "would not be a political trial." The only reason for the slide show, Keker charged, "is to inflame the jury with his dedication to the Resistance, which is not an issue in this case." But Gesell agreed with Sullivan that our conspiracy to defraud the IRS count, by referring to his "briefings" of potential donors, made the presentation relevant.

North could stage his show. Keker, Bromwich, and Zornow could barely conceal their shock as the defendant descended from the witness stand and accepted the pointer that his attorney helpfully offered to him.

"Excuse me, Mr. Smith," Sullivan said to Gesell's bailiff, "could you dim the lights a little?" Dim the lights? Was this a courtroom or a disco?

What followed may have been the oddest twenty minutes in the history of American jurisprudence. Pointer in one hand, slide carousel clicker in the other, North faced the jury and began his polished spiel as if he had done it the day before (which, given the W & C reputation for preparedness, he probably did). In a legal system generally meticulous about policing the reliability of witnesses' observations, North was given free rein. He made the most of it.

Names, places, numbers, facts—North lobbed bushels of them at the jury. "One hundred million human beings," North said at the beginning, are now threatened "by a communist government right here in the mainland of the United States"—which sounded more like Delaware than Nicaragua. The Soviet Union, he said, is outspending us, four to one, in this hemisphere alone. Here's a slide of the Kirov battleship group, "in sight of the coast of Louisiana." Here's a rocket launcher found in El Salvador, "serial number 308622, . . . made in the People's Republic of China, . . . which probably found its way into the hands of the North Vietnamese Army."

In one slide North identified a Nicaraguan "armored battalion staging area at El Tempisque," near Honduras. "As an infantry officer, a person in the military," North confided to the jury, "I can tell you that there is never a situation where you deploy armor as a defensive measure." (This observation, we later learned, was nonsense.) Children in Nicaragua, North explained, learn to count by adding up AK-47s and hand grenades. The pictures and the words kept coming and coming.

My seat in court on this day was near the front on the right side of the courtroom, so I could not see the slides at all, but I did have a perfect view of the jurors' faces as the show unfolded. Through North's presentation, they maintained the same impassive expressions with which they—like jurors in most cases—absorbed all the evidence. Many in the group did wince when North showed slides of a Father Baltadano, who "was bound hand and foot and thrown into his church and the church was set afire over him." But, in one respect, our fears seemed unfounded; neither the jury nor anyone else, it appeared, was "inflamed" by North's pitch.

North built to his climax by noting the severe shortages the Freedom Fighters were forced to endure. The last slide showed a small cemetery, the graves marked by simple crosses. "What you see here," North said to the jurors, is "what happens without support. It happens in any war. It just happens in this war that the only soldiers who get buried beneath the cross are with the Resistance. The ones who are being buried in Managua at the time were being buried beneath a plain stone slab without any reference to the fact that most of them are Christians."

And then—nothing. Applause had obviously been customary at this point, and the silence created a strange, uneasy void, like the space between rings of a telephone. "That was the briefing, Your Honor," North said, and he stepped back to the witness stand. The jurors rearranged their hands in their laps and turned without expression to hear the next piece of testimony.

I N the traumatic two-and-a-half years since his departure from the NSC, North developed what I came to recognize as "celebrity memory syndrome," a certain vagueness of recall common to those whose underlings remember details for them. For many years North served as a "Staff Guy" who kept track of the details for his superiors, but he had now transformed himself, perhaps consciously, into a "Big-Picture Guy."

That change was only the first of those that made him a less effective witness in court than he was before Congress. Detailed, factual exegesis sounds trivial and nit-picking under the loose evidentiary rules of a congressional hearing—where North could flick a troublesome question aside with a rhetorical sally instead of a straight answer. But that kind of gamesmanship wouldn't fly in court. Keker tried to keep a relatively low profile during North's direct testimony, but he bobbed up occasionally with timely objections. Repeatedly during his testimony North would say "I was told that . . ." and "It was my understanding that. . . ."

After several such claims, Keker arose and said, "Objection, Your Honor. Could we have who told him and some foundation?"

Gesell agreed, telling North, "I really think when you talk about 'understanding,' you're going to have to develop where it came from, who said what, the same rules we've had all the way through the trial." North invariably said his directions came from "Director Casey" and "Mr. McFarlane," but the times and places of these instructions remained conspicuously vague.

In one area, though, North did have direct, specific answers. On Friday morning, the second day of his testimony, Sullivan walked North through the drafting process of the letters McFarlane signed to Congress—the basis of the first four charges in the indictment. North said he had urged McFarlane to ignore the questions from Congress, "simply say we're not going to do this," and claim executive privilege. Yes, he admitted, he had written some of the drafts, but he had fought with McFarlane about the letters, with his boss eventually growing so fed up with him that he sent North a PROF note urging, "Ollie, don't send me any PROF notes about it." As North put it, McFarlane "didn't want to hear any more from me about it." North's testimony, on the McFarlane letters anyway, had the ring of truth.

He faced a much tougher road regarding count five of the indictment, which charged him with lying to the House intelligence committee on August 6, 1986. McFarlane had left the White House at this point, and North was then being supervised by John Poindexter. Press reports about North helping the contras had once again piqued congressional concern, and though the White House managed to forestall a full-scale hearing, Poindexter did agree to have North meet with the intelligence committee in the Situation Room—"on our turf," as North quoted Poindexter.

North's voice grew hushed as he discussed the August 6 testimony, which he said "was not billed as 'testimony' or anything like that. It would be an informal, off-the-record meeting in the White House Situation Room." North called it "informal" and "off-the-record" at least three times in five minutes on the stand, proving less the informality of the session than his defensiveness about his performance at it. He said he told Poindexter that he thought the whole idea of his speaking to the committee was not "a great idea, that he and I knew there were certain things . . . that just could not be revealed." His voice growing softer, North quoted Poindexter's instruction to him, " 'You can take care of it.'

"And so I went to that meeting with the belief that it was off the record, that it was informal, and . . . that there would be enough friends of the policy down there to vector the conversation away from the tough issues." And then he paused dramatically.

"And I was wrong."

Sullivan, too, hesitated before asking his next question. "Did you tell them the truth at that meeting on August 6, 1986?"

From my vantage point I believed I saw North's deep-set eyes fill with tears. He hesitated, then said: "No."

Sullivan asked, "Did you believe your conduct was unlawful?"

"No," said North, his voice barely more than a whisper, "I didn't think it was unlawful, but I was raised to know the difference between right and wrong. I knew it wasn't right not to tell the truth on those things, but I didn't think it was unlawful."

Sullivan then asked a very clever question, one that the jurors must have been thinking, "Why didn't Admiral Poindexter go to the meeting instead of you?"

"He was on leave," North said coldly—the boss on vacation, while the little guy twists in the wind.

Sullivan wanted North to make one last point. "How did you feel about being put in that situation? You knew that Mr. McFarlane had denied [Congress] the information in 1985 in three letters. . . . How did you feel about being told by your boss to go into a meeting on August 6, 1986?"

North waited again here, longer than before answering any other question. And when he finally spoke, his voice quivered once more, on the edge of weeping.

"I felt," said North, "like a pawn in a chess game being played by giants."

North's direct testimony could have ended there, and, as far as its dramatic impact, it did. As always, we wondered what the jury made of it. To our ears, the phrase echoed with the canned sentiment of a greeting card, coldly premeditated and unctuously executed. But we could not help but worry that our own cynicism and partisanship inured us to the appeal of North's cry. In one respect, North had a point: his boss Poindexter did hang him out to dry. Still, North had now admitted on the record that he walked into the Situation Room, looked those congressmen in the eyes, and lied to them. The jury, as always, sat expressionless in judgment.

In the aftermath of their "chess game" gambit, we wondered at the hazard Sullivan and North had risked. In this exchange and through much of his direct testimony, North simply admitted most of the prosecution case against him. Indeed, his own testimony rendered virtually all of our witnesses superfluous. Yes, he ran a resupply network for the contras. Yes, he solicited money. Yes, he made false statements to Congress. But no, he did not commit any crime.

From the beginning, the trial seemed headed for this pass. Disputes about the facts—what actually happened during North's years at the NSC—seemed insignificant. The jurors would have to look into North's heart, his "intent," in the legal argot, and weigh his responsibility.

The entire case—the *entire* case—would come down to John Keker's cross-examination of Oliver North.

CHAPTER SEVENTEEN

"That Was Truly a
False Statement"

As far as I was concerned, it turned out that what Keker meant by "defense team" really amounted to "North cross-examination team." Almost every day after court, Keker and I would talk about how the day's events shaped his plans for cross-examining North. After these discussions, I would then try to track down the ammunition—the evidence—Keker could use to make his points when the time came for the cross.

Keker saw that the trial was evolving into a personal judgment on North, rather than an assessment of competing versions of the facts. So Keker had me look to sources that might illuminate the persona that North presented to the jury, rather than provide evidence specifically about counts in the indictment. I tracked down the instruction material North received at the Naval Academy in the mid-1960s regarding an officer's duty to ignore an illegal order. So, too, I found copies of the oaths North signed in which he swore to uphold the Constitution. All of it was meant to illustrate that North knew that he had higher obligations than pleasing his superiors.

The colonel, we realized early in our investigation, had a reputation as a congenital liar among his colleagues. Keker believed this issue was crucial, especially after North admitted in his direct testimony that he deceived Congress. We felt we had to establish for the jury that the lies charged in the indictment did not represent North's momentary lapses under extraordinary pressures; rather, they fit within a long pattern of deceptions by North.

We ended up with a thick black binder that we came to call "Ollie's Tall Tales." I identified dozens of individual lies that North told and organized them by subject. Each tab had a summary of the lie and the back-up material to prove the statement was false. Some of the lies opened up classified information problems—like North's own violations of the classified information rules. Others seemed just too nutty to pursue—like when North told someone that he once sneaked into President Reagan's ranch to give him some information.

But Keker had one priority for the cross. North had portrayed himself as a selfless patriot, consumed by his desire to free the hostages and assist the Freedom Fighters in Nicaragua. That image, Keker believed, formed the single greatest impediment to obtaining a conviction of North. He would have to attack it head on and right away.

So Keker decided to shift the focus of the examination from the battlefields of Nicaragua and dungeons of Beirut to the showroom of Koons Pontiac in Vienna, Virginia.

SULLIVAN dragged out North's testimony through the full day of Friday, April 7, so as not to give Keker the last word before the jurors left for the weekend. The direct wrapped up quickly on Monday morning. Then Keker was on.

As Keker walked to the podium, the room crackled with excitement. Most people knew that the trial had come down to this moment. No one could predict what was going to happen now.

"Good morning, Colonel North."

Only hearing those words go unanswered fully prepares a listener for the strangeness of the resulting silence—like an unfinished musical scale. But North did not answer. He refused to greet Keker. North merely nodded, or, really, just jutted his square chin a few millimeters in Keker's direction.

On paper, they had much in common. Both ex-Marines and Vietnam War heroes, Keker and North were born within ninety days of each other during World War II. They even almost looked alike; both ruddy, trim, and handsome at the onset of middle age. But for all their similarities—indeed perhaps because of them—we had heard rumors that North had fixated his resentments on Keker personally. We heard a report that North had asked friends in the Marine Corps to check the veracity of the news reports about Keker's battlefield decorations in Vietnam—in hopes of discrediting the prosecutor. In the moment after Keker's "Good morning," we could see the stories were true.

Keker made it appear that he did not notice the snub, and proceeded calmly.

"Colonel North," he said, "you understand that you are not on trial for violating the Boland amendment, don't you?"

"I do."

"And you understand you're not on trial for trying to release hostages?"

"I do."

"Or for using the residual monies from the Iranian arms sales for the contras?"

"Yes."

"What are you on trial for, as you understand it?"

North stumbled a little, saying he didn't recall, and Sullivan properly objected to the question. North had no obligation to summarize the charges.

So Keker did. There are four "charges associated with the letters that Mr. McFarlane signed that went to Congress in 1985. . . . Do you remember those?"

North did. "And then there's a charge that you obstructed a congressional inquiry in August of 1986 by lying to it, do you remember that charge?"

He did. Keker worked through all twelve, trying to focus the jury on the specifics of the case rather than the vague and heroic story North told on direct.

"I'd like to ask you some questions about some of the very specific charges. . . . And I'd like to start with the traveler's checks, count ten."

Keker knew he had to start here—with the grubbiest, dirtiest count of all. First, he had to convince the jury this man was a petty thief. If he did that, the rest would be easy.

"You said that you had never committed while you were at the National Security Council an act that you considered criminal, is that right?"

"I—if I didn't say that, I'll say it now," North said, "I don't believe I ever did anything that was criminal."

"Fair enough," said Keker. Fair enough. It was Keker's conversational tic, which he fell into repeatedly during his cross-examination of North. So familiar did it become to the courtroom that even Judge Gesell started using it.

"You told us about the need to start an 'operational account' to support the contras toward the end of 1984 or the beginning of 1985. Do you recall that testimony?"

North repeated his contention that Casey told him to set up the fund. A total of about $300,000 passed through it, he said. On direct, North had admitted that he spent $4,300 from these traveler's checks for personal purposes, but he insisted that he had reimbursed the fund for the full amount.

Keker asked several polite questions about the operational account, but the tension between the two men was building. He moved to North's record-keeping practices for the account. North said that Director Casey "told me to keep very careful records as to the amount of money that came in, where it came from and how that money was expended."

"Where would you keep careful track of it, in what kind of book?"

"In a ledger," said North.

"Is that ledger still around?" Keker asked pleasantly.

"No," said North, "it is not."

Startled, Keker said, "Where is it?"

"It was destroyed."

"You say it was destroyed." Now Keker began to turn up the heat. "You make it sound like it might be in an earthquake or something," said the San Franciscan. "What happened to the ledger? Do you know who destroyed it?"

"Yes."

"Who?"

"I did," North said with a hard stare.

Keker paused and gave a smile that edged near to a smirk. "When did you destroy the ledger that accounted for what appears to be about $300,000 of cash and traveler's checks that came through your hands in 1985 and 1986?"

North didn't recall whether it was October or November 1986, but he was certain, as ever, that "Director Casey told me to, and I did so."

"That's the *late* director Casey who told you to destroy the ledger?"

"Yes."

Keker believed in making pictures for the jury, so he forced North to describe the ledger in detail ("a little spiral spring on the side") and then how he destroyed it. "I tore page after page out of it and put it into the shredder."

"Why did you destroy it?" Keker badgered.

"Because Director Casey told me to."

"This was the only record that existed of you spending about $300,000 over the last couple of years?"

"That's the only record I know of."

The words flashed hot and fast between the two men, but North knew Keker was building to something, holding something back, that would raise the temperature even more.

Keker turned to North's explanation for how he reimbursed the fund. Keker pointed to a chart on which we had posted all of North's personal uses of the traveler's checks. Here, Keker said, pointing, "at Giant Food on April 21, you cashed a $50 traveler's check for $41.05 in purchases, and you put the change in your pocket. You were reimbursing yourself for money that you had spent on contra or hostage initiatives, is that right?"

"Yes, correct."

"Where did you get the money that you spent on the contra- or hostage-related activities to begin with?"

"It was my money, my cash," said North.

"And where did you get cash?"

"Out of my house."

Keker, now incredulous, asked, "Did you have a stash of cash in your house?"

"You call it a stash," North said with the fastidious distaste he came to express frequently for Keker's colloquial language. "I call it a family fund and we had it since I was—before I was married."

"How large was the family fund?"

"I would say that by mid-1985," North said, searching his memory, "upwards of $15,000 in cash."

Keker was *really* incredulous. "Fifteen thousand dollars in cash that you kept in your house?"

"Yes." So Keker began pressing North about this large amount of cash in his home. How much did he have?"

"It would change almost every week, counsel, because when I would come home on a Friday, it was almost a ritual of the twenty-some-odd years I've been married, I would take my change out of my pocket and put it in that steel box that I'd been issued as a midshipman. And that's where it would go and that's how that fund was built over the course of twenty-plus years."

"The change in your pocket," Keker said slowly, almost mistily, "grew to $15,000 that you kept in your house."

"Yes."

Thus was born the Legend of the Little Metal Box. North's story about the box constituted one of the biggest "new" disclosures of the trial, and it was certainly news to us at the OIC. It also set off rounds of semiserious debate within our office about whether the jury would believe North's story. Many of us thought the jury would see North's oh-so-convenient explanation as a fraud—a desperate and phony attempt to account for his easy access to personal cash. North's story seemed almost intentionally designed to evoke comparisons with a legendary New York City pol of the depression era named Thomas Farley, who claimed, to great public amusement, that he accumulated $400,000 on a yearly salary of $8,500 by saving his change in "a little tin box."

Others in our camp disagreed with this cynical view, citing a class-based explanation for why the jury might buy North's story. While the thought of $15,000 in cash seemed outlandish to a group of upper-middle-class lawyers, they said, the accumulation of large amounts of cash was not at all uncommon for people who lacked charge cards or even checking accounts—people, in short, like our jurors. "No wonder you don't believe him," Zornow said to me, "your wife works for American Express."

Keker was not finished with the metal box. "In October of 1985, Mr. North," Keker asked, "did you buy a new car from Koons Pontiac?"

North was now anticipating Keker's sallies, so he tried to preempt them. Yes, he said, he had bought a "*used* GMC Suburban" and "paid for it from that family fund."

So, Keker said, "you just walked down and gave them" the cash?

Not exactly, said North. "As I recall, we were actually looking for another car, a station wagon, and I had brought with me $3,000 or $4,000, something like that, from the fund. I put a deposit down and a couple of days later I went back and paid for the rest of it."

"Where is J. Koons?" Keker asked, the question appearing out of the blue.

"It's in Tysons Corner"—a major shopping mall in the Washington suburbs.

"How far from your house?"

"Eight miles, ten miles, something like that."

Now it was Keker's turn to pause. "How far," he asked, "from General Secord's office?"

North, momentarily startled, said, "I don't know. About a mile or two."

"Did you go to General Secord's office that afternoon to get another $3,000 for the hostages that afternoon of October 5th?"

"I honestly don't remember."

The fruits of Bob Shwartz's long-ago compulsion about North's finances were about to be reaped. Shwartz had tracked down the receipts for the purchase of the van at Koons. The records showed that North had put down $5,000 in cash as a deposit on October 5—and paid the remaining $3,000 three days later. Secord's records showed that North had picked up $3,000 in cash from Secord, also on Saturday, October 5. The juxtaposition gave North some explaining to do.

"You had $5,000 in cash" at the auto dealer, Keker pressed. "You have got how much at home now, ten?"

"Sure."

"Ten in the metal box," Keker repeated. "Why not just go home" and get the balance and buy the car on Saturday?"

"Because I think I had to get to work. . . ."

"In any event, you showed up at Koons Pontiac a few days later and you had $3,038 in cash that you didn't have on Saturday?"

"That I didn't have *with me* on Saturday," North corrected.

"You hadn't gone to a bank account," Keker described, "you had gone someplace and gotten cash?"

By this time in his life, North had begun his career as a highly paid lecturer and he had, it appeared, become accustomed to a certain deference from his interlocutors. North plainly preferred his speech audience's admiring queries about the communist menace to Keker's brutal contempt about his petty cash.

"I had gone back to my box that was bolted to the floor of my closet and got the cash, Mr. Keker," North said in a tightly controlled fury.

The explosive first morning of the cross-examination concluded with this standoff. In just about an hour of work, Keker had developed a bumper crop of startling North claims: that he got his cash from a little box in his closet; that, notwithstanding having $15,000 in cash, he paid for his car in two installments because he had to get to work that Saturday; that Secord gave him $3,000 in cash—the precise amount owed on the car—at the exact time he needed to raise the money to complete the car purchase. In at least one respect, Keker had succeeded brilliantly: the focus had shifted a long way from fighting communism and saving hostages.

I N the afternoon Keker continued pounding at North's personal finances. His target this time: the Belly Button account that Secord and Hakim set up for North's benefit.

First Keker tried to make Secord's motives clear. North admitted that he knew Secord sold the contras about $11 million worth of weapons and that some unspecified amount of that sum went for Secord's profits. "Okay, let me ask you this, then," Keker said. "Was any of that money . . . set aside . . . for you and your family?"

"No—not one cent," North said emphatically. He had been waiting for the Button account to come up and he was ready.

"Colonel North," Keker said, "did you send your wife to Philadelphia to meet with Mr. Willard Zucker in March of 1986?"

North had. "Mr. Hakim," North said, "had noted the extraordinary danger" of the trip North was then planning to take to Tehran. "My wife, it was suggested, should meet with Mr. Hakim's lawyer in the event that something happened to me. . . . To my recollection, there was nothing discussed about money or accounts or amounts, simply that she would know the person who would come to her if I didn't return from that trip."

"Was there discussion about setting up a trust fund for the education of your children?"

"Not according to anything that I know about that, no."

North said that Zucker had called his home sometime in the summer of 1986, after the Philadelphia meeting, and he told his wife "not to call Mr. Zucker back, that there was no longer a need, that I had returned safely from Tehran."

Keker showed North a secret cable that Secord had sent to him, advising that the "$200,000 insurance fund" had been set up. What did North understand that fund to be? North said the money was for American pilots who were flying private resupply missions in Nicaragua. Keker then placed one of North's old schedule cards before him, the one for April 28, 1986. "Whose name is on the back of this schedule card?"

"It says Willard Zucker." It also had Zucker's phone numbers in Switzerland.

"Do you recognize the writing on the back of the schedule card?"

"I would guess," North stumbled, "it's either Fawn Hall's or—it's certainly not mine. I may not be fair. I don't know that it is."

"Why," Keker asked, "is somebody putting Mr. Zucker's overseas phone numbers at work and at home on your schedule card on April 28, 1986, after he's met a month and a half earlier with your wife to talk about your children and their educational plans?"

"I haven't the foggiest idea, Mr. Keker," North said with confidence. "All I can tell you is that I did not put that there and I did not realize it was there until you just showed it to me. The point is, I did not call Mr. Zucker. I don't believe my wife communicated at all again with Mr. Zucker until somewhat later in the summer, at which time he called and I told my wife not to call him back."

All of a sudden, North was taking control of the examination.

Unlike his morning sallies on the traveler's checks, Keker's version of the Button account story fell flat. North had a plausible answer for everything, and Keker lacked the documentation to make his insinuations stick. As it had so often during the past two years, the Button account promised more than it could deliver.

Keker sought the safe harbor of the story of the traveler's checks, where he had scored points earlier in the day. "Were you ever nervous," Keker asked, "about the fact that you and your ledger were the only thing that was keeping track of this $300,000 in cash and traveler's checks during the period that you were getting it?"

"Nervous?" North said earnestly. "I wouldn't use the word 'nervous.'" He was picking up both confidence and steam. Every time Keker asked a general, open-ended question like this one, North gave a sparklingly sincere (and lengthy) answer. "I was certainly very conscious of the fact that the money was not mine, that it needed to be strictly accounted for. Director Casey had emphasized that with me, and that's why I assume he gave me the ledger. . . . And I made every effort to make sure that the money was properly distributed for the purposes for which it was given."

I was on this day sitting with Larry Shtasel in the well of the courtroom, just behind our counsel table and within six feet of the jury box. As North pounced on Keker's question about whether he was nervous about the traveler's checks, Shtasel scribbled me a note: "This ain't no duck hunt."

The whole afternoon proved little short of a disaster for Keker. He lurched from subject to subject, and North held his ground on all of them. The colonel had all the answers. He knew Channell was fundraising, but he, North, never personally asked anyone for money. He did not know how much Secord made in profits. He did not believe he had violated the Boland amendment. Proud, confident, defiant—the North of the congressional hearings was back.

Our case, we feared, was coming apart. Walking back from the courthouse late that afternoon, a disconsolate John Barrett told me his view: "It's all over." We mostly left Keker to himself that evening, but worries percolated through the office.

KEKER approached the lectern on Tuesday morning with the same calm expression (and courteous greeting) as the day before.

"Colonel North, good morning," Keker said. Again he received only a glare in response.

Keker planned to ask North some more questions about the cable Secord sent to North on April 28, 1986, the message about the "insurance fund." By way of setting the stage, Keker said, "Just to orient the jury, April 28, 1986, is the day that Willard Zucker's home and office phone numbers appear on your appointment cards."

Keker was about to keep talking when North interrupted him. "If I may, counsel," he said, "I have learned something since last night about that card."

"Okay," said Keker, startled at North's volunteering.

North wore a satisfied, little smile as he began his explanation. "The card that you showed me yesterday has on it *my wife*'s writing, and it is her recollection that that writing was put there on or about the first of June. The card was sitting on my nightstand next to our bed in our bedroom which is where they stacked up, and that is the note she made when Mr. Zucker called on or about the first of June, and it is her writing on the back of that card."

At first Keker ignored North's explanation and pursued his questions about the Secord cable. But after about two minutes, Keker had a little epiphany.

Seemingly out of nowhere, Keker asked, "How long have you been married, Colonel North?"

"Twenty years."

"And do you recognize your wife's handwriting?"

North suddenly looked confused, hurt, angry. "I do," he said, "I did not recognize it yesterday."

"And your testimony is that the handwriting with Mr. Zucker's work and home phone numbers on government exhibit 137 on the back of your appointment card for April 28, 1986, is your wife's handwriting that you didn't recognize yesterday?"

"I did not recognize it yesterday, and I was apprised of that last night and I just told you about it."

"Fair enough," said Keker.

As much in hope as from experience, prosecutors say their defendants always wind up hanging themselves. Suddenly North made his convincing story implausible—and he wasn't even asked a question about it. Married for about twenty years himself, Keker knew that all spouses recognize each other's handwriting. The handwriting on that card may indeed have been Betsy North's, but this small exchange between Keker and North showed the jurors that North was, even now, still generating cover stories. For a short moment, the impact was devastating.

And it was just a prelude, because North soon found himself on the run. Using the April 28 cable, Keker got North to admit that Secord was planning on making a $300,000 profit over six months for the lease of a ship to the CIA. Then, in a bid to deflate North's supposed reverence for the CIA and its dear, departed Director Casey, Keker asked North about his code name for the CIA in his secret communications with Secord. At first North professed a faulty memory, but his reluctance only kindled more interest about the code word.

"What was the code for the CIA in yours and General Secord's and the Israelis' lingo?"

"As I said, the Israelis developed this," North said, continuing to stall, "and its name was 'FOOLS.' "

"And is that what you thought of them?"

"Not necessarily, no," North said, "I certainly didn't think that of the director."

But Keker had more ammunition. He showed North a PROF note he had sent to Vince Cannistraro around the same time. Keker asked, "You called the CIA people what?"

When pressed on matters he didn't want to discuss, North spoke in a strange, archaic style, like the subtitles to a silent movie. Reading the PROF note, North demurred. "It is a profanity that I would choose not to use in the presence of ladies. It was a male-to-male communication between friends. And if you would like to use the word in this courtroom, you may."

"Okay," said Keker, smiling. "Is it a word that starts with an 'A'?"

"Sure," said the straight-laced defendant.

Keker then abruptly changed gears to an exploration of North's background, specifically his training at the Naval Academy. He showed North some of the training material he had seen at Annapolis—some of it collected by me, some of it saved by Keker's poker-playing law partner who had graduated from Annapolis a few years before North. The lessons dealt with an officer's obligation to tell the truth. "The Naval Academy," said Keker, "is not a place where you are trained in deceiving people, is it?"

"No," said North, "and I wasn't raised that way, Mr. Keker. I knew [that] before I ever went to the Naval Academy, and my parents taught me that. I learned it in church. I knew that." But then he added, "But I also never learned at the Naval Academy or in the Marine Corps about running a covert operation. That was not something that I was briefed on or familiar with until I got to the National Security Council."

Keker pursued the issue of North's education and his values. "They taught courses about World War II when a lot of German officers at the end of the war would come and say, 'Yes, I committed all kinds of crimes, but I was ordered to do it.' You were trained that that wasn't a defense, right?"

Brendan Sullivan twitched with silent rage as Keker mentioned the defense used at the Nuremberg trials. As Keker (and I) did not then know, Sullivan had humiliated the congressional Iran-Contra committees when a questioner dared to compare North's defense with the one used by those accused of Nazi war crimes. Now, however, Sullivan could only watch.

"Training at the Naval Academy included training in what is an unlawful order," North said, hastening to add, "I don't believe I ever received an unlawful order."

"I just want to know about your training right now," Keker interrupted. Then, looking hard at North, Keker said, "You were trained that if an order is unlawful, you can't say something like, 'Oh, I felt like a pawn in a chess game among giants,' right?"

The courtroom gasped at Keker's bravado in ridiculing North's words of the previous week. North said only, "I don't believe that was ever mentioned to me by anybody."

From that point on, there was a profound change in North. He seemed smaller, weaker, quieter. By midmorning on Tuesday, he stopped giving speeches and began projecting an almost docile quality on the stand.

Having proved what he wanted about North's training, Keker

moved at last to the specifics in the charges. He established first that in the fall of 1985, North had been told by McFarlane only to "take a stab" at answering the congressional letters. It was hardly the direct order to lie that North had suggested under Sullivan's questioning. Keker confronted North with his own initial drafts of the letters—which were full of lies.

Almost unconsciously, Keker at one point referred to McFarlane as "Bud," and North jumped in to volunteer, "I didn't call him Bud."

"What did you call him?"

"McFarlane," said North.

Then Keker made another improvisation on the spot. He asked North, "Is Mr. McFarlane one of the giants that you felt like a pawn in a chess game, by the way?" As Keker knew it would, the question brought smiles from the jurors. Bud McFarlane—the pathetic figure who tried their patience for several days the previous month—scarcely seemed like a giant.

"Mr. McFarlane," North offered weakly, "was gone by the time I felt like that."

Keker continued moving through North's drafts, concluding with a series of answers North had prepared to certain specific questions Congressman Hamilton had asked.

Directing North's attentions to his draft, Keker said, "The answers to the questions that appear [there] are a pack of lies, right? I mean, there is no other way to say it. It is a pack of lies, right?"

Sullivan had obviously tried to train North not to quibble about the literal truth of his statements; the lawyer had to know that such attempts would look like nit-picking and probably fail in any event. But North once again rebelled at Keker's blunt words, saying, "If you want, I will go through each one of those, Mr. Keker. I am not going to admit that all of those are lies because I haven't read them in several years."

Keker eagerly took up the challenge and forced North to evaluate the honesty of his draft. One by one, he worked through North's statements. "That's a lie?" Keker asked. "Was that a one-hundred-percent lie?" "Now that was a false statement, wasn't it?" "That was false, wasn't it?" North caved in each time. Yes, yes, yes—North ultimately admitted that all of his statements were untrue. Or, as he answered one of these questions, "That was truly a false statement."

Gesell had watched most of North's testimony in uncharacteristic silence, allowing first Sullivan and then Keker free hands in their examinations. But near the end of this devastating day on the stand, after Keker had catalogued one North falsehood after another, the judge could not resist asking a single question—one that reached to the core of the issues in this case.

"Colonel North," Gesell said without expression, "did you at any time in this process consider in your own mind just not doing it?"

"Doing the memorandum, Your Honor?"—North seemed not to understand the question.

"Just saying, 'I won't do it,' " Gesell told him.

But the judge might as well have been speaking a foreign language. "No," said North, "I did not."

And Keker, realizing that he could add little to that seminal revelation, quickly brought the day's examination to a close.

For John Keker, it had been a day the likes of which few lawyers will ever know. North appeared on the stand on Tuesday morning full of confidence and left it in the afternoon a shattered man. There was no single moment when, as in the movies, the defendant cracked and confessed, but, gradually and inevitably, North's story fell into shards. This, the jury could now see, was a man who lied and cheated.

Walking back from the courthouse on this day, John Barrett, jubilant this time, informed me again, "It's all over."

THE next day, Wednesday, April 12, North once again interrupted with a new explanation, conjured up over night, that he wanted to share with the jury.

This one was based on one of the documents Keker had used from my book of Ollie's Tall Tales. In the fall of 1985, North had prepared two bland, nonsubstantive thank-you notes for President Reagan to sign personally for Carl Channell and Barbara Newington, one of Channell's biggest contributors. The letters had been run through the office of the White House Counsel, and one of the lawyers there had asked North whether Channell and Newington were involved in fundraising for the contras. In a cover memo for the president's inner office, Fred Fielding, the chief White House lawyer, stated that "Oliver North has advised my office that the recipients are not involved in raising private funds for the contras"—that is, North had lied to Fielding's colleague.

Keker breezed past the issue on Tuesday, and it did not make much of an impact. But on Wednesday morning, North's compulsion to explain surfaced again. "Having reread those documents," North said, unprompted, on Wednesday, "the letter . . . is addressed to Mr. Channell not in his role at NEPL, where he was raising funds for the Nicaraguan resistance. It is sent to Mr. Channell as the president of the American Conservative Trust," a different corporate shell from NEPL. Thus, North claimed, his statement to Fielding's colleague that Channell was not involved in fundraising was accurate.

Keker, incredulous, made North read Fielding's memo twice to the jury and let them realize that North was claiming this lie was in fact the truth. The difference in Channell's address, North said, made all the difference. "I am not trying to split hairs with you," North asserted, "but I don't think it is right for you to misrepresent what is really in this thing."

"Okay," said Keker. "Let's leave to the jury to decide where the misrepresentation is."

Keker's principal agenda for Wednesday was to explore North's final days at the NSC—and the cover-up that he helped conduct of the simultaneously unraveling Iran and Nicaragua programs. The crisp military bearing of North's days on direct had vanished by this point, and, indeed, the physical transformation in North during Keker's cross was remarkable. His eyes, deep set to begin with, sunk further into his head, and his face, always rough with stubble, took on a haunted, ashen look. He also began rambling, his answers wandering aimlessly over a landscape filled with self-justification and, now, self-pity. North was suffering.

North admitted with almost no prompting that he had shredded documents about Iran and Nicaragua without any instructions from McFarlane, Poindexter, or even the ever-present Casey. As for the chronology of the Iran arms sales he was preparing in November, he said he had originally intended for the document to be accurate but "Mr. McFarlane walked in and changed the story." North accepted McFarlane's false additions to the chronology even though the former national security advisor at that point held no government position and no official authority over North.

North agreed that he insisted the chronology say, "No one in the United States government" knew that the November 1985 shipment to Iran contained missiles. North conceded for Keker that the statement was false—he knew at the time missiles were shipped—but North said blandly that "I assumed that they all knew it was false." The meeting included the attorney general, the CIA director, the national security advisor, and several other high-ranking officials of the government, Keker said, and you just assumed that everyone was agreeing to telling Congress a false story?

Exactly, said North.

"Your feeling," said Keker, "was that there was nothing unusual about sitting in a room with high-level administration people and going over a false statement and making it even more false in preparation for congressional testimony? That just seemed like business as usual to you by that time?"

In essence, yes, said North—and not illegal.

The combination of both North's and Keker's fatigue—and the incredible story North was telling—gave the proceedings an almost hallucinogenic quality. North was saying that he assumed everyone he dealt with was lying, that cover-up was the standard operating procedure, and that he never thought to question the right or wrong of the practice.

The climax came when North described sitting in Poindexter's office and watching his boss remove from his office safe the only existing copy of the finding President Reagan signed in December 1985 to authorize the first arms shipments to Iran. Keker asked what happened to that copy of the finding.

"I am told," North said, "that it was destroyed."

"Where did you learn that Admiral Poindexter had destroyed the finding . . . ?"

"I was there."

"You were present when he destroyed it?"

"Yes," said North, "I was."

This revelation, piled on top of all the others made this day, tripped some switch in Keker's brain, and for just a moment, he lost his lawyerly reserve and allowed the outraged citizen in him to surface. The government North described in the waning days of November 1986 layered its lies in such complex, sedimentary formations that the truth seemed buried beyond recovery.

Keker stared at North and said, "Do you remember at the time that that happened, thinking, 'I'm in a den of thieves'?"

North, of course, said he believed nothing of the sort, but Keker's words seemed a fitting testimonial to the squalid immorality into which the White House fell in those fevered days.

B Y Thursday morning, the beginning of the fourth day of the cross-examination, Keker realized that his confrontation with the defendant had gone on long enough. There was, he thought, only one last piece of business to complete.

"Good morning, Colonel North."

For the seventh and final time—in four morning sessions and three afternoon—North gave an almost imperceptible nod in response to Keker's greeting. The courtroom, particularly the press, had come to look forward to North's twice-daily show of petulance, and there were audible titters this last time. Sitting again in the well, I saw the first alternate shake his head in disgust at North's failure to return Keker's good morning.

Keker reminded North that he had said, under Sullivan's questioning, that when he learned on the day he was fired that some of his actions might be considered criminal, it was "one of the most shocking things I had ever heard."

Keker said, "I would like to ask a few more questions and then I will be finished, about what you did after you heard this shocking news that somebody could consider, or might look into, any of your conduct as criminal."

Keker wanted to conclude with North's two phony letters to Robinette about the security system, and he planned a little theater to fix the scene in the jurors' minds. Sullivan had tried to take some of the sting out of the letters by asking North about them on direct. North called the fake letters the "stupidest thing I had ever done," but persisted in his assertion that he did not believe any of his actions were "unlawful."

Keker wanted to exploit our scientific report that in the second of the two letters North wrote, the typewriter ball had been intentionally defaced. Keker summoned me to find him an expendable typewriter ball from our office, and he asked John Barrett, a home do-it-yourselfer, to bring his tool kit to the courtroom. Keker was going to have North submit to the degrading spectacle of showing the jury how he hacked at the typewriter ball to advance his bungled deception scheme.

But Keker never had the chance. After he placed the first of North's two letters to Robinette on the overhead projector, the colonel volunteered a different and even stranger version of the letters story than the one we thought we knew.

"My recollection," North said, is that "I typed the two letters separately. My recollection is that this letter was typed first, and the other was typed second, because the ball, the wheel on the typewriter, was broken. . . ."

Keker then asked, "You didn't type them at the same time and then try to change the typewriter ball to make it look like it had been done at a different time?"

"No," said North, "my recollection is that this one was done, I believe, first and when I went back to the store to the second one, the little wheel . . . was broken. . . ."

The store? What store? I turned to Barrett in the last row, and we exchanged puzzled looks. Keker, too, was confused. "You say you went to a *store* to type it?"

Yes, he said, "a Best or a Bell store in Tysons Corner—about ten miles down the road from our house. . . . It was a display. . . . They had a whole series of display typewriters."

Keker usually did a good job of controlling his emotions in the courtroom, but now he yielded to an almost voyeuristic sense of curiosity about this newest North tale. Why type the letter in a store?

"Well, one, I don't recall we had a working typewriter at home at the time, and number two, I didn't want to do it at work. I didn't want the Marine Corps, which is where I was, involved in that kind of cover-up. And I went and did it at a store."

So why did the second letter have a damaged typeface?

"My recollection is that that was prepared several days later, when I went back to the store. . . . And the typewriter that I had used before was by now inoperable—someone had damaged it. And so I looked for another typewriter that had a similar type." But the first one "was all that was available, and it wasn't working properly."

North blew our carpentry demonstration, but he replaced it with a story that incriminated him every bit as much. By his own account, North wandered the shopping malls of suburban Virginia looking for a display typewriter to type a full-page, single-spaced, back-dated, cover-up letter to his friendly CIA agent. And he did it *twice*.

Or, as Keker put it to North, after writing the first letter to Robinette, "you went back to your house, and you thought about it for a few days . . . and then you decided that you would add to it" the second back-dated letter?"

"That's how I recall it now. . . ."

Keker gazed at North with a mixture of wonder and contempt—and perhaps even a touch of regret. Then he addressed Judge Gesell: "I don't have any further questions, Your Honor."

CHAPTER EIGHTEEN

A Tour of the White House

"There will be," Brendan Sullivan told the court, "no redirect."

Forgoing further examination of North was the right decision for Sullivan, but probably not a happy one. Keker's four days of cross-examination had ranged so broadly over North's story—and opened so many holes in it—that an attempt at a point-by-point refutation would have taken Sullivan at least several days. He sacrificed that opportunity because, for one thing, the gaunt and sagging defendant, his martial shine dulled, did not look ready to endure more testimony. In addition, to strike back in the area of North's greatest vulnerabilities, Sullivan might only have called more attention to them—as Keker could have done, in turn, in his recross. Better, Sullivan apparently thought, to try and leave the impression that Keker's cross did not merit a response.

The defense called only one more witness, Maurice Sovern, a CIA "document custodian," who testified that, according to his review of the relevant records, North and Casey had one hundred fifty-seven telephone conversations and twenty-six meetings between 1983 and 1986. As a mere record reviewer, Sovern could not report anything about what was said at these encounters. He did admit, under Bromwich's cross-examination, that many of these meetings included other people. He also lent some credence to North's repeated assertions of direction and authorization of his actions by Casey. When Sovern stepped down, the defense case was over.

We gave a good deal of thought to stopping right there, relinquishing our rebuttal case to show the jury that the defense case had not damaged our own. Keker sensed that the jurors were restless and, after about seven weeks of testimony, anxious to get on with their lives. But he was not quite ready to stop.

"Is there any rebuttal?" Judge Gesell asked on Friday morning, April 14.

"Yes, Your Honor," said Zornow. "The government calls William Howell."

The reporters, who had sat through the congressional hearings and these courtroom proceedings, had become experts on the case, and one could sense their pride in knowing every twist and turn in the Iran-Contra drama. But they came up short on William Howell. Nobody knew who he was.

He did not look like any of the other witnesses. In his late thirties, Howell had mounds of wavy strawberry hair framing an open, even gregarious countenance. But forget the face. What hypnotized the audience that morning was Howell's sport jacket. It looked like it had been cut from the tarpaulin that covers the infield during rain delays at Municipal Stadium in Baltimore—a sort of leatherized orange. If you believed in the stereotype, you would have said this guy made his living selling used cars.

"Mr. Howell," said Zornow, "I'd like to direct your attention to October of 1985 and ask you how you were employed at that time?"

Bill Howell answered, "I was a used car salesman for J. Koons Pontiac in Vienna, Virginia."

"Now I'd like to direct your attention, sir, to Friday, October 4, 1985, and ask you whether you recall receiving a telephone call from Oliver North on that date?"

"Yes, I do.

"Colonel North," said Howell, "had inquired about an ad that we had placed in *The Washington Post* concerning a particular vehicle"—a GMC Suburban.

"Can you briefly tell us," Zornow asked parenthetically, "what a Suburban is?"

Here the used car dealer's compulsion to sell took over. "A Suburban," he told Zornow with all the sincerity he could muster, "is a unique vehicle. It's like a large station wagon . . . [that] generally ends up being purchased by somebody who has a desire to tow something, things along that line."

"What was the price of the vehicle?" Zornow asked, fighting to keep a straight face.

"To the best of my recollection, $8,995." (Off the stand, Howell had confided to Zornow, "This deal had *juice*.")

Howell went on to say that North called him at Koons three times on October 4, pleading with him not to sell the vehicle before he had a chance to look at it. Demonstrating that he knew how to dangle his customers with the best of his profession, Howell said he told North "that with an ad in the paper like that, it was something that we generally did not do, but if he were to call before he left the White House, I would indicate whether or not it had been sold and would hold it for him until he arrived."

North finally showed up at the dealership around closing time, 9 P.M. North then "drove the vehicle around the parking lot," and sought permission to take it home to his wife, which Howell granted. The Norths then returned together, and the colonel and Howell agreed to meet the next morning to seal the deal.

The following morning, North "made an offer of $7,800," which Howell's boss accepted.

"Now," said Zornow, moving to the real point of Howell's testimony, "after the offer was accepted, was there any discussion about how payment would be made?"

Howell recounted that North said he wanted to make a down payment of $5,000 on that Saturday and pay the remainder the next week. "Did Colonel North say anything to you on that day about where he was getting the money?"

"It was my understanding that the money . . . was to come from the White House Credit Union—the balance of it was to come from the White House Credit Union."

"Did he say anything to that effect?"

Startled at the rustling in the courtroom caused by his last answer, Howell answered, "To the best of my recollection, yes, sir." North, Howell said, paid off the balance within a few days.

Zornow wanted to cover one more point. "Did there come a time after that when you saw Colonel North again?"

Howell looked a little uncomfortable. "After the delivery of the vehicle, through a conversation that I had with him," Howell said, North "had indicated that the White House was a particularly attractive place in the Christmas season, and he gave . . . a tour of the White House to myself, my daughter, and my mother and dad." With that Zornow stepped aside.

Howell had demolished North's story about the purchase of the van. North had testified that he intended to buy a different vehicle but settled on the van; Howell contradicted him. North had said that he didn't know the price when he arrived at the dealer; again Howell said otherwise. And North had told Howell that his money was going to come from his credit union. In fact, the jury knew at this point that he had gone to get cash—exactly the amount needed for the van—from Secord on that Saturday in October. Most importantly, if North had $15,000 in his little metal box, there would have been no need for any kind of partial payment plan for the vehicle.

But it was Howell's last answer, about the White House tour—a story that Zornow elicited only because he knew Sullivan would raise it on cross—that left an especially poignant remnant in the courtroom. This small insight into North's character showed a man eager, even compelled, to please others. North made this generous offer to a lowly car salesman just as he toadied to the wishes, even those he only intuited, of his superiors at work. There was, suddenly, a sadness about North—the sense that all that energy and enthusiasm had not been corrupt from the start, just hopelessly misdirected. North somehow knew it, too, and as he recognized his own failings, he lacked the inner resources to do anything except lie about them. And he kept on lying as he thrashed in the contradictions born of his own compulsive explanations.

Mary Dix came less than an hour after Howell began. She was a proper little lady, with a string of pearls, a collar of lace, and, one sensed, a will of iron.

She told Zornow she served as "director of administration" for the NSC starting in May of 1984, and in that role supervised "our petty cash fund." She said a primary purpose of the fund was to reimburse NSC employees for their taxi fares.

"Did you have any occasions," Zornow asked, "to have contact with Lieutenant Colonel North regarding reimbursement for monies that he had expended for taxi fare?"

"Yes," Dix said daintily. "There were troubles at times in keeping money in the cash box. We sometimes would run out and we'd have to wait until we had a resupply of money, and if something happened and we didn't have the money on hand, Colonel North would get very upset if we didn't have the cash right there when he needed it."

Zornow asked if Dix recalled any specific encounters with North.

"Yes," she said with the same equanimity, "there were occasions when I would be walking down the hallway to leave work at night and I would hear him yelling, 'Mary! Mary!' And he would need cash to go home; that he didn't have enough cash to pay for gas. And so I would go back into the office.

"Most likely," she continued, "I would be the last one out so the safes would all be closed. Everything was locked up. So lots of times I just gave him some of my own cash. And then I replenished myself when the cash box was open. . . ."

Twice, she said, North ran into her office, "his face was red, and he was very upset with my staff because they didn't have money. . . . He either would say he didn't have enough money for gas to go home or he didn't have enough lunch money."

"Did there come a time," Zornow asked in his final question, "when Colonel North did not approach you with problems concerning the petty cash box?"

"I would say it totally stopped, the best I can recollect, in the middle of 1985."

"Thank you," said Zornow, "I have no further questions."

Dix's testimony, like Howell's, was brief and brutal. The most obvious question raised by her was, if North had $15,000 in cash at home, why did he sob to Dix that he lacked money for a sandwich? But even better for the prosecution was her statement about when North's demands ceased. According to North's own testimony, he created the "operational fund" of cash and traveler's checks in the middle of 1985. Dix's testimony left the strong impression that the proceeds of his fund made up for his heretofore severe cash shortages.

Sullivan had left Howell more or less alone, but he sought to limit the effect of Dix's testimony with a vigorous cross. He questioned how many times North actually complained about his reimbursements, and Dix informed him that it was five—"I can remember distinctly because it was sort of dramatic." And Dix added, in a revelation that did not make it into her direct, that she grew so concerned about North's financial situation that she reported him to the NSC authorities as a possible security risk. Sullivan attempted to show that Dix's story had changed between the grand jury and the trial, but Dix explained that she "wanted to be as fair as I could," so she checked her vouchers and records and was now certain of her testimony. Recognizing that each question was only sinking his client deeper into trouble, Sullivan finally slunk off, like a scolded pupil.

Howell and Dix put sharp exclamation points at the end of our case. More than any other witnesses in the trial, they demonstrated on a small scale one of the larger themes of our investigation: the futility of using the criminal process to expose or correct governmental misdeeds. These two individuals neither illuminated policy failures, nor suggested alternatives. They taught no "lessons" of the Iran-Contra affair. Rather, their stories offered nothing more and nothing less than insights into the character and behavior of one man, Oliver North.

We should have stopped right there, but we called three more, equally concise witnesses, and their testimony did not leave nearly as memorable imprints as did the other two. We summoned Willard Zucker back to testify about his meeting with Betsy North and the creation of the Button account, but his appearance got bogged down in legal disputes. Steven Berry, a Republican House intelligence committee staffer, testified that North told the committee that he had installed the security system in his home "at his own expense." However, Berry larded up his brief appearance with so many testimonials to North's high character that the impact of the North lie was probably minimal. So, too, the final witness, John Richardson of Attorney General Meese's staff, added little to his previous testimony. With

Dix we could have ended with a bang; with Richardson, the sound more resembled a thud.

Still, as Richardson left the stand, Keker was allowed to say the words that he often thought he would never have the chance to utter. "Your Honor," the prosecutor told Gesell, "the government rests."

Sullivan, too, seemed to have an uncharacteristic lilt as he added, "The defense rests."

As always, Gesell's first thoughts were for the jury. "All the evidence is in, ladies and gentlemen," he told them. "That's what that means in nonlawyer's talk."

Sitting in my remote outpost of the courtroom that day, my only thought was, "Hallelujah."

M Y joy initially derived from the most personal of reasons. Gesell said the lawyers' closing statements would come on the following Tuesday and Wednesday, April 18 and 19, his instructions to the jury on April 20, and then the jury would be sequestered for their deliberations. That meant that I could almost certainly see the case through to a verdict and keep my promise to McIntosh to leave the OIC by the end of April. So many times over the previous four months I had thought the goal of an April finish was slipping beyond reach— whether it was the Justice Department's attempted appeal of our CIPA arrangements, the prosecutorial misconduct hearing, or Brendan Sullivan's off-hand mention, early in the trial, that the defense case might take three months (it took less than two weeks). Thanks to Gerhard Gesell's insistence on completing the case "in my lifetime," as he joked on several occasions, it looked like I would make it.

My exultation at the end of the trial came also from my optimism about the result. By my accounting, I believed the jury stood ready to convict North on virtually all of the twelve charges:

> *Counts one through four:* The McFarlane letters to Congress. I thought Keker had established convincingly that North played a significant (and willing) role in their creation.
>
> *Count five:* The most solid of them all. I was betting that North

stood almost no chance of an acquittal based on his face-to-face lie to the House intelligence committee on August 6, 1986. "Pawn in a chess game" or not, North admitted lying to the congressmen, and I thought the jury would convict him for it.

Count six: Likewise, I believed Keker demonstrated that North played an important and independent role in the creation of the false chronology of the Iran arms sales, the basis of this charge.

Counts seven and eight: North's defense to these counts, his lies to Attorney General Meese on November 23, 1986, was based entirely on his technical and legalistic claim that Meese's investigation did not constitute an "official" inquiry; because North all but admitted his statements to Meese were false, I thought the jury would convict on those two counts as well.

Count nine: The shredding—the charge of destruction of documents in count nine—also seemed one of the strongest counts. Since his very first moment before the jury, Keker had painted in vivid hues the picture of North and Fawn Hall crouched over their shredder working to keep papers away from the attorney general's team. North's claim of authorization here was particularly vague and insubstantial.

Count ten: This count, which charged his illegal acceptance of the security fence, also seemed impervious to an authorization claim, as North's two phony letters to Robinette shouted the defendant's criminal intent.

Count eleven: The traveler's check count was something of a mystery all the way to the end. We poked any number of holes in North's story. North's claim of his little metal box as the source of family cash did have some inherent implausibility. Also, Howell and Dix showed North himself did not act as if he had a box full of cash in his home. But still the question remained: had we proved beyond a reasonable doubt that North's explanation was false? Had we *proved* that North had *not* reimbursed the "operational account" for his personal expenses? I was not sure.

Count twelve: On the last count, for conspiracy to defraud the IRS, I was betting acquittal. Depriving the treasury of the money that Spitz Channell's contributors deducted from their taxes always seemed to me a little too obscure for the jury to convict North of a five-year felony.

KEKER had just completed four grueling days of crossexamining the defendant, an event that took almost as much out of him as it did North, and he then had to turn around, almost immediately, and summarize nearly two months of evidence for the jury. Fortunately for Keker, he had a weekend to recover, and he spent the bulk of it alone in his office scribbling inside his three-ring trial binder. After a half-hearted run-through with Bromwich and Zornow on Monday—Keker lacked the energy for a full-scale rehearsal—he was ready to leap the final hurdle.

As Keker moved to the podium on Tuesday morning, the courtroom was strangely subdued. North's testimony had packed such an emotional wallop that everyone—the lawyers, the judge, and especially the jurors—still seemed drained by the encounter. Everything else seemed like filler.

Still, Keker wore a big courtroom smile when he greeted the jurors. "Good morning, ladies and gentlemen."

"Good morning," they said together, their first public sounds in more than two months.

"On behalf of the government of the United States, represented in this case by Mr. Bromwich, Mr. Zornow, and me," Keker began, "I want to first thank you for what has been extraordinary service by you in this case."

Keker's first task was to rivet the jury on the guilt or innocence of Oliver North rather than the larger governmental Iran-Contra drama. "This is not a case," Keker continued, "about wise or unwise government policies. It is not a case . . . where you have to resolve any dispute between Congress and the president of the United States. It's not a case really about Nicaragua or the contras or whether or not Mr. North and his colleagues in the government violated the Boland amendment.

"What this case is about is something one hundred times more important than any of that. It's about what law, what standards of conduct, are to be applied to the highest-ranking public servants in this country. Is it the law that Judge Gesell is going to give you, the law that applies to every single person in this country, or is it some law, some standard of conduct of their own?

"The charges in this case, you well know by now, are very serious ones. They go to the very heart of our system of self-government. They involve the need for honesty in the government, especially between the branches of government, between the Congress and the president. The laws that the government claims . . . were broken here are fundamental laws. They are the laws that say that an executive branch official who is sworn to uphold the law, to uphold the Constitution of the United States, cannot lie to Congress, cannot obstruct congressional inquiries into what that executive branch official is doing.

"Government by deception," Keker continued, "is not a free government. Government by deception is not a democratic government. Government by deception is not a government under the rule of law. Telling the truth is an important principle in this government. . . . The fact that telling the truth is not always honored in our government makes it *more* important, . . . not less important, that the laws against lying, laws requiring truth-telling, be enforced. If those laws are enforced," Keker said, "the 'government of the people, by the people, for the people shall not perish from the earth.' "

Keker then turned to the defendant and the sight of North seemed to energize him. Unlike North, Keker did not wear hatred of his adversary like a row of ribbons on his chest, but neither did Keker view the defendant as a neutral observer. So Keker picked up both the pace of his delivery and the heat of his rhetoric.

"The tragedy of Oliver North," Keker said, "is that a man who says he cared so much about freedom and democracy in Nicaragua forgot about the demands of freedom and democracy at home.

"By his own testimony," Keker explained, "Oliver North describes himself as a man of great power, a man who met with kings and presidents, a man who guided cabinet officials. . . . But Oliver North . . . wants all that power without any of the responsibility, the personal responsibility that goes with it. When he's confronted with his own wrongdoing, instead of purging his guilt by admitting it, he blames other people. McFarlane made me do it. Casey made me do it."

Here, Keker was taking on the heart of North's defense—authorization—and he began on a controversial tack: "Well, as usual, ladies and gentlemen, the Bible says it best: 'The wicked walk on every side when the vilest men are exalted.' Fingerpointing is not an excuse. Sharing the blame is not a defense. Saying McFarlane and Casey made me do it is no more a defense to man's law than saying the devil made me do it is a defense to God's law."

Appealing to the Bible is a high-stakes play for any lawyer, and Keker was going all out. Importing so personal a subject as religion into the courtroom risks alienating those who believe it does not belong there. But Keker's decision to leaven his closing with biblical references came with his recognition that this was no ordinary case. He thought it was folly to try and convince the jury that this trial was like any other. Through their very appearance, the jurors signalled their own understanding of the case's importance. About midway through the trial, they all started coming to court dressed in their finest clothes, something they did not do in the early stages. Church clothes, Keker believed, called for oratory of the pulpit.

Moving to the specific counts, Keker said, "Most of the elements of most of the charges are not really in dispute in this case." North did not deny that the statements to Congress were false; nor did he suggest that the shredding—or even his acceptance of the fence and the traveler's checks—did not occur. What "it really comes down to on most of these charges," said Keker, "is what was in Oliver North's mind, what was his intent."

On the letters North drafted for McFarlane to send to Congress, Keker pounded away at North's admission that McFarlane only told him to "take a stab" at preparing the answers—hardly a direct authorization to lie.

"All right," Keker said almost parenthetically, "so far in this drama, in August and September of 1985, North and McFarlane are following Adolf Hitler's old strategy. He was the one who said, the victor will never be asked if he told the truth. And the idea was, if the lies work, Congress will stop asking questions."

History has placed certain epithets off limits in civilized discourse, and "Hitler" is one. ("Slave" is another.) The remark prompted a swirl of publicity (all of it bad) and gave Sullivan a terrific opening for a response. To the extent that the reference to Hitler remains the defining public memory of John Keker, it is a shame that he tarnished his valiant performance in the trial with this momentary error.

Keker did pause at one point to explain, "Let me say a word at this point about Mr. McFarlane, because Mr. McFarlane is, to put it mildly, a troublesome witness. It seems to me, that the evidence shows him to be a man in some agony. You know about the suicide attempt. . . . You know that he has got a memory that seems to dredge up very little. . . . At least, though, Mr. McFarlane has been man enough to admit that he is guilty in connection with these letters"—admit, that is, in misdemeanor form. Keker suggested that North and McFarlane "both lied to Congress and they both knew perfectly well what they were doing and why they were doing it. The only difference between them is that at least McFarlane admits it."

After the McFarlane reference, Keker moved once more to the attack. On North's August 6 testimony, Keker hammered away remorselessly. "There is no question—there is no dispute—he admitted it. . . . There were twelve, thirteen congressmen there plus staff. Colonel North lied, lied to them. He lied to them about fundraising, lied to them about Owen, lied to them about Singlaub—lied to them about things they didn't even ask about." Keker said North tried to make the congressmen "feel sorry for him, the threats he had been receiving, and insisted that he put up the security fence *at his own expense*. He didn't have to tell them that lie, but he did.

"By mid-1986, ladies and gentlemen, lying had become a habit for Oliver North." Keker told the jury, "Lies start on your tongue, but pretty soon they eat at your heart." With that he turned to the corruption issue—as symbolized by the traveler's check count and the testimony of Mary Dix. "On this one," Keker said, "you don't need to be an accountant, you don't need to be a lawyer, you just need to be a person who has lived in this world. . . . North was desperate for cash in 1984. And then suddenly in mid-1985 he was no longer desperate for cash.

"Do you believe that?" he asked the jurors. "He lied about that tin box because he knew, and he knew that we knew, that he had paid cash, completely impossible-to-explain cash for his car in October of 1985—$8,000 in cash. And he knew he couldn't explain where he got the cash. So he made up a story about $15,000 in a tin box that only he and his wife knew about, nailed to the floor of his closet. Only one man who has ever lived can create out of nothing, something—loaves and fishes, enough to feed everybody.

"And that man," Keker explained in a voice filled with contempt, "is not Oliver North. He created the cash to explain his cash expenditures."

In North's final days at the NSC, Keker said, "[L]ying had become a habit. Deceit had become his watchword. His first reaction when confronted with a problem was to lie or to cover it up."

The shredding, the false chronologies, the lies to Meese—Keker parsed them all. Dozens of times Keker pointed to specific lies that crossed North's lips. With lunchtime approaching, Keker wound to a rather abrupt close, reminding the jurors that he would be responding to Sullivan's closing statement the following day.

Keker had done his job. He had challenged the jury to treat North like any other citizen. The Oliver North of his summation was a big man, an important man, one who flouted our constitutional system and then dared that system to catch up with him. The jury's job, Keker said, was to do just that.

CHAPTER NINETEEN

Lying, Cheating, and Stealing

At forty-seven, Brendan Sullivan was a only year older than North and Keker, but Sullivan's haunted pallor made him seem at least a decade their senior. With hair the color of the Capitol dome and skin tone to match, Sullivan lacked the proud defiance of North or the easy grace of Keker. By the end of the trial Sullivan seemed even to have stopped talking to his colleagues at the defense table. Wordlessly, he declined their daily offers of Life Savers. Sullivan always looked angry—as he did when took the stand to close.

"Ladies and gentlemen," Sullivan said just after lunch on the day of Keker's summation, "today is the day that we look at what the jigsaw puzzle has shown. And I would suggest to you that what the government has said is a far cry from what the evidence has shown in this case. If you listen to the government, you believe that Colonel North went into work every day to decide what kind of crime to commit in each meeting."

He moved quickly to his theme: "The government has overreached in this case in order to get a conviction of Colonel North beyond anything you can imagine. And the best way I can describe to you what they did is to just take a moment and look at" Keker's closing statement.

"You heard a couple of hours ago references to Colonel North as having forgotten about principles of freedom and democracy. Well, no matter what happens in this case, there is one thing that's for sure, and that is that Colonel North is devoted to freedom and democracy, and he has proved it, unlike many people. He worked for twenty years as a Marine Corps officer. He put his life on the line in Vietnam. He is a highly decorated soldier. . . .

"Those words by the government are insulting, and they demonstrate to you the extraordinary overreaching of this case. They will do anything to get Colonel North, that's what their argument demonstrates. But that's not the worst of it."

Sullivan then cited Keker's reference in his closing to how North cried on the stand during his "pawn-in-a-chess-game" speech. Sullivan angrily denied that North shed tears and added, "That's only the beginning of the cruelty that they have imposed on this man in their argument and in this case."

"What about the biblical reference to wicked men?" Sullivan asked. "Do you buy that? Wicked? Is that what Colonel North is supposed to be, wicked?" Sullivan's own voice was cracking at this point, but he had not quite reached his peak.

"But worse still and beyond anything I have heard in a courtroom, and outrageous to the extent that it should send a course of rage through everyone in this room, is the reference to Adolf Hitler.

"This Marine, retired, was linked in this courtroom to Adolf Hitler. Some in this room have fought Adolf Hitler. [One juror was a World War II veteran.] They know what Adolf Hitler was. And this man is not Adolf Hitler, and he doesn't do things like Adolf Hitler, and to suggest it indicates the extraordinary drive, the force, the power of the government to put its might on top of Colonel North, to see what they can say is a crime.

"You should be offended by it," Sullivan almost yelled, "because anyone that will link Colonel North to Adolf Hitler is not credible and should not be believed."

Then, as it did so often throughout the case, the energy of Williams & Connolly burst the dams of prudent restraint. Sullivan, again, pushed too far. The lawyer raged and screamed. "The view of the evidence expressed in this courtroom is sick and twisted."

It was one thing to criticize Keker and the prosecution, but here Sullivan offended Gerhard Gesell. Sullivan impugned the fairness of the trial. Sick and twisted? When Sullivan uttered those words, the judge gathered his robes in irritation and fired an epochal scowl toward the trembling attorney. Few in the audience (and none in the jury) missed it.

Sullivan may have sensed the rebuke because he soon circled back to pay obeisance to the "extraordinary" service of the jurors. Then he reminded them of BARD, beyond a reasonable doubt, which, he said, "is like climbing Mount Everest. The government has the burden of climbing Mount Everest, and they have to get up to the top and they have to plant the flag in the top, and they have to say, we have proved it beyond a reasonable doubt." Their verdict, Sullivan reminded the jurors, must be unanimous. "It is not majority rule," he said. "In here, for the government to be entitled to a conviction against one of our citizens, it has to be twelve people, all twelve. . . . And if one person believes in their conscience and in their mind, after fully deliberating and fully listening to all other jurors, that there should not be a conviction, then that one person says no conviction, and there is no conviction." It was Sullivan's clever plea for a hold-out and a hung jury.

His arguments were familiar by now. The first three counts, Sullivan said, related to "three letters that Colonel North's boss wrote and signed;" North's statements to the congressmen had "no oath, no court reporter." "There have got to be one hundred thousand meetings a year in the Justice Department," Sullivan said of the charges based on the Meese interview, "but they pick this meeting to make a crime out of."

The one common theme of all the counts, Sullivan said, was that North was a scapegoat: "I say to you that the evidence is overwhelming here that it is the government that's blaming Ollie North for everything. To me, that's clear. The thrust of the charges is almost childlike in that sense. Blame Ollie North. Blame Ollie North for McFarlane's letters. Isn't that what this is about?"

Sullivan dwelled for a long time on what he called, not a little defensively, "the absolute, most ridiculous count in this case"—the traveler's check charge. Sullivan said "it was perfectly permissible for Colonel North to reimburse himself out of the" operational fund. The lawyer said he wanted to discuss the financial proof "more generally," because of "all the things the government wants to try to use to dirty up Ollie North . . . a trial tactic that's used when they don't have evidence for the count itself." As for the notorious cash purchase of the GMC Suburban, Sullivan bet that the jurors would be less shocked about it than the charge-card-bearing attorneys: "You know, a lot of Americans buy cars with cash. A lot of honest Americans have cash at home, and to suggest that because Colonel North had cash at home he should be charged and convicted . . . is a little bit absurd. . . ."

Sullivan went on for more than an hour just about the traveler's checks, and by the time he reached the other counts, he sensed the courtroom's postlunch drowsiness settling in. Like Keker, he let himself peter out rather than build to a crescendo. That would come the following morning.

In the morning session, Sullivan started by doing the best he could with count five—North's lies on August 6, 1986, to the House intelligence committee. "You know the old phrase," Sullivan asked, "a rock and a hard place?" That was North's quandary as his boss, Poindexter, left him to face the congressmen. The fault, Sullivan said, was clearly Poindexter's. North "shouldn't have been put in that circumstance. In fact, he was abused. . . . His boss shouldn't have sent him into that meeting. . . . So what does Ollie North opt to do when he's between a rock and a hard place? He opts to protect the secrets." Sullivan conceded that "maybe they shouldn't send an operational officer into such a meeting, but that's what happened. But to call it criminal doesn't make sense."

As he built to his finale, Sullivan refined his scapegoat theme. When North was fired on November 25, Sullivan said, he was "offered as a sacrificial lamb, so to speak, to the raging Congress." In support of this thesis, Sullivan drew special attention to one of the best-known events of the Iran-Contra affair. We had known about it for so long that we tended to discount its impact, but for jurors chosen largely for their ignorance about the scandal, it probably had great significance. "You remember," Sullivan reminded the jury, that later on November 25, after North had been fired, "the president of the United States called him.

"That's something for you to figure out and use a little common sense about in that jury room as well. How can you be fired at noontime and have the president of the United States call you in the late afternoon and tell you that you are an American hero? What do you suppose that's about? What conclusion do you draw from that?

"I draw the conclusion," Sullivan offered, "that the president was using Ollie North as a scapegoat. They threw him overboard to get some political peace, along with a couple of others. It doesn't sound like the kind of thing the president would do unless he knew fully well what Ollie North was doing."

Sullivan concluded with the obvious, a hymn to North the man. He read snatches of the testimonials that came from the stand. Calero: "I trusted him with my life." Quintero: "I couldn't believe that anyone could put so many hours in trying to help these people." McFarlane: "The hardest-working person I have ever seen, gave every bit of his heart." This was no ordinary criminal defendant.

"The man who held the lives of others in his hands," said Sullivan, "now puts his life in your hands."

Sullivan looked at last to the PROF note North sent to Poindexter on the day he was fired. The lawyer read it slowly to the jury. "There's an old line about you can't fire me, I quit," North wrote. "Well, I do want to make it official so that you know I sincerely meant what I said to you over the course of these last several difficult weeks. I am prepared to depart at the time you and the president decide it to be in the best interests of the presidency and of the country.

"I'm honored to have served the president, you, and your predecessor these five-and-a-half years," North continued. "I only regret I could not have done so better. My prayer is that the president is not further damaged by what has transpired and that the hostages will not be harmed as a consequence of what we do now. Finally, I remain convinced that what we tried to accomplish was worth the risk. We nearly succeeded. Hopefully, when the political fratricide is finished, there will be others in a moment of calm reflection who will agree. Warmest regards. Semper fidelis. Oliver North."

"That's Oliver North," said Sullivan, his voice breaking, "the day before he's fired.

"One more thought," he said, almost whispering. "I've never in twenty years of practice used a biblical quotation. I don't know why. Somehow it didn't seem right or seemed too personal, too religious. But in this courtroom we've had Bible quotations used against the defendant, which I've never seen before. So I'm going to use one in return for the first time in twenty years, and probably the last.

"They pick out the quote about the wicked man. I'll pick out the quote from the Apostle John, chapter fifteen, verse thirteen. The quote is: 'Greater love hath no man than he be willing to lay down his life for another.' That's Ollie North. That's the kind of man he is. Not the kind of man that commits crimes. Now he cries out for an end to his agony after two-and-a-half years. I ask for a verdict on the evidence because it's the right thing, because it hasn't been proved beyond a reasonable doubt.

"In a sense, he's been a hostage. I ask you on the evidence to set him free. Thank you."

KEKER knew the time for fireworks had passed. He knew that Sullivan's closing scored more than a few points. A little chastened by the fallout from his Hitler reference, Keker sought a restrained and moderate tone for his rebuttal. In some respects, he thought, the tone would matter more than the substance—because Sullivan had harped so incessantly on the image of a desperate, wanton prosecution. Keker wanted to be, and to sound, fair.

So it was a quieter Keker who spoke on Wednesday afternoon, his manner expressing more sorrow than anger. "As you have learned," he said at the outset, "criminal trials are not happy occasions. A trial at which the government proves a citizen guilty of a crime is not a pleasant proceeding, and a decision by the jury is not an easy or pleasant decision to make." But it was a decision, Keker said, that the jury must make "according to the rule of law . . . without passion, without prejudice, without bias."

Keker wasted little time, for he had agreed to limit his remarks to an hour. He turned to the fall-guy theme. He did point out that

Poindexter, Secord, and Hakim were all presently under indictment, but then reminded the jurors, "This case is about what Oliver North did. . . .

"Please don't be misled by . . . the emotional content of this 'fall guy' sort of word. Remember what a fall guy was." And then Keker gave a little history of the term. "It comes from boxing, and it deals with crooked fights. The fall guy is the guy that agrees to fall over and then the fake winner is the guy that is going to be standing up. It is a fix so that the gamblers can make money.

"The fall guy is guilty," Keker said, "the winner is guilty, and the people that pay him are guilty. They are *all* guilty."

He focused on a few of the most obvious areas of factual rebuttal. In response to Sullivan's claim that North was so meticulous about the traveler's checks, he pointed to the testimony that North gave $1,000 worth of them to Rob Owen as a wedding present, and lent Fawn Hall $60 for a weekend at the beach. He noted how North's recollections of the Meese interview conflicted with those of three other people who were there—Meese, Cooper, and Richardson. Keker pointed to the witness stand and said, "From that chair Colonel North contradicted just about every witness that had important testimony that was contrary to him."

Keker was tired, the jury was tired, and the judge was tired. The prosecutor wanted to leave only one last thought. "Ladies and gentlemen, I said in the opening statement in this case eight, nine long weeks ago that there's a time and place for everything. There's a time for me to stop talking and for Mr. Bromwich and Mr. Zornow and me to thank you for your attention throughout the case and to rest. The evidence is before you. The arguments are before you.

"For you it's time to deliberate, and it's time to decide this case. You're the representatives of the people of a free society, and it's time to decide whether or not the evidence in this case proves beyond a reasonable doubt that Oliver North is guilty of each one of these charges.

"For Colonel North, it's a time for judgment. We've heard a lot about courage in this trial. There's another kind of courage that's required, to admit when you're wrong, to admit your personal responsibility and indeed to admit guilt where that's appropriate.

"He has not admitted any of those things—it is time for you to do it for him.

"The government asks you to return a verdict of guilty as to each one of these twelve charges. Thank you very much."

A L L through the last weeks of the trial, the two sides had fought one final legal dispute—over the instructions Judge Gesell would issue to the jurors. The point of greatest contention: the authorization defense.

Confusion about the authorization defense arises from a fundamental ambivalence in criminal law. The system is based on the notion of individual responsibility—the idea that everyone is responsible for his or her own actions. Still, judges persist in allowing some flexibility in weighing the conduct of low men or women on the totem poll. The "just following orders" defense received its most celebrated rejection in the Nuremberg war crimes trials, yet it has never been fully expunged from our legal system.

The key precedent on the issue in the federal appeals court for the District of Columbia—from a trial growing out of Watergate—illustrated just how muddied the issue had become. The case arose when E. Howard Hunt, the head of the White House "plumbers" unit, hired Bernard Barker and Eugenio Martinez, two of his former subordinates at the CIA, to burglarize the office of Dr. Louis Fielding, Daniel Ellsberg's psychiatrist. When the pair was prosecuted for violating Fielding's civil rights, they claimed that their good-faith (if mistaken) belief that Hunt had the right to authorize these actions entitled them to an acquittal.

Barker and Martinez were convicted in the district court, but the three-judge appeals panel voted two-to-one that they should go free. The three judges wrote three separate, extremely long opinions explaining their reasons. One judge said that if a defendant was "acting out of good faith reliance upon the apparent authority of another," and that reliance was "reasonable," he should not be convicted. The second judge in the majority also believed that authorization was a valid defense, but under more limited circumstances—only when a defendant acted on the basis of a "statement of law issued by an official charged with interpretation, administration, and/or enforcement responsibilities in the relevant legal field." The third judge entirely rejected the authorization defense, saying that if the defendants were misled by the actions of their superior, that factor should be considered in sentencing, not in determining guilt. To complicate the situation even further, most courts since the mid-1970s had generally tended toward the third judge's narrow view of the defense.

In short, then, the law relating to "authorization" was full of vague phrases about objectivity, subjectivity, reasonability, and other squishy concepts. Judge Gesell was left to sort out the mess. He did so as clearly as he could—and he did it our way.

Gesell did not entirely rule out an authorization defense, but he came close. "Authorization," Gesell told the jury, "requires clear, direct instructions to act at a given time in a given way. It must be specific, not simply a general admonition or vague expression of preference. It must be sufficiently precise to assure a reasonable person that it was intended to apply in the given circumstances that develop subsequently. . . . A person's general impression that a type of conduct was expected, that it was proper because others were doing the same, or that the challenged act would help someone or avoid political consequence, does not satisfy the defense of authorization."

Driving his point home, Gesell concluded that "if an authorization can be satisfied by two different courses of action, one clearly legal and one illegal or of dubious legality, and a person chooses the illegal or dubious course when other, legal action would comply, authorization cannot be viewed as affecting intent." In these words one could hear the echo of Judge Gesell's question to North on the stand: "Colonel North, did you at any time in this process consider in your own mind just not doing it?" The instructions, we thought, paved the road to a conviction.

Gesell read these and the rest of the instructions to the jury on Thursday morning, April 20, and for once the toll of the thirteen months since indictment showed on the almost seventy-nine-year-old judge. Hard as the lawyers in this case worked, Gesell had to work harder. Each issue in the North case—immunity, classified information, the notebooks subpoena, authorization, to name only the most prominent—required extensive legal research by the judge and his single law clerk. These difficult questions also forced on Gesell the rigorous exertion of making up his mind. By the day of the verdict, Gesell had issued an astonishing *one hundred ninety-three* separate written opinions in the case—all of which came on top of the scores of informal rulings he made during the trial and more than one hundred pages of jury instructions. And all of it, too, was subjected to the most searching public scrutiny.

On April 20, the strain showed. On that spring morning, the ruddy cast to Gesell's cheeks had faded to a chalky pallor. His hands shook. And as he reached the second of his two hours of reading, he began slurring some of his words. The jurors leaned forward, trying, with evident strain, to catch them all. The case was in the jury's hands.

''I WARN you,'' Keker said to us on that Wednesday, "I'm not good at this."

He meant the waiting. Suddenly, after all those months (in this case, years) of frantic activity, there was nothing else to do.

Judge Gesell even limited the one activity that might have given the lawyers somewhere to go during jury deliberations. Many judges allow jurors to return to the courtroom for "read-backs" of testimony that they want to hear again. Not Gesell. He believed that the practice emphasized one section of the trial more than was appropriate, so he simply counted on the memories of the jurors. In addition, Gesell preempted the need for the jurors to ask to see individual trial exhibits; he sent all of them in with the jurors to their deliberation room. He also gave them a copy of his instructions on the law. More than most juries, this group was on its own.

All of this meant that we had our days entirely free for one of the trial lawyer's most maddening (if inevitable) pastimes: speculating and debating about how the deliberations were going. A guessing game is what it was. So we guessed.

The conventional wisdom on jury deliberations holds that a very brief review of the case by the jurors—say, less than a day after a long trial—means an acquittal is coming. If they are considering convicting, says the theory, the jurors usually like to take a little time, working element-by-element, count-by-count, if only to convince themselves that they are giving the defendant a fair deal. When the deliberations stretch beyond four or five days, the received wisdom breaks down. Long deliberations, says one school of thought, are good for the government because it means that the jurors will probably compromise—and convict on at least some counts. Not so, says another group. Long deliberations mean that some jurors feel passionately that the defendant should be acquitted, and they are willing to wait out their peers. Both sides cite examples. In this kind of pointless speculation, we occupied our days waiting.

After the instructions on Thursday, the jurors gathered their belongings for sequestration at an unidentified hotel, and they began their deliberations with an all-day session on Friday, April 21. The first hint of things to come, though, came in a note from the forewoman, Denise Anderson, that first afternoon. "Right now we are reading through documents that pertain to charges," she wrote. "Time is flying in here. Can you help with a bigger room?" The massive pile of exhibits, along with the twelve bodies, were apparently too much for the twelve-by-eighteen-foot jury room just behind Courtroom Six. Gesell let the jurors take over the courtroom itself, though, as he did in the CIPA hearings, he asked the courthouse marshals to cover the windows on the door with colored paper. No one was to see the jury at work.

Saturday, when the jury was scheduled to work half a day, brought a minicontroversy. The Washington bureau of NBC News sent letters to all the jurors at home, asking them to give the network interviews after the verdict. The jurors learned of the NBC request when one of the marshals assigned to the jury picked one up on a mail run to a juror's home and (unaccountably) passed it on to the juror at the hotel. When Gesell informed both sides of the contact, he issued a brusque denunciation of NBC for meddling. Barry Simon, obviously fidgety with the time on his hands, made a strident demand for a hearing on the issue, but no one took it too seriously. The letters may have been a bad idea, but it was hard to see how they hurt North's chances for a fair trial. Still, Carl Stern, the NBC correspondent covering the trial, gave Reaganesque denials that he knew anything about his own office's letters. "What," we wondered, "did Stern know and when did he know it?"

Gesell gave the jury Sunday off. After church, they reportedly watched movies on video at their hotel. The real tension began the following week. Monday, Tuesday, Wednesday all passed without so much as a note from the jury.

"This," Zornow told me, "is like a Borscht Belt resort. You kill time between meals."

The two of us often took walks from Thirteenth Street down to the courthouse on Third Street to see the forest of antennae that the television journalists had erected so they could give live reports on the verdict. With nothing to do once their satellite dishes were correctly aligned, the crews sunned themselves on the courthouse plaza. Zornow and I looked with covetous eyes on the elaborate lunch buffet CBS had put on for its people—but we kept walking.

Keker seemed to have disappeared. When the jury went out, he bought a stack of bestsellers—*Chaos* (by James Gleick), *Love in the Time of Cholera* (by Gabriel García Marquez), a few others—and each day he would arrive at 9 A.M., close his office door and start reading. Judge Gesell's chambers kept us apprised of the jury's comings and goings, when they arrived, went to lunch, and left for the day, and Keker would take a long walk by himself during the jury's lunch hour. He said little to anyone.

At around 4 P.M., Keker would receive a call from one of Gesell's assistants, poke his head out of his door and say, "They're gone." The news would empty our office faster than a fire drill—until the next day's round of waiting began.

FRIDAY, April 28, 1989. That was the day. We could feel it. After a full week of sequestration, the jurors would not want to spend a second weekend away from their families. They had spent enough time so that they would not be accused of acting precipitously. Friday. It *had* to be.

For my own selfish reasons, I hoped more than anyone else that it would be so. I was still thinking about my April deadline. My plan was to drive home to New York and then fly out to Phoenix on that last weekend of the month. But as the hours passed without any word on Friday the 28th, I realized that an April finish was not going to happen. So, in the best lawyer's tradition, I negotiated. I called

McIntosh and we agreed that this would be our last weekend apart, but that I would give the jury four more days. I would leave Washington for New York on Thursday, May 4, and fly west the next day. That, I promised, was *it*.

The team grew surly and the days long during my final week. Rumors sprouted unaccountably. On Tuesday, May 2, we learned from reliable sources that the jury took only thirty-five minutes for lunch. Were they winding up? The day passed without more news. What were they *doing* in there? Reporters, we learned from the grapevine, were telling jokes about the jurors' living it up in their hotel, perceiving no hurry to give up room service.

Somewhere around midday on Wednesday, I pretty much gave up hope of seeing a verdict. After almost two-and-a-half years, it was terribly frustrating to exit with the principal business of the office unfinished—like leaving a ball game in the top of the fourteenth inning. Yes, it would probably end soon, but it could also, theoretically, go on for several more weeks. I had to live my life. For me, Thursday was it.

On my last night in town, I fulfilled one of my principal goals in moving to Washington—seeing a baseball game at Baltimore's Memorial Stadium. Better yet, John Keker had procured seats in the owner's box, next to the Orioles dugout. Even better *still*, the tickets came courtesy of a longtime friend of Keker's who was a partner at Williams & Connolly. I stayed up late many nights courtesy of W & C. I enjoyed this one most of all.

On Thursday, May 4, the twelfth day of deliberations and my last at the OIC, I rented a car for the drive to New York and spent the rest of the morning packing the last of the boxes in my office. Then a group of my pals treated me to lunch at one of the awful Chinese restaurants in our office neighborhood. One last time, John Barrett, Mike Bromwich, Larry Shtasel, David Zornow—better friends I will never find—and I shared a meal as colleagues.

We arrived back at the office at 1:35, and Keker's phone was ringing. Bromwich walked into Keker's office to pick up.

When he returned, his skin had gone pale against his black beard.

"That was Doris Brown"—Judge Gesell's secretary—"she said we have a verdict on all counts."

PANIC. Frenzy. Rummaging and pacing. Everyone was trying to not look too excited. The OIC had reclaimed the courtroom passes from John Barrett's "spies," the members of the Inter-Agency Group who had sat through the whole trial, so we had enough to admit all the lawyers. Shtasel distributed these precious tokens, and we jumped on the subway for the two-stop trip to the courthouse.

Until I entered Courtroom Six that final time, I never imagined how solemn the day of judgment would be. Packed tighter than any time during the trial, the crowd was still hushed, respectful, and somber. Even the reporters, who had affected a wisecracking insouciance throughout the proceedings, sat tense and still awaiting the judge and jury. All of us, at some level, were invested in the fairness of this proceeding. Almost unconsciously, it seemed, we wanted this last occasion to appear just, to satisfy us that the right result had been reached. All of us treated the moment with deference.

At 2:18, North's four lawyers walked grimly to their places. North, expressionless, followed them, with Betsy and a clergyman. North held the Bible that he had brought to court each day.

Gesell assumed his place in front of the sheer wall of green marble at 2:22. "As I notified counsel," Gesell said, "I received a note from the foreperson at twenty-nine minutes after one stating, 'We the jury have come to a unanimous decision on all counts. We have finished our deliberations.' So I gather we're ready to take a verdict. You may bring in the jury."

We stared as the twelve walked in—at first for a hint about their verdict, but then simply at the amazing transformation in them. They looked entirely different from the congregation we last saw almost two weeks earlier. Gone was the semibored torpor with which they absorbed the evidence. They were now profoundly, utterly drained. Water filled the eyes of at least half of them. Denise Anderson's cheeks were streaked with unashamed tears. Beverly Turner, always so full of smiles during the trial, looked drawn and exhausted. Patricia Bennett, proud and haughty, who rolled her eyes during North's testimony, stared into the empty middle distance. Earl Williams, in his seventies and ever drowsy, looked pained. In only a moment, one could tell that this jury did not spend twelve days playing with room service. They had worked.

"Madam foreperson," Gesell asked Denise Anderson, "have you filled out the verdict form?"

"Yes," Anderson said, "I have." She then handed the verdict form, two pages, folded, to the bailiff, who passed it to Judge Gesell. The form actually called for the jury to make eighteen separate determinations about North's guilt. For six of the counts, North was charged, in the alternative, with a substantive count and "aiding and abetting." For purposes of sentencing, a conviction for "aiding and abetting" is identical to a verdict of guilty on the substantive count.

In an era of tracking polls, exit polls, point spreads and odds-makers, few events can match the announcement of a jury verdict for sheer unpredictability. No one—no one—knew what Gesell was going to say.

"I will study this, if I may, for a moment," said Judge Gesell, prolonging the agony. Then he began reading.

"As to count one," he said, "the verdict is not guilty, both of the substantive count and aiding and abetting." I was shocked, and the jolt was compounded when I recognized instantly that an acquittal on the first McFarlane letter meant that the jury would reject the first four counts.

"As to count two, the verdict is not guilty of the substantive count and of aiding and abetting.

"On count three, the verdict is not guilty as to the substantive count and not guilty as to aiding and abetting.

"As to count four, the verdict is not guilty as to the substantive count and not guilty as to aiding and abetting.

"As to count five, the verdict is not guilty."

Worse than the results was Gesell's rhythm. *That rhythm.* It sounded like he was reading a list: not guilty, not guilty, not guilty. Was he ever going to stop? He had to get out of that cadence. Not guilty on count five? That was North's lie to the House intelligence committee. He lied in their face. My mind racing, I thought with a weak smile of the low-budget science fiction movies of my childhood, the ones where the scientist says gravely, "Something is terribly wrong here."

"As to count six, the verdict is not guilty of the substantive count, *guilty* of aiding and abetting."

Finally! The false Iran chronologies.

"As to count seven, the verdict is not guilty of the substantive count, and not guilty of aiding and abetting.

"As to count eight, the verdict is not guilty." That damned Ed Meese.

"As to count nine, the verdict is guilty." The shredding.

"As to count ten, the verdict is guilty." The fence, of course.

"As to count eleven, the verdict is not guilty." Not guilty on the traveler's checks, little metal box and all.

"As to count twelve, the verdict is not guilty."

Throughout the brief recitation, North looked blank, unmoved. As with everyone else, I think, the events happened too fast for him to process their meaning. But after Gesell dismissed the jury and began to walk toward the door behind him, the courtroom erupted in a fit of swirling action. Reporters stampeded for the door—the pounding of their feet alone making a bigger racket than anything heard in Courtroom Six during the trial—and raced to broadcast the news first. Republican Congressman Henry J. Hyde of Illinois vaulted, uninvited, into the well and grabbed North's hand, giving a too-loud "congratulations" and demonstrating that Washington spin doctors will deprive a man of even a single private moment at a crushing time.

From the courtroom the action shifted to the plaza in front of the courthouse where about thirty microphones, almost as many television cameras, and more than a hundred people awaited the principals. A small group of right-wing congressmen (not Hyde), drawn like moths to the lights of the minicams, denounced the verdict and sang North's praises. How could North be judged, they asked with indignation, by this uninformed group of citizens? It was almost entertaining to watch these legislators struggle to avoid saying what they were so obviously thinking—that these . . . these . . . *black people* had no right to condemn "our Ollie."

Keker had retreated with Bromwich and Zornow to our courtroom headquarters to prepare a statement. About half an hour after the verdict, the three of them approached the nest of microphones. Keker, too, had learned something about media management in his tenure on the job, so he resolved to refuse to answer any questions and deny the reporters any choice in what to report.

"Some said our system of justice could not deal fairly, if at all, with this case," Keker said. "Some even said that it couldn't be tried. Colonel North has been convicted of three very serious felony charges. The jury has spoken, after a long and difficult trial.

"And the principle that no man is above the law has been vindicated."

Keker said the words slowly, almost morosely, and one could sense immediately his disappointment. North had been convicted of three of twelve charges—Keker wanted more.

Not me. As I basked in the sun of that early summer day, I exulted in our success. True, North had not been convicted of all the charges, but we had surmounted almost unimaginable hurdles to convict him of three felonies. The jury chose three of the strongest counts—and from three very different parts of the case. The jury went for the most elemental of crimes, North's most compelling moral transgressions. He wrote a false chronology for Congress; he lied. He shredded important documents before others could see them; he cheated. He took a valuable home improvement to which he was not entitled; he stole.

Lying, cheating, and stealing—I could think of no better epitaph for *United States v. Oliver North.*

THE team gathered that night one more time at David Zornow's house for pizza and postmortems. The dominant emotion: relief. We all realized that we could have lost this case. Many of us dwelled on the jury's refusal to convict North on count five—his face-to-face lie to the House intelligence committee. Judge Gesell's instructions had all but told the jurors that North had not been "authorized" to tell untruths, but the jury, as was its right, simply nullified the instruction. They believed that Poindexter put North, as Sullivan said, "between a rock and a hard place," and they weren't going to punish him for it. Oh, my, I thought—this case had been a close one.

Shortly after nine, Zornow answered the bell to find Lawrence E.

Walsh standing outside. He had been repeatedly invited to join us but many of us bet that he would not show. Just this once, he shed his lonely cloak and lifted the party and our spirits. Everyone was openly, visibly delighted to see him. And as Judge Walsh engaged in enthusiastic conversation with one Samuel Zornow, who was a mere three-quarters-of-a-century Walsh's junior, I allowed myself a moment's thought that all was right with the world.

I set off the following morning before five to drop my things at our New York apartment, which had, with McIntosh in Phoenix and me in Washington, the look of a yuppie Miss Havisham's. To make my 1:10 P.M. flight from Kennedy Airport to Phoenix, I sped through the predawn rain—alternating on the radio among high-decibel Top Forty, talk radio verdicts on the verdict, and Nina Totenberg of National Public Radio.

Totenberg had spoken with Earl Williams of the jury, a retired security guard in his seventies. As Williams described it, the jurors' discussions had been every bit as exhausting as their faces portrayed in court on Thursday. Until the final hours, Williams said, some jurors were still holding out in favor of acquittal on all counts. But then one of the jurors convened the group for a "powerful" prayer, and that had brought them together.

The verdict, said Williams, "made us feel that in our democracy, in our country, . . . it doesn't matter any more the color of your skin. It doesn't matter how many degrees you've got. It's what you got in your heart that can help your fellow man."

Williams recalled the jury's last moment together in the courthouse elevator, just before they gave their verdict. At that time, Williams said, "we got together and sang, 'God Bless America.' We hugged and held hands. The ladies cried—men did, too."

And so, at that point, did I.

Fair Enough

Then we lost. The judgment in *United States v. Oliver North* belongs, ultimately, to the defendant.

The first blow to the OIC came with Judge Gesell's sentencing of North: a $150,000 fine, two years probation, 1,200 hours of community service—and no jail time. In practical terms it amounted to no punishment at all. The Colonel's supporters immediately stepped forward and offered to pay the fine, and in any event North reportedly made enough on the lecture circuit in about a week to cover his bill to the government. Probation meant only a small disruption in his life. And, working at his usual frenetic pace, North fulfilled his community service obligation before the appeal of his case was even argued. North's conviction served to bar him from holding federal office; but that penalty came automatically with his conviction on the shredding charge, not from any decision by Judge Gesell. The sole consolation, it seemed at the time of his sentence, would be that the label "convicted felon" would dog North for a lifetime.

But even the paltry sentence vanished with the decision of the United States Court of Appeals for the District of Columbia Circuit. On July 20, 1990, a three-judge panel voted two-to-one to reverse

North's conviction. Fourteen months after the jury rendered its verdict, Oliver North was no longer a convicted felon.

The three judges on the appeals panel did not represent propitious choices for the OIC. One judge—Patricia Wald, a former official in President Carter's Justice Department—seemed likely to wind up in the OIC's corner. But there were only small hopes for the other two: David Sentelle, a North Carolinian who owed his appointment to the patronage of Senator Jesse Helms; and Lawrence Silberman, who wrote the opinion striking down the Independent Counsel law in 1988, a decision that was itself overturned by the Supreme Court later that year.

Sure enough, the panel split along partisan lines: two Reagan appointees for North, one Carter for the OIC—a tawdry coda to Gesell's doggedly unpolitical conduct of the trial. The reversal was based on *Kastigar:* the majority ruled that Judge Gesell had not held enough hearings to determine if North's immunized testimony before Congress had been used against him. All of our efforts to avoid North's testimony—the canning, the insulation, the instructions to the grand jurors—had not been enough for Sentelle and Silberman.

The appeals court did *not* hold that we had used North's testimony against him. Rather, it said that Gesell did not look hard enough to see if we did. In this the decision was a major departure from current trends in criminal jurisprudence during the tenures of Warren Burger and William Rehnquist as Chief Justices of the United States—and, except for the North opinion, Sentelle and Silverman are leading exponents of these trends. Defendants generally must show that they suffered some harm, some prejudice, from a supposed procedural defect in their trials. Not so Oliver North. Sentelle and Silberman ruled that Gesell's failure to hold what they regarded as complete *Kastigar* hearings doomed the entire prosecution. (The appeals court did not find fault specifically with Gesell's pretrial *Kastigar* hearing, the one that Herbert J. Stern conducted for the OIC. According to the judges, Gesell should have done more after the trial to see that North's immunized testimony had not been used against him.)

In addition, the judges in the majority rejected Gesell's instructions on the count that charged North with destroying, altering, and removing documents—the shredding charge. They said that the jury should have asked specifically whether North destroyed *or* altered *or* removed documents—even though the judges acknowledged that there was evidence that he did all three. Because Gesell did not instruct the jury this way, the court held, the jury might not have been unanimous in their view of what North actually did. It was not enough for the jury to find that North merely engaged in a course of conduct that included all these forms of deception. The court also said that Gesell should have allowed the jury to consider whether North's superiors had authorized him to shred documents—even if such instructions were "incredible" or if they came from "incompetent or venal" superiors.

As a result of these rulings, North's convictions on all three counts were reversed. On the shredding count, because of the faulty instructions, the court ordered a full new trial. But before any new trial could be held, the appeals court ordered Gesell to hold a new round of *Kastigar* hearings to determine if the remaining two convictions, for obstruction of justice and receipt of the security fence, could stand. In these new hearings, Gesell must examine, "witness-by-witness," all those who testified in the trial *and* in the grand jury to see if they were at all influenced by North's statements before Congress. If at the end of this "line-by-line and item-by-item" review, Gesell found that North's immunized testimony played any part in shaping that testimony, the case must be dismissed once and for all. "We readily understand," the appeals court noted dryly, "how court and counsel might sigh prior to such an undertaking."

Sigh, indeed. Such a massive hearing would probably have taken at least six months to complete; in fact, the action of the appeals court was designed to force Gesell to dismiss altogether the case against North. The judges acknowledged as much when they noted that their admonitions to Gesell would apply only "if this prosecution is to continue."

The prospect of a defendant forced to yield his Fifth Amendment rights, testify publicly, and then face prosecution on the same subject matter as his testimony is a troubling one. No one—least of all the OIC—underestimated the hazards of such a case. Still, the majority's insistence on a "line-by-line" review of the transcripts for any hint of the immunized testimony was more than merely unprecedented in the scores of cases in which courts have interpreted *Kastigar*. More important was the fact that the decision missed the point of the protections afforded by the Fifth Amendment: that involuntary statements may not be *used* against the speaker.

The judges in the majority ignored the fact that the OIC located all of its trial witnesses *before* North gave any immunized testimony. Indeed, these witnesses told essentially the same story before and after North appeared before Congress. Yes, North was forced to give immunized testimony, and yes, it received wide publicity. But Judge Gesell supervised the trial, examined the record, and found that neither the prosecution, the grand jury, the trial jury, nor the trial witnesses "used" that testimony against North. Even Sentelle and Silberman did not claim that North's immunized testimony was actually used against him. These judges did not say that the trial was unfair; they merely sought an extended replay of it, without showing how this second run would provide any greater insights than those contained within the already enormous record of this case.

More outrageous than the appeals court's *Kastigar* holding were its two grounds for reversing the shredding count. The first basis for the reversal was that Gesell's instruction risked a nonunanimous jury. The judge repeatedly told the jury that, on all counts, they must agree on which acts formed the basis for their verdict. No sensible laymen, like the members of the North jury, would have noticed or cared that Gesell did not repeat the admonition for this specific count. The second ground for the court's action—that the jury should have been allowed to consider authorization—was chilling. "The open-ended invitation for juries to exonerate defendants who simply follow orders," Chief Judge Wald noted in her dissent, "runs counter to a most fundamental tradition of our criminal law, which is based on the notion that citizens, big and small, insider and outsider, have some independent responsibility to find out and conform to what the law requires of them." The reversal of the shredding charge revealed two judges who decided first and found reasons later.

Walsh asked the Supreme Court to review the appeals court's ruling, but the justices declined to enter the Iran-Contra thicket and, without comment in May 1991, let the reversal of the conviction stand. The following month, Michael Bromwich appeared before

Judge Gesell to begin the process of holding the new round of hearings demanded by the appeals court. Recognizing that the appeals court's ruling amounted to a mandate to throw out the North case—and frustrated that Walsh did not seem to get the message—Gesell treated Bromwich with testy contempt. More than three years after the indictment, more than two years after the verdict, Gesell counseled Bromwich that "people lose cases."

Rather than bow promptly to the by-then-inevitable end of the case, Walsh actually began the hearings demanded by the appeals court. The OIC called Robert McFarlane to testify about whether his words at the trial had been influenced by North's immunized testimony. McFarlane turned in a predictably squalid performance, doing his bit for his former protegé by saying that North's testimony did have an impact—though McFarlane could not say what it was. In truth, if McFarlane had not said that he was influenced by North's Congressional testimony, then any of several dozen other trial or grand jury witnesses would have. But McFarlane's admissions alone meant the end was *really* inevitable, so Walsh made his only choice. On September 16, 1991, he asked Gesell to dismiss the remaining charges against North. Gesell did so.

The D.C. Circuit opinion will at least deprive Congress the luxury of pretending, in future national scandals, that they can immunize witnesses and still expect that these people will be criminally prosecuted. Now it will be one or the other. In some cases it may well be worthwhile for Congress to act quickly and air the facts at the cost of criminal prosecutions down the line. But the Congressional committees in the Iran-Contra affair won meager rewards for the actions that torpedoed our case: days of elected officials and witnesses hectoring one another for the cameras rather than exploring the facts for the common good. The goal of educating the public about the misdeeds of its government may well be as important as assuring that the criminally culpable go to jail. But with its precipitous immunity grants and vacuous hearings, Congress assured that neither goal would be fulfilled.

SO, IN THE END, it appears that no one will ever spend a day in prison because of what he did in the Iran-Contra affair. (John Poindexter, sentenced to six months, may also have his conviction reversed based on the appeals court's decision in the North case.) No one was convicted of diverting money from the Iran arms sales. (Secord and Hakim pleaded guilty to lesser charges after North's conviction.) No one even stood trial for providing illegal assistance to the Contras. (The case of the CIA's Joe Fernandez was dismissed because the Bush Administration refused to declassify enough information to allow him a fair trial.)

The Office of Independent Counsel did not "solve" the Iran-Contra affair. We did not even "get to the bottom" of it. That was not our job. Anything we learned to guide future administrations was incidental to our principal assignment. As Judge Harold Greene told the jury in John Poindexter's trial, "This court and this jury do not sit in judgment on the President or the Congress or on . . . who's got the right policy. We are here to determine whether this defendant is guilty of certain specific offenses."

That was our job. This more modest conception of the OIC's mission did not come easily (or immediately) to me. When I arrived in Washington, I wanted to see us expose the fatal arrogance of a corrupt administration. But arrogance, I learned, is no crime. Nor is reprehensible policy in Central America or an inept attempt to free American hostages. Only crimes are crimes.

I came to see that the most "important" documents we found involving Oliver North were his two phony letters to Glenn Robinette about the security fence—texts that illuminated nothing at all about the practice of foreign policy but enormous amounts about one person's conduct. The investigation of the latter, not the former, defined our mission.

Our office sought and obtained convictions for crimes, and that is all we did. In a way, the OIC was at its best in the trial of John Poindexter, which took place the year after North's. The lead prosecutors, Dan Webb and Howard Pearl, distilled the case down to its essentials: Poindexter lied to Congress. By forcing Oliver North to admit to both his own and his boss's role in the Iran-Contra coverup, Webb made the most of this reluctant witness. (And in this successful use of North, Webb also vindicated our decision to try North before Poindexter.)

Webb defused President Reagan's testimony by zeroing in on the key issue. Did the president authorize Poindexter to commit crimes? No, Reagan had to admit, he did not. Indeed, the former president's rambling and embarrassing answers advised the jury that he remembered little of his eight years in office. Webb made sure that Reagan's impact was marginal.

With Poindexter or even before his trial, the OIC did not attempt (nor should we have) to assign moral, rather than criminal, responsibility for the disasters of the Iran-Contra affair. Who set the tone of contempt for Congress that made others feel they had a license to lie? Whose careless thinking motivated the trading of arms for hostages? Whose sloth and inattention to duty allowed his subordinates to behave without restraint? To my eyes, in any moral or philosophical sense, the "fault" for the Iran-Contra affair lay with President Reagan.

Arrogance and intolerance will never be prosecuted out of existence. Personal moral judgments about morality and philosophy— about what constitutes arrogance and intolerance—are just that: personal, idiosyncratic, individualistic. Criminality, in contast, must be weighed by standards far more broadly shared among us; crimes transgress our very lowest common denominator of behavior. Only when that standard is breached should we impose criminal penalties, and by that measure Ronald Reagan committed no crimes. Knowing (and preserving) the difference between the assignment of moral as opposed to criminal responsibility will preserve the integrity of both.

My initial ambitions for the job were more those of an adolescent than a prosecutor. Prosecutors thinking broadly put all of us at peril. To expand the criminal law into anything less fundamental than enforcement of specific statutes—into the realms of honest disagreements, policy tussles, and close calls—jeopardizes the whole edifice of the law.

We had not prosecuted anyone for the diversion of funds to the Contras, but I had eventually to ask myself: was the diversion a crime at all? The diversion was clearly *wrong,* and those who made it happen should certainly have been fired and condemned. But one can say all those things and still believe that those people did not commit a *crime.* President Reagan's indifference to his responsibilities well earned him derision and contempt. But not jail.

What Oliver North did, in contrast, deserved imprisonment. North flouted the values that, as John Keker told the jury, you "learned at your mother's knee." He lied, cheated, and stole—one count of each, in fact. *Crimes*.

LONG AFTER I LEFT the OIC, Walsh was still looking for crimes. In July 1991, he obtained a guilty plea from Alan Fiers, the former chief of the CIA's Central American Task Force and a colleague of North and Elliott Abrams in the Restricted Interagency Group (RIG), to two misdemeanor counts of withholding information from Congress. Once widely regarded as the most promising covert operative in the entire CIA, Fiers admitted that he had misled Congress about the extent of his knowledge of North's operations on behalf of the Contras and on the exact time when North told him about the diversion of funds to the Contras. As part of his plea, Fiers also agreed to cooperate with the OIC's continuing investigation.

The Fiers plea put new life into Walsh's probe, which was well into its fifth year. Apparently based on Fiers's testimony, Walsh obtained an indictment of Clair George, the former chief of covert operations at the CIA, on felony charges of lying to Congress about what he knew of North's activities. Then on October 7, 1991, Elliott Abrams pled guilty to two crimes under the same misdemeanor statute that had laid the basis for Fiers's plea—and, before that, Robert McFarlane's. Aware that Fiers was, at long last, giving Walsh a full picture of what went on inside the RIG, Abrams chose to admit "withholding information" from Congress about his knowledge of North's work for the Contras and his own efforts to solicit money from the Sultan of Brunei. The plea came less than a week before the five-year statute of limitations on these crimes expired—and, presumably, just before Walsh was about to bring felony charges against Abrams.

More pitiful than sinister as he offered a few tepid words of self-defense in a postplea news conference, Abrams looked out on a world transformed from the one he saw from his office at the State Department. This former dark prince of *Nightline*—who, like North, warned of Communism skipping from Nicaragua to New Orleans —pled guilty on a day when he could scarcely find a Communist in Moscow, never mind Managua. A misdemeanor plea will certainly not land Abrams in jail, but the conviction will probably bar Abrams from returning to high government office. Good.

As Walsh winds down his investigation, it can be said that the real offense at the heart of the Iran-Contra affair was something that Judge Barrington Parker grasped instinctively at the hearing on North's civil suit in 1987. As Parker suggested with his sidelong glance at the Colonel, North was a vigilante. He did not so much violate the law as vault around it; he did not so much break the rules as pretend they didn't exist. North admitted that he lied repeatedly to Congress, acknowledged that he knew lying was wrong, but insisted that it never occurred to him that he was violating the law. By reversing North's conviction, the appeals court missed an opportunity to send the message that proximity to power, like power itself, is a responsibility, not an excuse.

AS THE GROOM loped to the front of the room, the wedding guests set aside their wineglasses. Larry Shtasel accepted the microphone from the bandleader and turned to the assembled family and friends.

"Many of you here know David Zornow," he began. "He was the one handing out his business card as you all walked in. Well, David once told me that you'll never have a better audience than at your own wedding, so I'm going to take advantage.

"You know," Shtasel continued, "some people said I had a fear of commitment, but that's not true at all. I just had a few *conditions* that had to be met before I got married." He paused.

"The Berlin Wall had to come down. . . . McDonalds had to open in Moscow. . . . The Sixers had to win twelve straight. . . . Mike Tyson had to get knocked out. . . . And Nelson Mandela had to be freed. . . .

"And *then* I would get married."

Shtasel's wedding in 1990 amounted to the first unofficial reunion of the OIC staff, which began scattering soon after the North verdict. John Keker headed home to San Francisco almost as fast as I left

Washington. Zornow, as Shtasel implied, had not so much arrived at a celebrated New York law firm as hurled himself at it.

Mike Bromwich had also become a law firm partner, but, unlike Zornow, he appeared almost to covet the smaller paychecks of his days as a public servant. In fact, he retained part-time duties with the Walsh staff. Prosecutors have a word for people like Bromwich, those who switch sides but not allegiances. In spirit, Bromwich was a "lifer."

Cliff Sloan was writing briefs to the Supreme Court for the solicitor general. Bill Hassler was about to start enforcing environmental laws in Denver. Bruce Yannett, a prosecutor in the District of Columbia, missed the wedding because he and his wife were expecting their first child at any moment. Shtasel himself was exploring private law practice in his home town of Philadelphia.

John Barrett and Geoff Berman remained with the office of Independent Counsel in Washington.

Lawrence Walsh, although invited to the wedding, did not attend.

We didn't talk too much about the case. The subject wasn't exactly painful, but we never knew how to handle it either. It was easier to chat about new jobs, new homes, and the quality of the *hors d'oeuvres* (high).

Still, seeing that splendid group together one more time, I could not help but wonder: had any thirteen-year-olds watched the televised jaunts of Keker, Bromwich, Zornow (and, if they had sharp eyes, Toobin) up the courthouse steps in Washington, as I once gaped at the Watergate prosecutors, and marveled at our invincibility?

I doubt it. And that is okay with me.

TODAY, McIntosh and I are back in New York. Sometimes we go to work together, though she, characteristically, usually leaves the house first. But when I keep pace with her, we wedge into the subway next to one another. I lose McIntosh at the World Trade Center and almost everyone else at Wall Street. On the final leg of my journey, beneath the East River, I sometimes have a whole car to myself.

My destination is Brooklyn, where I am today a junior assistant United States attorney. I am learning to try my own cases. An elderly

Nigerian woman who arrived at Kennedy Airport with 107 condoms full of heroin in her stomach. A doctor in Staten Island who sold prescriptions for thirty dollars apiece. Videotape bootleggers, mail thieves, counterfeiters—drug dealers by the bushel.

I work in front of juries and almost no one else. Rows of empty benches greet my every appearance. We see crowds in our courthouse only on the days when new citizens assemble to pledge their new allegiance.

Gone is the desire—much less the expectation—for my work to change the course of history, but I celebrate, rather than regret, my enlightenment. I know better my own limits and those of all prosecutors.

On good days—which include most of them—I still see our potential: to catch bad guys, to right wrongs, to do justice.

But only a little. And not always. And one case at a time.

Acknowledgments

I am grateful to Lawrence Walsh for allowing me the privilege of serving on the Office of Independent Counsel staff. To my splendid colleagues at the OIC, I offer my thanks for the education they provided me—and for the pleasure of their company.

This book is based principally on my diary, notes, and recollections. All quotations from court proceedings come from official transcripts. The book—as well as my decision to write it—was in no way endorsed, authorized, or supported by Judge Walsh, the Office of Independent Counsel, or any of its current or former employees.

Aaron Marcu made indispensable contributions to the publication of this book. David Boies and Robert Baron, along with their colleagues Brooks Burdette and Andrew Hayes, generously provided advice and assistance. They know—and I know—how important they were.

This is my first book. I had a lot of help.

Day in and day out, my agent Esther Newberg has been a model of dedication and loyalty.

My editors Al Silverman and Dan Frank lavished thoughtful attention on every word of my manuscript, including many that, thanks to their wisdom, have now disappeared from it. They were—and are—teachers, boosters, and friends.

Andrew J. Maloney, United States Attorney for the Eastern District of New York, has never mentioned the name Oliver North in my presence without adding, "that great American." My thanks to him for his broad-mindedness in bringing me aboard. My gratitude also to Bill Muller, Peter Norling, Tom Roche, and Mary Jo White of the U.S. Attorney's office. It should go without saying (but won't) that this book does not necessarily represent the views of these good people or the Department of Justice.

Several other friends provided important support along the way: among them are Ed Barber, Joel Blumenthal, Mike Kinsley, the National Security Archive (particularly Scott Armstrong and Tom Blanton), Lisa Pliscou, Cathy Pohl, John Savarese, and Dorothy Wickenden.

I first met Amy McIntosh when she edited my copy at *The Harvard Crimson*. On this book, ten years later, she performed the same function—with similar regard for the product and disregard for the ego. An unsparing editor still, she is now also my true love and best friend.

Index